"John Kenneth White, one of the nation's foremost political scientists, skillfully and with deep insight explores in *Barack Obama's America* the social and cultural upheavals that have produced a new political era—supplanting 40 years of conservative domination. White's lively and highly readable account of changing mores culminates in the 2008 election which, in his words, 'represented a moment when a new demography caught up to a new politics.' White's literary skills make his description of how 'the Reagan era has come to a close and the Obama era has begun' attractive and accessible to both the layman and the specialist. *Barack Obama's America* is essential reading for all those seeking to make sense of the transformation of American politics in the past few years."

—THOMAS EDSALL, Columbia Journalism Professor and Huffington
Post Political Editor and author of *Building Red America*

"There are only a few authors that are on top of the big themes that define this country. I put John Kenneth White at the top of the list with Garry Wills, Alan Wolfe, and Richard Florida. I can always count on John for meticulous research, historical context, and the best trend analysis."

—JOHN ZOGBY, President/CEO of Zogby International
and author of *The Way We'll Be*

"John Kenneth White has been well ahead of the rest of us in identifying the societal transformations in progress and then developing their lasting political consequences. *Barack Obama's America* is a major contribution to the study of social transformation and political change, one that sets the standard for understanding such developments."

—WILLIAM CROTTY, Thomas P. O'Neill Chair in Public Life and
Director, Center for the Study of Democracy, Department
of Political Science, Northeastern University

D1538571

Barack Obama's America

CONTEMPORARY POLITICAL AND SOCIAL ISSUES

Alan Wolfe, Series Editor

Since at least 1973, when the U.S. Supreme Court issued its *Roe v. Wade* decision legalizing abortion, American politics has been dominated by the contest between red states that lean conservative and blue ones that vote Democratic. The results have all too often included bitter partisanship, sharp polarization, and gridlock.

Many observers believe that Barack Obama's 2008 election to the U.S. presidency has changed the contours of American politics. In this book, John Kenneth White, an expert on polling and public opinion, shows that this belief is true and explains how these changes came to pass. White's detailed analysis of recent U.S. political life proves that what makes Obama distinctive is not just his race. Fundamental changes in who we are—the importance of young voters, the changing racial profile of the country, shifts in basic American values—are all at play.

This book, the most detailed of its kind, will go a long way toward helping Americans understand their political present and their future.

—Alan Wolfe

Barack Obama's America

HOW NEW CONCEPTIONS OF RACE, FAMILY, AND RELIGION ENDED THE REAGAN ERA

John Kenneth White

THE UNIVERSITY OF MICHIGAN PRESS • ANN ARBOR

Copyright © by the University of Michigan 2009
All rights reserved
Published in the United States of America by
The University of Michigan Press
Manufactured in the United States of America
⊛ Printed on acid-free paper

2012   2011   2010   2009   4   3   2   1

A CIP catalog record for this book is available from the British Library.

Library of Congress Cataloging-in-Publication Data

White, John Kenneth.
    Barack Obama's America : how new conceptions of race, family, and
religion ended the Reagan era / John Kenneth White.
        p.   cm.
    Includes bibliographical references and index.
    ISBN 978-0-472-11450-4 (cloth : alk. paper)
    ISBN 978-0-472-03391-1 (pbk. : alk. paper)
    ISBN 978-0-472-02179-6 (ebook)
        1. Family—United States—History.   2. Coalitions—United States—
History.   3. United States—Social conditions—1980–   4. Obama,
Barack.   5. Reagan, Ronald.   I. Title.

HQ535.W47   2009
306.8509730905—dc22   2009018645

For

REVEREND DOUGLAS J. SPINA, PH.D.

Pastor, Counselor, Friend

"Yesterday's strangest dreams are today's headlines, and change is getting swifter every moment."

—LYNDON B. JOHNSON, NOVEMBER 7, 1967

Contents

Acknowledgments

DOING A BOOK OF SUCH VAST SCOPE means that my list of debts is unusually large. I especially thank Phil Pochoda, director and executive editor of the University of Michigan Press, who guided this book to production and spurred its author to tell him (and you) more about the vast changes taking place in contemporary politics. I am also indebted to Jim Reische, former acquisitions editor at the Press, who commissioned this project and followed it through with helpful advice. I also thank the Press's Contemporary Political and Social Series editor, Alan Wolfe of Boston College, for his unwavering and steadfast support, helpful feedback, and continuous encouragement. Anne Lesher, reference librarian at the Catholic University of America's Mullen Library, fielded innumerable requests for books and documents. Carol Therese Young served as my initial research assistant and ably provided the information I sought (and much more). Stergos Kaloudis became my second research assistant and cheerfully handled a barrage of queries. Anne Roan Thomas of Catholic University compiled the index. Ann Kasprzyk, formerly of the Life Cycle Institute at Catholic University, also cheerfully assisted in a number of research tasks. My colleagues at the Life Cycle Institute and in the Politics Department at the Catholic University of America listened to drafts of these chapters and gave plenty of good commentary. I am also indebted to my students at Catholic University, who heard various versions of these chapters in my classes and whose questions helped sharpen my thinking.

I am especially beholden to my family, especially my wife, Yvonne, and my daughter, Jeannette. The period in which this book was written was an especially difficult one, and without their love and constant support, you would not be reading this now.

John Kenneth White
Washington, D.C., April 2009

Introduction

THE POLITICS OF DISCOMFORT

"Shall we be a great nation? That is the question for the third century."
—LYNDON B. JOHNSON, NOVEMBER 20, 1967

AT PRECISELY 7:46 A.M. on October 17, 2006, the United States passed an important milestone. According to the U.S. Census Bureau, the U.S. population exceeded the magic 300 million mark.[1] If people represent power, then the United States remains a world force, with only China and India superseding it in terms of sheer number of people. Despite the terrible terrorist attacks of September 11, 2001, the two subsequent wars in Afghanistan and Iraq, and a widespread perception (at least in hindsight) that the presidency of George W. Bush was a failure,[2] the United States continues to grow exponentially. Indeed, surpassing the 300 million mark was an especially speedy occurrence: 139 years elapsed between the nation's inception and 1915, when the U.S. population hit 100 million; only 52 more years went by before the population surpassed 200 million; and just 39 more years passed until the number of people eclipsed 300 million. Estimates show that by 2045 (a mere 39 years from the 2006 touchstone), the United States will top 400 million.[3]

But when it came time to honor the arrival of the 300 millionth American, the rejoicing was muted, a sharp contrast to the celebrations that greeted the birth of the 200 millionth American on November 20, 1967, when loud cheers rang through the lobby of the Commerce Department and applause repeatedly interrupted President Lyndon B. Johnson's speech marking the occasion. Johnson extolled the greatness of America, a splendor that he claimed was unequaled in world history: "Today we see a nation that is ready to fly to the moon and ready to explore the depths of the ocean. We see a nation fiat, having begun its own climb up the mountain, [that] has neither forgotten nor has it forsaken those people throughout the world who want to grow and who want to prosper in their own ways. . . . To put it in a sentence, we have seen success in America beyond our wildest dreams."[4]

Johnson was not the only one in a triumphant mood. *Life* dispatched a cadre of photographers to find the 200 millionth American, anointing a baby boy in Atlanta with the title.[5] *Newsweek* welcomed the newborn, proclaiming, "'The bigger the better' is almost an article of faith, as American as turkey on the Thanksgiving table." The Commerce Department concurred: "We are a relatively busy and prosperous people . . . living better and better in a growing economy."[6] In an article marking the occasion, former Census Bureau director Richard M. Scammon predicted that when the 1967 newborn turned twenty-one in 1988, he or she would face a bright future:

> The bourgeois, accomplishment-oriented middle-class values will still predominate, despite the hippies' protestations. Most people will still like their creature comforts and the better life and, as they always have, will be trying to get what they can out of them. . . .
>
> [A] backyard swimming pool will be as common as a color TV set is today, and central home air conditioning will be the norm. With the shorter work week, most people will be able to get a second job to help them pay their bills.

Scammon invented the word *demophobia* to describe those people who feared a country overgrown with people.[7] Among the demophobes was John W. Gardner, secretary of the Department of Health, Education, and Welfare, who warned, "If our society continues to become less livable as it becomes more affluent, we shall all end in sumptuous misery."[8]

Gardner's admonition was lost amid the national celebration. Yet his sentiments were commonplace when the 300 millionth American arrived.

Few cheers marked that milestone, and President George W. Bush gave no address in honor of the occasion. A day before the 300 million mark was reached, a Census Bureau spokesperson told reporters that plans to observe the occurrence were "still being finalized," adding, "I don't yet know what, if anything, we are going to do in the way of an event."[9] The bureau ultimately treated its employees to a slice of a hastily purchased cake and a glass of punch before sending them back to their counting.[10] Dowell Myers, a professor of urban planning at the University of Southern California, noted the contrast between this milestone and those that had preceded it: "When we hit 100,000,000, it was a celebration of America's might in the world. When we hit 200,000,000, we were solidifying our position. But at 300,000,000, we are beginning to be crushed under the weight of our own quality-of-life degradation."[11]

For some Americans, having 300 million residents means rethinking how the United States should use its precious resources. Gregg Easterbrook, a visiting fellow at the Brookings Institution, invoked Gardner's memory, writing that having more Americans means having more of everything in life, including those things that are less desirable: "More people, more sprawl, more creativity, more traffic, more love, more noise, more diversity, more energy use, more happiness, more loneliness, more fast food, more art, more knowledge, maybe even more wisdom."[12] Novelist Paul Theroux found that the news about the arrival of the 300 millionth American "gave me no pleasure." Instead, Theroux mourned the passing of "a country of enormous silence and ordinariness—empty spaces not just in the Midwest and the rural South but in the outer suburbs of New England, like the one I grew up in, citified on one margin and thinning to woods on the other. That roomier and simpler America shaped me by giving me and others of my generation a love for space and a taste for solitude."[13]

Today, doubts about the future abound. But it is not the scarcity of land, food, or fuel or the presence of too many people that creates our present-day discomfort. Rather, our political dissent is amplified by who these new Americans are and the question of whether they embody the ideas associated with becoming an American. Though no one can say for sure, it is probable that the 300 millionth American is the child of immigrants. In Queens, New York, the Elmhurst Hospital Center decided it should lay claim to the precedent-setting birth. So when Gricelda Plata, aged 22, gave birth to a six-pound, five-ounce boy at 7:46 A.M. on October 17, 2006, the hospital presented her with an oversized T-shirt that announced, "I delivered America's 300 millionth baby." Plata and the boy's father, Armando Jimenez, aged 25, immigrants from Puebla, Mexico, reside in Brooklyn.[14]

At precisely the same moment, another New York City hospital also claimed credit for producing the 300 millionth American. Zoe Hudson was born at 7:46 A.M. at New York–Presbyterian/Weill Cornell Hospital in Manhattan. Her parents were of mixed racial heritage. Her father, Garvin Hudson, aged 29, was an investment banker and the son of a Jamaican couple. Her mother, Maria Diaz, aged 28, was a teacher of Puerto Rican and Dominican heritage. When asked how the family would celebrate having the 300 millionth American in its midst, the baby's maternal grandmother replied, "We're Hispanic, and we celebrate so many different holidays. But how do you celebrate being the 300 millionth American born in a family of Hispanics, Jamaicans, Puerto Ricans, Dominicans? It's just so Americanized."[15]

Other hospitals made similar claims to having the celebrated newborn in their nurseries. In Atlanta, Kiyah Boyd of Mableton, Georgia, was welcomed by a film crew from ABC's *Good Morning America*. Kiyah's father, Kristopher Boyd, aged 28, was in the U.S. Navy and had been stationed in Bahrain but came home to join his wife, Keisha, also 28, whom he met in the service. Both are American-born. In San Francisco, hospital spokesman Kevin McCormack announced the 300 millionth American was an Asian American baby delivered at 4:42 A.M. Pacific time in California's Pacific Medical Center. William Frey, a demographer at the Brookings Institution, dismissed all of these claims, telling the *New York Times*, "I'm still going with the Latino baby boy in Los Angeles. This is the symbol of where we're heading: the new American melting pot."[16]

Today, a new American is born every 7 seconds, another one dies every 13 seconds, and every 31 seconds a new immigrant sets foot on American soil.[17] The presence of so many immigrants of Hispanic or Asian descent has relegated the largely white America of the 1950s to the dustbin of history. To say that Ozzie and Harriet don't live here anymore is an understatement. Even the quintessential institutions of white America have been upended by the rapid ticktock of the immigrant clock. The Miss America pageant, for example, had only white winners until the 1980s. Yet even it has been sublimated as other ethnic pageants have gained in popularity— for example, Miss Liberia USA, Miss Vietnam USA, Miss India USA, Miss Asian America, Miss Latina U.S., and Miss Haiti. *Washington Post* reporter Darryl Fears vividly depicts the differences between these shows and Miss

America: "At the immigrant pageants, beauty has a browner, more worldly tinge. Noses are wider and eyes are a gooey chocolate brown, framed in almond-like contours. Hips sway more in talent segments, such as an adaptation of a Bollywood performance at Miss India, or a belly dance at Miss Liberia."[18]

These new immigrants have made many white Anglo-Saxon Protestants, along with lots of white Catholics and Jews, uncomfortable in their own skin. Conservative commentator Patrick J. Buchanan writes that uncontrolled immigration threatens to ruin his vision of what America has been and should be: "This is an invasion, the greatest invasion in history . . . , and if this is not stopped, it will mean the end of the United States."[19] Historian Alan Brinkley reminds us that fear of the Other is deeply rooted in American history: "Diversity is something we claim to value, but diversity is difficult. When diversity suddenly and rapidly increases in new ways, it is especially difficult."[20] Buchanan ominously warns that the ongoing arrival of immigrants both legal and illegal means that "America is being transformed. [There is] the death of faith, the degeneration of morals, contempt for the old values, collapse of the culture, paralysis of the will."[21]

In his remarks commemorating the birth of the 200 millionth American, Johnson observed that during the course of history, Americans asked themselves three fundamental questions: "At the beginning, we said, 'Shall we be a free nation?' A hundred years ago we asked ourselves, 'Shall we be one nation?' Thirty-five years ago we asked ourselves, 'Shall we then be a humane nation?'" Each generation, Johnson noted, had answered these queries in the affirmative. But then LBJ posed a fourth question, "Shall we be a great nation?" and posited that the ultimate answer to this "difficult" challenge would be provided in "the third century [by] the next 100 million Americans."[22]

Searching for a Politics of Comfort

In times of despair, Americans yearn for past comforts. For example, in 1939, in the midst of the Great Depression, 63 percent of respondents told the Gallup Organization that their fellow countrymen were "happier and more contented during the horse and buggy days than they are now."[23] While the Depression was terrible, a hardscrabble existence was a frequent feature of American life long before the stock market collapsed. Nonetheless, whenever a crisis arises, it brings with it a strong desire for the creature comforts of the past. Such was the case after the horrific September 11 attacks. Following the collapse of the World Trade Center, the burning of the Pentagon, and the plane crash in the Pennsylvania hills, Clear Channel Communications, which owns 1,170 radio stations and has 110 million listeners each week, issued a list of 150 songs it considered inappropriate for airplay, including the Gap Band's "You Dropped a Bomb on Me," Soundgarden's "Blow Up the Outside World," the Beatles' "Ticket to Ride," the Drifters' "On Broadway," all songs by Rage against the Machine, and even John Lennon's anthem, "Imagine."[24] MTV took to playing what it called "comfort videos, " including Lenny Kravitz's "Let Love Rule," Bob Marley's "One Love," Sting's "If You Love Somebody Set Them Free," and U2's "Walk On." Head programmer Tom Calderone explained, "This is a weird word to use, but we're trying to find videos that are soothing and compatible with what the country is feeling right now."[25] The major network executives were astounded when compilations of *I Love Lucy* and *The Carol Burnett Show* scored big ratings. Television programmers almost immediately began scouring their vaults for more "comfort programs" that could be repackaged and reaired.

This search for a politics of comfort considerably aided George W. Bush's political standing. On September 10, the Gallup Organization found Bush holding the lowest job-approval rating of his young administration, 51 percent.[26] But three weeks later, his approval scores had jumped to an astounding 90 percent.[27] MSNBC commentator Chris Matthews depicted Bush prior to 9/11 as "an easy-going Prince Hal" who, thanks to the terrorist attacks, was "transformed by instinct and circumstance into a warrior King Henry."[28] This image was both consoling and comfortable. All the controversy surrounding Bush's election in 2000 and the Supreme Court's subsequent actions in *Bush v. Gore* disappeared, and few Americans felt buyer's remorse. A Zogby poll taken shortly after the attacks found that 67 percent of those surveyed did not believe the country would be better off if Al Gore had been president.[29] Similar percentages were happy that Bill Clinton was no longer in the White House and that Dick Cheney rather than Joe Lieberman was vice president.[30]

Bush's King Henry persona lasted long after the 9/11 attacks were seared into the public's memory. In a February 2003 *Los Angeles Times* poll, 71 percent of respondents characterized Bush as a "strong and decisive leader." The same poll also showed that more than three-quarters of respondents liked Bush as a person, and a remarkable 50 percent described themselves as either "hopeful" or "happy" that he was president.[31] The Iraq debacle, Hurricane Katrina, and the subsequent financial crisis eventually erased the public persona that Bush and the voters had so happily constructed. In its place came a new politics of discomfort.

The New Politics of Discomfort

Today's politics is highly personal. When Americans speak about race, family, religion, or homosexuality, many say, "Hey, you're talking about me," causing a profound level of both personal and political discomfort. A 2007 Pew Research poll illustrates the point. Many of those who responded condemned various social trends as "bad things": 66 percent thought single women should not have children; 59 percent thought unmarried couples should not have children; 50 percent said gay and lesbian couples should be discouraged from raising children; 44 percent disapproved of people living together without marrying; 41 percent frowned on mothers of young children working; 29 percent objected to women choosing not to have children; 23 percent believed that women should not wait until after age 35 to have their first child; 21 percent said it was not right for fathers to stay home with their children; and 4 percent objected to people marrying at older ages.[32] Most Americans are not particularly comfortable talking about race, family lifestyles, gay rights, or religion, yet these transformations are reshaping present-day politics.

At the same time, most Americans remain very comfortable talking on a one-to-one basis with their neighbors. They may say, "Oh, that's Sally and Joan," or, "There goes Cheryl, the single mom," or "Say hello to Bill and Jack," or "Those are the Joneses, a blended family with lots of kids," or "Those are the Smiths, our good Mormon [or Buddhist or Muslim or atheist] neighbors." In each case, Americans are essentially saying that the person they know is okay. That, too, resembles a politics of yore, when ethnic groups carved out particular urban neighborhoods as their own—a reality Jimmy Carter acknowledged in 1976, when he promised not to use the power of the federal government to alter the "ethnic purity" of these communities.[33] Carter later apologized for this remark, but it reassured voters that as president, he would not disrupt the comfortable politics of race and ethnicity to which they had become accustomed: "People have a tendency—and it is an unshakable tendency—to want to share common social clubs, common churches, common restaurants. I would not use the forces of the Federal Government to break up the ethnic character of such neighborhoods."[34]

We long to be creatures of comfort. Americans take pride in their melting pot of values, which creates an image of uniformity. Becoming an American means becoming one with each other. Prior to the Civil War, for example, it was grammatically correct to say, "The United States are . . ." After that conflict, it became grammatically correct to say, "The United States is . . ." To Americans, "E Pluribus Unum" (Out of many, one) is not just a slogan but a desire. Yet a country whose contemporary slogan might be "E Pluribus Duo" (Out of many, two—or more), thrusts everyone into a politics of discomfort. While we may like (and even be comfortable with) our neighbors, our neighborhoods often are relatively homogenous. Abraham Lincoln's infamous "mystic chords of memory" seem to have hit a discordant note.[35]

This is a book about discomfort. Today, the parameters of political conflict are in the midst of a significant redefinition. Conservatives look at the changing U.S. racial makeup, the decline of the "traditional" family (with its working dad, stay-at-home mom, and requisite two kids), the emergence of gay rights, and new forms of religious practice and say, "See, I told you things are awry in this country." A plethora of authors make these points, including former Pennsylvania senator Rick Santorum in *It Takes a Family*, Buchanan in *The Death of the West* and *State of Emergency*, and conservative radio talk show host William J. Bennett in *The Death of Outrage*. All proclaim the death of something—the death of a national memory that they once shared and that they believe has somehow been lost. The death they see is less about a romanticized past than it is mourning the loss of certainty in life itself. Indeed, it is the demise of universal definitions of right and wrong. Conservative historian Gertrude Himmelfarb observes that contemporary liberal Protestant theologians avoid using words associated with an older morality (*sin, shame,* and *evil*) in favor of less harsh words (*inappropriate, unseemly,* or *improper*).[36]

Liberals are equally discomforted. While many celebrate a new politics of rights, Democrats are hardly anxious to have referenda on gay marriage appear on state ballots. When she took control of Congress in 2007, House speaker Nancy Pelosi decided that she would advocate programs that made Democrats of every stripe comfortable: raising the minimum wage, implementing the recommendations of the 9/11 Commission, doing something about health care, enacting ethics reforms, proposing new monies for stem cell research, making college tuition tax deductible, and asking Bush administration officials tough questions. Deciding to engage in their own politics of comfort means that Democrats often dodge issues that make them uncomfortable. Paraphrasing John F. Kennedy, Democrats Rahm Emanuel and Bruce Reed criticized the comfort level their party found during the George W. Bush years by using the mantra, "Ask not what your country can do for you, ask focus groups what they want you to do for them."[37]

This new politics of discomfiture is likely to continue for some time to come. In *The Audacity of Hope*, Barack Obama describes a nation where too many citizens appear to be fellow strangers: "In an era of globalization and dizzying technological change, cutthroat politics and unremitting culture wars, we don't even seem to possess a shared language with which to discuss our ideals, much less the tools to arrive at some rough consensus about how, as a nation, we might work together to bring those ideals about."[38] Since his emergence on the national stage, Obama has sought to bridge the cultural gap between the so-called red states and blue states. In his 2004 keynote address to the Democratic Convention, for example, Obama pleaded with his fellow citizens to find common ground:

> The pundits like to slice and dice our country into Red States and Blue States: Red States for Republicans, Blue States for Democrats. But I've got news for them, too. We worship an awesome God in the Blue States, and we don't like federal agents poking around our libraries in the Red States. We coach little league in the Blue States and, yes, we've got some gay friends in the Red States. There are patriots who opposed the war in Iraq, and there are patriots who supported the war in Iraq. We are one people, all of us pledging allegiance to the stars and stripes, all of us defending the United States of America.[39]

Compounding the difficulty of finding a common vocabulary is a new sense of moral freedom that Americans have used to reconfigure their personal lives. The emergence of this moral freedom began with the civil rights and women's rights revolutions of the 1960s and 1970s. Today, these revolutions are largely over, and their aftereffects are increasingly interwoven into the fabric of American life. But the consequences of these revolutions go far beyond greater opportunities for minorities or equal pay and better jobs for women. These revolutions have given birth to something even more momentous: the opportunity for all Americans to make more moral choices than ever before in their personal lives. The discomfiture this new-found freedom has created has given our politics its renewed passion.

Historian Henry Adams said that American politics "is at bottom, a struggle not of men but of forces."[40] This book is about new forces that are reshaping American politics as it was previously understood. Chapter 1 describes how the nation has been transformed from the 1950s, occasionally using my own family as an example. Chapter 2 tells the story of new immigrants and how their presence is making the United States a less white, more diverse, and sometimes even more angry country. Chapter 3 explains how the traditional family structure of the 1950s has been split apart and reconstituted into innumerable mutations. Chapter 4 builds on this theme by telling the story of one important redefinition of the family—that is, how homosexuals have been increasingly accepted into American life and are creating families, whether or not a state gives them either the right to marry or enter into a civil union. Chapter 5 describes how the location of religion has moved away from the church pews to more interior (and private) expressions of faith. Chapter 6 discusses how these trends have resulted in the demise of the grand Republican coalition that Ronald Reagan constructed in the 1980s and that culminated with the 1994 Republican takeover of Congress. Chapter 7 explains how the 2008 election gave the nation not just a new president but the beginnings of a fresh and potentially powerful coalition favoring Obama and the Democrats.

The forces that made Obama the 44th president of the United States continue to swirl as we mark the first decade of the new century. Whether President Obama can use the transformations in how Americans think about race, family, and religion to develop a new politics of comfort is an open question. California, often a trendsetter, gave conflicting answers to this dilemma in 2008. Its citizens took to Obama's message of hope and change, giving him 61 percent of their votes. But at the same time, Californians overturned a state supreme court decision legalizing gay marriage by a margin of 52 percent to 48 percent. One-third of Obama's supporters backed Proposition 8, leading many homosexuals in California (and elsewhere) to conclude that they remain the Other in our society and that their presence (particularly at the altar) makes many of their fellow citizens uncomfortable.[41] African Americans and Hispanics were at the forefront of the opposition to Proposition 8 even as they overwhelmingly supported Obama and his call for national unity.[42]

These contradictory results raise the question of whether we have become so discomforted that we remain comfortable opposing what Brinkley calls the Other. In his masterful study of Richard M. Nixon's political career, historian Rick Perlstein argues that Nixon's legacy was the creation of two kinds of Americans:

> On the one side, that "Silent Majority." The "nonshouters." The middle-class, middle American, suburban, exurban, and rural coalition who call themselves, now, "Values voters," "people of faith," "patriots," or even, simply, "Republicans"—and who feel themselves condescended to by snobby opinion-making elites, and who rage about un-Americans, anti-Christians, amoralists, *aliens*. On the other side are the "liberals," the "cosmopolitans," the "intellectuals," the "professionals"—"Democrats." Who say they see shouting in opposition to injustice as a higher form of patriotism. Or say "live and let live." Who believe that to have "values" has more to do with a willingness to extend aid to the downtrodden than where, or if, you happen to worship—but who look down on the first category as unwitting dupes of feckless elites who exploit sentimental pieties to aggrandize their wealth, start wars, ruin lives. Both populations—to speak in ideal types—are equally, essentially, tragically American. And both have learned to consider the other not quite American at all.[43]

As we begin the Obama years, will we drop our comfort with an old politics associated with the Nixon and Reagan eras and enter a postpartisan era that does not revolve around the usual questions of race, gender, or religious affiliation? And in so doing, will we find new areas of discomfort? Answers to these questions will not come quickly. There will be fits and starts. But contained in these responses are surely going to be new interpretations of the old values of freedom, individual rights, and equality of opportunity. Seymour Martin Lipset notes that those "who focus on moral decline, or on the high crime or divorce rates, ignore the evidence that much of what they deplore is closely linked to American values which presumably they approve of, those which make for achievement and independence."[44] Lipset identifies this phenomenon as "American exceptionalism," meaning that while citizens may disagree about how the core values of the American experience should be applied to present-day life, Americans have never challenged the premises that have underpinned their democratic experiment. Instead, each generation has posited new answers to the ancient question of what it means to be an American by using the old values of freedom, individual rights, and equality of opportunity.

At the onset of a new presidency, this all-important and historic question takes on a new resonance. This book tells the story of how we arrived at our present-day condition and in the process how we are rethinking once more the notion of what it means to be an American.

One · One Family, Two Centuries

> *"Life belongs to the living, and he who lives*
> *must be prepared for changes."*
> —JOHANN WOLFGANG VON GOETHE

LIKE MANY AMERICANS OF A CERTAIN AGE, I have succumbed to the temptation to reach for a newspaper and examine the leading stories on my date of birth. In my case, the chronicle of choice was the *New York Times*, and the headlines for October 10, 1952, read, "South Korean Unit, Bayoneting Reds, Regains Key Peak"; "Work Completed on U.N. Buildings"; "Stevenson Taunts Rival for Backing McCarthy, Dirksen"; "U.S. to Give France $525,000,000 in Aid and Hints at More."[1] Perusing these stories draws the reader to a distant world that no longer seems pertinent. For me, the headlines reflect the fact that I am a child of the Cold War, a conflict that lasted nearly 40 years and ended as the twentieth century neared its close.

That decades-long struggle with the Soviet Union gave Americans an easy political and cultural shorthand. The world was divided in two: the "Free World" (the United States and its allies) versus those held captive behind the "Iron Curtain" (the Soviet Union and its Eastern European neighbors and later the People's Republic of China). Depending on how the Cold War was progressing, Americans either felt good about themselves (e.g., during the Eisenhower and Kennedy regimes in the 1950s and early 1960s) or didn't (e.g., when the Vietnam War produced a stalemated quagmire during the Johnson and Nixon regimes in the 1960s and 1970s).

13

Throughout the Cold War, answers to the all-important question, "What does it mean to be an American?" were easily forthcoming. Simply put, most Americans believed that communists hated individual freedom, while Americans celebrated it with ever greater fervor. As Hollywood film director Sydney Pollack observed, the Cold War "was very good fodder for drama, because you had what was perceived as a clearly virtuous position against what was seen as clearly bad."[2]

Because communism was viewed as being so throughly dastardly—in Ronald Reagan's words, "an evil empire"[3]—conformity of thought was not only welcome but seen as a political necessity. Arthur Larson, an undersecretary of labor during the Eisenhower administration, summarized the prevailing view: "Principles that we have always taken for granted as the air we breathe are now flatly denounced and denied over a large part of the world—the principles, for example, of the preeminence and the freedom and the sovereignty of the individual person." Larson described the emergence of an "Authentic American Center" that was sustained by the struggle with the Soviet empire: "We are playing for keeps now, with staggering world responsibilities that we cannot escape."[4] Sociologist Daniel Bell echoed Larsen's arguments, writing that between 1930 and 1950, several intense ideological conflicts emerged as a consequence of the rise of fascism and communism abroad, the Great Depression at home, and the brutally bureaucratized murder of millions in Adolf Hitler's concentration camps. The aftermath, Bell claimed, left the United States both politically and intellectually exhausted: "For the radical intellectual who had articulated the revolutionary impulses of the past century and a half, all this has meant an end to chiliastic hopes, to millenarianism, to apoplectic thinking—and to ideology. For ideology, which once was the road to action, has come to be a dead end."[5]

Without the fervor of ideology to guide them, Americans spent the 1950s engaged in the politics of personal self-improvement. Political scientist Robert Lane wrote that in their personal journeys, Americans would pat themselves on the back when they achieved a modicum of success and excoriate themselves when they suffered personal failures. Two of Lane's respondents—one a blue-collar worker, the other a mechanic—captured these countervailing trends:

BLUE-COLLAR WORKER: My God, I work where I want to work. I spend my money where I want to spend it. I buy what I want to buy. I go where I want to go. I read what I want to read. My kids go to the school that they want to go to, or where I want to send them. We bring them up in the religion we want to bring them up in. What else—what else could you have?

MECHANIC: I could have been better off but through my own foolishness, I'm not. What causes poverty? Foolishness. When I came out of the service, my wife had saved a few dollars and I had a few bucks. I wanted to have a good time, I'm throwing money away like water. Believe me, had I used my head right, I could have had a house. I don't feel sorry for myself—what happened, happened, you know. Of course you pay for it.[6]

During the 1950s, self-improvement became coupled with an intense desire for personal security, as symbolized by a family structure dominated by wage-earning fathers and homemaker mothers. In *Living History*, Hillary Rodham Clinton wrote that her stay-at-home mom was "a woman in perpetual motion, making the beds, washing the dishes and putting dinner on the table precisely at six o'clock."[7] Established gender roles not only created a sense of group loyalty but were viewed as essential to the national defense. For example, one 1950 civil defense project put men in charge of firefighting, rescue work, street clearing, and rebuilding; women tended to child care, hospital work, social work, and emergency feeding.[8] Still, the need for personal security was never-ending. A 1957 Ford Foundation study called for families that were "stronger emotionally and morally" to meet the dangers from abroad.[9] In the authors' eyes, family renewal meant that parents should set good examples for their children, view divorce as unthinkable, and associate with other wholesome families. Most Americans agreed. In 1950, just 90,992 divorces took place, with 54 percent of them not involving children.[10]

The emphasis on conformity inside the home became pervasive outside its boundaries, too. In 1956, William H. Whyte Jr. described the emergence of a new "organization man" whose social ethic stressed collaboration rather than confrontation and sublimation rather than expressions of individualism.[11] This emphasis on conformity extended not only to social and political thought but even to the means of production itself. California entrepreneur Ray Kroc, for example, used the bromides of factory life to begin his McDonald's hamburger empire. Meanwhile, on the other side of the country, William Levitt brought Ford Motor Company's techniques for mass-producing cars to the Long Island, New York, housing market.

In each case, the intent was clear: sell to families. And that market was immense. Clinton recalled that her mother counted 47 kids living on her square block in the Chicago suburbs.[12] So when Kroc advertised his hamburgers as a chance to "Give Mom a Night Off"—a precursor to its more famous slogan, "You Deserve a Break Today"—millions of harried mothers agreed."[13] And that was only the beginning. In Lakewood, California, returning GI's and Douglas Aircraft Company workers purchased 17,500 homes in just 33 months. The bargain was irresistible: an 800-square-foot, two-bedroom home for $7,575—or $595 down and $43 a month. (A three-bedroom, 1,100-square-foot home went for $8,525.)[14] According to architectural critic Paul Goldberger, these Levittown-style homes were much more than instant architectural wonders: "[T]hey turned the single detached single-family house from a distant dream to a real possibility for thousands of middle-class American families."[15] Whyte described these newly built suburbs as "the packaged villages that have become the dormitory of the new generation of organization men."[16]

The suburban Rhode Island neighborhood in which I grew up featured cookie-cutter houses built in 1954 by one of Levitt's many imitators. My parents paid $12,000 for their house, a three-bedroom, one-level ranch. Only two variations were available: some with a front peak, others without. In 1957, my sister, Janet, was born. As our neighborhood grew, its residents lived up to the American penchant for inventiveness and individual expression by making major modifications to the prefabricated designs, often by adding "family rooms" (as our family did in 1964) or a second floor with more bedrooms, especially when more than the conventional two children necessitated the renovations. Amid all this construction, family togetherness remained a theme. As one 1954 advertisement for a prefabricated home read, "When Jim comes home, our family room seems to draw us closer together."[17]

Inside the home, family life followed conventional patterns. My parents paralleled the working dad and stay-at-home mom of the era. In fact, it was not convention so much as an adherence to a strict schedule that characterized life in many 1950s households. My mother, a devoted record keeper, codified in my baby book the routine that I was to observe (and undoubtedly did) when I was two years old:

Breakfast at 7:30 A.M.

Play outside: 10:00–noon.

Lunch: noon.

Nap: 1:00–3:00 P.M.

Play outside till 4:30 P.M.

Supper at 5:30 P.M.

Bedtime at 7:30 P.M.

The 1950s penchant for avoiding controversy and maintaining order meant that when it came to male-female roles, relatively few differences existed between my grandparents—also a homemaker woman and employed man—and my parents. The chief distinctions were that my paternal grandparents shared their rented home with my grandmother's father, and my grandfather worked in the textile mills. My grandfather's only son, my father, acquired a college education and eventually secured a white-collar job as an accountant. Although the movement away from a workforce that used its hands to manufacture goods to one in which productivity meant using one's intellectual skills was gaining momentum, the status of women remained largely unchanged.

Despite the interregnum of World War II, which saw many single women enter the workforce for the first time, white women remained mostly inside the home. For many 1950s-era homemakers, leaving home was an impossibility—they did not drive. My mother, for example, did not learn to operate a car until the early 1960s. Only one family on my childhood street had a working mother, since transportation to and from work often required an automobile, especially in the suburbs, where mass transit had yet to make much of an impact. State laws also kept many women from working. During the Great Depression, more than half of the 48 states enacted statutes prohibiting employers from hiring married women. In 1937, Muriel Humphrey, wife of the future U.S. senator and vice president, took off her wedding ring (a necessary prerequisite for employment) and found a job as a bookkeeper.[18] Many of these laws—and their accompanying prejudices—remained on the books long after the Great Depression ended. For example, a 1954 *Esquire* magazine article called working wives a "menace."[19] The reasoning was simple: "undeserving" females would get lower-paying jobs that would otherwise go to male breadwinners at much higher salaries.[20]

Instead of entering the workforce, women were incessantly advised to find men and be helpmates. In a 1955 issue of *Better Homes and Gardens* magazine, Mrs. Dale Carnegie, wife of the famed individual motivator, told readers, "The two big steps that women must take are to help their husbands decide where they are going and use their pretty little heads to help them get there. Let's face it, girls. That wonderful guy in your house—and in mine—is building your house, your happiness and the opportunities that will come to your children." Carnegie added that while split-level homes were fine for the family, "There is simply no room for split-level thinking—or doing—when Mr. and Mrs. set their sights on a happy home, a host of friends, and a bright future through success in HIS job."[21]

Even when inflation prompted many mothers to find work during the 1960s and 1970s, their roles inside the household did not change much. For example, when my mother sought employment in 1965, she took a job at a local public school so that her working hours and vacations coincided with those of her children. But even as she worked outside the home, Mom continued the routines she established as a homemaker, including preparing the family meals and making sure the children adhered to their familiar schedules. Meanwhile, my father's authority remained firm, and his roles as principal breadwinner and home handyman went largely unquestioned.

Religious practices also stressed conformity. In the Roman Catholic Church, masses were said in Latin, as had been the practice for centuries. Devotion to ritual was an important part of Catholic life. Part of that devotion meant going to confession. In *Roman Catholicism in America*, Chester Gilles offers a vivid description of the 1950s confessional experience: "[M]any Catholics would go to confession weekly, usually on Saturday afternoons in a dimly lighted church. Penitents would wait, kneeling in pews alongside a confessional box where a priest would sit for hours hearing confessions, forgiving sins, and meting out penances usually requiring the penitent to say a certain number of Hail Marys and Our Fathers."[22] So it was in the White household, as confession became a weekly Saturday ritual. Once, having run out of sins to confess, I made up a few, only to have the priest accuse me of lying in the confessional booth. My mother, noting the unusual length of time it took for what was normally a quick ritual, wondered what horrible sin I had committed. (I avoided her questions.) Other church rules were also faithfully followed. For example, eating meat on Fridays was a definite no-no. Likewise, fasting before communion was lengthy: a 12-hour refrain from eating was recommended. Women were expected to cover their heads while attending mass, and attire for both sexes was always formal. The same dress code applied to the religious: priests always wore their Roman collars, while nuns were covered from head to toe in their black-and-white garments.

In enunciating these rules, the Catholic hierarchy reminded those in the pews of its command of eternal truths and saw fidelity to the church as the best means of attaining salvation. Sometimes this led to resentments among non-Catholics: in one 1952 survey, 43 percent of respondents said that Catholics tried too hard to get people to join their church, though 42 percent disagreed with that idea.[23] Alexis de Tocqueville once observed that while the doctrines and practices of the Roman Catholic Church astonished many Americans, "they feel a secret admiration for its discipline, and its extraordinary unity attracts them."[24] In this respect, Catholics and non-Catholics were far more alike than different. I can recall occasionally attending my father's Presbyterian Church and hearing the minister give one of his hellfire-and-brimstone sermons, full of certitude about the Almighty and the failings of his earthly servants.

As the social and cultural revolutions of the 1960s and 1970s gathered momentum, many Americans, especially within the Roman Catholic Church, longed for the certainty of the old-time religions. Instead of the universal Latin rite, contemporary masses are said in a multitude of languages, although Pope Benedict XVI has once again made the Latin liturgy an option, delighting older Catholics, who welcomed the reappearance of the familiar ritual in many parishes. Dressing for church is increasingly less formal for both priests and laity. Even eating meat on Fridays is permissible, and the fasting time prior to receiving Holy Communion has been reduced to a mere hour. Many faithful Catholics practice birth control despite Pope Paul VI's 1968 publication of *Humanae Vitae*, which denounced the Pill as violating the sanctity of human life. *New York Times* religion columnist Peter Steinfels maintains that the publication of *Humanae Vitae* created a Vietnam War–like credibility gap between the Catholic hierarchy and those sitting in the pews: "Theologians publicly dissented from official teaching; priests quietly or not so quietly resigned from the priesthood to marry; nuns shed not only their peculiar head-to-foot-garb but, in many cases, their traditional roles as schoolteachers and nurses, and not a few left their strife-ridden religious orders altogether."[25]

Not surprisingly, a conservative Catholic backlash has ensued and is increasingly vocal and attracting a loyal cadre of followers. Archbishop John J. Myers of Newark, New Jersey, says that the Second Vatican Council, which began a period of institutional reform within the church, "watered down the true teachings of Catholicism." While Myers's opinions have evoked strong criticism, his moral certitude draws more than a few admirers. Christine Flaherty, executive director of Lifenet, an antiabortion group, says of her bishop, "It is so uplifting to hear him, because he is teaching the truth. And the truth is like a magnet. It attracts people to it."[26] Myers's rigid interpretation of a bygone era has found significant support. For example, during the summer of 2004, the U.S. Conference of Catholic Bishops declared that Catholics "should *not honor* those who act in defiance of our fundamental moral principles [with] awards, honors, or platforms which would suggest support for their actions."[27] At the Catholic University of America, a furious debate ensued after the administration banned a speaker at a film symposium, and the college president barred all politicians from appearing on the campus during the 2004 and 2008 campaigns.

The 1950s image of a nation that was both righteous and surefooted is found not only in yellowed newspapers, musty magazines, or old black-and-white photographs but on the TV Land cable channel, which reruns programs from the era. The plots of these shows vary slightly, but the families depicted are always the same. One can watch the Nelsons, Andersons, or Cleavers in Any Town, USA, and see a working dad, a homemaker mom, and the requisite two children. Divorce was unmentionable, especially since the dads represented security while the moms were perfect hostesses. In 1947, the Screen Actors Guild, led by Ronald Reagan, organized "a series of unprecedented speeches . . . to be given to civic groups around the country, emphasizing that the stars now embodied the rejuvenated family life unfolding in the suburbs." It was said that Reagan's repeated evocations of family values were especially "stirring."[28] But speeches by actors defending the family paled in comparison to the power of the televised images espousing family virtues. For example, when Ward Cleaver of television's *Leave It to Beaver* asked his wife, June, what type of girl their son should marry, she responded, "Oh, some very sensible girl from a nice family . . . one with both feet on the ground, who's a good cook, and can keep a nice house, and see that he's happy." At this, her husband responded, "Dear, I got the last one of those."[29] Today, some observers might say that Ward Cleaver's statement was prophetic.

Even that most famous television program from the 1950s, *I Love Lucy*, strictly adhered to conventional thinking about the sexes. Although Desi Arnaz broke the mold by becoming the first hyphenated American television star in his role as Ricky Ricardo (a decision that CBS executives resisted), the Cuban-born Arnaz told his television (and real life) spouse, Lucille Ball, in the pilot episode, "I want a wife who's just a wife."[30] Throughout the series, Lucy resisted Ricky's demands that she stay home by devising lots of wacky ways to get into show business. Lucy eventually succumbed to conventional realities, first by getting pregnant in 1952 (a show that was viewed by 44 million Americans, more than twice the number who watched Dwight D. Eisenhower's inauguration)[31] and later by following audience trends and moving her television family from a small New York City apartment to a single-family home in the Connecticut suburbs.

Half a century later, television programs such as *I Love Lucy* still find appreciative audiences. David Halberstam, whose book on the 1950s is the definitive work on that decade, believed that these shows created images that were so sharp that they became objects of considerable nostalgia as the composition of families and the roles the sexes played within them changed radically in the decades that followed.[32] A few years into the twenty-first century, Lynn Jensen, a 33-year-old married mother with two children, expressed a widely shared longing for the stability of a bygone era: "This is going to sound silly, but I wish things were like they were when we were growing up. I wish we could go back in time. We had stable lives. Mom could stay home, and we could afford it. Life was slower. God, I'm sounding like my parents—all nostalgic for the old days. But it's true: There wasn't trouble then like there is today. Take my kids—they're growing up too fast. My daughter is only five, and she knows too much."[33] This longing for a lost past transcends partisanship. Brink Lindsey, a vice president for research at the Cato Institute, writes that "in the first decade of the twenty-first century, the rival ideologies of left and right are both pining for the '50s." "The only difference," Lindsey concludes, "is that liberals want to work there, while conservatives want to go home there."[34]

Of course, not all family life in mid-twentieth-century America was idyllic. In 1953, one physician wrote that under a feminine "mask of placidity" often lay "an inwardly tense and emotionally unstable individual seething with hidden aggressiveness and resentment."[35] A decade later, Betty Friedan published a classic study of the daily drudgery she described as "a problem with no name": "The problem lay buried, unspoken, for many years in the minds of American women. It was a strange stirring, a sense of dissatisfaction, a yearning that women suffered in the middle of the twentieth century in the United States. Each suburban wife struggled with it alone. As she made the beds, shopped for groceries, matched slip-cover material, ate peanut butter sandwiches with her children, chauf-feured Cub Scouts and Brownies, lay beside her husband at night—she was afraid to ask even of herself the silent question—'Is this all?'"[36] Capturing the sentiments of the moment, *The Feminine Mystique* sold more than two million copies and launched Friedan as a spokesperson for the feminist movement. As futurist Alvin Toffler memorably remarked, publication of *The Feminine Mystique* "pulled the trigger on history."[37]

In my home, the issue was not a problem with no name as much as a struggle with illness. I vividly recall my father having a severe heart attack in 1960. My mother, then a homemaker, pleaded with the local bank to al-low our family to pay only the interest on the home mortgage while my fa-ther recuperated. (She was turned down.) Dad eventually went back to work, but our brush with poverty struck a powerful chord, prompting Mom to learn to drive a car and eventually to return to the workforce. My father's numerous hospitalizations from 1960 until his death in 1977 be-came a subtext of life in our household, a plot very familiar to viewers of the popular television programs *Ben Casey* and *Dr. Kildare* but hardly the subject of the family sitcoms that are so frequently reaired in the half cen-tury since they first debuted.

Even now, despite all of the horrors hidden behind the suburban Levitt-towns of the 1950s, Americans retain a collective longing for a past that was certain of its moral values. The first signs of nostalgia came in 1962, when the Students for a Democratic Society (SDS) issued a manifesto that called on society's elders to reaffirm society's traditional mores: "Making values explicit is an activity that has been devalued and corrupted. . . . Un-like youth in other countries, we are used to moral leadership being exer-cised and moral dimensions being clarified by our elders."[38] The young members of the SDS, who became such strident critics of the Vietnam War and the Establishment they saw as its cause, charged that their parents had abandoned their role as moral authorities. Put another way, the children of the 1950s sought the clear voices heard in the fatherly television personas of Ozzie Nelson, Ward Cleaver, and Jim Anderson.

Enter the Twenty-first Century

Today, images of the prototypical 1950s-era nuclear family are quickly fading from public memory, and a new, more varied picture of the family is developing, even in my household. I married Yvonne Prevost in 1995, a late, first-time marriage for both of us. This alone was quite different from the social patterns of the post–World War II era into which we were born. In a 1947 bestseller, *The Modern Woman: The Lost Sex*, authors Marynia Farnham and Ferdinand Lundberg described feminism as a "deep illness" and called the notion of an independent woman a "contradiction in terms."[39] Sociologist David Riesman notes that a woman's failure to bear children went from being "a social disadvantage and sometimes a personal tragedy" in the nineteenth century to being a "quasi-perversion" in the 1950s.[40] Men who remained bachelors were also demonized as being "immature," "infantile," "narcissistic," "deviant," and even "pathological."[41] Family advice expert Paul Landis wrote, "Except for the sick, the badly crippled, the deformed, the emotionally warped and the mentally defective, almost everyone has an opportunity to marry."[42]

Given these pressures, it is not surprising that by 1959, 47 percent of brides were under 19 years of age. Women who remained unmarried flocked to colleges to find husbands.[43] In one popular guidebook, *Win Your Man and Keep Him*, marketed to these lonely women, the authors emphasized the cultivation of good looks, personality, and cheerful subservience: "If you are more than twenty-three-years-old . . . perhaps you have begun to wonder whether Mr. Right would ever come along for you. Your chances are still good; you can increase them appreciably by taking actions which this book advocates."[44] Another tract offered similar advice: "A girl who reaches the middle twenties without a proposal ought to consider carefully whether she really wishes to remain single. If she does not, she should try to discover why marriage hasn't come her way, and perhaps take steps to make herself more interesting and attractive."[45] My mother followed this advice, marrying my father when she was 21. But my mother did defy the conventional norms in one very important sense: she was a Catholic and wed a white Anglo-Saxon Protestant, a practice largely frowned on in 1944 and a decision that caused her parents to skip the wedding, performed by an army chaplain.

My marriage has adhered to today's social and cultural mores in other ways that are quite different from the patterns of a half century ago. For starters, my wife decided to keep her maiden name, thereby horrifying my 1950s-minded mother. Today, any weekly perusal of the "Weddings/Celebrations" page in the Sunday *New York Times* finds lots of women who have made similar decisions. Yet these pages capture not only the resolve of many women to retain their birth names but also the very different nature of family life itself. For example, on February 9, 2004, the *Times* reported the wedding of New Yorkers Norma Fritz and Michael O'Brien. The paper described the couple's romance: how she heard him walking up the stairs and pacing the floor in the apartment above hers as he visited his ex-wife and their two children, Dana, aged 13, and Jack, aged 11. Fritz and O'Brien spied each other in the hallway. Phone numbers were exchanged, and the two began dating. While the story may seem reminiscent of the 1950s, the circumstances have a decidedly twenty-first-century twist. Fritz, aged 45, had concluded some five years earlier that marriage was not in her immediate future. She decided to have a baby, conceiving her son, Noah, with sperm provided by an anonymous donor. According to Fritz, "I had opportunities to get married, but I never felt like any of them was 'the one.'" A friend, Nancy Brandwein, told the *Times*, "She has taken leaps and made bold decisions that others seldom would."[46]

When the couple began dating, O'Brien's two children babysat Fritz's son. According to Fritz, "Mike's ex-wife has been very, very gracious and his kids have been amazing." But as the romance blossomed, O'Brien, a software developer with J. P. Morgan Chase, began having doubts. The couple separated for two months. The relationship finally resumed when O'Brien knocked on the door of Fritz's apartment and four-year-old Noah answered and asked, "Oh, you love her again?"[47] After the wedding, the newly married couple immediately began house hunting in the suburbs.

David Brooks captures the differences between today's wedding announcements and those of a half century ago. Sentences that would never appear in contemporary newspapers include, "She is descended from Richard Warren, who came to Brookhaven in 1664. Her husband, a descendant of Dr. Benjamin Treadwell, who settled in Old Westbury in 1767, is an alumnus of Gunnery School and a senior at Colgate University." Or "Mrs. Williams is an alumna of Ashley Hall and Smith College. A provisional member of the Junior League of New York, she was presented to society in 1952 at the Debutante Cotillion and Christmas Ball." Even the captions seem quaint: "Mrs. Peter J. Belton, who was Nancy Stevens."[48] In

The Feminine Mystique, Friedan wrote that after World War II, women—like the newly married Mrs. Peter J. Belton—"lived their lives in the image of those pretty pictures of the American suburban housewife, kissing their husbands goodbye in the front of the picture window, depositing their stationwagonsful of children at school, and smiling as they ran the new electric waxer over the spotless kitchen floor." According to Friedan, these newlyweds "gloried in their role as women, and wrote proudly on the census blank: 'Occupation: housewife.'"[49]

In 2002, the wedding pages of the *New York Times* were revamped in a way no one could have dreamed of a half century earlier. That year, the paper's editors decided to publish reports of same-sex commitment ceremonies. Even the name was changed from "Weddings" to "Weddings/Celebrations." The paper's executive editor, Howell Raines, explained, "In making this change, we acknowledge the newsworthiness of a growing and visible trend in society toward public celebrations of commitment by gay and lesbian couples—celebrations important to many of our readers, their families, and their friends."[50] The first such announcement printed, tucked away in the corner of the page, heralded the marriage of Hillary Goodridge and Julie Goodridge, who had been granted permission to wed by the Massachusetts State Supreme Judicial Court.[51] Although the decision was controversial, what is striking about the first official lesbian wedding is how typical it was compared to those of other heterosexual couples. In an interview the day before the ceremony, Julie Goodridge described herself as being consumed by details, not the history she was making: "I'm thinking about whether or not the shoes are going to look good with the suit I picked out. Is the tailor going to be done, and have we ordered enough flowers, and are we going to have fried calamari at the reception, and how much is enough?"[52] Much like its announcements of heterosexual weddings, the *Times*'s first lesbian wedding announcement emphasized the résumés, accomplishments, and romance that had brought together the two women.

HILLARY GOODRIDGE, JULIE GOODRIDGE

Hillary Smith Goodridge and Julie Wendrich Goodridge, the lead plantiffs in the case that led the Massachusetts Supreme Judicial Court to extend marital rights to same-sex couples in that state, were themselves married on Monday in Boston. The Rev. William G. Sinkford, the president of the Unitarian Universalist Association, officiated at the organization's building there.

Hillary Goodridge, formerly Hillary Ann Smith, and Julie Goodridge, formerly Julie Neil Wendrich, changed their surnames eight years ago when their daughter, Annie, was born.

Hillary Goodridge, 48, is the director of the Unitarian Universalist Funding Program, a grant-making arm of the Universalists. She graduated from Dartmouth. She is the daughter of Ann Kiernan Smith of Vero Beach, Fla., and of Ralph K. Smith Jr. of Locust Valley, N.Y., who is a partner in Snow Becker Krauss, a New York law firm.

Julie Goodridge, 46, owns NorthStar Asset Management, an investment advisory firm in Boston. She graduated from Boston University and received a master's degree in education from Harvard. She is the daughter of the late Carolyn S. Wendrich and the late Kenneth A. Wendrich, who lived in Nashville. Mr. Wendrich was the executive director of the W. O. Smith/Nashville Community Music School in Nashville; before that he was dean of the Musical Arts at Bowling Green University in Ohio.

The couple met in 1985 at a seminar at Harvard about disinvestment from South Africa.

"I had just read a book by my friend Amy Domini on socially responsible investing," Julie Goodridge said. "At the seminar, Amy, who was speaking, introduced me to Hillary, who was dressed like a Republican stockbroker."

Julie Goodridge added, "For two years I pursued Hillary, but she would have nothing to do with me." She worked hard at making an impression, she said, volunteering to cook a meal in Hillary's apartment in Somerville, Mass., in the spring of 1987, when the two were working into the night on a speech to introduce Gloria Steinem at a conference at Radcliffe.

"When she told me that all she had in her refrigerator was raw chicken and some beer, I said, 'That's no problem,'" Julie Goodridge remembered. "I threw it together in an aluminum baking pan. Of course it was disgusting. We went out for ice cream instead."

A few months later, Julie Goodridge said she convinced Hillary to attend a gay pride parade with her, and their relationship finally blossomed. Now they live in a leafy Boston neighborhood that their friend Ms. Domini described as "fairly ordinary."

Ms. Domini, speaking at their wedding, said, "You introduce a couple of people, you maybe encourage them a bit, and what happens? A national crisis. The fault line for the presidential election. The coming of Armageddon."[53]

And when the Goodridges announced their separation in 2006, that, too, seemed typical. Mary Breslauer, a spokesperson for the couple, asked for privacy: "Julie and Hillary Goodridge are amicably living apart. As always, their number one priority is raising their daughter."[54]

As the Goodridges' wedding and subsequent split suggest, signs of change are all around us. In the life of the Whites/Prevosts, more changes arrived on the cusp of the new century when our daughter, Jeannette, was born. The childhood she enjoys today is quite different from the experiences of her parents half a century ago. While she is hardly of an age to go to the library and look up old newspapers, I retrieved a copy of the *New York Times* for her date of birth, April 14, 1997, in an effort to contrast her childhood experiences with mine. The front page headlines read, "Tiger Woods, in a Blaze, Rewrites Masters' History"; "Pope in Sarajevo, Calls for Forgiveness"; "Women in Washington State House Lead U.S. Tide"; "Smaller Investors Keeping Faith, Despite Stock Market Tumbles."[55] These stories reflect enormous transformations—among them, the nation's increased racial diversity, the tensions between ethnic groups that have characterized post–Cold War international conflicts, the enhanced role of women in politics, and the emergence of a new, more individualized, investor class. Most of these headlines would have been unthinkable in the 1950s, thereby vindicating the wisdom of eighteenth-century philosopher Johann Wolfgang von Goethe: "Life belongs to the living, and he who lives must be prepared for changes."[56]

As our daughter ages—and she will most likely spend the rest of her life in the twenty-first century—the sociological trends captured on her birth date will only accelerate. For example, in the Montgomery County, Maryland, public school system she attended from grades 1 to 4, just 45 percent of the students enrolled in 2003 were white. In fact, 2003 marked the last year that a majority of the county's graduating high school seniors were white, a stark contrast to thirty years earlier, when 90 percent of the total student population was white.[57] Watching high school graduates traverse various stages to receive their diplomas and knowing that many got their start in such diverse places as Kenya, El Salvador, Vietnam, and Iran, school superintendent Jerry D. Weast observed, "Sometimes you see an 'aha' in the crowd, the realization of what we've been saying all along: 'It's not coming. It's here.'"[58] Since 1991, Montgomery County schools have added 16,000 Hispanics, 12,000 blacks, and 7,000 Asians while losing 3,000 white students.[59] In her local primary school, Jeannette was a racial minority: the student population was 38 percent Hispanic, 33 percent African American, 18 percent white, and 10 percent Asian.[60] And that is only the beginning. Estimates show that by 2010, most residents of the Washington, D.C., metropolitan region will be minorities.[61]

Many of Jeannette's peers are not just brown-skinned but from very different family structures. The Census Bureau has tracked the changes.

- In 1960, 88 percent of children under 18 years of age lived with a married parent. Forty years later, that figure fell to 69 percent, a decline that continues each year.[62]

- From 1960 to 2000, the divorce rate more than doubled. Forty years ago, there was a one-in-four chance that a child would witness a parental split; today, the odds are one in two.[63]

- In 1960, just 5.3 percent of newborns had unmarried mothers. By 2000, that figure had increased more than sixfold to 33.2 percent. Among whites, the number of single mothers expanded tenfold, from 2 percent to 27 percent, while the ratio among blacks tripled from 22 percent to 68.5 percent.[64]

- Between 1960 and 2000, the number of single-parent families tripled from 9 percent to 27 percent of all households.[65]

- The number of cohabitating couples grew from 439,000 in 1960 to 4.7 million in 2000. Two-thirds of those born between the years 1963 and 1974 say that their first union was a cohabitation.[66]

Explaining these changes to children is sometimes challenging. In 2004, the *Washington Post* ran an article on its "Kids Post" page describing young Justin McGwire's lesbian parents. The 10-year-old was so perplexed as to why his two moms were prohibited from marrying that he went before the Maryland state legislature to ask, "[I]sn't this whole entire country supposed to be about freedom and equality and 'everybody's created equal?'" When describing his family to his peers, Justin says it is "no big deal," adding, "I've been over at friends' houses who have moms and dads, and it's no different than at my house."[67] Justin McGwire is just one sign of a radical transformation of the American family. In 2001, David Smith, a communications director for a national gay-rights organization, predicted, "I think the next decade is basically the decade of the gay family."[68]

Popular culture fully reflects the revolutions of our time. Television programs are a far cry from the married heterosexual couples with two children that dominated the 1950s and 1960s. Today, every variation of family life—from the singles who proliferated on *Seinfeld* to the father and son who shared an apartment on *Frasier* to the various couplings depicted on *Friends*—has been shown on network television. The 2003–4 season featured the ABC sitcom *It's All Relative*, featuring a heterosexual couple in which the wife was the daughter of two upscale gay men and the husband's family had a blue-collar background. The plots revolved around how these two families interacted with each other and their children.[69] During the 2005–6 television season, none of the top twenty-five rated television programs depicted a happily married couple. And in 2007, the major cable networks debuted several new programs, none of which celebrated marriage: HBO's drama series *Tell Me You Love Me* chronicled marital strife among several couples; VH1's reality series *Scott Baio Is 45 and . . . Single* described the inability of the former *Happy Days* television star to enter into marriage with any number of past lovers; Showtime's *Californication* depicted a man who regretted not marrying the mother of his child and decided to commence a series of unromantic hookups with several attractive young women.[70] Instead of married couples who might serve as updated 1950s-era role models, programmers prefer dysfunctional marrieds like *The Sopranos* or the Henricksons on HBO's *Big Love*, with its more-is-better polygamy setting.

Perhaps the most significant change is the prevalence of gay television characters. Surveying the airwaves, Focus on the Family founder James Dobson says, "It seems as if every episode of every sitcom on television now includes a gay character portrayed in a sensitive light. . . . It's gay, gay, gay, wherever you look."[71] Hyperbole aside, Dobson has a point. Things have changed. Thirty years ago, homosexuality was virtually banned from the airwaves. If it was mentioned at all, it was always with a negative connotation. For example, on *Marcus Welby, M.D.* (1969–76), starring Robert

Young, the doctor told his gay patient to "win that fight" against his homosexual feelings.[72] The contemporary airwaves feature several gay-oriented popular programs, including *Ellen, Will and Grace,* and the surprise 2003 summer hit, *Queer Eye for the Straight Guy. Ellen,* the first network series to depict a real-life gay character playing the lead, attracted 36 million viewers for its 1997 "coming out" episode.[73] One television critic described *Will and Grace,* with its gay/straight couple pairing, as the *I Love Lucy* of twenty-first-century programming.[74]

The success of *Queer Eye* is especially remarkable: in its first broadcast, the program drew 1.6 million viewers on the Bravo cable network, the largest audience in that channel's history. NBC, the parent company of Bravo, quickly decided to air the show on its main network, drawing 7 million viewers and earning second place in the time slot. In another sign of the times, *Queer Eye* had no trouble attracting first-rate sponsors, including Bausch and Lomb, Levi's jeans, Volkswagen, and promos for the hit summer flick *Seabiscuit.*[75] Only three NBC affiliates balked: WITN (Greenville, South Carolina) and WAGT (Augusta, Georgia) did not broadcast the program in its allotted prime-time slot, relegating it instead to 1:35 A.M. and 2:35 A.M., respectively. WCNC (Charlotte, North Carolina) did not show it at all.[76]

Another cultural barrier was broken in 2005 when an episode of *The Simpsons,* "There's Something about Marrying," featured a plot wherein Marge Simpson's sister, Patty Bouvier, came out of the closet while Homer Simpson conducted dozens of same-sex marriages after the town voted to legalize gay weddings as a means of garnering tourists. Ray Richmond, a television columnist and coeditor of *The Simpsons: A Complete Guide to Our Favorite Family,* noted that the episode represented a cultural milestone for the long-running program, which has become a billion-dollar franchise: "The issue [of gay marriage] was mainstream to some degree, but now that they've deigned it worthy of the show it is interwoven into the popular culture. *The Simpsons* bestows upon something a pop culture status it never had before, simply by being ripe for a joke."[77]

Max Mutchnick, cocreator of *Will and Grace,* explains the success of these gay-themed shows: "Television is catching up with society at large. These new gay shows are a reflection of what everyone sees now in their jobs, in their families, in their schools. The Brady Bunch never lived next door to anyone in America. Gay people do live next door."[78] In a 2000 Henry J. Kaiser Family Foundation survey, a surprising 52 percent of respondents believed that television programs and books had the "right amount" of gay themes and characters; only 37 percent answered "too many."[79] We are a long way, indeed, from the days when Lucy and Ricky Ricardo slept in separate beds and avoided the word *pregnancy* in favor of the term *expectant mother.*[80]

Institutional Change and Social Response

These societal transformations are dynamic. But change is hardly a new story in the American saga. In 1832, Tocqueville described meeting an American sailor and asking him why the ships made in his country were built to last only a short time. The man replied that "the art of navigation was making such quick progress that even the best of boats would be almost useless if it lasted more than a few years." From this and other observations, Tocqueville concluded, "Everyman sees changes continually taking place. Some make things worse, and he understands only too well that no people and no individual, however enlightened he be, is ever infallible. Others improve his lot, and he concludes that man in general is endowed with an indefinite capacity for self improvement."[81] Change and the optimism that often accompanies it are key elements of the American saga.

While Tocqueville focused on technological improvements, demographic changes have become a consistent theme in the American story. From 1890 to 1930, more than 15 million people from Central, Eastern, and Southern Europe came to American shores—roughly the number who emigrated to the United States from *all* countries from 1820 to 1890.[82] Many of these new arrivals found work in the industrial mills. Not surprisingly, a check of the 1920 Census found that my paternal grandfather, best described as a swamp Yankee, was working as a spinner in the Rhode Island textile mills. The Industrial Revolution and the immigrant hands whose labor gave that revolution its endurance touched every household. Old-timers took notice. In 1926, Massachusetts Yankee Daniel Chauncey Brewer authored a book appropriately titled *The Conquest of New England by the Immigrant.*[83]

Not surprisingly, the social and political institutions of the early twentieth century adhered to an old maxim: adapt or die. Most adapted. For example, neighborhood churches, many of them Roman Catholic, quickly assimilated the newcomers. New urban-based parishes were created, many with schools attached. According to author Peter Steinfels, the Catholic

Church also responded in a myriad of other ways to the needs of its newly arrived parishioners: "Catholic fraternal societies provided insurance while preserving ethnic cultures. Catholic reading circles and Catholic summer school programs of lectures, concerts, and dramas mirrored the nineteenth century Chautauqua Movement for cultural improvement. Catholic newspapers by the hundreds were printed in a babel of languages, often for small ethnic readerships but sometimes with national impact. Catholic publishers sprung up to serve a growing market for Bibles, prayer books, catechisms, religious novels, and pious nonfiction."[84]

Political parties also gave immigrants a place to turn. Party machines arose as a direct response to bosses' desire to tie their fortunes to those of the newcomers. As Richard Croker, a one-time head of Tammany Hall, put it, "Think of what New York is and what the people of New York are. One-half are of foreign birth. . . . They do not speak our language, they do not know our laws. . . . There is no denying the service which Tammany has rendered to the Republic, there is no such organization for taking hold of the untrained, friendless man and converting him into a citizen. Who else would do it if we did not?"[85]

Political scientist Robert D. Putnam describes how many twentieth-century institutional leaders wanted the immigrant newcomers to immerse themselves in the nation's civic life. In 1916, L. J. Hanifan, state supervisor of rural schools in West Virginia, coined the phrase *social capital*, explaining how he wanted his schools to enhance it:

> The individual is helpless socially, if left to himself. . . . If he comes into contact with his neighbor, and they with other neighbors, there will be an accumulation of social capital, which may immediately satisfy his social needs and which may bear a social potentiality sufficient to the substantial improvement of living conditions in the whole community. The community as a whole will benefit by the cooperation of all its parts, while the individual will find in his associations the advantages of the help, the sympathy, and the fellowship of his neighbors.[86]

Hanifan's views became commonplace. A 1920 Massachusetts conference on immigrant education held the education process responsible for ensuring "that our American institutions may endure. . . . We believe in an Americanization which has for its end the making of good American citizens by developing in the mind of everyone who inhabits American soil an appreciation of the principles and practices of good American citizenship."[87]

Social Change and Political Response in the 1950s

Even the less demanding and seemingly placid 1950s saw more institutional adaptations to new realities than is commonly understood. One important transformation came when returning nonwhite servicemen from World War II and Korea attempted to relocate in predominantly white neighborhoods. In 1951, Harvey Clark, a black man, tried to move into Cicero, Illinois, a largely white community. A mob of more than 4,000 whites spent four days tearing apart his apartment while police stood by and joked with them. Two years later, when the first black family moved into Chicago's Trumbull Party public housing project, neighbors "hurled stones and tomatoes" and trashed stores that sold groceries to the new residents. Despite the unfavorable publicity, prejudices against blacks remained strong. *Life* magazine reported in 1957 that in Dearborn, Michigan, nearly 10,000 Negroes worked at the Ford Motor plant but that "not one Negro can live in Dearborn itself."[88]

In 1954, the Supreme Court formally ended segregated public education in its *Brown v. Board of Education* ruling. That change engendered strong resistance, especially in the states most affected by the decision. In 1957, a federal court ordered nine black students admitted to Central High School in Little Rock, Arkansas. The state's governor, Orval Faubus, resisted and summoned the National Guard to prevent the order's enforcement, rationalizing that the Guard members were attempting "to maintain or restore the peace and good order of this community [and] not act as segregationists or integrationists."[89] But when mobs gathered to prevent the Little Rock Nine from entering the school, President Dwight D. Eisenhower federalized the Arkansas Guard, noting that his constitutional duty required him to implement Supreme Court decisions. This, too, represented a change of heart. Only two months earlier, Eisenhower had announced at a news conference, "I can't imagine any set of circumstances that would ever induce me to send federal troops . . . into any area to enforce the orders of a federal court."[90] Although the black students ultimately were enrolled, Faubus's actions won him an unprecedented third term in the governor's mansion. Forty years later, however, another former Arkansas governor, Bill Clinton, honored the Little Rock Nine with the Congressional Gold Medal. Their courageous actions had begun a profound transformation.

In 1957, Congress responded to the brewing civil rights revolution by enacting the first civil rights law since Reconstruction. Senate majority leader Lyndon B. Johnson believed that passage of a civil rights bill was essential to the well-being of two of the nation's most vital institutions: the Senate and the political parties that inhabited it. According to Johnson biographer Robert Caro, the Texas Democrat cajoled his colleagues, saying, "We've got the *world* looking at us here! We've got to make the world see that this body *works!*" To Republicans, Johnson pleaded, "You're the party of Lincoln. That's something to be proud of. You're the image of Lincoln." To Democrats, LBJ warned, "Our party's always been the place that you can come to whenever there's injustice. That's what the Democratic Party's *for*. That's why it was born. That's why is survives. So the poor and the downtrodden and the bended can have a place to turn. And they're turning to us now. We can't let them down. We're down to nut-cutting now, *and we can't let them down.*"[91] After considerable wrangling, the bill passed by an overwhelming vote of 72 to 18.

The 1950s also saw the growth of movements outside the existing constitutional structures that were altering both the scope and direction of political conflict. In 1960, political scientist E. E. Schattschneider wrote, "We have had difficulty perceiving change because we have looked for the wrong kind of conflict (conflict *within* the government) and we have underestimated the extent to which *the government itself as a whole* has been in conflict with other power systems."[92] While the civil rights revolution qualified as an example of a struggle that began outside the traditional constitutional tripartite separation of federal powers, it was not the only one. In his 1961 farewell address, Dwight Eisenhower acknowledged the growth of the "military-industrial complex," whose growing power threatened to disrupt the artful arrangements so carefully constructed by the founding fathers: "Today, the solitary inventor, tinkering in his shop, has been overshadowed by task forces of scientists in laboratories and testing fields. In the same fashion, the free university, historically the fountainhead of free ideas and scientific discovery, has experienced a revolution in the conduct of research. Partly because of the huge costs involved, a government contract becomes virtually a substitute for intellectual curiosity. For every old blackboard there are now hundreds of new electronic computers."[93]

During the 1950s, the family itself was also changing, despite the many societal pressures to conform. For example, the rate of teenage pregnancy peaked in 1957.[94] Moreover, even as the nuclear family was being celebrated in the popular culture, the Cold War required more mothers to be employed in defense-related industries. The 1952 Democratic platform contained the promise, "Since several million mothers must now be away from their children during the day, because they are engaged in defense work, facilities for adequate day care of these children should be provided and adequately financed."[95]

In his Farewell Address, Eisenhower observed that "it is the task of statesmanship to mold, to balance, and to integrate these and other forces, new and old, within the principles of our democratic system."[96] In other words, society's leaders must capture and control the transformations at work. A major theme of John F. Kennedy's quest for the presidency was that Eisenhower had failed to manage conflicts sparked by societal change. Accepting the 1960 Democratic nomination, Kennedy charged that "a slippage in our intellectual and moral strength" had occurred, adding, "Seven lean years of drought and famine have withered a field of ideas."[97] Kennedy's mantra, "It's time to get this country moving again," not only referred to a reinvigorated presidency but also called on the American polity to heed the many metamorphoses of change already at work within it.

The Scope and Intensity of Change in the Twenty-first Century

While changes in the nation's social and cultural life are hardly new, as even the seemingly placid 1950s demonstrate, the scope and intensity of today's transformations are impressive. Changes in the definition of the family itself, the question of what people of mixed racial heritage call themselves, and new ways religion is practiced all characterize life in the twenty-first century. For example, my wife and I own a duplex home in Fall River, Massachusetts. A few years ago, we searched for a tenant for our one-bedroom furnished apartment. Those who came were either unmarried couples—usually in their first cohabitation experience—or singles who had previously been married. Some cohabitating applicants had the encouragement of their parents. One especially memorable example was a young man who had just broken up with his girlfriend. Together they had one child, but the child's mother had three other offspring by three different men. We had nearly ninety inquiries from persons of many different racial backgrounds, but few came from either single people who had never been married or from married couples with or without children.

In the twenty-first century, there are numerous examples of institutions that are bending—sometimes in surprising ways—to the social and cultural transformations that are taking place. One is the Christian Coalition, the organization formerly headed by the Reverend Pat Robertson. While its current president, Roberta Combs, finds her conservative political views akin to Robertson's, she is cut from a very different cloth. Combs believes that to survive in the twenty-first century, the Christian Coalition must seek alliances with unlikely partners. Thus, she teamed up with New York Democratic senator Charles Schumer to support antispam legislation that severely restricts the use of e-mail to distribute pornography. In another sign of apostasy, Combs met with then-Senator Hillary Rodham Clinton to discuss prescription drugs and how the elderly could be helped by federal coverage. While Clinton remains anathema to the Christian Coalition's members, Combs believes that the group's antipathy must give way so that the legislation they jointly seek can become law. Says Combs, "If you are going to make progress, you have to be tolerant. You have to be willing to work with Democrats. If there is legislation that affects the family, you have to work with both sides of the aisle."[98]

Governments are also responding to society's changes, in some cases molding them to fit new circumstances. In 2001, the San Diego City Council saw the blurring of racial and color lines and banned the word *minority* from all city documents.[99] Other state and local governments have also jettisoned antiquated rules to adapt to new social realities. In 2000, 60 percent of Alabamians voted to repeal the portion of the state's constitution forbidding interracial marriages, making Alabama the final state to remove the official prohibition on miscegenation.[100] In 1952, twenty-nine states prohibited interracial marriage, which was a particularly entrenched taboo.[101] When the Supreme Court was asked to overturn these statutes following *Brown v. Board of Education*, it refused. As one law clerk advised a justice, "In view of the segregation cases, it would be wise judicial policy to duck this question for a time."[102] Thus, the Supreme Court acknowledged a binary world that divided people into black and white, although such a world never really existed in practice and was inevitably going to bend in the decades to come.

Yet for every institution that is adapting to changing times, others remain sclerotic. Chief among these is the U.S. military and its attitude toward gays. Cathleen Glover, a 1999 graduate of Miami University of Ohio, chose to attend the Defense Language Institute (DLI), the U.S. military's premier language school, after a U.S. Army recruiter came to her home and enticed her to join. The army offered to pay for her postgraduate education, and she was told that if she studied Arabic and liked to travel, her military career would be long and rewarding.[103]

The DLI, located at the Presidio in Monterey, California, is one of the nation's most prestigious institutions of higher learning. Founded on the eve of World War II, when the army established a secret school to teach Japanese, the institute expanded during the Cold War, and native speakers of more than 30 languages were recruited to teach there. Russian quickly emerged as the largest program. But as U.S. security needs changed, so did the school's offerings. For example, during the Vietnam War, more than 20,000 service personnel studied Vietnamese there. With the advent of the all-volunteer forces and the opening of most specialties to women in the 1970s, the DLI again adapted, admitting women.[104] After September 11, officials placed a priority on teaching Arabic, which is now the DLI's most popular language, with 832 students. Korean (743 students), Chinese (353 students), and Russian (301 students) are also studied extensively.[105] Through the years, the institute has shown itself capable of responding to the nation's changing security needs.

In a moment of severe stress, however, Glover penned a letter to the *Monterey County Herald* describing how she had been leading a double life: one on the base; the other sharing a nearby apartment with her gay partner. The torment had taken its toll, and the relationship ended, prompting Glover to write, "What if a married person in the military couldn't tell anyone that his wife exists?" Her immediate superior, not wanting to lose yet another gay student, initially refused to acknowledge Glover's homosexuality. But Glover was soon found to be in violation of the military's "Don't ask, don't tell" policy. The words "HOMOSEXUAL ADMISSION" were written in large capital letters on her discharge papers.[106]

The security risks posed by dismissing gay Arab linguists are grave. Since "Don't ask, don't tell" was instituted in 1993, fifty-eight Arabic linguists have been discharged from military service despite repeated warnings from various government agencies that training more Arab linguists was a national security priority.[107] An October 2001 House Intelligence Committee report discovered that "thousands of pieces of data are never analyzed, or are analyzed 'after the fact' because there are too few analysts, even fewer with the necessary language skills."[108] A 2002 General Accounting Office study disclosed that staff shortages in Arabic and Farsi had "adversely affected agency operations and compromised U.S. military, law enforcement, intelligence, counter-terrorism, and diplomatic efforts."[109] Former congressman Marty Meehan, a Massachusetts Democrat whose bill to repeal "Don't ask, don't tell" had 124 cosponsors in the 110th Congress, says, "At a time when our military is stretched to the limit and our cultural knowledge of the Middle East is dangerously deficient, I just can't believe that kicking out able, competent Arabic linguists is making our country any safer."[110]

Bill Clinton's 1993 introduction of the "Don't ask, don't tell" policy was controversial. General Colin Powell, then serving as chair of the Joint Chiefs of Staff, told the president that having gays in the military would be "prejudicial to good order and discipline."[111] In a poll taken at the time, 48 percent of respondents opposed the policy, while 45 percent approved. But the passion lay with the opposition: only 16 percent of respondents strongly approved of lifting the ban, while 33 percent strongly disapproved.[112] Yet Clinton insisted on the change, telling Powell that the government had spent $500 million ousting 17,000 gays from the military during the previous decade.[113] Clinton managed to find a lonely Republican ally in Barry Goldwater, who told reporters, "You don't need to be straight to fight and die for your country. You just need to shoot straight."[114] But not even the iconic Goldwater could convince his fellow Republicans to support Clinton. Even though the president ultimately prevailed, the military continued to resist, and "[m]any anti-gay officers simply ignored the new policy and worked even harder to root out homosexuals, costing the military millions of dollars that would have been far better spent making America more secure."[115]

The institutional rigidity of the U.S. military remains costly. According to military estimates, the cost of training each DLI graduate is $33,500, excluding room, board, and the stipend each student receives.[116] According to the Government Accountability Office, more than 11,000 military personnel—including 800 in crucial jobs such as Glover's—have been dismissed for being gay since 1993.[117] Other countries have shown themselves more facile in making changes to their military policies. For example, Canada officially ended its ban on gays in the military in 1992, while Britain did so in 2000.[118]

The Search for an "Axial Principle"

In the early days of the twenty-first century, an old slogan has taken on new meaning. During the 1960s and 1970s, a commonly heard phrase was, "The personal is political." Advocates of women's rights and civil rights maintained that gender and race were not merely private affairs. Politicians ultimately resolved controversies about when people should marry, have sex, and work or stay at home with their children and about whether blacks could obtain equitable housing, attend biracial schools, or even enter polling booths. As these struggles illustrate, societal change and political conflict go hand in hand. But identifying the changes at work (and the resulting conflicts) has proven more difficult than previously imagined. Twenty-five years ago, Everett Carll Ladd Jr. wrote that the "student of American government and politics needs to know which links between the political and social spheres have the greatest influence on politics and how changes in the larger social environment are reshaping politics, molding it, and moving it in new directions. What aspects are the most consequential? We need an 'axial principle' that identifies the primary features of American society that together form the distinctive setting for political life."[119]

The search for an "axial principle" still continues, often unsuccessfully. Today's changes have resulted in some confusion about the most elemental matter of conflict: how to label it. One reason for this muddle is the confusion that surrounds the sense of self and which identities are most important. This state of affairs is in sharp contrast to the 1960s, when race rose to the forefront, as the Kerner Commission concluded in 1968: "Our nation is moving toward two societies, one black, one white—separate and unequal."[120] Racial identification became part of an emerging political equation: whites were whites; blacks were blacks. Even those of mixed racial heritage were forced to choose. Thus, during the nineteenth century, Virginia's governors began the practice of identifying someone as black if he or she met the "one drop" test.[121]

Today, there is a growing lack of racial self-definition. In the 2000 Census, Levonne Gaddy of Tucson, Arizona, checked 3 of the 19 available racial categories: white, African American, and American Indian. Said Gaddy, "When I see the word 'race,' I cringe, because I don't see there is much connected to the word."[122] Gaddy's lack of association with the word *race* would have astonished her nineteenth- and twentieth-century ancestors. Whether it be race, sex, or other controversies, conflict is both a matter of definition and of choice. As Schattschneider wrote in *The Semi-Sovereign People,*

> Political conflict is not like an intercollegiate debate in which the opponents agree in advance on a definition of the issues. As a matter of fact, *the definition of alternatives is the supreme instrument of power*: the antagonists can rarely agree on what the issues are because power is involved in the definition. He who determines what politics is about runs the

country, because the definition of the alternatives is the choice of conflicts, and the choice of conflicts allocates power. It follows that all conflict is confusing.[123]

One illustration of using outmoded conflicts in a futile attempt to understand the political dynamics at work is the role John F. Kerry's Roman Catholicism played in the 2004 presidential election. It stands in stark contrast to the influence of Roman Catholicism played in another, long-ago contest featuring another Catholic candidate, John F. Kennedy.

Conflict and Choice: JFK and Religion in 1960

When Kennedy was contemplating whether to seek the presidency in 1960, he had one especially enthusiastic supporter: his father. Joseph P. Kennedy told his son that being a Roman Catholic would make him a powerful contender: "Just remember, this country is not a private preserve for Protestants. There's a whole new generation out there and it's filled with the sons and daughters of immigrants from all over the world and those people are going to be mighty proud that one of their own is running for president. And that pride will be your spur, it will give your campaign an intensity we've never seen in public life. Mark my words, it's true." Hearing this, the young Kennedy had just one question left: "Well, Dad, when do we start?"[124]

The elder Kennedy's analysis proved correct, and JFK's Roman Catholicism became a political crucible. Voters made it their conflict du jour and divided accordingly. During the Democratic primary contest in Protestant-dominated West Virginia, the response of one elderly woman to Kennedy's candidacy was echoed by several others: "We've never had a Catholic president and I hope we never do. Our people built this country. If they had wanted a Catholic to be president, they would have said so in the Constitution."[125]

For their part, Catholics decided to make religion a key factor in their decision making. On August 1, 1960, *U.S. News and World Report* stated, "There is, or can be, such a thing as a 'Catholic vote,' whereby a high proportion of Catholics of all ages, residences, occupations, and economic status vote for a well-known Catholic or a ticket with special Catholic appeal."[126] History supported that analysis. In 1928, New York governor Alfred E. Smith, a Democrat and the first Catholic ever to receive a major party's presidential nomination, lost to Republican Herbert Hoover in a landslide. Smith's religion became the campaign's major focus, and white southerners broke their historic Democratic Party ties to vote for Hoover, giving rise to the widespread belief that a Catholic could never become president. But Smith won overwhelming support from Catholic voters. In key Irish-Catholic wards in Boston, for example, he received 91, 71, and 60 percent of the votes, respectively. Smith campaigned in Boston before 750,000 people, a larger crowd than those drawn by aviation hero Charles Lindbergh and Pope John Paul II during their visits to the city.[127] But the Eisenhower years saw the waning of the fervent support Catholics had previously given to the Democrats, and Eisenhower's 1956 reelection bid captured 54 percent of the Catholic vote.[128]

John F. Kennedy was determined to get Catholics back into the Democratic fold, and his religious identification played a crucial role in doing so. Kennedy's rival, Vice President Richard M. Nixon, "could not dismiss from my mind the persistent thought that, in fact, Kennedy was a member of a minority religion to which the presidency had been denied throughout the history of our nation and that perhaps I, as a Protestant who had never felt the slings of discrimination, could not understand his feelings—that, in short, he had every right to speak out against even possible and potential bigotry."[129] Many Catholics had vivid memories of religious and ethnic discrimination and bonded with Kennedy.

During the campaign, Kennedy tried to allay voter fears about a Roman Catholic president. Accepting the Democratic nomination, he noted that his party had taken a "hazardous risk" in choosing him. He reiterated his pledge to uphold the Constitution and his oath of office, regardless of any religious pressure or obligation "that might directly or indirectly interfere with my conduct of the presidency in the national interest." In a nationally televised speech before the Greater Houston Ministerial Association, Kennedy told voters, "I am not the Catholic candidate for President. I am the Democratic Party's candidate for President, who happens also to be a Catholic. I do not speak for my church on public matters—and the church does not speak for me. Whatever issue may come before me as President— on birth control, divorce, censorship, gambling, or any other subject—I will make my decision in accordance with these views, in accordance with what my conscience tells me to be the national interest, and without regard to outside religious pressures or dictates. And no power or threat of punishment could cause me to decide otherwise."[130]

In Kennedy's view, voters could choose from among plenty of other conflicts: "the spread of communist influence, until it now festers only ninety miles off the coast of Florida; the humiliating treatment of our president and vice president by those who no longer respect our power; the hungry children I saw in West Virginia; the old people who cannot pay their doctor's bills; the families forced to give up their farms; an America with too many slums, with too few schools, and too late to the moon and outer space."[131] Nixon agreed. Appearing on *Meet the Press*, the Republican nominee said the best way to avoid having religion become a campaign issue was not to talk about it: "As far as I am concerned, I have issued orders to all of the people in my campaign not to discuss religion, not to raise it, not to allow anybody to participate in the campaign who does so on that ground, and as far as I am concerned, I will decline to discuss religion."[132]

But Americans stubbornly resisted the candidates' pleas to choose other conflicts. Newspaper headlines stressed Kennedy's Catholicism: "Democrats Hit Back on Religion" (*New York Times*); "Johnson Blasts 'Haters' Attacks on Catholics" (*Washington Post*); "Creed Issue Must Be Met, Bob Kennedy Says Here" (*Cincinnati Enquirer*); "Mrs. FDR Hits Religious Bias in Talk to Negroes" (*Baltimore Sun*).[133] For its part, the National Association of Evangelicals sent a distressed letter to pastors, warning, "Public opinion is changing in favor of the church of Rome. We dare not sit idly by—voiceless and voteless."[134] These headlines reflected and shaped the public's views of the candidates: 78 percent of Catholics voted for Kennedy; 63 percent of white Protestants backed Nixon.[135] The morning after the long election night, Nixon's daughter, Julie, awakened the exhausted candidate to ask, "Daddy, why did people vote against you because of religion?"[136]

Three years later, the old Catholic-Protestant divide was already losing its salience. On November 13, 1963, John F. Kennedy presided over his final White House political meeting, focusing on the movement of many city dwellers—including Catholics—to the suburbs. Census Bureau director Richard M. Scammon suggested that Kennedy focus on the new suburbanites in his upcoming 1964 reelection campaign. Kennedy was fascinated by Scammon's analysis and wanted to know at what point in their upward climb these former urban dwellers became Republicans. Scammon promised to find out, but that assignment was shelved when Kennedy was assassinated just nine days later.[137] Kennedy understood that a new "axial principle" was forming around a set of conflicts that transcended the old

Catholic-Protestant divisions. This new conflict became fully developed (but not fully understood) when another Catholic Democrat, also from Massachusetts and also with the initials JFK, sought the presidency in 2004.

Conflict and Choice: JFK and Religion Redux, 2004

In 2004, the Democratic Party nominated only the third Roman Catholic in history for the presidency of the United States. But unlike 1928 and 1960, anti-Catholicism was not an issue in 2004. In the four decades since 1960, Catholics have joined white Protestants to become haves in American society. In the words of sociologist William V. D'Antonio, "Proportionately, Catholics nowadays are just as likely as Protestants to have attended and graduated from college, and even slightly more likely to enjoy above-average incomes. For example, Catholics represent 26 percent of the overall population, but 30 percent of those with incomes of $75,000 or more."[138]

Social advancement meant that Catholics no longer saw themselves as objects of discrimination, as evidenced by George W. Bush's 2000 visit to Bob Jones University, the self-described "World's Most Unusual University." The school's eponymous founder once likened the Pope to the biblical Antichrist. On its Web site, university officials expressed their belief that "[a]ll religion, including Catholicism, which teaches that salvation is by religious works or church dogma is false. Religion that makes the words of its leader, be he Pope or other, equal with the Word of God is false."[139] The campus bookstore stocked Catholic materials under the heading "Cults." William Donohue, head of the conservative Catholic League, denounced Bush's choice of Bob Jones University for his speech making: "He just doesn't get it." But, Donohue quickly added, "I don't think he's a bigot."[140]

Indeed, many Catholics hardly seemed outraged that George W. Bush used an anti-Catholic venue to rally support from southern white Protestants. In the 2000 general election, only 47 percent of Catholics backed Bush.[141] But among observant Catholics, Bush's support stood at 57 percent.[142] This is a far cry from the Catholic/Democratic unity that existed in 1960. Pollster John Zogby notes that Catholic voters today "go to the polls as something else: veterans, union members, residents of the northeast, young, old. Being Catholic is not the major identifier."[143] *Washington Post* columnist E. J. Dionne agrees: "The differences among us are rooted in ideas and impulses only marginally connected to the fact that we are Catholic. For this reason, one cannot talk about a Catholic vote. One can talk, at most, about a Catholic tendency."[144]

In the emerging culture wars, religion has become a crucial factor. But instead of the old Catholic-Protestant split, church attendance is the new axis for the values divide. On one side are those who believe that there are absolute truths—the idea that there is an eternal sense of right and wrong. On the other are those who, in Alan Wolfe's phrase, like their "morality writ small"—meaning that morals and values are a personal matter and not a guide for others.[145] Church attendees are on the side of absolute truth; those who find their spirituality elsewhere like their morality writ small. Not surprisingly, frequent churchgoers understood and applauded when George W. Bush explained during a 2000 Republican candidate debate that Christ was his favorite philosopher "because he changed my heart."

This new divide has turned the old Protestant-Catholic split on its head. In 1960, Americans wondered whether a Catholic could become president. But in 2004, many wondered if John F. Kerry was Catholic enough to serve as president. One man interviewed after leaving the 8:00 A.M. daily mass at St. Matthew's Cathedral in Washington, D.C., said of Kerry, "It's really character, personal integrity. And a man who does not seem committed to his faith, I don't see why he would be committed to his ideas or, necessarily, even his country."[146] Billy Graham's magazine, *Christianity Today*, a staunch opponent of John F. Kennedy's candidacy in 1960, completely reversed itself in 2004. In a June editorial, the magazine opined that it is "certainly appropriate" for bishops to expect a Catholic president to submit to Vatican authority on values matters, especially abortion.[147] Gary Bauer, a Republican presidential contender in 2000, observes, "When John F. Kennedy made his famous speech that the Vatican would not tell him what to do, evangelicals and Southern Baptists breathed a sigh of relief. But today, evangelicals and Southern Baptists are hoping that the Vatican *will* tell Catholic politicians what to do."[148]

Kerry sought to allay religiously observant people's worries that he was inattentive to their values concerns. In fact, Kerry had long equated his religiosity with his public service: at a February 4, 1993, National Prayer Breakfast, for example, he said, "Jesus tells us that the real spiritual renewal that we need requires a faith that goes beyond even accepting the truth of His message. It requires literally a movement toward the person of Jesus, an attachment that requires us to live our lives in a manner that reflects the fullness of our faith and that allows Jesus to become for us truly a life-saving force, so that ultimately it may even be said of us that he who does what is true comes to the light, that it may be clearly seen that his deeds have been wrought in God."[149]

A decade later, Kerry described himself in an autobiography, *A Call to Service*, as "a believing, practicing Catholic, married to another believing, practicing Catholic."[150] But during his long political career, Kerry had been reluctant to provide a strong public voice to his religious beliefs, perhaps believing, as many New Englanders do, that religion should be a private matter. National Public Radio reporter Barbara Bradley Hagerty unearthed his National Prayer Breakfast speech and played excerpts from it on the radio during Kerry's 2004 presidential campaign. In the absence of any religious dialogue from Kerry, churchgoing Catholics focused on his public record and especially on his strong support for abortion rights, including "partial-birth" abortions. Kerry's stances caused considerable friction with Catholic hierarchy. Catholic prelates in Camden, New Jersey; St. Louis; Lincoln, Nebraska; Denver; and Colorado Springs issued statements forbidding the Democratic nominee from receiving Holy Communion in their dioceses. The Colorado Springs bishop, Michael Sheridan, went further, noting that Catholics who backed Kerry were jeopardizing their salvation by supporting a proponent of abortion rights.[151] And Denver bishop Charles Chaput described Catholics for Kerry as "cooperating in evil."[152]

The 2004 election results show that Catholic identity no longer exerted a powerful hold. According to the exit polls, Kerry received a mere 47 percent of the Catholic vote, while George W. Bush (a Methodist) got 52 percent. Among white Catholics, Kerry garnered an even more dismal 43 percent to Bush's 56 percent. And in the all-important state of Ohio, Bush won 55 percent of the Catholic vote, a shift of 172,000 votes into the Republican column, enough to give Bush the electoral votes for another term.[153] Back in 1960, John F. Kennedy told the Southern Baptists that he dreamed of a country "where there is no Catholic vote."[154] Forty-four years later, Kennedy's wish had come true.

But the lack of a Catholic vote did not signify the absence of conflict. Forty years ago, Schattschneider wrote, "The substitution of conflicts is the most devastating kind of political strategy."[155] In this case, the Catholic-Protestant conflict gave way to a conflict over the internalization and exposition of religious values. Those who attended church weekly gave Bush 58 percent of their votes, whereas 62 percent of those who never went to church voted for Kerry.[156] Republicans understood the new political realities and sought to mobilize churchgoers. In Pennsylvania, for example, the Bush-Cheney team sent an e-mail seeking to identify 1,600 "friendly congregations" where voters "might gather on a regular basis."[157] A new form of conflict emerged, pitting those who believe religious values should inform public life against those who are more secular. This new axial principle gave the Bush team, as Schattschneider might have predicted, a "most devastating kind of political strategy."[158] A new axial principle—now fully understood by Republicans and Democrats alike—has appeared, and it is redefining twenty-first-century political conflicts.

Demography, Conflict, and the New Twenty-first Century

In 1970, Richard M. Scammon and Ben J. Wattenberg observed that "demography is destiny"—that is, demography helps shape future political conflicts. For them, the conflicts of the 1970s revolved around newly formed values concerns—including crime, pornography, and drug use—that bothered the white, middle-aged, middle-income, married persons with kids living at home who, Scammon and Wattenberg claimed, constituted the "real majority" of the voting public, Americans who were "un-young, un-poor, and un-black."[159] Demography was indeed destiny.

As the remainder of this book outlines, twenty-first-century demography will surely mold the political conflicts of our time. For young Jeannette White, the questions include:

What conflicts will she deem to be important?

How will demography influence her choices?

How will institutions respond to the decisions made by her and the rest of her generation?

How will those institutions manage the new conflicts?

Her answers (and those of her peers) undoubtedly will differ substantially from those of her parents, who, though carried by the forces of nature into the twenty-first century, remain products of the previous century. The ongoing saga of the White family is not only personal but also uniquely American.

Two • Twenty-first-Century Faces

"Tomorrow is right now."

—CISCO MONTANEZ, A 15-YEAR-OLD DAIRY QUEEN
EMPLOYEE IN ATLANTA

IT WAS A BEAUTIFUL SEPTEMBER 1967 morning in Palo Alto, California, where a wedding was taking place at the Stanford Union Memorial Church. Precisely at 11:00 A.M., the bride arrived, radiantly dressed in an empire gown of white peau de soie, with bodice and elbow-length sleeves of chantilly lace and a short tulle veil. Carrying a bouquet of roses and white daisies, the young lady walked down the aisle hand in hand with her father. The bride and groom had met three years earlier at Rock Creek Park in Washington, D.C., where they discovered their mutual interest in horseback riding. On this special day, they had the usual wedding jitters. Outside the church, a nervous groom struggled to put on his jacket. But he was not nervous merely because of the tension associated with the day; the couple's future was very uncertain. The bride's father worried that his 18-year-old daughter was too young to marry her 22-year-old sweetheart, a second lieutenant in the Air Force Reserve. The groom, proudly hailed by the bride's uncle as "a real gung-ho type," was about to be deployed to a war zone as a combat helicopter pilot.[1] After leaving the chapel, the father of the bride, his anxieties now forever set aside, was photographed grinning from ear to ear and was overheard to say, "Just two young people in love."[2]

This particular love story was atypical for its time because the bride was white and the groom was black. Margaret Elizabeth Rusk was the daughter of Secretary of State Dean Rusk, who hailed from Cherokee County, Georgia, and was the grandson of two Confederate soldiers, and Virginia Foisie Rusk, a homemaker. Guy Gibson Smith was the son of Clarence L. Smith, a chief analyst with the Army Correction Program, and Arlenia Gibson Smith, a public school guidance counselor. During the 1960s, such white-black weddings were both rare and extremely controversial. Shortly after Rusk and Smith tied the knot, the minister who married them told one of several reporters present, "I wanted to be sure they had thought about this. They had looked at it from every angle and had an awareness of the difficulties. If any couple can make it, this pair can, I believe."[3]

But that was easier said than done. Only nine years earlier in Caroline County, Virginia, another biracial couple, Richard and Mildred Loving, had been jolted out of bed at 2:00 A.M. by sheriff's deputies, who had stormed into the home of Mildred's parents, with whom the young couple resided. Shining flashlights into the Lovings' eyes, the sheriff demanded of Richard Loving, who was white, "Who is this woman you're sleeping with?" Mildred Loving, a woman of Native American and African descent, responded, "I'm his wife," and her husband pointed to the wall, where the certificate attesting to their June 2, 1958, marriage in Washington, D.C., hung. Said the sheriff, "That's no good here." Next, Mildred Loving recalled, "They told us to get dressed. I couldn't believe they were taking us to jail." The sheriff advised the Lovings that they were being arrested for violating the 1924 Racial Integrity Act, a felony punishable by a year in prison. After pleading with her mother to make the police officers "go away," Mildred and Richard Loving surrendered and were taken to a local jail. Following a brief trial, they were convicted and sentenced to a year in prison, with punishment suspended if they left Virginia and promised not to return to the state for twenty-five years. And if they returned to Virginia as a married couple after 1984, they would again be subject to prosecution. The judge told the Lovings that they would be known as felons for the rest of their lives and added a final condemnation: "Almighty God created the races white, black, yellow, malay, and red, and he placed them on separate continents. And but for the interference with his arrangement there would be no cause for such marriages. The fact that He separated the races shows He did not intend for the races to mix."[4]

Three months before Guy and Margaret Smith exited that Palo Alto chapel, the U.S. Supreme Court had issued a decision overruling the ban against interracial marriages. Speaking for a unanimous court in *Loving v. Virginia*, Chief Justice Earl Warren declared, "The freedom to marry has long been recognized as one of the vital personal rights essential to the orderly pursuit of happiness by free men."[5] The justices undoubtedly were moved by Richard Loving's simple directive to his attorney: "Tell the court I love my wife, and it is just unfair that I can't live with her in Virginia." After hearing the decision, an overjoyed Mildred Loving told reporters, "I feel free now." In August 1967, Leona Eve Boyd (white) and Romans Howard Johnson (black) became the first interracial couple to legally marry in Virginia.[6]

But the powerful language used by the Supreme Court and the Lovings did little to alter public opinion. Virginia had not been the only state to ban interracial marriages; in addition to all 11 states of the former Confederacy, miscegenation was prohibited in Delaware, Kentucky, Missouri, Oklahoma, and West Virginia.[7] Asked in 1963 whether interracial marriage would eventually become widespread, former President Harry S. Truman bluntly responded, "I hope not. I don't believe in it."[8] In an April 1968 poll, 53 percent of respondents believed that laws should prohibit black-white marriages, and in 1971, 51 percent of those surveyed agreed with the statement, "Any white girl who goes out with a black man is going to ruin her reputation as far as I'm concerned."[9] President Barack Obama, the son of a black African man and white, native-born American woman, recalled that his parents' 1960 decision to marry after learning that his mother was pregnant could have had life-threatening consequences: "In many parts of the South, my father could have been strung up from a tree for merely looking at my mother the wrong way; in the most sophisticated of northern cities, the hostile stares, the whispers, might have driven a woman in my mother's predicament into a back-alley abortion—or at the very least to a distant convent that could arrange for adoption. Their very image together would have been considered lurid and perverse, a handy retort to the handful of softheaded liberals who supported a civil rights agenda."[10]

Thus, it was not surprising that when the secretary of state and his daughter made their way into the Stanford Union Memorial Church, security was extraordinarily tight. An armada of State Department officers and campus police scrutinized the guests, each of whom carried an admission pass. Only 50 of the church's 2,000 seats were filled, most of them with friends of the Rusk family. In fact, no blacks other than the groom and his parents attended. The tension outside was just as palpable. On a tour of the Midwest, an anxious Lady Bird Johnson expressed the hope that "everything will go well." Traveling with the First Lady, the wives of the vice president and secretary of agriculture also extended their best wishes.[11] But the First Lady and everyone else in her party knew that the potential for violence was very real.

Behind his public display of bravado, Dean Rusk believed that his daughter's marriage might mean that his tenure as secretary of state was at an end. Rusk telephoned President Lyndon B. Johnson to inform him of Margaret Rusk's intentions and asked if the impending marriage would compromise the administration's relations with Congress, especially with southern Dixiecrats. Johnson initially said no but later telephoned Georgia senator Richard Russell to confirm the assessment. Russell reassured the president, "It won't make any difference at all."[12]

The Rusk-Smith nuptials did not stop the march of history, which, among other things, saw the unpopular Vietnam War result in Lyndon Johnson's involuntary retirement. But on that late summer day in 1967, when the newlyweds descended the chapel steps to have their pictures taken, history paused when one of the photographs landed on the cover of *Time*. Inside the magazine, a grande dame at Florida's Orlando Country Club delighted in the secretary of state's public predicament: "It will serve the old goat right to have nigger grandbabies." Rusk's cousin, Ernest Stone, expressed a popular sentiment: "I think he should've done something about it, not let it get this far. He should've prevented it." Many blacks were equally dismissive, and some, including Black Power activist Lincoln Lynch, saw a sinister motive: "I wonder to what lengths Dean Rusk has to go in order to gain support for his and Johnson's war in Vietnam." Only Martin Luther King Jr. captured the couple's sentiments: "Individuals marry, not races."[13]

The wedding haunted Rusk for years. Following Johnson's decision to abdicate the presidency in 1968, the former secretary of state returned to his native Georgia. There, regents at the state university named him to fill the newly created Samuel H. Sibley Professorship. But one board member, Roy Harris, who had served as the state chair of George Wallace's 1968 presidential campaign and president of Georgia's White Citizens' Council, vociferously objected. As Rusk later recalled, Harris was outraged not by "policy like Vietnam, or U.S.-Soviet relations, or even my lack of a law degree or a Ph.D."; rather, Harris apparently "objected to my appointment because my daughter, Peggy, had married a black man."[14] The regents ignored Harris, voting nine to four to give Rusk the appointment. Harris responded by filing a bill in the state legislature reducing the university's appropriation by the amount of Rusk's salary. That gambit also failed and Rusk held onto his professorship until his death at age 85 in 1994.[15]

Looking back at the 1967 brouhaha over the marriage of two people from different races is akin to perusing an old, sepia-toned photograph. American teenagers today strongly support interracial marriage, with 91 percent agreeing with Warren's assertion that marriage is an essential right in the orderly pursuit of happiness. This endorsement is not surprising, given that 4 in 10 teens report dating someone of the opposite race and that 3 in 10 describe these as "serious" relationships.[16] A survey of teenagers in the Washington, D.C., area confirms these findings: 97 percent have friends of different races; 45 percent say these friendships eventually turned into dating relationships; and 80 percent would consider marrying someone of a different race.[17] South Korean–born Kristin Spring for one, says that race is no longer an issue: "Most people in this generation know that race does not matter. And we'll pass [tolerance] on to our children."[18] Ricky Reiter, a 17-year-old Maryland high school senior, agrees. Reiter, who is white, dates only black women: "I prefer black girls, and don't ask me why, 'cuz I don't know why. I mean, how can you explain who you're attracted to? You just *are*." When Reiter was reminded about state laws that once banned interracial marriages, he exclaimed, "I can't believe all of that actually happened." Reiter's 43-year-old mother noted that the dating scene is very different for her teenage son than it was for her: in the past, "the Italians stuck together . . . the Russians stuck together. It was very narrow-minded, what people believed in. The change has been just amazing—*amazing*."[19] Indeed. As recently as 1970, interracial marriages accounted for fewer than 1 percent of married couples (about 300,000 total). At the dawn of the twenty-first century, the number of interracial marriages has climbed to 5.4 percent (more than 3 million couples).[20]

Barack Obama describes *miscegenation*—that antiquated word once used to categorize interracial marriages—as being "humpbacked, ugly, portending a monstrous outcome: like *antebellum* or *octoroon*, it evokes images of another era, a distant world of horsewhips and flames, dead magnolias and crumbling porticos."[21] Today, *miscegenation* has become a linguistic artifact whose meaning has been overwhelmed by a racial revolution with profound implications for the nation's demographic and political futures. Nowhere is this transformation more pronounced than in Georgia. Just seventy-one miles away from Rusk's grave in Athens stands Atlanta, a city that is a thriving multiracial, multicultural, and multilingual metropolis and a symbol of the race revolution that has obliterated old patterns of thought.

Atlanta: A New South Meets the Newer South

The first signs of the new racial revolution appeared in 1970. That year, a peanut farmer from Plains, Georgia, sought and won his state's governorship. The soft-spoken Jimmy Carter appealed to whites and blacks alike based on their shared economic interests and conservative cultural values. In his Inaugural Address, Carter won instant acclaim by setting himself apart from his segregationist predecessors:

> At the end of a long campaign, I believe I know our people as well as anyone. Based on this knowledge of Georgians north and south, rural and urban, liberal and conservative, I say to you quite frankly that the time for racial discrimination is over. . . . No poor, rural, weak, or black person should ever have to bear the additional burden of being deprived of the opportunity of an education, a job, or simple justice.[22]

As governor, Carter removed Roy Harris from his post as a University of Georgia regent.

During the 1970s, a host of other southern progressives also won their state governorships, including Democrats Reuben Askew (Florida), John West (South Carolina), Dale Bumpers (Arkansas), and Bill Clinton (Arkansas) and Republican Linwood Holton (Virginia). All echoed Carter's plea for racial tolerance. As Bumpers told *Time*, "My election and the victories of Governors Carter and Askew . . . weren't coincidences. There has been a cry for new leadership in the South."[23] In 1978, Arkansans affirmed Bumpers's analysis by electing the 32-year-old Clinton as the youngest governor in the state's history. In his 1979 Inaugural Address, Clinton echoed Carter's call for racial justice: "For as long as I can remember, I have believed passionately in the cause of equal opportunity, and I will do what I can to advance it."[24] Clinton, Carter, and their fellow progressives helped the South turn away from the race-baiting politics of the past.

That politics had been especially vituperative. In 1966, Democrat

Lester Maddox won the Georgia governorship by decrying integration as "un-American, un-Godly, and even criminal."[25] Maddox first won statewide notice when three black activists attempted to desegregate his fried chicken restaurant and he chased them away with axe handles and a pistol, creating a memorable televised scene that established his political appeal. The protesters turned to the courts, which eventually ruled that Maddox had violated the public accommodations provision of the 1964 Civil Rights Act. In response, Maddox closed his Atlanta chicken emporium and began campaigning for governor by giving axe handles to his many admirers. Although Maddox lost the popular vote, the state legislature chose him as governor.[26]

More than four decades later, the Maddox saga has faded from memory. After serving one term, he was succeeded by his lieutenant governor, Jimmy Carter, and Maddox died, nearly forgotten, in 2003. But the racial politics Maddox espoused still echo in Dixie. In 2001, Mississippians voted to keep their state flag with its Confederate design rather than replace it with one without such an overt symbol of slavery.[27] The following year, Georgians elected their first Republican governor, Sonny Perdue, after the incumbent Democrat eradicated the Confederate emblem from that state's flag.[28] Yet the winds of change are blowing. In 2000, the South Carolina legislature lowered the Confederate battle flag from its perch atop the statehouse, where it had flown for nearly 40 years after the National Association for the Advancement of Colored People began a boycott that cost the state $20 million.[29] Speaking in favor of removing the offensive flag, Democratic state representative Todd Rutherford alluded to the Civil War and asked his recalcitrant colleagues, "I mean no disrespect, but isn't that war over?"[30]

As Rutherford's query suggests, race-baiting politics is increasingly part of the nation's past. During the 2008 campaign, surprisingly few Americans saw Barack Obama's candidacy through the prism of race. In a remarkable speech at the National Constitution Center in Philadelphia, Obama noted, "Despite the temptation to view my candidacy through a purely racial lens, we won commanding victories in states with some of the whitest populations in the country."[31] One reason for race's relative impotence in Dixie is that the faces of twenty-first-century southerners differ substantially from the black and white visages that dominated the region from the nation's founding until very recently. One good place to see the area's new racial complexion is Atlanta's Hartsfield-Jackson Airport, the world's busiest, accommodating more than 78 million passengers and 900,000 takeoffs and landings each year.[32] The facility employees 44,800 people, many of them new immigrants to the United States.[33]

Adama Camara is one of them. An émigré from Mali, Camara arrived in the United States at age 19. In lilting English accented by his native French, Camara succinctly explained why he left Mali, "I fled a dictator." For Camara, one of thirteen children, life in Atlanta began inauspiciously. He settled into the city and shared an apartment with a cousin, sleeping on the floor, as he had in Africa. He first found employment as a day laborer working alongside other immigrants, most of them Mexican, but got more steady work when he became a daytime custodian at one of Hartsfield-Jackson's large concourses and a nighttime utility worker at the airport's Budweiser Brew House.[34]

Camara is part of a swelling migration of native Africans to metropolitan Atlanta. These African immigrants—the vast majority of them black—now constitute 2 percent of the region's 4.1 million residents.[35] By 2010, those numbers are expected to grow even more as refugees from Ethiopia, Nigeria, Somalia, Mali, and Sierra Leone flee hostile dictatorships, drought, famine, and economic deprivation for new lives in the United States. Most of these immigrants take whatever work is available: in Atlanta, for example, many drive taxicabs or work in fast food restaurants.

Yet even as the African newcomers quickly adapt to the popular culture, many—including Camara and his three Malian roommates—retain their strong Muslim religious beliefs. Atlanta has 23 mosques serving an estimated 32,469 Muslims. A 2003 study published by the Glenmary Research Center found that the city is the tenth-most religiously diverse metropolitan area in the United States, with 149 different religious organizations, 87 of which have established houses of worship.[36] In 2005, the Catholic Church took note of the changing racial composition and named Wilton D. Gregory as the region's first black bishop. One black Catholic exalted, "As an African-American, it's great seeing other African-Americans in hierarchical positions within the church."[37]

Increased racial and religious diversity is a direct consequence of the more than 256,000 immigrants who have come to metropolitan Atlanta during the past decade.[38] At the Hartsfield-Jackson Airport, the janitorial service is 70 percent foreign born, a stark contrast to the 1970s, when most of its employees were single African American women.[39] Signs of the new immigrant presence have spread far beyond the airport's boundaries. For example, the drive down Buford Highway away from the airport and toward downtown Atlanta features road signs advertising the Pho 79 Restaurant, the Pho Bac Restaurant, and the Saigon Noodle House, all of which specialize in Vietnamese cuisine. Then there is the Havana, a Cuban-style establishment. Nearby is the Machu Picchu, featuring a Peruvian-based menu, while diners at the Abbay can savor Ethiopian food. Adding to the diverse culinary palate are Pancho's and the Mariscolandia Seafood House, both featuring Mexican cuisine; the Phuket, a Thai restaurant; the Peking and Red China; and Lawrence's Café, which trades in Lebanese food. Even fast food restaurants are not exempt. One Sikh-owned former Baskin-Robbins ice cream store has been renamed the Basket Rabbit.[40] Of course, other restaurants associated with traditional southern cuisine remain, including Folks, which features southern soul food. Likewise, the Atlanta Diner and Chicago Sports Bar and Grill are conventional meat-and-potatoes establishments. But the smorgasbord of ethnic eateries is a sure sign that the market for such fare is increasing. The *Atlanta Journal-Constitution* has taken note: on Wednesdays, it publishes a special "Cab Market" section that spotlights foods and recipes from around the world.

More important than changing menus and restaurant names are the stories of their patrons and owners. One of the most compelling is that of Nallely Ortiz, who on one Fourth of July was discovered by a *Washington Post* reporter eating hot wings under the watchful eyes of the Confederate faces carved into Stone Mountain, Georgia. Born in Mexico and just six years old when she arrived in the United States in 1991, Ortiz and her family were lured to Atlanta by the construction boom associated with the 1996 Olympics. As another Hispanic man who came to the city at the time recalled, "Only I know Georgia for Atlanta, the Olympic games. Maybe this city is more rich. People is rich."[41] Although the Ortizes arrived on a tourist visa, sightseeing was hardly their reason for coming. Making money and a better life for themselves were, and to that end, Ortiz's father got a job working in a restaurant, while her mother operated a snack stand.[42]

But life in their newly adopted country proved difficult. By the time Ortiz reached fifth grade, her parents had divorced. Money, which had been an overriding family objective, became even more scarce. On the best days, the snack stand brought in $75, hardly enough to support Nallely and her five siblings. With her father gone, her brother, Reuben, became the primary breadwinner, working as a full-time restaurant cook. Reuben eventually graduated from high school with a technical degree in the culinary arts. Even so, money remained elusive, and when it appeared, the coveted dollars were stuffed into envelopes and even into bras, meticulously (and reluctantly) doled out when the rent and other bills came due.[43]

Nallely Ortiz's story is hardly unique. The South's estimated Hispanic population grew from 562,663 in 1990 to 2,400,000 in 2005. In Georgia alone, 20 percent of the population is Hispanic, and estimates show that between 350,000 and 450,000 illegal immigrants—including Ortiz and her family—reside in the Peach State.[44] Ortiz's life changed dramatically in 2002, when she received U.S. citizenship. One reason for her altered status was the birth of her son, Sebastian, which reflected another twenty-first-century trend: from 1990 to 2000, Georgia's teenage birth rate increased 50 percent among Latinos, 30 percent among blacks, and 1 percent among whites. Born out of wedlock, Sebastian lives with his parents in an apartment they share with another unmarried Hispanic couple and their child. To make ends meet, Ortiz's boyfriend, Eduardo, works as a prep cook, while she holds several part-time, minimum-wage jobs, including one at a sandwich shop and another as a supermarket cashier. They get by on their meager salaries and assistance from the federal and state governments. Because Sebastian is a U.S. citizen by birth, he is eligible for nine cans of government-subsidized milk each month. The State of Georgia also offers health care to low-income children through Peach Care for Kids. But Ortiz has one asset that most illegal Hispanic immigrants lack: she finished high school; half of the Latinos who enroll in Georgia's high schools do not graduate.[45]

Variations on Nallely Ortiz's story are replayed in a thousand other locations across Atlanta. At a Dairy Queen 14 miles south of Hartsfield-Jackson Airport, a Porsche is parked outside while its owner, Rizwan Momin, counts the day's receipts inside the restaurant. Momin arrived in Atlanta in 1985 from the Indian state of Gujarat with only $310 in his pocket. He quickly found employment after his uncle purchased a white-owned Dairy Queen in a mostly black neighborhood. Mopping and sweeping the floors, Momin pocketed most of his take-home salary by living frugally, including sleeping on the floor. By 2002, Momin owned nine Dairy Queens in the greater Atlanta area and was one of the company's largest franchise owners in the southeastern United States. He is hardly alone: Indian immigrants own 60 of Georgia's 208 Dairy Queens. According to Momin, his employees, most of whom are Indian immigrants, are inspired to re-create his version of the American Dream: "Indians are gonna work for you. At the beginning, they work for minimum wage. Then little raise, little raise, slowly, slowly. Everyone live together; they are saving money, six people in household working, they bank 80 percent of their money and use 20 percent for expenses. They don't drink, no clubs, no fancy clothes. Suddenly, they have $60,000 in the bank. Then they will buy the Subway or the Blimpie."[46]

In 2002, Momin expanded his holdings by opening a chain of As Seen on TV stores; they have become a shopping-mall staple. Inside, customers can purchase a Flowbee Haircutting System, a Bug Wand, Bye-Bye Blemish, or a Juice Man II—products often spotlighted on late-night cable television infomercials.[47] Momin is one of thousands of Indians who have achieved the American Dream. According to one estimate, 300,000 Indians work in California's Silicon Valley, earning a median income of $200,000 per year; another figure estimates that Indians own 30 percent of the nation's hotels and motels.[48] Commenting on the fact that Indian Americans are the fastest growing minority in his adopted home state of Delaware, Vice President Joseph Biden observed, "You cannot go into a 7-11 or a Dunkin' Donuts unless you have a slight Indian accent."[49]

The racial transformation of Atlanta into a southern-style Los Angeles has not been without tension. William Morton, a 38-year-old white kitchen worker in Gainesville, Georgia, says, "This country's not right."[50] Even some black Georgians are disturbed by the changing demography. In Atkinson County, where Hispanics outnumber blacks 21 percent to 19 percent, black county commissioner Jimmy Roberts Jr. finds the immigrant presence disconcerting: "They done took over the population. I don't think it's right."[51] Yet the faces of the twenty-first century are not those of these Georgia stalwarts but those of Adama Camara, Nallely Ortiz, and Rizwan Momin. They represent a Newer South that is standing alongside the black-white New South of old that spawned the likes of Carter, Clinton, and other racial progressives. In 2008, Obama overwhelmed John McCain in the metropolitan Atlanta area, winning 68 percent of the vote in Fulton County (which includes part of Atlanta) and 79 percent support in De Kalb County (which also includes part of Atlanta). As one of Momin's Dairy Queen employees, 15-year-old Cisco Montanez, succinctly put it, "Tomorrow is right now."[52]

Another sign of the changing times came in 2000 when the Census Bureau relented in the face of growing public pressure and agreed to list 21 different racial categories on its forms.[53] This push for a more realistic racial count began a dozen years earlier when the Association for Multi-

Ethnic Americans lobbied to have multiracial categories listed on all government documents. Soon, other like-minded organizations—including Project RACE (Reclassify All Children Equally) and A Place for Us—took up the cause. In 1997, these groups won powerful backing from speaker of the U.S. House Newt Gingrich, who endorsed "phasing out the outdated, divisive, and rigid classification of Americans."[54] Thanks to Gingrich's support, the Office of Management and Budget mandated that people be allowed to mark more than one race on all federal forms. After the new rules were promulgated, Census director Kenneth Prewitt noted that the millennial count "will go down in history as the event that began to redefine race in American society."[55] Other government agencies are playing catch-up. In 2006, for example, the Department of Education finally allowed students to circle more than one racial category on its surveys.[56]

For some of Atlanta's immigrants, racial self-identification is a matter of argument. Montanez, for example, is the son of a single Puerto Rican mother and black father who left shortly after Montanez was born in the racially troubled Bronx, New York. His mother believed that the South would be a "gentler" experience for her young child, so they moved to Atlanta. But Atlanta proved to be no panacea. Montanez was suspended from eighth grade and went to work in the fast food industry, telling friends, "I like ice cream." After quarreling with his mother about his use of language and culture, he has become fully black-identified. He tells his mother to use the word *sausage*, not *chorizo*. His erratic work habits ultimately got him fired from the Dairy Queen, and he returned to high school.[57] But Adama Camara, Nallely Ortiz, Rizwan Momin, and Cisco Montanez are a part of the Newer South.

"The Third Great Revolution"

Speaking at the 1998 commencement exercises at Portland State University, Bill Clinton cast his eye toward the impending new century and saw a nation transformed. The president told the student body that the nation was experiencing a "third great revolution," one as powerful as the American Revolution, which gave birth to the democratic ideas of the eighteenth and nineteenth centuries, and as imposing as the civil rights and women's rights revolutions that broadened the definition of personal liberties in the late twentieth century. According to Clinton, this gathering revolution was being fought by an army of immigrants: "Today, largely because of immigration, there is no majority race in Hawaii or Houston or New York City. Within five years there will be no majority race in our largest state, California. In a little more than fifty years, there will be no majority race in the United States." Hearing this, the crowd of mostly white students applauded.[58]

The facts bear out Clinton's argument. When Richard M. Nixon took the presidential oath in 1969, there were approximately 9.6 million foreign-born persons residing in the United States. Thirty-two years later, when George W. Bush raised his hand to repeat the same oath, that figure had grown to 28.4 million.[59] During the 1970s, approximately 400,000 persons entered the United States each year; a decade later, the number was 800,000; by the end of the twentieth century, it topped 1 million.[60] Today, there are more foreign-born people living in California (8.4 million) than there are people residing in all of New Jersey, and New York state has more foreign-born people than there are in the entire population of South Carolina.[61] Many of these arrivals are nonwhite. A 2005 Zogby International poll provides one small shard of evidence that the United States is inexorably moving toward a new multiracial, multiethnic society: 75 percent of respondents said that a person of a different race lived within one block of their home; 91 percent had invited a person of another race to a dinner or a party; and 78 percent had close friendships with someone outside of work or school who did not share their racial background.[62] In another sign of the times, 36 percent of those surveyed told the Gallup Organization in 2006 that they had personal contact with recent immigrants whom they either know or suspected were illegal.[63]

The September 11, 2001, terrorist attacks hardly slowed the immigration tide. In fact, the number of immigrants subsequently has increased rapidly. In 2006, according to the Pew Hispanic Center, the United States had 37 million resident immigrants, of which 11.1 million were illegal, 1.3 million were temporary legal residents, 2.6 million were refugees, 11.5 million were naturalized citizens, and 10.5 million were legal permanent residents.[64] This proliferation of immigrants even extends to the U.S. military. Today, 69,300 soldiers are foreign-born, including 33,000 non-U.S. citizens who are on active duty.[65] Their names often appear on roll calls of the dead in Afghanistan and Iraq—Falaniko, Valdez, Perez, Ramos, and Le.[66]

Army private first-class Diego Rincon is one. Rincon was only 19 years old when he was assassinated in 2003 by a suicide bomber on the streets of

Baghdad. A native of Colombia, Rincon fled a country torn apart by drug warlords in 1989, arriving in the United States with his family when he was only 5 years old. After September 11, Diego and his father, Jorge, impulsively entered an army recruiter's office. The army rejected 40-year-old Jorge but immediately signed up 18-year-old Diego, even though he was not a U.S. citizen. After his death, Jorge Rincon lobbied Congress to pass legislation granting citizenship to his dead son.[67] Congress obliged, approving a measure that granted preferred status in obtaining citizenship to the foreign-born parents of any immigrant killed in combat.[68] Today, Diego Rincon's framed citizenship papers are prominently displayed on a wall of remembrance at the family home in Conyers, Georgia.[69]

Stories like Rincon's are altering stereotypes about ethnic enclaves and the people who populate them. For example, in Boston, the home of the Kennedy dynasty, nonwhite immigrants populate the once Irish-dominated neighborhoods. For the first time since 1790, whites are now a minority group in the old colonial city: 297,850 Bostonians list themselves as either minority or multiracial, whereas only 291,561 are white. According to Cheng Imm Tann, director of the Mayor's Office of New Bostonians, "In the beginning here, the people of color—the Native Americans—were in the majority. Now the people of color are again the majority. The diversity is amazing."[70] Nowhere is that diversity more apparent than in the city's Jamaica Plain section, where Spanish is replacing the Irish brogue. One reason is that two-thirds of the families in Miraflores, a small Dominican Republic village with a population of 4,000, have relatives living in Jamaica Plain. Author Peggy Levitt characterizes the two-way communication that occurs between these once-distant lands: "Because someone is always traveling between Boston and the island, there is a continuous, circular flow of goods, news, and information. Thus, when someone is ill, cheating on his or her spouse, or finally granted a visa, the news spreads as quickly in Jamaica Plain as it does on the streets of Miraflores."[71]

The ethnic recasting of Boston has found its way into the voting booths. In 2005, Sam Yoon, a Korean immigrant, ran for an at-large seat on the city council. Locating his headquarters near Fields Corner, an area heavily populated by immigrants from Vietnam, Cape Verde, and elsewhere, Yoon developed a Web site that was a virtual Tower of Babel, with portions translated into Chinese, Korean, Spanish, Vietnamese, Haitian Creole, and Cape Verdean Creole.[72] Thanks to the strong support he received from Boston's immigrant newcomers, Yoon became the first Asian

American to sit on the city council. Basking in victory, he acknowledged various Asian American groups: "This is for the Chinese Americans! This is for the Japanese-Americans!"[73] Yoon's win, along with that of Puerto Rican–born city council member Felix Arroyo, underscores the city's metamorphosis. Arroyo's triumph was particularly impressive, as he garnered enough votes to finish near the top of the ticket, losing to incumbent council president Michael Flaherty, an old-time Irish Democrat, by a mere 5,700 votes.[74]

Other cities have witnessed similar transformations in their immigrant populations and politics. Cook County, Illinois, which encompasses the city of Chicago and is home to Barack Obama, has more Hispanics than does Arizona, Colorado, or New Mexico.[75] A similar phenomenon has occurred in Hartford, Connecticut. In 2003, more than 40 percent of that city's population was Hispanic, outnumbering blacks (38 percent) for the first time. According to Hartford's Puerto Rican–born mayor, Eddie Perez, "Hartford has become a Latin city, so to speak. It's a sign of things to come."[76]

Perez's personal story is illustrative. He came to Hartford in 1969 at age 12 from Corozol, Puerto Rico. Perez and his single mother, Felicita, and siblings William, Orlando, Wilfredo, Moses, Nelson, Ruben, Noel, and Jeanette moved from apartment to apartment, searching for a safe neighborhood. The *Hartford Courant* described this 10-member family as a "living metaphor for survival, continually evolving." Perez fell into a street gang before coming under the positive influence of a Catholic priest, Father Thomas Goekler, and joining Goekler's Sacred Heart Church Youth Group. Goekler eventually became president of Trinity College, where he hired Perez as director of community relations. In 2001, Perez left that job to become Hartford's first Hispanic mayor, and he has held the office ever since. As chief executive of an increasingly multiracial city, Perez "danc[es] between worlds, pretending it ain't nothing to be forever negotiating among white, black, and Puerto Rican—rich and poor, landlord and tenant."[77]

Unlike the nineteenth and twentieth centuries, when immigrants often settled in the major ports of call, today's migrants are found not only in "traditional" urban settings (often displacing older white ethnics) but also in the formerly white-dominated suburbs. David Brooks writes that when he once opened a local newspaper in Loudoun County, Virginia, National Scholar Award winners announced included Kawi Cheung, Anastasia Cisneros Fraust, Dantam Do, Hugo Dubovy, and Maryanthe Malliaris.[78] In fact, from 1990 to 2005, enrollment in the county's public schools tripled from 14,633 to 47,361, while the number of Asian students increased by a factor of 12 and the number of Hispanics grew by a factor of 17.[79]

The same phenomena are replicated in many other suburban communities. For example, Marshalltown, Iowa (population 30,000), has seen natives from Villachuato, Mexico (population 15,000) hold 900 of the 1,600 jobs in the Swift and Company meatpacking plant, the town's largest employer.[80] Similarly, in Saline County, Kansas, the Hispanic population has grown by 20 percent between 2000 and 2008. Hispanics in this rural area work at Tony's Pizza, the frozen food plant, the Exide Technologies battery plant, and the Phillips Lighting plant. County clerk Dan Merriman credits Hispanics with saving his community: "A lot of local companies either wouldn't be here or wouldn't have expanded the way they have. Phillips Lighting would've gone overseas. It's that [Hispanic] labor force. If we didn't have that here, they could pull that thing and take it wherever."[81]

Today, the immigrant march into unexpected places continues: from 2000 to 2005, the number of immigrants living in Indiana rose 34 percent; in South Dakota, 44 percent; in Delaware, 32 percent; in Missouri, 31 percent; in Colorado, 28 percent; and in New Hampshire, 26 percent.[82] And Obama won four of these six states, in part because of their enhanced immigrant presence.

A Bilingual (and Bifurcated) Nation

Everywhere one looks, the evidence overwhelmingly shows that the United States is rapidly becoming a multiracial, multicultural, and multilingual polity. Los Angeles County, to cite one instance, provided special ballots in 2008 for its Latino, Chinese, Filipino, Japanese, Korean, and Vietnamese voters. But this new cultural diversity hardly signifies an ethnic "melting pot."[83] In the twenty-first century, two distinct Americas are coming into focus: one is mostly white and English speaking, while the other is mostly Hispanic and Spanish speaking. Nationwide, 47 million Americans speak a language other than English, with 26 million conversing in Spanish. Of these 47 million foreign-tongued speakers, 21.3 million claim to know English less than "very well." In some states, the demand to learn English is acute: in Massachusetts, 460,000 people (7.7 percent of the population) are not conversant in English, and entry into English as second language courses can take as long as two or three years.[84]

Yet that Hispanic and Spanish-speaking portion of the populace will dominate twenty-first-century politics. During the 1990s, an estimated 2,249,000 Mexicans came to the United States, 3.5 times the number who came during the 1970s.[85] By 2006, the Census Bureau reported that Latinos totaled a record 44.3 million. For the first time in U.S. history, Latinos outnumber blacks (population 36.7 million), making Hispanics the nation's number one minority group.[86] Latinos are predicted to account for 60 percent of the U.S. population growth between 2005 and 2050, and in 2008, the Census Bureau issued a bulletin stating that by 2042 (eight years earlier than previously anticipated), whites will be the nation's new minority.[87] Thus, as the twenty-first century progresses, the binary white-black racial politics of the past will become increasingly obsolete as the term *minority* will stop meaning "black" and instead come to be associated with "white."

As always, children are harbingers of the future. According to the Census Bureau, 70 percent of the population increase among children aged five and younger is Hispanic.[88] California is a trendsetter. In 2002, Hispanics constituted 71.9 percent of the students in the Los Angeles Unified School District, while just 9.4 percent of students were white. One year later, in another historic first, a majority of all California newborns were Hispanic. Nationwide, the 2002 fertility rates were estimated at 1.8 for whites, 2.1 for blacks, and 3.0 for Hispanics.[89] In light of such numbers, it is not surprising that *José* has replaced *Michael* as the most popular name for baby boys.[90] Should present trends continue, Hispanics will approach 29 percent of the total population in 2050 and could even reach 33 percent by 2100.[91]

Today, the nation's skin complexion is rapidly changing from white to a shade of beige. As whites decline in population—thanks to what Ben J. Wattenberg describes as a "birth dearth"—racial intermixing will only increase.[92] According to Peter Brimelow of *Forbes* magazine, the proportion of whites nationwide could fall to an all-time low of 61 percent by 2020.[93] In some places, the decline has been striking. California, for example, saw its Anglo population fall by nearly 500,000 during the 1990s as a consequence of low birth rates and a white exodus, even as the total statewide population increased by 3,000,000, mostly Hispanics.[94] Today, only 46.7 percent of Californians are white, while 32.4 percent are Hispanic.[95]

California's new demography helped give Barack Obama a solid victory in the Golden State in 2008. Whites constituted just 63 percent of the Californians casting ballots, and they were tepid in their support for Obama, giving him just 52 percent of their votes. But nonwhites made up for Obama's relative lack of support among whites: blacks constituted 10 percent of the total vote, and 95 percent of them backed Obama; Hispanics were 18 percent of the total vote, and 74 percent of them supported Obama; Asians comprised 6 percent of the votes cast, and 64 percent of them backed Obama; and those of some other race were 3 percent of the vote and named Obama on 55 percent of their ballots.[96] Thanks to such overwhelming nonwhite backing, Obama overwhelmed McCain statewide, 61 percent to 37 percent. With each election, the number of whites casting ballots in California will decline. Unless Republicans find a way to compete with this demographic reality, California will remain a Democratic bastion in presidential politics and will provide the party with a crucial bloc of electoral votes.

Los Angeles has become a microcosm of the changes taking place in California politics. Today, 44.6 percent of Los Angeles County residents are Hispanic, a figure that is getting ever closer to the 48.7 percent who are white.[97] The city of Los Angeles is already "majority-minority": 48 percent of its residents are Latino, 11 percent are Asian, and 10 percent are black, while just 31 percent are white.[98] Writer Joan Didion observed some years ago that for many Los Angeles Anglos, Spanish had become "part of the ambient noise, the language spoken by the people who worked in the car wash and came to trim the trees and cleared the tables in restaurants."[99] That "ambient noise" has now reached a crescendo as Hispanics not only grow in numbers but acquire both cultural and political power. In 2005, Antonio Villaraigosa became the city's first Latino mayor since Cristol Aguilar left that office in 1872.[100] Villaraigosa, the Mexican American son of a single mother, handily defeated white incumbent James Hahn, 59 percent to 41 percent. Villaraigosa won 86 percent of the Hispanic vote and 77 percent of the votes from people aged 18 to 29 but only 48 percent of the votes from whites residing in the suburban middle-class enclave of the San Fernando Valley.[101] Leaving the polls, 26 percent of Villaraigosa supporters said they liked their candidate because he "understands multi-cultural Los Angeles."[102] Striding to the microphone on election night, the new mayor thrilled the crowd by shouting, "Sí, se puede! [Yes, we can!]"[103] Villaraigosa's victory made him an instant celebrity, as witnessed by the attendance of former vice president Al Gore and California governor Arnold

Schwarzenegger at his inauguration. In 2008, Obama found gold in Los Angeles County's changing demography, swamping McCain 69 percent to 29 percent.

Australian writer and critic Clive James has said, "Call Los Angeles any dirty name you like. . . . The fact remains that you are already living in it before you get there."[104] Today, James's observation holds special resonance. In the nation's 20 fastest-growing cities during the past decade, the proportion of blacks has risen 23 percent, while the proportion of Asians has jumped 69 percent and that of Hispanics has grown by 72 percent.[105] In some areas, the increase has become an explosion. In Loudoun County, Virginia, one of the many suburbs that ring Washington, D.C., the Hispanic population rose an astounding 368 percent from 1990 to 2000.[106] Neighboring Fairfax County also saw a rapid rise in its Hispanic numbers, and 27 percent of the county's residents are now foreign born, while the number of Hispanics in Prince William County doubled from 2000 to 2006.[107] Obama's win in Virginia was fueled by the solid support he received in all three of these counties: 54 percent in Loudoun, 60 percent in Fairfax, and 58 percent in Prince William. Virginia's new demography enabled the Democratic presidential candidate to carry the Old Dominion for the first time since 1964.

Politics is not the only venue in which the increased Hispanic presence is making itself felt. On a cold January day in 2005, Washington, D.C., radio station WHFS-FM, an alternative rock outlet featuring songs from the White Stripes, Green Day, and Jet, played Jeff Buckley's "Last Goodbye" and abruptly switched to a Spanish-language pop music format. After 36 years of airing rock and roll, the first words broadcast on the new El Zol were "WHFS tranmitiendo desde la ciudad capital de America: Esta! Es! Tu! Nueva! Radio! [Transmitting from America's Capital City: This! Is! Your! New! Radio!]."[108] Longtime listeners were stunned: one told the *Washington Post*, "This is the end of an era. I feel like I just lost my parents."[109] But the demographics motivating the change were obvious: from 1998 to 2005, the audience for Spanish-language radio stations jumped 37 percent. As for WHFS, the audience grew by an astounding 69 percent in the first three months after the switch, lifting the station into a tie for twelfth place in the city's Arbitron ratings.[110]

Other cities have witnessed similar changes. In New York, La Mega (WSKQ-FM), a Spanish-language station, regularly beat shock jock Howard Stern in the competition for listeners.[111] Sensing that the world had changed, Stern abandoned commercial radio in 2006 and moved his racy program to Sirius, a satellite operation modeled after pay-cable television. Meanwhile, the number of Spanish stations on traditional broadcast dials continued to grow, from 297 in 1990 to 686 in 2005.[112] One Hispanic host explained the newfound popularity of an old medium: "Recent immigrants use radio as their principal source of information. It is a forum that people are familiar with from back home."[113]

The proliferation of Spanish stations has helped boost record sales by popular Hispanic artists including Ricky Martin, Marc Anthony, Gloria Estefan, Julio and Enrique Iglesias, Selena, Juan Luis Guerra, and Victor Manuelle. Their success has resulted primarily from their young listeners and their ever-expanding pocketbooks. In 2003, Hispanic purchasing power totaled $580 billion, of which $249.5 million went to record purchases. By 2010, Hispanics will spend an estimated $900 billion.[114]

Young people not only like music but watch lots of television, a fact that in 2003 led Spanish-language cable television company Univision to launch TeleFutura, a cable outlet aimed exclusively at young Hispanics. That year, TeleFutura had the youngest audience of any 24-hour broadcast network, with half its viewers aged between 12 and 34.[115] Nationwide, Univision reports that in the top three television markets—New York, Los Angeles, and Chicago—Spanish-speaking local news broadcasts outscore their English competitors among the key demographic of adults between 18 and 49.[116] Keeping tabs on these trends, NBC bought the Spanish-language cable network Telemundo in 2002 for a record $2.7 billion.[117] Every major U.S. market now has at least two Spanish-language radio and television stations.

Hispanics and many other Americans also eat lots of Mexican fast food. One of the most popular restaurants, Taco Bell, has more than 6,500 franchises serving 35 million customers each week. In 2003, the company generated sales of $5.4 billion.[118] Taco Bell's success has not been lost on its competitors. Hamburger giant McDonald's acquired Chipotle, a Mexican-style fast food restaurant. The lunchtime crowd at the Chipotle on Manhattan's 34th Street—the company's 419th franchise, opened in 2005—includes not only hungry Latinos but also whites and members of other races. There are now more than 500 Chipotle franchises.[119]

Nowhere is the changing face of the United States more evident than in Miami. As early as 1987, Didion wrote that "an entrepreneur who spoke no English could still, in Miami, buy, sell, negotiate, leverage assets, float bonds, and if he were so inclined, attend galas twice a week in black tie."[120] By 1999, the chieftains of the city's largest bank, real estate development company, and law firm were Hispanic, and this economic status has translated into substantial amounts of both cultural and political power. In 1998, a Spanish television station became the city's most-watched channel, the first time a foreign-language station achieved such prominence there.[121] The same year, Alberto Ibarguen became the first Hispanic publisher of the *Miami Herald*, a post he held until 2005. A native of Puerto Rico, Ibarguen had previously held the top job at the *Herald*'s sister newspaper, *El Nuevo Herald*, which has 227,000 daily and 289,000 Sunday subscribers.[122] Simply put, Miami is the de facto economic, social, and political capital of Latin America. As political scientist Michael Jones-Correa observes, Miami, New York, and Los Angeles are "required campaign stops for politicians in national and even state and local campaigns across Latin America."[123]

But the infusion of Hispanics has produced a powerful political backlash. A white Miami resident unable to communicate with government bureaucrats exclaimed, "My God, this is what it's like to be the minority."[124] In California, author Dale Maharidge interviewed several whites who described their fear of living in a state with a population that is mostly minority:

> Whites are scared. The depth of white fear is understood and misunderstood by progressive thinkers and the media. Whites dread the unknown and not-so-distant tomorrow when a statistical turning point will be reached that could have very bad consequences for them. They fear the change that seems to be transforming their state into something different from the rest of the United States. They fear losing not only their jobs but also their culture. Some feel that California will become a version of South Africa, in which whites will lose power when minorities are the majority.[125]

Campaigning for president on the Reform Party ticket in 2000, Patrick J. Buchanan reported that many voters approached him and said, "Pat, we're losing the country we grew up in."[126] In Gainesville, Georgia, described as the Poultry Capital of the World, longtime resident Joe Merck describes his city as being "overrun" with Hispanics: "I don't blame 'em coming up here, but half of 'em are illegal. We're taking care of 'em.

They're having all these babies one right after another. You can go buy your credentials. It's a known fact, but nobody does anything about it. We need to send 'em back home."[127] Respondents in numerous national polls echo these sentiments:

- 83 percent want federal authorities to crack down hard on noncitizens by using fingerprinting and random interviewing;[128]
- 81 percent believe illegal immigration is out of control;[129]
- 74 percent agree it is either extremely or very important to halt the flow of illegal immigrants;[130]
- 66 percent say illegal immigrants cost taxpayers too much;[131]
- 58 percent maintain that immigrants contribute to a worsening crime situation;[132]
- 56 percent oppose new laws making it easier for illegal immigrants to become legal workers;[133]
- 52 percent believe immigration hurts the nation;[134]
- 46 percent agree that immigration is contributing to a worsening economy;[135]
- 37 percent believe immigrants are making social and moral values worse.[136]

In many communities, the immigrant backlash has become a springboard for aspiring politicians. In 2006, the mayors of Hazelton, Pennsylvania, and Avon Park, Florida, supported legislation that would fine landlords $1,000 for every illegal tenant. The mayors, both of them Republicans who grew up in the 1960s and 1970s, speak wistfully of the days when traditional nuclear families occupied single-family homes, all residents paid their taxes, and English was the only language heard on the streets.[137] In 2008, Hazelton's mayor lost his bid for the U.S. House of Representatives seat held by Democrat Paul Kanjorski. Tom Tancredo, a Colorado Republican congressman whose anti-immigrant views briefly propelled him into the 2008 presidential contest, believes that illegal immigrants are "a scourge that threatens the very future of our nation."[138] In a television commercial promoting his presidential candidacy, Tancredo linked the flow of illegal aliens to the terrorist threat:

Hi, I'm Tom Tancredo, and I approve this message because someone needs to say it. There are consequences to open borders beyond the twenty million aliens who have come to take our jobs. Islamic terrorists now freely roam U.S. soil, jihadists who froth with hate, here to do as they have in London, Spain, Russia. [This is] the price we pay for spineless politicians who refuse to defend our borders against those who come to kill.

The ad concludes with a loud explosion and the tag line, "Tancredo—before it's too late.[139]

Anti-immigration measures have increasingly frequently won approval on state ballots. In 2004, 56 percent of Arizonans supported Proposition 200, which required proof of citizenship to vote and receive public benefits, despite public opposition from two of that state's top officials, Democratic governor Janet Napolitano and Republican U.S. senator John McCain.[140] Phoenix mayor Phil Gordon believes the measure creates "the equivalent of a police state" where citizenship papers could be required at public parks and bus stops to obtain police and other local services.[141] But Republican state representative John Allen emphatically disagrees: "The question is when do we stop this activity of illegal immigration? Right now, it's like Groundhog Day. You wake up every day and there's more of them. It will be this way until we have a closed border."[142]

Other xenophobic initiatives that have won widespread support have made English the official state language. By 2005, 27 states had approved so-called English-only laws buoyed by such sentiments as, "We have to go to the bank, and it says do you want this in English or Spanish? Well, phooey. This is America, you want to live here, you speak the language."[143] In one 2004 poll, 82 percent of respondents—including 76 percent of Democrats, 92 percent of Republicans, and 76 percent of independents—said that they wanted a nationwide English-only law.[144]

The backlash against Hispanic immigrants is so great that some social commentators have questioned whether the newcomers have a greater loyalty to their birthplaces than to their newly adopted homeland. Political scientist Samuel P. Huntington describes Hispanics as "sojourners," coming to the United States to work for a few years before returning home.[145] Even some Hispanics claim that they do not feel comfortable even after years of residing in the United States. Olga Contreras-Martinez was 12 years old when she and her family illegally migrated from Mexico to Florida, where Contreras-Martinez picked fruits and vegetables. Despite having obtained a college degree and U.S. citizenship and despite her current position as a teacher in Georgia, Contreras-Martinez does not feel especially welcome: "I call [Georgia] home, but I know I'm not welcome in my own home. Maybe that feeling of home will be something that will always be missing for me."[146]

While the backlash against immigrants is considerable, it is slowly bending to present-day realities. Many politicians realize that they must adapt to the inevitable changes that will be coming. In 2001, George W. Bush became the first president to utter a few Spanish words before a joint session of Congress. Pleading for support of his domestic agenda, Bush told lawmakers, "Juntos podemos [Together we can]."[147] A few months later, he paid tribute to the Mexican holiday Cinco de Mayo by becoming the first president to broadcast his weekly radio address in both English and Spanish.[148] Later that year, the White House Web site was modified to include Spanish translations of the administration's press briefings, biographies of the president and First Lady, and Bush's radio addresses.[149] Accepting renomination at the Republican National Convention Bush referred in Spanish to his signature educational reform: "No dejaremos a ningun nino atras! [We will leave no child behind!]"[150]

Bush backed these symbolic gestures by proposing policy changes designed to benefit Hispanics and foster a Republican realignment that would renew the GOP majority. In May 2006, he endorsed an overhaul of the nation's immigration laws, championing a plan offered by John McCain and Edward M. Kennedy that tightened border restrictions and offered a path to citizenship for the 11 million illegal aliens residing in the United States. In a nationally televised address, Bush pleaded with recalcitrant House Republicans and GOP voters to forgo their misgivings and embrace the future:

> There is a rational middle ground between granting an automatic path to citizenship for every illegal immigrant and a program of mass deportation. That middle ground recognizes there are differences between an illegal immigrant who crossed the border recently, and someone who has worked here for many years, and has a home, a family, and an otherwise clean record.
>
> I believe that illegal immigrants who have roots in our country and

want to stay should have to pay a meaningful penalty for breaking the law, to pay their taxes, to learn English, and to work in a job for a number of years. People who meet these conditions should be able to apply for citizenship, but approval would not be automatic, and they will have to wait in line behind those who played by the rules and followed the law. What I've just described is not amnesty; it is a way for those who have broken the law to pay their debt to society, and demonstrate the character that makes a good citizen.[151]

Bush's appeal was prompted in part by outcries from immigrants (both legal and illegal) who suddenly found their collective voices. Arturo Hernandez, an illegal immigrant from Mexico, was one. He and a half million others took to the streets of Los Angeles to support citizenship for illegal migrants. For Hernandez, it was a seminal moment: "I have lived for fifteen years in America. All that time I have lived with my head down, you know. [At the protest], all these people were telling me to put my head up."[152] As the protests multiplied, organizers proclaimed May 1, 2006, "A Day without Immigrants." Over one 24-hour period, millions of immigrants left work or school. At Chicago's Benito Juarez High School, for example, just 17 percent of the student body showed up. In California and Arizona, scores of lettuce, tomato, and grape growers gave their workers a day off. Tyson Foods closed several of its plants because of the lack of employees. In Phoenix, 150,000 people waved signs that read "Somos America [We Are America]."[153]

The demonstrations were sparked by the 2005 passage of a Republican-sponsored measure that made assisting illegal immigrants a felony. José Martinez, a 43-year-old illegal immigrant from El Salvador, retorted, "A criminal is a person who kills or steals. If I had come here to kill, I would understand. But I came to work."[154] Marcella Calderon, an 18-year-old Mexican migrant, agreed: "I want people to know we're not criminals. We're here to work. We're coming here to make the American Dream."[155] Adelina Nicholls, an organizer of a massive demonstration in Atlanta, acknowledged that the bill "was the ignition that is giving fuel to all community and grassroots groups." Illegal immigrants, Nicholls declared, had "decided not to be invisible anymore."[156] Another illegal migrant, marching with 4,000 others in tiny Lake Worth, Florida, held a sign that read "Let Me Love Your Country."[157] Other signs captured the coming of a new revolution: "Immigrant Nation"; "I'm an Immigrant and I Vote"; "Brown and Proud." Crowds chanted, "Hoy, marchamos; mañana, votamos [Today, we march; tomorrow, we vote]."[158]

But the Republican-controlled 109th Congress ignored the marchers and passed the Secure Fence Act, creating a 700-mile, double-layered fence stretching along the United States–Mexico border from Brownsville, Texas, to San Diego, California. The legislation also authorized the use of unmanned aerial vehicles, ground-based sensors, satellites, radar, and an array of security cameras at a cost of $1.2 billion.[159] The bill won over-whelming approval from congressional Republicans, who seemed intent on thwarting the rising tide of immigrants by yelling, "Stop!" California representative Dana Rohrabacher, for one, vividly described his opposition to the McCain-Kennedy immigration reform bill: "I would hope the American people are smart enough to smell the foul odor that's coming out of the United States Senate. . . . Those people in the Senate who are look-ing out for the interests of somebody else other than the American people will have to pay the political price and I'm sure Senator McCain, when he runs for president, will find that out."[160] An Arizona Republican state leg-islator was even more emphatic, labeling McCain "treacherous" and "trea-sonous" for even suggesting such legislation.[161]

Although the racial revolution received the attention of a war-weary White House as Bush's stay there drew to a close, the president's inability to sign comprehensive reform delayed the day of reckoning when policy-makers will have to bring immigration laws in line with present-day reali-ties. Bush was unable to either capture or control a central demographic reality of his time.

A Blurred Future

In 1992, several hundred self-described multiracialists gathered in Bethesda, Maryland, for the first national gathering of the multiracial com-munity. The Loving Conference, named in honor of the Supreme Court's decision in *Loving v. Virginia*, marked the beginning of a potent political movement.[162] Mildred Loving, the widow whose marriage spawned the Supreme Court decision, said, "Since the older generation is dying, the younger ones . . . realize that if someone loves someone they have a right to marry."[163] Four years later, the first "multiracial solidarity march" was held on the Mall in Washington, D.C.[164]

The movement spawned by the Loving Conference owed its potency to the ever-larger number of children living in interracial families, a number that quadrupled from 900,000 in 1967 (when *Loving v. Virginia* was decided) to more than 3,000,000 in 2007.[165] Mildred and Richard Loving's grandchildren were among them. Peggy, the youngest and fairest of the Loving children, married someone of "mixed race" and classifies herself as such. Donald, the middle child, married a white woman, and their children are seemingly white in appearance. Sidney, the oldest and darkest of the Loving children, whose color most resembles her mother's, lives as a self-identified black. In reality, all of the Loving children are part white, part black, and part Native American.[166] The removal of racial restrictions on the right to marry has put an end to the binary black-white world view of the 1960s and has created a contemporary rainbow of people whose racial origins and skin tones form a multitude of colors.

One effect of more interracial marriages is the growing number of offspring who have trouble labeling their racial backgrounds. Pattia Rodriquez, the light-skinned 31-year-old sales director for a New York–based woman's magazine, does not think of herself as either black or white: "I acknowledge that I have both black and white ancestry in me, but I choose to label myself in nonracial terms: Latina. Hispanic. Puerto Rican. Nuyorican. I feel that being Latina implies mixed racial heritage, and I wish more people knew that. Why should I have to choose? White means mostly privilege and black means overcoming obstacles, a history of civil rights. As a Latina, I don't try to claim one of these [for myself]."[167]

Rodriquez is hardly alone. When asked to complete the 2000 census form, 42 percent of Hispanics checked the box labeled "some other race," while 48 percent marked "white."[168] Kathia Mendez, a migrant from the Dominican Republic, explained that she chose "some other race" because "I am not black and I am not white. We don't define ourselves that way."[169] When asked to identify themselves in a 2002 survey, 30 percent of those of Latin American descent chose "Hispanic," 12 percent selected "Latino" or "Latina," 5 percent opted for "Mexican," another 5 percent selected "Mexican American," 5 percent simply said "American," 4 percent chose "brown," 1 percent "mestizo" or "mestiza" (mixed race), another 1 percent answered "human being" or "universal race," 1 percent chose "Puerto Rican," 1 percent selected "Latin American," 5 percent listed no category, and 2 percent had no reply.[170]

With the dawn of the twenty-first century, defining the term *race* is a linguistic challenge. Eduardo Diaz, a social service administrator, finds labels imposed by others especially demeaning: "There is no place called Hispanica. I think its degrading to be called something that doesn't exist. Even Latino is a misnomer. We don't speak Latin." One Mexican American office worker says that when she is called a "Latina," it makes her think "about some kind of island."[171] The complexity of racial self-identification prompted Ellis Cose, author of *Color Blind: Seeing beyond Race in a Race-Obsessed World*, to observe, "Tomorrow's multiracial people could just as easily become the next decade's something else. A name, in the end, is just a name. The problem is that we want those names to mean so much—even if the only result is a perpetuation of an ever-more-refined kind of racial madness."[172]

Cose's observation has special resonance for the Goderich family. Mario Goderich is a Miami police officer with light brown hair, green eyes, and the white skin of his Puerto Rican mother. When filling out the 2000 census form, Goderich checked the boxes labeled "Hispanic" and "white." His father, Rene, a refugee from Santiago, Cuba, made a different choice, describing himself as "white." Rene Goderich explained that in Cuba he would be called a *jabao* (a light-skinned mulatto): "Over here there's no 'jabao' or 'mulatto,' so I say white. We are all mixed." Letvia Arza-Goderich, a Los Angeles lawyer and Mario Goderich's cousin, has likewise lived along the edge of the racial divide. After fleeing Fidel Castro's Cuba in the late 1960s, Arza-Goderich grew up in white-dominated Wisconsin. Although she thought of herself as white, her neighbors did not, as she remembers: "We were Cubans, and that wasn't white. My answer was 'Not that it matters, but I'm white just like you because the people I come from were from Spain.' They'd look at you in disbelief. If you're Latino, you're not white-white in the eyes of white Americans." Arza-Goderich married a Cuban; she and her husband never discuss race with their three teenage sons because they believe it is no longer relevant. Her 16-year-old son, Ray, has had Vietnamese, Indian, Chicano, white, and black girlfriends as a consequence of his intense interest in the hip-hop culture.[173] Rodolfo de la Garza, a political science professor at Columbia University, marvels at what Arza-Goderich and her children now take for granted: "Interracial, interethnic dating isn't even a question. It's hard for people over forty to really understand that. And people my age—I'm sixty—people were killed for that."[174] Today, there are 2,000,000 couples in which one partner is Hispanic while the other is of a different race.[175]

Those numbers will steadily grow. A 1994 study provides important clues to the racial future. While only 8 percent of first-generation Hispanics marry outside of their race, that figure increases to 26 percent among second-generation Hispanics and to 33 percent by the third generation.[176] Further complicating the question of racial identity are the one-third of Asian marriages, 13 percent of black marriages, and 7 percent of white marriages that include partners of different races.[177] Susan Fu, a white woman married to a Chinese American man, has fielded numerous queries about the mixed race of their three children. One person asked if her daughter was "one of the children of China," while another wondered if the girl spoke English. Fu told one woman who asked where the children were from, "They're mine." The woman replied, "I know they are *yours*, but where did they come *from?*" prompting an exasperated Fu to nearly shout, "They're from my uterus."[178]

The complexity of racial self-identification is clear in a 2001 poll: 9 percent of respondents reported using different terminology to describe their race in different social situations; 28 percent described themselves as being of mixed race; and 48 percent always self-identified with one race.[179] As these results suggest, racial self-identification is both a semantic and emotional problem. In "High Yellow White Trash," Lisa Page, whose father is black and mother is white, wrote, "There are a lot of names for people like me. Bright-skinned, mixed, café au lait, high yellow white trash. The last one I made up myself. It sums up for me what it is to be black yet aware of a white heritage. You get a double consciousness that never goes away. You are forever light-skinned, no matter how black you feel on the inside." When Page was born in Chicago in 1956, her mother was situated in the white section of the hospital, but with the baby's arrival, hospital officials moved her to the colored section, and Page's "mother lost a piece of her identity that day; her status as a white woman, something she'd taken for granted all her life." Later, when Page and her siblings visited relatives in Michigan, family members explained the children's skin color by claiming their father was East Indian, and "during one family reunion, the pictures weren't taken until my sister, brother, and I were out of the room."[180]

But times are changing. Patty Alexander is white; her husband, Todd, is black. They live in a suburban Baltimore subdivision with their two children. The Alexanders claim they encounter little if any racial discrimination. Says Todd, "We're in the twenty-first century. And interracial relationships are just a fact."[181] Statistics confirm his argument: the number of black-white married couples rose from 51,000 in 1960 (when only 1.7 percent of black Americans had white spouses) to 363,000 in 2000 (when 4.3 percent of blacks had white spouses).[182] With that increase came a shift in racial attitudes, as Todd Alexander explains: "It's about getting beyond race and looking at people for who they are inside. When I was young, I remember Martin Luther King, Jr. saying that it's about the content of your character. That's what it's all about." Perhaps not surprisingly, three of Todd's four siblings have white spouses, and none of the nuptials brought the sort of controversy that attended Margaret Rusk's 1967 wedding.[183]

Yet racial self-identification remains an issue. When one of the Alexanders' young sons asked his mother, "What is my skin color?" she replied, "It's skin color." But the questions kept coming until Patty finally responded, "What color do you see?" Recognizing that the lack of racial discrimination the couple encounters and what race may mean for their children are two different things, Todd points out, "I know what it is like to be a black man in America. Patty knows what it's like to be a white woman in America. But neither of us knows what it is like to be biracial. When the kids come to me one day and say, 'You don't understand,' I won't be able to understand. But hopefully when they're older, things will be different. That is a concern I have for their future—that they don't get hurt or feel that they have to choose what race they are."[184]

But changing skin tones may give the Alexanders' children more role models from which to choose. The Miss America Pageant illustrates what is coming. For more than 50 years after it began as a swimsuit contest in 1921, persons of color were not permitted to participate. In 1974, blacks were allowed to enter. A decade later, Vanessa Williams became the first black contestant to wear the crown. In 2000, Angela Perez Baraquino, the reigning Miss Hawaii, became the first Asian to win the title, beating out a black woman from Louisiana, a Vietnamese American contestant from California, and white women from Mississippi and Kentucky. Three years later, the pageant chose its first multiracial winner, Erika Harold, who is of black, American Indian, Russian, Greek, German, Welsh, and English descent.[185]

As the face of America turns from white to beige, more multiracial achievers are winning national acclaim. Golfer Tiger Woods has compared himself to a living United Nations, a concession to the fact that he is Thai, black, white, and American Indian. When the young Woods asked his father for advice on navigating among his many racial worlds, his black father responded, "When you're in America, be black. When you're in the

Orient, be Asian."[186] Woods has labeled himself a "Cablinasian," a word he coined from the the terms *Caucasian, black, Indian,* and *Asian.*[187] Woods might have to invent another racial term for the children born to him and his wife, white, blonde-haired Swedish model Elin Nordegren.[188] Like Woods, Barack Obama has siblings of various races, courtesy of his mother's marriages to a black man and an Indonesian man. According to Obama, "I have got a sister who is half-Indonesian, who is married to a Chinese Canadian. I have got a niece who looks like, you know, she's all mixed up. . . . I have got family members that look like Margaret Thatcher. I have got family members that look like Bernie Mac."[189]

Other prominent Americans of mixed race include actress Halle Berry, the child of a white mother and black father who in 2001 became the first person from a multiracial background to win an Oscar in seventy-four years. In her acceptance speech, Berry thanked Dorothy Dandridge, Lena Horne, Diahann Carroll, and Oprah Winfrey "for being the best role model[s] any girl can have."[190] Hollywood has increasingly acknowledged the talents of nonwhites. In 2005, a record five nonwhites—four blacks and one Colombian—received Oscar nominations. Morgan Freeman won Best Supporting Actor, and Jamie Foxx was named Best Actor, only the second time in seventy-seven years that blacks had captured two of the major awards. Accepting his prize, Freeman told reporters that his victory "means Hollywood is continuing to make history."[191] Foxx, who won for his portrayal of musician Ray Charles in *Ray,* believes that his honor "says to those kids in chocolate cities like Chi-Town and south Dallas that things are changing. Things are getting better. I was just in Washington, D.C., screening *Ray* for the Black Caucus, and afterward this young kid stands up—jersey on, with some bling—and he says, 'Yo, Foxx, you think you might get a nod?' He's asking about an Oscar nod. That's a beautiful thing."[192] The same year, the Oscar for Best Song went to "Al Otro Lado del Rio," a Spanish tune from a movie *The Motorcycle Diaries,* about Che Guevara. A Spanish song had never before even been performed at the Oscars, much less won.

Two Marriages, Different Centuries

Just before 5:00 P.M. on a sunny August day in 2004, a bride entered a 100-year-old stone church to marry a man she met in a trial advocacy class in law school. The couple's story was like many others—they had sat next to each other and passed notes, and in one of them he asked her if she would like to play a round of golf.[193] And as at so many other weddings, the newlyweds had their pictures taken before heading off to a reception under a tent pitched behind a local inn. This wedding was different, however, because of the the presence of former president George H. W. Bush and his sons—Jeb Bush, the governor of Florida, and George W. Bush, the current president—as well as numerous Secret Service agents. Reporters commented on the attendance of so many political luminaries but did not mention the race of the bride, Amanda Williamson, a white woman, or the groom, George P. Bush, son of Jeb Bush and his Mexican-born wife, Columba.[194]

George Prescott Bush's Hispanic roots are well known, and within his family, he has come to symbolize the multiracial future. In 1988, George H. W. Bush referred to his grandson as one of the family's "little brown ones," a depiction Democrats criticized as racially insensitive.[195] The Bush family later came to see George P. as a campaign asset, and he was dispatched to plead his father's and uncle's cases to Hispanic voters. Addressing the delegates at the 2000 Republican National Convention, George P. extolled George W. as "un hombre con grandes sentimientos . . . who really cares about those he was elected to serve, including those of us whose faces look different."[196] The same year, *People* magazine ranked the young Bush number 4 on its list of the 100 most eligible bachelors.[197] *USA Today* noted the excitement he generated and dubbed him a hybrid of John F. Kennedy and Ricky Martin.[198] Frank Guerra, whose Austin-based marketing company has worked for the Bush family, says of George P., "He is intelligent, he's articulate, he's handsome, he has a very clean, clear communication style, and he has the kind of charisma you can't buy."[199] Angela Figueroa, managing editor of *People en Espanol* (the popular magazine's Spanish-language version) concurs: "He just popped out of nowhere, and now it's like, 'Ooh, la-la!' He's hunky. There's definitely a buzz."[200]

But on his wedding day, neither the mixed race of George P. Bush nor Amanda Williamson's race was mentioned. Instead, reporters noted the couple's impressive resumes. The *Austin American-Statesman* announcement was typical: "She works for the Jackson Walker law firm in Fort Worth. He works as an assistant to U.S. Judge Sidney Fitzwater in Dallas, but he plans to leave that post in the fall to work for the Dallas office of Akin, Gump, Strauss, Hauer, and Feld."[201] After the ceremony, a proud Jeb Bush echoed Dean Rusk's sentiments decades earlier: "I am very happy for my son. He is marrying a wonderful young woman. Life can't get any better."[202] For his part, George P. declared that he wanted to "start a family as soon as possible," adding, "I want a lot of kids."[203]

One month later, the future manifested itself when the newlyweds campaigned—in Mexico—for the reelection of the groom's uncle. As George P. explained to an accompanying reporter in Spanish, "It was a surprise for me [to learn] that there are over one million U.S. citizens living in Mexico, and that hundreds of thousands of them vote each election."[204] On Election Day, George W. Bush received an astonishing 44 percent of the Latino vote, giving him crucial margins in key states.[205]

There are many differences between the weddings of Guy and Margaret Smith and George P. and Amanda Bush. Though both couples were harbingers of the future, the Smiths were ahead of their time while the Bushes were of it. The Bush-Williamson wedding did not make the cover of *Time* magazine; rather, it was just another noteworthy item (among many) mentioned in the celebrity gossip columns. Yet that union and others like it are sure to change American politics. Shortly after their nuptials in Kennebunkport, Maine, the *Portland Sunday Telegram* warned its readers to adopt a more cosmopolitan outlook, an admonition the paper described as especially pertinent in a place whose population is 97 percent white: "Imagine the white Maine kid growing up in an all-white community, going to a virtually all-white university or college, getting a job in an all-white establishment, and someday leaving the state to learn that most of the world is composed of people of color. . . . [T]he culture shock could be severe."[206]

That culture shock is already here. A changing racial makeup means that the definition of race itself is now in question, even as a growing number of people acknowledge the irrelevancies of past racial stereotypes. In a poll taken a few months prior to George P. Bush's wedding, 83 percent of respondents said that they would not be concerned if their child were to marry someone of another race or religion.[207] Thanks to the increased propensity of interracial marriages, Henry Pachon, president of the Tomas Rivera Policy Institute at the University of Southern California, says, " 'White' is going to get darker over the coming decade. People will legitimately call themselves white, but they may be a shade darker, a café au lait sort of look."[208] As old racial stereotypes become obsolete, patterns of discrimination shift from skin tones to other attributes. For example, a 2003 survey of Hispanics who claimed to have experienced some form of discrimination found that only 8 percent attributed their misfortune to skin color.[209] Changing skin tones have also revolutionized the black-white racial politics of the past, and the only lagging indicators seem to be our language and political paradigms. The question of who we are will become an increasingly important matter of both private self-definition and public policy.

Signs of a new twenty-first century future are popping up everywhere. In 2005, the New York City police department had its first graduating class composed mostly of nonwhites: 18 percent of the recruits were black, 28 percent were Hispanic, and 8 percent were Asian American. These numbers have changed remarkably since 1979, when 87 percent of the force was white. This diversity reflects the promise of good pay and benefits, along with the sense of belonging to an institution that many immigrants (like their predecessors) find attractive. As Rafael Pineiro, the chief of police personnel, observed, "When I came on the job in 1970, there were only 300 Hispanics on the job." Today, there are 8,000.[210]

The changing makeup of the New York City police force reflects changes to the city as a whole: for the past 15 years, a majority of residents have been nonwhites. Today, 60 percent of New York City's residents are foreign born, and the number of Mexicans living there has increased 36 percent since the turn of the twenty-first century. More than half the residents of Queens and the Bronx do not speak English at home.[211] Police commissioner Raymond Kelley believes that the integrated, multiracial, and multilingual police force has improved police-community relations: "There is less tension in the streets and among the police than we have seen in my career."[212]

New York City has caught the wave of the future. So, too, did the United States itself in 2008, when Obama joined the parade of white-faced presidents. During the campaign, Obama half-jokingly said that he did not look like the presidents on the dollar bills. Indeed, he did not. But race did not become the issue in 2008 that old thinking about skin tones would have suggested. Like the Bush-Williamson wedding, Barack Obama is of his time, not ahead of it.

Three · Redefining Relationships

"The twenty-first century will be the century of moral freedom."
—ALAN WOLFE, AUTHOR OF *MORAL FREEDOM: THE IMPOSSIBLE IDEA THAT DEFINES THE WAY WE LIVE NOW*

HALFWAY THROUGH HIS thousand-day presidency, John F. Kennedy was exasperated. With the Cold War suddenly turning hot, the Soviet threat had never seemed more ominous. Expecting the worst at any moment (including a thermonuclear World War III), Kennedy desperately wanted unity at home. But that was not to be. Negroes (as they were called then) were demanding racial justice, with school desegregation a top priority. As southern streets filled with civil rights protesters and the National Guard was summoned to keep order, Kennedy complained bitterly behind closed doors to a black adviser, Louis Martin, "Negroes are getting ideas they didn't have before. Where are they getting them?" Martin shouted, "From you! You're lifting the horizons of Negroes."[1] Martin reminded Kennedy of his Inaugural Address, with such stirring phrases as, "My fellow citizens of the world, ask not what Americans can do for you, but what together we can do for the freedom of man."[2] Though Kennedy had uttered these words in the context of the Cold War, blacks took their meaning to heart and decided that freedom began at home.

At the turn of a new century, the transposition of presidential words into a different context than originally intended has repeated itself. In his second term, George W. Bush echoed Kennedy's call for a world filled with freedom. For Bush, enhancing liberty at home meant creating a twenty-first-century "ownership society," which meant more freedom to make more varied choices. In his Second Inaugural Address, Bush declared, "By making every citizen an agent of his or her own destiny, we will give our fellow Americans greater freedom from want and fear, and make our society more prosperous and just and equal."[3] And in his final State of the Union Address, Bush returned to his familiar theme: "As Americans, we believe in the power of individuals to determine their destiny and shape the course of history. We believe that the most reliable guide for our country is the collective wisdom of ordinary citizens. And so in all we do, we must trust in the ability of free peoples to make wise decisions, and empower them to improve their lives for their futures."[4] From a governing perspective, these speeches signaled Bush's desire to privatize a portion of Franklin D. Roosevelt's Social Security program, thereby giving citizens the option of investing some of their government savings in privately held accounts, an idea that received little congressional support and was eventually shelved.

As with Kennedy, Americans are reading something more into Bush's profreedom rhetoric. To them, his ringing second-term Inaugural Address meant not just having more economic choices but more moral choices. The desire for greater moral freedom began in the mid–twentieth century with the civil rights and women's rights revolutions. To poor blacks and disenfranchised women, more freedom meant exercising more options in life's economic and political marketplaces. At the same time, citizens of all races and both sexes began experimenting with a sexual revolution that provided increased moral selection in private life. In 2001, political scientist Alan Wolfe wrote, "Never have so many people been so free of moral constraint as contemporary Americans." He concluded, "The twenty-first century will be a century of moral freedom."[5]

At the onset of a new century, Americans are taking the Declaration of Independence's promises of "life, liberty, and the pursuit of happiness" and endowing them with heretofore unthinkable meanings. Political scientist Francis Fukuyama believes that this hyperindividualism in the private realm has produced a profound shift in public values: "Traditional societies have few options and many ligatures (i.e., social bonds to others): people have little individual choice concerning a marriage partner, job, where to live, or what to believe, and are tied down by the often oppressive bonds of family, tribe, caste, religion, feudal obligation, and the like. In modern societies, options for individuals vastly increase, while the ligatures binding them in webs of social obligation are greatly loosened."[6]

One byproduct of this newfound moral freedom is a narrowing of what constitutes the common good. Many Americans previously believed that defending the common good necessarily meant sacrificing some of their personal liberties. As John Adams put it, "We have no government armed in power capable of contending with human passions unbridled by morality and religion. Our constitution was made only for a religious and moral people. It is wholly inadequate for the government of any other."[7] Andrew Jackson was even more succinct: "Individuals must give up a share of liberty to preserve the rest."[8] Traveling across the continental United States in the 1830s, Alexis de Tocqueville found most citizens willing to marry their ideas about liberty to other values—including morality, law, and civic responsibility—that they deemed essential to preserving the common good.[9] But in the twenty-first century, few people are willing to sacrifice their personal liberties to uphold commonly held public values.

This redefinition of morality has produced a powerful political backlash, particularly among conservatives. According to social commentator Irving Kristol, "The consequence of such moral disarray is confusion about the single most important question that adults face: 'How shall we raise our children? What kind of moral example shall we set? What moral instruction should we convey?' A society that is impotent before such questions will breed restless, turbulent generations."[10] Former U.S. senator Rick Santorum, a conservative Pennsylvania Republican, blamed 1960s-era "secular liberals" for the dwindling of the nation's moral capital: "We now have a generation that has grown up with a belief, inspired by the Sixties' free-love assault on sexual mores, that true love is a *feeling*, and that it should not be resisted or constrained—rather, its ultimate validation is through sexual relations, without regard to the outdated social convention of marriage."[11]

For decades, a conservative consensus existed that constrained the most personal of private behaviors to preserve a semblance of "common decency." A 1939 poll found 8 in 10 respondents vehemently opposed to having sexual relations before marriage. Of the 5,000 men and women separately surveyed, 47 percent of females described premarital sex as "wicked," while 52 percent of males said it was "unfortunate" (see table 1). Three decades later, societal condemnation of premarital sex continued unabated. For example, in a 1963 survey, 67 percent of respondents strongly disagreed with the idea of men having premarital sex even if they were in love with the women involved. Likewise, 71 percent found it completely unacceptable for women to engage in such behavior (see table 1). A similar taboo existed concerning abortion. According to a 1969 survey, 78 percent of those polled believed abortion should be illegal if the parents "simply have all the children they want, although there are no major health or financial problems involved in having another child" (see table 1).

In the twenty-first century, some commonly understood limits to private moral behavior remain. For example, one study found that 93 percent of people believe polygamy is morally wrong.[12] Such condemnation is hardly surprising. For decades, an overwhelming majority of people have viewed fidelity in marriage as an important social value. Polls conducted by the National Opinion Research Center since 1972 show a consistently large majority that says that marital infidelity is "always wrong." And the number of people universally condemning this behavior increased 10 percentage points between 1972 and 2004 (see table 2).

Another area of public consensus is disdain of pornography, especially when it involves children. From the 1970s to the 1990s, a decisive majority of those surveyed said that pornography of all stripes contributed to a breakdown of public morals. While the percentage of those wanting all forms of pornography banned has declined slightly, there has been a nine-point increase in those who believe persons under eighteen years of age should not receive any pornographic materials (see table 2). Moreover, an overwhelming 97 percent of respondents reject equating child pornography to free speech.[13]

But when Americans are asked about nearly every other aspect of private behavior, many are unwilling to pass judgment. According to surveys conducted by the National Opinion Research Center from 1972 to 1982, the public was divided on the question of premarital sex: 31 percent believed it was "always wrong"; 34 percent said it was "not wrong at all." By 2006, only 25 percent thought premarital sex was "always wrong," while 45 percent replied that it was "not wrong at all." A similar pattern emerges on the subject of cohabiting heterosexual couples. In 1994, the public was split: 41 percent thought it was "all right" if a couple lived together without intending to get married; 41 percent disagreed. By 2005, those favoring cohabitation outnumbered dissenters, 49 percent to 46 percent (see table 3). When marriage is introduced into the equation, there is a greater likelihood of public approval: in 1994, only 33 percent approved of a pre-

TABLE 1.   A Regnant Moral Consensus, 1939–69 (in percentages)

Question: "Do you consider it all right, unfortunate, or wicked
when young men have sexual relations before marriage?"
(1939, males only)[a]

All right	11
Unfortunate	52
Wicked	28
Don't know	9

Question: "Do you consider it all right, unfortunate, or wicked
when young women have sexual relations before marriage?"
(1939, females only)[a]

All right	10
Unfortunate	35
Wicked	47
Don't know	7

Question (Agree/Disagree): "I believe that full sexual relations are
acceptable for the male before marriage when he is in love." (1963)[b]

Strongly agree	5
Agree	6
Slightly agree	6
Slightly disagree	8
Disagree	7
Strongly disagree	67

Question (Agree/Disagree): "I believe that full sexual relations are
acceptable for the female before marriage when she is in love." (1963)[b]

Strongly agree	4
Agree	5
Slightly agree	5
Slightly disagree	8
Disagree	7
Strongly disagree	71

Question: "Do you think abortion operations should or should not
be legal in the following case: where the parents simply have all the
children they want although there are no major health or financial
problems involved in having another child?" (1969)[c]

Should be legal	15
Should not	78
Don't know (volunteered)	8

[a]Roper Poll for *Fortune Magazine*, September 1939.
[b]National Opinion Research Center, July 1963.
[c]Gallup Organization poll, September 17–22, 1969.

TABLE 2. A Persistent Moral Consensus: Marriage and Pornography, 1972–2006 (in percentages)

	1972–82	1983–87	1988–91	1993	1994	1996	1998	2000	2002	2004	2006
Marital Infidelity											
Always wrong	71	72	77	76	78	77	78	78	79	81	81
Almost always wrong	14	16	13	14	12	15	12	11	13	12	11
Wrong only sometimes	11	8	6	6	6	5	6	7	4	5	5
Not wrong at all	3	2	2	2	2	2	2	3	2	2	2
Don't know (volunteered)	1	1	2	2	1	2	2	2	2	1	1
Pornography Laws											
There should be laws against the distribution of pornography whatever the age.	41	41	42	42	37	37	38	36	38	38	38
There should be laws against the distribution of pornography to persons under 18.	49	54	54	54	59	58	57	60	56	57	58
There should be no laws forbidding the distribution of pornography.	8	4	5	3	3	4	4	3	5	4	3
Don't know (volunteered)	2	1	2	1	0	1	1	1	1	0	1

Source: National Opinion Research Center polls, 1972–2006.

Text of first question: "What is your opinion about a married person having sexual relations with someone other than the marriage partner—is it always wrong, almost always wrong, wrong only sometimes, or not wrong at all?"

Text of second question: "Which of these statements comes closest to your feelings about pornography laws? There should be laws against the distribution of pornography whatever the age. There should be laws against the distribution of pornography to persons under eighteen. There should be no laws forbidding the distribution of pornography."

marital cohabitation that resulted in an eventual marriage; 11 years later, 40 percent favored premarital cohabitation under such conditions (see table 3). Familial backgrounds appear to be a contributing factor for the change of heart. One study of college-aged women whose parents had divorced found that 65 percent concurred with the statement, "It is a good idea to live with someone before deciding to marry him." Just 49 percent of women from intact families agreed.[14]

TABLE 3. An Emerging Moral Freedom, 1972–2006 (in percentages)

	1972–82	1983–87	1988–91	1993	1994	1998	2000	2002	2004	2006
Premarital Sex										
Always wrong	31	27	26	26	25	25	27	27	27	25
Almost always wrong	11	9	10	10	9	9	8	8	9	9
Wrong only sometimes	22	22	21	20	20	20	21	20	19	19
Not wrong at all	34	40	40	41	42	42	40	44	43	45
Don't know (volunteered)	3	3	3	3	3	4	4	2	2	2

	1972–82	1983–87	1988–91	1993	1994	1998	2000	2002	2004	2005
All right for a Couple to Live together without Intending to Get Married										
Strongly agree	N/A	N/A	N/A	N/A	10	17	N/A	16	N/A	28
Agree	N/A	N/A	N/A	N/A	31	26	N/A	30	N/A	21
Neither agree nor disagree	N/A	N/A	N/A	N/A	16	21	N/A	17	N/A	4
Disagree	N/A	N/A	N/A	N/A	25	16	N/A	19	N/A	13
Strongly disagree	N/A	N/A	N/A	N/A	16	18	N/A	17	N/A	33
Don't know (volunteered)	N/A	N/A	N/A	N/A	2	2	N/A	2	N/A	2

	1972–82	1983–87	1988–91	1993	1994	1998	2000	2002	2004	2005
Good Idea to Live together before Marriage										
Strongly agree	N/A	N/A	N/A	N/A	10	15	N/A	21	N/A	22
Agree	N/A	N/A	N/A	N/A	23	24		27	N/A	18
Neither agree nor disagree	N/A	N/A	N/A	N/A	23	26		19	N/A	6
Disagree	N/A	N/A	N/A	N/A	27	17		18	N/A	17
Strongly disagree	N/A	N/A	N/A	N/A	15	16		14	N/A	34
Don't know (volunteered)	N/A	N/A	N/A	N/A	2	2		2	N/A	2

Source: The responses for 1972–2004, and 2006 are from National Opinion Research Center, General Social Surveys, 1972–2006. Text of first question: "There's been a lot of discussion about the way morals and attitudes about sex are changing in this country. If a man and woman have sex relations before marriage, do you think it is always wrong, almost always wrong, wrong only sometimes, or not wrong at all?" Text of second question: Agree/Disagree: "It is all right for a couple to live together without intending to get married." Text of third question: "It's a good idea for a couple who intend to get married to live together first."

The responses for 2005 are from Greenberg Quinlan Rosner Research, July 25–August 7, 2005. Text of first question: "Now I am going to read to you a list of statements. For each of the following, please tell me if you agree or disagree with the statement. If you neither agree nor disagree with the statement, please say so. . . . It is all right for a couple to live together without intending to get married." Text of second question: "Now I am going to read to you a list of statements. For each of the following, please tell me if you agree or disagree with the statement. If you neither agree nor disagree with the statement, please say so. . . . It is a good idea for a couple who intend to get married to live together first."

Note: N/A = not asked.

Other surveys suggest a greater public tolerance of various sexual behaviors. For example, a 2001 poll of 1,000 unmarried women attending four-year colleges found that 87 percent agreed with the statement, "I should not judge anyone's sexual conduct except my own."[15] This newfound moral freedom was evident in a 2005 online survey that found 25 percent of men and 13 percent of women have had more than 25 sexual partners during their lifetimes.[16] These findings echo those of the National Center for Health Statistics, which also reported in 2005 that men aged 30 to 44 had a median of 6 to 8 sexual partners, while women in the same age bracket had 4. Nonwhite males were especially apt to engage in a variety of short-term relationships: among men aged 15 to 44, 18 percent of Hispanics, 22 percent of whites, and 34 percent of blacks revealed that they had had 15 or more female partners. (For women of the same age, 4 percent of Hispanics, 10 percent of whites, and 9 percent of blacks had an equal number of male partners.)[17]

The sexual revolution is no longer a revolution. Twenty-first-century teenagers provide abundant evidence of this point. According to a 2004 study, half of high-school-age adolescents have had intercourse, with a comparable proportion of senior girls and boys (62 percent and 61 percent, respectively) being sexually experienced.[18] A similar survey conducted by the Centers for Disease Control found the proportion of young people having sex rises nearly 10 percent with each passing grade:

32.8 percent of ninth-graders have had sex;

44.1 percent of tenth-graders have had sex;

53.2 percent of eleventh-graders have had sex;

61.6 percent of twelfth-graders have had sex.[19]

As young people become more sexually adventurous, some parents have reacted by strongly endorsing abstinence education. In Anaheim, California, students receive ATM cards. But these are hardly the conventional banking cards—rather, the abbreviation stands for "Abstinence Til Marriage." But Anaheim is the exception, as only 35 percent of school districts nationwide provide abstinence-only sex education. An additional 51 percent teach abstinence-plus—that is, courses that teach that chastity is preferred but that also provide information about contraception. Only 14 percent of districts have comprehensive programs that include discussions about abortion, homosexuality, premarital sex, oral and anal sex, and masturbation.[20]

But whatever the curriculum taught in the schools, teenage sexual activity is rampant. One poll of 600 abstinence-pledging teenagers found that 61 percent had broken their vows within a year.[21] Another study found that 88 percent of middle and high school students who promised to remain virgins until marriage had engaged in premarital sex.[22] And 40 percent of twelfth-graders reported having sex outside of any romantic relationship.[23] With numbers like these, it is no wonder that 82 percent of adult parents with teenagers agreed with the statement, "Waiting to have sex is a nice idea, but not many teens really do wait."[24] Reflecting on her teenage years, one adult woman recalled abstinence as a whim of her childhood:

> If someone had asked me when I was twelve if I wanted to remain a virgin until marriage, I would have said, "Of course I do."
> At thirteen, I would have said, "I think so."
> By fourteen, I would have replied, "Maybe."
> At age fifteen, my response would have been, "I don't see how that is possible."[25]

Parents are hardly oblivious to what their children are doing. One study found that two-thirds of parents believed their teenage children had engaged in sexual intercourse.[26] This does not mean that parents subscribe to an "anything goes" philosophy. When asked about teaching sex in schools, 47 percent of parents agreed with the statement, "Teenagers need to have limits set, they must be told what is acceptable and what is not." At the same time, 51 percent believed that "teenagers need to make their own decisions, so their education needs to be more in the form of providing information and guidance."[27] Parents Ed Gold and Amy Robinson neatly captured the majority sentiments: "What if [teenagers] just can't say no? What if they are overwhelmed, or think they are in love, or their bodies overrule their heads? The reality is that children are having sexual experiences younger and younger. I don't understand the concept of not wanting the child to have all the available information. I don't think that's any way to make a child whole."[28]

But with so many once-forbidden sexual taboos falling by the wayside, it is not surprising that today's intimate relationships are incredibly diverse.

The varieties include married couples, cohabiting couples (straight or gay), singles, blended families, "friendships with privileges" (meaning sex with no enduring commitment), civil unions, and gay marriages. Today, only 24 percent of households have a traditional family structure of a mother, father, and children living with them, and only one-third of all U.S. households have children under 18 years of age.[29] Other statistics echo these figures. In 2004, nearly 1 in 5 women over 40 years of age was childless, compared to 1 in 10 in 1976.[30] A 2005 Census report revealed that 36.8 percent of all U.S. births were to unmarried women.[31] And a 2007 Pew Research poll found that 47 percent of adults in their 30s and 40s have spent a portion of their lives in cohabiting relationships.[32] Thus, when pollster Stanley Greenberg asked respondents to define the term *family*, only 34 percent replied that it was "mother, father, and children," "husband, wife, and children," or "parents and children," a sure sign as any that what once passed for the nuclear family is no more.[33]

Simply put, we are as far away from the 1950s (with that era's conventional stay-at-home mom and working dad) as the 1900s (with their Model-T Fords and urban tenements teeming with European immigrants) were from the mid–twentieth century, as statistics show:

- In 1950, 78 percent of U.S. households were headed by married couples; today, 54 percent.[34]
- In 1950, 93 percent of families with minor children had married couples as parents; today, 73 percent.[35]
- In 1950, 9.3 percent of households consisted of people living alone; today, 26 percent.[36]
- In 1950, 1 in 20 children were born to unmarried mothers; today, more than 1 in 3.[37]

Reflecting on these transformations, Daniel Patrick Moynihan observed, "The biggest change, in my judgment, is that the family structure has come apart all over the North Atlantic world." And, he added, this phenomenon had happened in a "historical instant."[38] Indeed, it seems so. Back in 1965, Moynihan, then the assistant secretary of labor in the Johnson administration, warned that black families were trapped in a "tangle of pathology" as fathers abandoned households, leaving bereft mothers to cope with raising children. Years later, sociologist Stephanie Coontz observed that this troubling phenomenon was only "a rehearsal for something that was going to happen in the white community."[39] Today, white women under 25 years of age are just as likely to have children out of wedlock as are black women of the same age. Among Hispanics, the percentage of unwed births has increased from 19 percent in 1980 to 48 percent in 2005.[40]

The destruction of the nuclear family has provoked outrage among many conservatives. In 1992, Vice President Dan Quayle won plaudits from the Religious Right when he criticized television's Murphy Brown for having an out-of-wedlock baby, saying that the character mocked "the importance of fathers by bearing a child alone, and calling it just another 'lifestyle choice.'"[41] Quayle believed the program's subtext reflected a "poverty of values" among the nation's cultural elites, who, he declared, "sneer[ed] at the simple but hard virtues—modesty, fidelity, integrity."[42] Sixteen years later, the Republican Party nominated Sarah Palin for vice president despite the fact that her teenage daughter, Bristol, was pregnant and not married to the father of her child. The situation hardly caused a ripple. In fact, it endeared Palin to the party's conservative wing, since her daughter had not had an abortion. And on the Democratic side of the aisle, 38-year-old Representative Linda Sanchez made history in 2008 when she became the first House member to become pregnant without being married. Sanchez defended her pregnancy, saying, "I'm not a high school kid, it wasn't an accident. I'm financially stable, in a committed relationship." Sanchez told the *Washington Post* that she had always wanted children and that the public reaction to Bristol Palin's pregnancy led her to conclude that her constituents would not object: "We've evolved as a society so much. The reality of single working moms is such a powerful reality." Her boyfriend, who, like Sanchez, is divorced (and who is the father of five other children), welcomed the news. Marriage, said Sanchez, would have to wait.[43]

The fact that so many Americans from both political parties are having children out of wedlock has led Coontz to conclude that marriage itself has come to an inevitable end: "It took more than one-hundred-fifty years to establish the love-based, male breadwinner marriage as the dominant model in North America and Western Europe. It took less than twenty-five years to dismantle it. No sooner had family experts concluded that the perfect balance had been reached between the personal freedoms promised by the love match and the constraints required for social stability, than people began to behave in ways that fulfilled conservatives' direst predictions."[44]

A decade after Quayle excoriated Murphy Brown, another vice president, Democrat Al Gore, described how varied interpersonal moral choices made for intricate family arrangements. In *Joined at the Heart*, Gore and his wife, Tipper, introduced readers to a prototypical twenty-first-century family headed by Dick and Susan Fadley, who were raising six children from four different partnerships.

> Dick married Dee.
>
> Dee previously had a child, Jacob, whom Dick adopted.
>
> Dick and Dee had two children of their own.
>
> Dick and Dee divorced, and Dick fell in love with Caitlin. They had one daughter, although they never married.
>
> Dick married Susan, and they had two children.[45]

Explaining how each child is related to the other is to describe a tangle of relationships. As Susan Fadley said, "This family is definitely a crazy mixed-up family. . . . It would have been nice to have a family with two parents and children from those parents, but life's choices did not happen that way, unfortunately—or fortunately, because then we wouldn't have [become] who we are now." Susan described the Fadleys' choices as "okay."[46] That's just the point. In the twenty-first century, personal relationships—straight, gay, married, cohabitating, single—are all about making choices, and those choices are just as diverse as the country itself. The 1950s version of the family has been ripped apart and redefined in a myriad of ways.

The Postmarriage Century

In its 1966 mission statement, the National Organization for Women (NOW) declared, "We believe that a true partnership between the sexes *demands a different concept of marriage*, an equitable sharing of the responsibilities of home and children and of the economic burdens of their support."[47] NOW's marital critique was not the first. Four years earlier, *Cosmopolitan* magazine founder Helen Gurley Brown advised women that marriage was "insurance for the *worst* years of your life."[48] By the late 1960s, protests against the conventional roles associated with marriage began to spread. In 1968, supporters of women's liberation gathered outside the Miss America Pageant in Atlantic City and tossed bras and pictures into garbage cans, saying that they "degraded" women as "sex objects."[49] Yet despite such occasional uproars, husbands remained the dominant partners and often had the law on their side. Until the 1970s, men could force their wives to have sex. As Coontz reminds us in *Marriage: A History*, men had complete authority over the family finances and did not legally have to consult with their wives about where the couple would live.[50]

When the members of NOW penned their founding document, marriage was—as it had been for centuries—an arrangement formed as much by economics as by love. Molly Yard, a former president of NOW, joined the organization because she was determined to overturn the economic and social constraints that defined her marriage. In 1938, Yard married Sylvester Garrett, a fellow classmate from Swarthmore College. She immediately defied social convention by choosing to keep her maiden name, but when she and her husband attempted to open a joint checking account with their different last names, bank officials said no. When Yard protested, they told her that if she had been Garrett's mistress, there would have been no problem with their opening a joint account.[51]

Yard was far ahead of her time. When respondents to a 1955 study were asked what they had sacrificed by marrying and raising a family, an overwhelming majority replied, "Nothing."[52] The promarriage sentiment was so strong that four out of five respondents believed that anyone who remained single was "sick," "neurotic," or "immoral."[53] A 1962 survey of more than 2,000 women conducted for the *Saturday Evening Post* painted an idyllic Norman Rockwell–esque portrait of marriage cast in the bounty of economic materialism: 47 percent of respondents said that they dreamed of marrying hardworking, ambitious men who could give them material benefits they otherwise could never afford; only 15 percent said there should be only "affection or love between" husbands and wives. In return for economic security, most women believed that their duty was to provide emotional stability: 60 percent said their chief purpose in life was being a good mother, 32 percent chose being a good wife, and 20 percent selected making a good home for the family. Only 1 percent believed having personal financial success was life's most important goal.[54]

Prominent public figures and the national media echoed these sentiments. Two-time Democratic Party presidential nominee Adlai Stevenson told graduates of Smith College that "most of you" are going to assume "the humble role of housewife," and "whether you like the idea or not just now, later on you'll like it."[55] In 1956, *Life* magazine commented that women "have minds and should use them . . . so long as their primary interest is in the home."[56] *Ladies' Home Journal* ran a regular feature under the title, "Can This Marriage Be Saved?" Inevitably, the answer was an emphatic yes, especially if women became faithful domestic partners and let their husbands be the breadwinners. In one case, "Marilyn" saved her marriage by giving up her "glamour girl" fantasies about becoming a movie star to do volunteer work in a local church. In another, "Ava" learned to control her bossiness, telling a therapist that her husband "now feels that he is the head of the family."[57]

Today, those old magazines have been relegated to dusty bookshelves. No aspiring politician would ever give Stevenson's commencement address. And even the Miss America Pageant, replete with its celebration of 1950s-era family values, has been demoted to Country Music Television after drawing just 9.8 million viewers in its final outing on a major network.[58] The demise of the Miss America Pageant is an especially notable cultural touchstone. During the 1950s, the extravaganza captured nearly 40 percent of television viewers on the second Saturday in September. Contestants competed in the bathing suit competition, for such titles as Miss Congeniality, and of course for the overall crown.[59] *Washington Post* staff writer Libby Copeland explains the reasoning lurking behind the judges' final selection: "Miss America is not expected to be beautiful. Rather, she is aggressively cute. Her values are also cute, which is why Miss America and Country Music Television are so perfect for each other. The pageant is heartland entertainment for a heartland channel, and by 'heartland' we never mean a place but a state of mind. An irony-free state of mind. A cute state of mind."[60]

The shunting of the Miss America Pageant to Country Music Television symbolizes a values revolution that encompasses the institution of marriage, which is no longer an economic contract with its guarantees of financial primacy for the male and emotional stability for both partners. As *New York Times* columnist Maureen Dowd observes, the feminist revolution had the "unexpected consequence of intensifying the confusion between the sexes, leaving women in a tangle of dependence and independence as they entered the twenty-first century."[61] Gone are the predetermined male-female married roles of the past. In 2001, for example, one in four wives earned more than their husbands.[62]

Moreover, many married couples are experimenting with reversals of 1950s-era gender roles: in 2003, 5.6 million couples had stay-at-home dads and working moms.[63] Since the mid-1990s, the number of men suing their employer for family leave has grown from 5 percent to 11 percent. A survey found that the most important reasons men gave for staying home were "showing love and affection to kids," followed by providing "safety and protection," "moral guidance," "tak[ing] time to play," and "teaching and encouraging."[64]

Divorce, American Style

Emotional stability is no longer part of the marriage contract. In polls taken by the National Opinion Research Center from 1973 to 1976, 70 percent of respondents described their marriages as "very happy." But when respondents were asked the same question between 1998 and 2004, the number of happily marrieds fell to 64 percent.[65] Moreover, only 39 percent of first-time married couples in a 1999 Rutgers University study characterized their unions as "happy."[66]

These extraordinarily low figures correspond to a significant increase in the divorce rate. Although divorce has increased in every decade since the Civil War, the yearly rate held steady throughout the 1950s and early 1960s at fewer than 10 partings per 1,000 couples.[67] Correspondingly, only 11 percent of children born in the 1950s saw their parents either divorce or separate by the time they turned 18. But in 1965, the divorce rate sharply increased, peaking at 23 divorces per 1,000 marriages in 1979.[68] Today, a 25-year-old marrying for the first time has a 52.5 percent chance that the marriage will end in divorce.[69]

All marriages end. During the colonial era, most conjugal unions ceased because one spouse died.[70] But today, most marriages end as a matter of choice.[71] According to a study conducted by sociologists Barbara Dafoe Whitehead and David Popenoe, men aged 25 to 33 attribute prevalent divorce rates to narcissism, consumerism, and having "too many choices." Observed one, "You used to fall in love with the girl in your high school English class. Now you have more choices and you get married and then three years later, a better one comes along."[72] Sociologists Norval Glenn and Elizabeth Marquardt see an emerging "divorce culture" based on the freedom to make varied moral choices: "The divorce culture arose when shifts in attitudes about the importance of lasting marriage began to have an impact on *everyone's* marriage. In a divorce-oriented culture, then, not only are troubled marriages more likely to end in divorce, but more marriages are likely to become troubled."[73]

Still, the choice to end a marriage is not without cost. Children are often the unwitting victims, with more than 1 million watching their parents part each year.[74] One by-product is an enhanced teenage angst. Mary Eberstadt, a fellow at the Hoover Institution, believes that today's popular music contains more than the usual dose of anomie. In an influential article, "Eminem Is Right," Eberstadt cited several examples of popular music that reflect teenagers' pain following a family divorce:

- Papa Roach, "Broken Home": "I know my mother loves me / But does my father even care?"
- Blink 182, "Stay Together for the Kids Sake": "What stupid poem could fix this home / I'd read it everyday."
- Good Charlotte, "Little Things": "We checked [Dad's] room / His things were gone / We didn't see him no more."
- Everclear, "Sick and Tired": "I blame my family / Their damage is living in me."[75]

The success of these million-selling songs has even caught the artists who composed them off-guard. According to Blink 182's Tom DeLonge, "We get e-mails about 'Stay Together,' kid after kid saying, 'I know exactly what you're talking about! That song is about my life!' And you know what? That sucks. You look at statistics that 50 percent of parents get divorced, and you're going to get a pretty large group of kids who are pissed off and who don't agree with what their parents have done."[76]

The founding members of Good Charlotte concur. When Benji and Joel Madden were teenagers, their father abandoned them, leaving behind a financially precarious and emotionally devastated family. Benji recalls, "It was pretty traumatic. We went from working class to poverty, and it was probably at the worst time possible. It's happening when I'm in the ninth grade, which is a really tough year, and my mom is having health problems, and my older brother Josh, he was like: 'I'm outta here.' We didn't know what the [expletive] we were going to do. I was angry." Joel had similar thoughts: "I didn't know where my dad was. I was living in this [bad] little town, where nobody knows what's cool. I wanted to play sports, but I wasn't good. I wanted chicks, and chicks didn't like me. I wanted to have friends, but I didn't get to go to the parties. I had to work forty hours a week to help my mom pay the bills. It was like a tornado."[77]

Joel and Benji Madden translated their emotional losses into popular music. On the song "Emotionless," they sing of their father,

It's been a long hard road without you by my side
Why weren't you there all the nights that we cried?
You broke my mother's heart, you broke your children for life
It's not okay, but we're all right
I remember the days you were a hero in my eyes
But those are a long-lost memory of mine
I spent so many years learning how to survive
Now I'm writing to let you know we're still alive.[78]

Music journalist William Shaw writes that these lyrics reflect the feelings of a generation that sees itself as "uniquely fractured."[79] Eberstadt agrees, citing an important qualitative difference between today's teens and their baby boomer parents: "Baby boomers and their music rebelled against their parents *because* they were parents—nurturing, attentive, and overly present (as those teenagers often saw it) authority figures. Today's teenagers and their music rebel against parents because they are *not* parents—not nurturing, not attentive, and often not even there."[80]

The death of so many marriages clearly causes substantial emotional pain for the children involved. Marquardt reports that children growing up in divorced families often feel like different people with each parent, while kids whose parents stay married remain at the center of family life and feel emotionally secure.[81] As one acquaintance told Marquardt, "When I was a kid it would really stress me out when my divorced parents were in the same room together . . . because I didn't know who to be."[82] To relieve some of the emotional upheavals caused by divorce, the mushrooming "collaborative law" movement has sought to bring parents and lawyers to terms without resorting to family court. Even after divorces, many ex-partners turn to "parent coordinators" who can mediate decisions involving children.[83]

In this morally free environment, the social stigma previously associated with divorce has all but disappeared. In a 2006 poll, two-thirds of respondents considered divorce morally acceptable, while 58 percent of those who participated in a 2007 study said that divorce is "painful but preferable to an unhappy marriage."[84] These opinions represent quite a change of heart. In 1936, only 23 percent of those surveyed thought divorces should be easier to obtain; 77 percent disagreed.[85] Two books neatly capture this shift toward no-fault divorce. One mid-1940s text tersely asserted, "Children are entitled to the affection and *association* of two parents, not one." Thirty years later, another popular book proclaimed the opposite: "A two-parent home is not the only emotional structure within which a child can be happy and healthy. . . . The parents who take care of themselves will be best able to take care of their children."[86]

The latter attitude now prevails. According to *Nation* magazine writer Katha Pollitt, divorce has become "an American value."[87] A 2008 *Time* magazine report found that businesses aimed at the newly divorced are booming. New Orleans resident Renee Savant, for example, bought a hearse, thinking that she would rent it out for over-the-hill parties. Instead, customers often hire it to celebrate the end of their marriages. According to Savant, "I would never in a million years have thought the fad would be divorce parties." Other companies have found success with ex-wife toilet paper, ex-husband voodoo dolls, wedding ring coffins, and the like.[88] Even Hallmark cards has gotten into the "let's celebrate the divorce" spirit with greetings such as, "Think of your former marriage as a record album. It was full of music—both happy and sad. But what's important now is . . . YOU! The recently released HOT, NEW, SINGLE! You're going to be at the TOP OF THE CHARTS!"[89] Divorce parties, replete with upside-down wedding cakes with the legs of the bride and groom sticking out at the bottom/top, are also popular. At one, Lesley Rogers, a Seattle communications director whose five-year marriage ended in 2006, met her current boyfriend.[90]

The failure of so many marriages has created a crisis of confidence in the institution itself. In a 2005 survey of women aged 18 to 24, 45 percent said, "You see so many unhappy marriages that you begin to question it as a way of life."[91] One New York University student typified the prevalent thinking: "You see so [many] people getting divorces. . . . I just don't see the necessity [of marriage]. I think that I don't have to be married to [the] person that I'm with. . . . You know like [movie stars] Goldie Hawn [and Kurt Russell]? They're not married."[92] In a 2006 interview on *Larry King Live*, Hawn said that she and her long-standing live-in boyfriend had considered and rejected marriage:

We had both been married. I've been married twice. It didn't work. He was married once. That didn't work either. And we were at a time where we had kids and thought well, you know, what actually would it do to get married? I like being independent. I like being his girlfriend. I like that notion. I think it's sexy and I do think that it's a way of saying I don't own you and there's no paper that says that. My union with you is in my heart and it's in my promises and that's the best you can do. . . . And the kids didn't want us to get married either by the way. After about five years [together] we said, "You know, guys, do you want us to get married?" And they went, "No, it's working great just the way it is."[93]

The dissolution of marriage is hardly a phenomenon pitting Republicans versus Democrats, conservatives versus liberals, red states versus blue states, or Hollywood versus the rest of America. While the country has chosen sides in a values war that defines how citizens should live, the plethora of interpersonal choices people make in real life knows no party or ideology. For example, a 1999 poll found that divorce is relatively commonplace—5.1 per 1,000 people—in eleven conservative, southern, Republican-dominated states. But in nine liberal, pro-Democratic, northeastern states, divorce was less frequent: 3.5 per 1,000 persons.[94] Texas and Massachusetts—home states to the 2004 presidential nominees, George W. Bush and John Kerry, respectively—showed the same pattern. In Texas, the 2000 Census pegged the divorce rate at 4.1 per 1,000; in Massachusetts, the figure was 2.4 per 1,000.[95]

A similar phenomenon occurs when marriage trends are analyzed. The areas with the greatest decline in marriage from 2000 to 2005 were not limited to either red or blue states. In Boone County, Kentucky, for example, the marriage rate fell an astounding 11.6 percent, yet the county gave Bush 72 percent of its votes in 2004. Similarly, in Nash County, North Carolina, marriages dropped by 9.7 percent, yet Bush won 58 percent of the ballots. And in Webb County, Texas, Kerry received 57 percent of the vote although the number of married households fell by 9.6 percent.[96]

A comparison of divorce rates among conservative Christians and members of other religious groups shows a similar pattern. According to one study, Baptists are most prone to divorce, with 29 percent having dissolved their marriages; among born-again Christians, that figure was 27 percent; and Catholics, Lutherans, atheists, and agnostics all had divorce rates of 21 percent.[97] Similarly, 23 percent of evangelicals have been married more than once, while only 15 percent of people with no religious preference have entered into more than one union.[98] According to pollster George Barna, the old saying that the family that prays together, stays together finds little validity in the social science data:

> While it may be alarming to discover that born-again Christians are more likely than others to experience a divorce, that pattern has been in place for quite some time. Even more disturbing, perhaps, is that when those individuals experience a divorce many of them feel their community of faith provides rejection rather than support and healing. But the research also raises questions regarding the effectiveness of how churches minister to families. The ultimate responsibility for a marriage belongs to the husband and wife, but the high incidence of divorce within the Christian community challenges the idea that churches provide truly practical and life-changing support for marriages.[99]

In Arkansas, the divorce rate became so high that former Governor Mike Huckabee declared a "marriage emergency."[100] Thirty-six other states joined Arkansas to fund programs to reduce the divorce rate and encourage couples to stay together.[101] Even so, the divorce rate nationwide remains at nearly 50 percent. Many observers blame the transient nature of contemporary commitments and the range of family choices. As Harry Pearson, a former history teacher, told Wolfe, "When it is convenient for us to be committed, we are to another person. When it becomes inconvenient . . . the other person gets dumped along the way. I'm gonna get in trouble for this, but families work when there's a way to make sure that children, particularly until they're ten or eleven or twelve years old, are well cared for, are well directed, and are the prime focus of the family as a social unit. That doesn't happen when both parents work sixty-five hours a week."[102]

Redefining Marriage

Rather than a contractual arrangement that provides economic security and emotional stability, today's marriages represent declarations of love by both parties at a given moment. As the French often say, "Le coeur a sa raison [The heart has its reason]." Thus, when 18- to 24-year-olds are asked, "Regardless of how you may currently feel about marriage, which one or

two of the following represent the best reasons to get married?" the answers represent affairs of the heart:

- to have a partner for life—74 percent;
- to start a family—58 percent;
- to make a visible commitment to another person—51 percent;
- to obtain financial security—10 percent;
- to avoid being alone—10 percent.[103]

In the twenty-first century, these heart songs involve all types of voluntary choices. By renegotiating the marriage contract to have its primary
clauses premised on love (transitory or permanent), the concept of marriage itself has been transformed. Coontz writes that love-struck heterosexuals have involuntarily promoted the "disestablishment" of their once-
stable conjugal unions: "Marriage is no longer the institution where people
are initiated into sex. It no longer determines the work men and women do
on the job or at home, regulates who has children and who doesn't, or co-
ordinates care-giving for the ill or aged. For better or worse, marriage has
been displaced from its pivotal position in personal and social life, and will
not regain it short of a Taliban-like counterrevolution."[104]

For many Americans, disconnecting love from marriage has meant
foregoing marriage altogether. A milestone was reached in 2006, when for
the first time, only a minority of the nation's households (49.7 percent)
consisted of married couples. Demographer William H. Frey notes that
the continued decline of married couples closes "the book on the Ozzie
and Harriet era that characterized much of the last century."[105] A 2007 Pew
Research poll shows that even having children is no longer viewed as a primary reason for entering into a marriage: 65 percent of those surveyed believed that mutual happiness and fulfillment should be the main purpose of
entering into a marriage; only 23 percent thought bearing and raising children should be the reason to get married. Moreover, only 41 percent believe children are very important to a successful marriage, a 24-point decline from 1990.[106]

Disconnecting love from marriage does not mean that marriage itself is
dead. But it is a choice more Americans are making later in life. Today, the
average age for men entering into first-time marriages is 27; for women, it
is 25.[107] And many of these "starter marriages" will end in divorce. Politi-

cal essayist and social critic Barbara Ehrenreich believes that marriage has become so transitory that couples should have "renewable marriages," with reevaluations occurring every five to seven years to give couples opportunities to revise, recelebrate, or dissolve their unions.[108]

The dissolutions and reformations of the marriage contract have affected both adults and children alike. Today, nearly half of all children live in households that do not include both biological parents. And some children reside with both biological parents, but those adults are not married. Jim and Michelle Fitzhenry thought that they were following the common path when they created their family situation but ultimately realized that this road is becoming less traveled: "By getting married and having a kid, we just assumed we were doing what everyone else in the country was doing. We thought we were normal."[109]

But what once passed for a "normal" family is no more. In one survey, 36 percent of 18- to 24-year-olds likened their families to television's *The Simpsons*—an intact but somewhat dysfunctional unit. Only 30 percent said their families reminded them of the Huxtables from *The Cosby Show*—a close family with two working parents.[110] Today a majority of Generation Y children report that by the time they graduate from high school, one of their biological parents has left home.[111] Correspondingly, a majority of adults report spending most of their adulthood outside the bonds of marriage.[112] Andrew Cherlin, a sociology professor at Johns Hopkins University, says, "Marriage used to be the first step into adulthood." Now, however, "it's the last."[113]

The dissolution of so many marriages makes many Americans uneasy, and their political leaders have taken notice. Assuming office in 2001, George W. Bush launched the Healthy Marriage Initiative to discourage divorce and encourage fathers to be more responsible.[114] In 2003, Bush proclaimed Marriage Protection Week and proposed spending $200 million to help couples form and sustain more durable unions through marriage education and counseling programs offered by faith-based and other organizations. These programs would provide information on parenting, financial management, conflict resolution, and career skills. As Bush observed, "Marriage is a sacred institution, and its protection is essential to the continued strength of our society. . . . By supporting responsible child-rearing and strong families, my Administration is seeking to ensure that every child can grow up in a safe and loving home."[115] Two years later, Bush redoubled his efforts. In his 2005 State of the Union Address, the president announced a three-year effort to help young people foster stronger family and community relationships.[116] At the inaugural Helping America's Youth Conference, First Lady Laura Bush, chair of the new initiative, declared, "We all know that mothers and fathers are the most important influences in a child's life. Children whose parents show them love and support and stay active in their lives have an enormous advantage growing up. Yet too many children grow up in homes where one parent is absent, most often their father. Young people who grow up without their dads suffer a profound loss."[117]

And the Bush administration backed up the First Lady's words with money. In 2006, Congress approved spending $500 million over the next five years to promote healthy marriages through programs including anger and stress management, premarital assessments, conflict resolution, and communication skills. Congress also authorized an additional $250 million to promote responsible fatherhood.[118]

But despite these entreaties from their political leaders, more Americans are choosing not to marry even if they have children. One separated 30-something woman observed, "If Jesus Christ bought me an engagement ring, I wouldn't take it. I'd tell Jesus we could date, but we couldn't marry."[119] One reason for the unwillingness of so many women to marry is the abundance of birth control pills, which permit people to delay or avoid having children. Prior to the 1971 passage of the Twenty-sixth Amendment, which lowered the age of majority to 18, birth control pills were largely unavailable. In 1969, for example, an 18-year-old woman could legally obtain birth control pills in just nine states.[120] One unintended consequence of the amendment was to make the Pill widely available.

Another reason many women delay taking their vows is the emergence of an Information Age economy that places a high premium on obtaining college and advanced degrees. Returning World War II GIs, most of them men, entered college classrooms en masse thanks to the 1944 GI Bill of Rights, which gave them full financial assistance. Staggering increases in college enrollments resulted. In 1941, the University of Michigan had fewer than 10,000 students; four years later, it had more than 30,000.[121] Women soon followed men into the college classrooms. In 1958, only 35 percent of all females attended college.[122] But during the 1960s and 1970s, more women began sitting in college classrooms in pursuit not of dream men but of dream jobs. In 1978, a cultural milestone was reached as college-bound women outnumbered men.[123] The ratio of female/male college graduates subsequently has sharply tilted toward women: by 2010, the Department of Education projects, 142 females will graduate for every 100 males.[124] Jen Smyers, a junior at American University, where just 36 percent of the students are male, says, "The women here are on fire." Smyers should know: she won a dean's scholarship and held four internships and three jobs during her college years. Asked to explain her motivational drive, Smyers responded, "Most college women want a high-powered career that they are passionate about. But they also want a family, and that probably means taking time off, and making dinner. I'm rushing through here, taking the most credits you can take without paying extra, because I want to do some amazing things, and establish myself as a career woman, before I settle down."[125]

But for many college-bound women, marriage and children never happen. Many women graduate expecting to launch their careers, which often means postponing marriage. As one female Howard University student explained, "By the time I'm actually established and making the kind of money that I want to be making before I start a family, I'll be in my early thirties. So I'm kind of confused about how marriage is going to fit into all of this."[126] M. Belinda Tucker, a psychologist and coeditor of *The Decline in Marriage among African Americans*, says that the experiences reported by female college graduates typified her conversations with her peers while in college: "You were essentially consigning yourself to being unmarried. . . . That's what we said to each other and that's what we were told."[127] Joy Jones, a single sixth-grade teacher, describes her epiphany about marriage:

> The turning point in my own thinking about marriage came when a longtime friend proposed about five years ago. He and I had attended college together, dated briefly, then kept in touch through the years. We built a solid friendship, which I believe is a good foundation for a successful marriage.
>
> But—if we had married, I would have had to relocate to the Midwest. Been there, done that, didn't like it. I would have had to become a step-mother and, although I felt an easy camaraderie with his son, step-motherhood is usually a bumpy ride. I wanted a house and couldn't afford one alone. But I knew that if I was willing to make some changes, I eventually could.
>
> As I reviewed the situation, I realized that all the things I expected marriage to confer—male companionship, close family ties, a house—I

already had, or were within reach, and with exponentially less drama. I can do bad by myself, I used to say as I exited a relationship. But the truth is, I can do pretty good by myself, too.[128]

Census Bureau statistics reflect what Jones says. In 2000, 27.2 million Americans were living alone, the highest number in U.S. history. Eight years later, presidential election exit polls showed that more than one-third of voters were not married, and members of that group voted overwhelmingly for Barack Obama.[129]

Many of these single heads of households are women. In Manhattan, which has the nation's largest percentage of single households, 56 percent of families are headed by single women.[130] But women are not alone in making conscious decisions to eschew marriage. James Conaboy, a 35-year-old musician, chooses to live alone because, he says, "If you want to make a mess, you can make a mess. If you want to paint the walls a certain color, you can do it." Thomas F. Coleman, executive director of Unmarried America, notes that singles no longer experience discrimination and low self-esteem: "Self-esteem isn't based on having children and being married anymore."[131] Indeed. As of 2004, nearly one in four college-educated women between ages 40 and 44 were childless.[132]

Single Motherhood: The Murphy Browns Take Center Stage

At the dawn of the twenty-first century, more Americans than ever before are voting no on marriage. Transient relationships are surely one reason, as fewer first-time lovers take their vows. Today, both sexes can find sexual fulfillment without having a 1950s-style marriage and the children that once accompanied it. According to one study, 50 percent of those aged 18 to 24 believe that they "can lead a perfectly fulfilled life without having children."[133] But some people are adding a twist to this view: young women giving birth without the security of marriage. In 2005, a record 4 in 10 babies were born outside of marriage, many to women between ages 25 and 29, a group for whom unwed births have risen 30 percent since 1991.[134] While many of these unwed mothers were poor women, a substantial number were highly educated, well-to-do females—like the mythical Murphy Brown—who could easily support one or more children. When asked to explain why she chose to have an out-of-wedlock baby, one chiropractor from Avon, Connecticut, admitted, "It is selfish, but this was something I needed to do for me."[135] A female student at the University of California at Berkeley concurred: "I like the idea of kids more than I like the idea of a husband."[136]

Yet for every well-paid, self-fulfilled, college-degree-holding single mother, there are many more women who lack a college education, are not married, and have children. Today, one in three women becomes pregnant by age 20, and half of these pregnancies are out-of-wedlock births to teenagers. Startlingly, one of every five out-of-wedlock births to teenagers is a repeat birth.[137] While more than 80 percent of unmarried mothers say they hope to marry the fathers of their children, fewer than one in seven do so before the child turns three years old. Shenia Rudolph, a 42-year-old divorced mother living in the Bronx, is one. Shortly after graduating from high school, Rudolph and the father of her two-week-old baby married. When that marriage foundered, Rudolph had three children by another man before ending that relationship after learning he was married to someone else. Now, she says, "I don't trust men [enough] to marry them."[138]

Some men readily admit that Rudolph is right. Joe Callender, a retired 47-year-old New York City corrections officer, has had two long-term relationships and fathered four children but has never married. He says, "Marriage, that's sacred to me; I'm committed to you for the rest of my life, my last breath. I'm not cheating, looking. Work, home, that's it. It's you and me against the world."[139] Not surprisingly, the children of unmarried relationships often eschew marriage based on their unhappy experiences. As one 12-year-old black boy told his teacher, "Marriage is for white people." His classmate agreed: "We're not interested in the part about marriage. Only about how to be good fathers."[140] Not surprisingly, as marriage becomes the choice of fewer citizens, more single women are opting to adopt. Of the 50,000 children adopted in 2001, one-third found homes with single women.[141]

But the increasing elusiveness of marriage has been caused by more than a mutual lack of female-male trust and single-mother adoptions. More women are deciding to have children knowing that marriage is not part of the bargain. And more Americans than ever before find out-of-wedlock births morally acceptable. A 2007 Pew Research survey discovered that 67 percent of those aged 18 to 29 thought the idea of unmarried women having children was either only "sometimes wrong" or "not wrong at all."[142] Brookings Institution scholar Isabel V. Sawhill notes that these changing attitudes have eclipsed the model family of married parents with

kids living at home: "Before [1970], if you looked at families across the income spectrum, they all looked the same: a mother, father, kids, and a dog
named Spot."[143]

As the approbation against out-of-wedlock births abates, other attitudes have also changed. For example, when one pollster asked whether
"one parent can bring up a child as well as two parents together," respondents were about evenly split: 42 percent agreed, while 45 percent disagreed.[144] As one unwed 20-year-old mother told the *New York Times*, "I
wanted to have a baby. It wasn't, like, because everybody *else* had a baby.
. . . I wanted somebody to take care of." A 21-year-old single mother agreed:
"I'm gonna make sure I have my own stability. I mean, because they're *my*
kids. I don't care who the fathers are, they're *mine*. For the rest of my life,
they're gonna be my kids and I'm gonna have to take care of them, with or
without their fathers."[145] According to sociologists Andrew Cherlin and
Frank Furstenburg, "Through divorce and remarriage, individuals are related to more and more people, to each of whom they owe less and less."[146]

Cohabitation without Marriage

Many Americans prefer to live together without legal entanglement.[147] Between 1960 and 2005, the number of unmarried couples cohabitating in
the United States grew from 439,000 to more than 5,368,000.[148] Today,
nearly 4 in 10 adults under age 50 have entered into cohabitating relationships.[149] As Whitehead and Popenoe write, "When blushing brides walk
down the aisle at the beginning of the new millennium, well over half have
already lived together with a boyfriend."[150] Amanda Hawn, a 28-year-old
writer living in San Francisco, explained why she set up housekeeping with
her boyfriend: "Owning three toothbrushes and finding that they are always at the wrong house when you are getting ready to go to bed wears on
you. Moving in together has simplified life."[151]

In his pathbreaking 1987 book, *The Closing of the American Mind*, Allan
Bloom wrote, "The kind of cohabitations that were dangerous in the twenties, and risque or bohemian in the thirties and forties, have become as normal [today] as membership in the Girl Scouts."[152] In a bow to the redefinition of family, nearly half of the 500 largest U.S. corporations extend
health care and other benefits to unmarried partners.[153] Jennifer Lynch
and her live-in, divorced boyfriend typify the trend. Lynch told the *New
York Times* that she and her partner will not marry because unmarried co-

habitation makes their union stronger: "Cohabitating is our choice, and we have no intention to be married. There is little difference between what we do and what married people do. We love each other, exist together, all of our decisions are based upon each other. Everyone we care about knows this. [If anything,] not having the false security of wedding rings makes us work even a little harder."[154]

Cohabitation is one more example of the moral freedom many Americans prefer to exercise.[155] But these new liberties sometimes provoke controversy. In Black Jack, Missouri, for example, the city council rejected a motion allowing unmarried couples to cohabitate. Under the law, couples who are not married face eviction. Olivia Shelltrack and Fondrey Loving, the parents of three children, were denied an occupancy permit after moving into their new home.[156]

But even as the Black Jack city councillors try to turn back the clock, the number of Americans who find cohabitation morally acceptable rises. A 2007 Gallup poll found that 55 percent of respondents approved of unmarried men and women living together.[157] Among the younger age cohort, the onus once associated with the term *living in sin* has evaporated. According to a 2001–4 survey of high school seniors, 64 percent of boys and 57 percent of girls said, "It is usually a good idea for a couple to live together before getting married in order to find out whether they can really get along."[158]

Cohabitation has become so commonplace that pollsters routinely ask whether respondents are "married, single, divorced, in a civil union, or together." One 2002 survey found that 37 percent of all married couples reported living together prior to their marriages.[159] Chris and Gabrielle Wagener typify the trend. Long before their wedding, they decided to live together so that, according to Gabrielle, they could "test things out beforehand." As Chris put it, "We wanted to spend as much time as we could together, but we weren't ready to get married. The next thing I knew there was a hair dryer and all this stuff." After two and a half years together, Chris and Gabrielle married in May 2001.[160]

As cohabitation increases, more couples have children without rushing to the altar. Today, 43 percent of unmarried couples are raising children, just a trace behind the 46 percent of married couples who have children living with them at home.[161] In Mississippi, New Mexico, and West Virginia—all red states that supported George W. Bush in 2004—a greater proportion of unmarried couples are raising children than are married couples. In fact, the former Confederate states have the highest share of unmarried couples and the lowest share of married households with children.[162] In such places, marriage, with all of its entanglements and commitments, has become passé. And in the cohabiting relationships involving children, three-quarters will see their parents split up before they reach age 16.[163] It is no surprise, therefore, that 57 percent of young people believe "the institution of marriage is dying in this country."[164]

"Friendships with Privileges"

Perhaps the fastest-growing type of relationship goes by the names *friendships with privileges*, *friends with benefits*, or *hookups*. These affairs involve virtually no mutual long-term commitment and are especially commonplace on college campuses. One New York University student describes the typical encounter: "Some people are just friends with benefits. Like I know this girl, oh God, this disgusted me. There's this guy on my floor and she lives upstairs and they'll just call each other at random times and they'll, you know, just have sex and then leave. Knock on each other's doors, satisfy themselves, and go home."[165] One female senior at George Washington University defended the practice: "I don't have time or energy to worry about a 'we'" in relationships.[166] A Colby College sophomore tacitly agreed, telling an investigative team of sociologists, "I would like to meet my husband here. . . . But . . . I don't really think that it will happen. . . . A lot of [the guys] don't want relation[ships]. They . . . want little freshman girls . . . to hook up with [and it's] almost [about] the numbers."[167]

One study found that just 50 percent of college senior women had been asked on six or more dates, while one-third had had just one or two dates. A University of Virginia undergraduate explained, "Hookups happen way more than just dates. Dates, you're actually interested in the person. A hookup it's like you just want to get something." Not surprisingly, 49 percent of college women agreed with the statement, "At this time in my life, I am not ready to be serious about romantic relationships." As one University of Washington student said, "I think the goal at this point for most women my age is just to have a good time [and] maybe have a boyfriend."[168] Amy Kass, a University of Chicago scholar, bemoans the loss of a "courtship culture": "The very terms—'wooing,' 'courting,' 'suitors'—are archaic; and if the words barely exist, it is because the phenomena have all but disappeared. Today there are no socially prescribed forms of conduct that help guide young men and women in the direction of matrimony. This is true not just for the lower or under classes even—indeed especially—the elite, those who in previous generations would have defined the conventions in these matters, lack a cultural script whose denouement is marriage."[169]

Rather than committing to a courtship following prescribed rules of behavior, men and women simply "hook up." According to one poll of college undergraduates, 78 percent have hooked up at least once.[170] In another survey, 50 percent of college females said that hookups happened "very often" or "fairly often" at their schools. The same survey also found that a surprising 12 percent of women agreed with the statement, "Sometimes it is easier to have sex with a guy than to talk to him."[171] According to one male Duke University student, "The girls made all the effort. *The guys* didn't have to do anything."[172] Says a Yale University student, "Women know within the first five minutes of meeting a man whether they are going to hook up with him or not. But . . . women don't want the guy to know he'll be hooking with [her] until he's actually doing it. . . . Post hookup is when guys tend to get ambiguous [they ignore you]. It's their payback. Do they want to hook up again? Dunno. Do they want to date? Dunno. Are they straight? Dunno. Name? Dunno."[173]

Despite the impersonal nature of these relationships, many people welcome them. As one Rutgers University student explained, "I think hooking up with different people and seeing what you like and don't like is a good idea. Because eventually you're going to have to . . . marry someone and I'd just like to know that I experienced everything."[174] The college practice of hooking up is increasingly spreading to high schools. Josey, a 17-year-old student from New Jersey, told a reporter that hooking up has few, if any, social ramifications: "As a senior I've noticed a lot of people hooking up. Not just hooking up, but getting out of control with hooking up. They don't feel one should have romance together to have sex with somebody. And the guys enjoy it. Nobody gets a bad reputation from it either."[175]

Living in Two Parallel Universes

The weakening of marriage and the plethora of personal relationships that has replaced it have created another values division. To cite but one example, nearly half of married men aged 25 to 34 attend religious services several times a month, while less than one-quarter of their unmarried peers do so. Similarly, 75 percent of married men believe that children should be raised in a religion, compared to just 59 percent of unmarried men.[176] These findings accord with other polls. Stanley Greenberg finds that when respondents from traditional families (i.e., married men and women with children under age 18) are compared to those from nontraditional ones (i.e., unmarried parents with children under 18), the values gaps are enormous (see table 4). Those in traditional families are more likely to frown on cohabitation (with or without the intention of getting married), divorce, different family formulations (including homosexual parents or a single parent raising a child), and having women find fulfillment outside the home in the workplace. Nontraditional families are far less likely to make moral judgments on these matters.

TABLE 4.   Marriage and Family Values, Traditional vs. Nontraditional Families (percentage answering "agree")

Issue	Traditional Families	Nontraditional Families
Married people are generally happier than unmarried people.	51	27
It is all right for a couple to live together without intending to get married.	46	59
It's a good idea for a couple who intend to get married to live together first.	38	61
Divorce is usually the best solution when a couple can't seem to work out their marriage problems.	38	54
It is better for children if their parents are married.	81	57
Love is what makes a family, and it doesn't matter if parents are gay or straight, married or single.	56	74
The law should define marriage as a union between one man and one woman.	61	50
Having a job is the best way for a woman to be an independent person.	38	65
Both the man and the woman should contribute to the household income.	60	83

Source: Greenberg Quinlan Rosner Research poll, July 25–August 7, 2005. Text of question: "Now I am going to read you a list of statements. For each of the following, please tell me if you agree or disagree with the statement. If you neither agree nor disagree with the statement, please say so."

As interpersonal relationships become even more varied and nonjudgmental, the connections between traditional families and nontraditional ones become even more frayed. Fukuyama writes that the "moral miniaturization" of adult relationships has resulted in fewer sources of authority, fewer common values, and more competition among individuals and groups.[177]

Despite the unwillingness of those in nontraditional families to render moral judgments about themselves or anyone else, that reluctance does not mean that they do not worry about their family's or the nation's values. In fact, the worries expressed by nontraditional family members exceed those who belong to traditional households on a variety of issues—including the negative influences of other kids on their own children, paying bills and making ends meet, and obtaining health insurance and good medical care for their offspring. Moreover, a substantial minority fret about juggling the demands of work and family, making sure their children learn the right values in school, and having their child watch too much sex or violence in the popular media (see table 5). In all cases, the concerns expressed by these nontraditional family members strikingly outdistance the worries of those in traditional families.

TABLE 5. Family Concerns Compared, Traditional vs. Nontraditional Families (percentage answering "a lot")

Issue	Traditional Families	Nontraditional Families
The negative influence of other kids on your child	40	53
Paying bills and making ends meet	34	60
Juggling the demands of work and family	28	49
Getting health insurance and good medical care for your child	36	58
Your child learning the right values from his/her teachers at school	37	49
Your child seeing too much sex or violence from video games, television, and movies	38	46

Source: Greenberg Quinlan Rosner Research poll, July 25–August 7, 2005. Text of question: "Now I am going to read you a list of things some parents worry about. Please tell me how much you worry about each of the following: a lot, some, only a little, not at all."

As the variety of interpersonal relationships expands, so, too, does the feeling that the nation has divided into two parallel universes. On the one side are those who like their "morality writ small." As Wolfe has written, "There *is* a moral majority in America; it just happens to be unwilling to follow anyone's party line about what morality ought to be."[178] On the other side are those who like their "morality writ large"—having absolute certainty about what is right and what is wrong. Many people in traditional families are more apt to take the morality writ large view; those in nontraditional families like their morality writ small.

This divide has become so great that each side accuses the other of not getting it. On occasion, the split even tears apart those who otherwise share a common faith and background. Jimmy Carter and his fellow Southern Baptists provide just one of many examples. For 70 years, Carter was a member of the Southern Baptist Convention. But in 2000, the organization adopted a new "Baptist Faith and Message" that mandated that men "provide for, protect, and lead [the] family" and ordered wives to "submit graciously" to their husbands based on what Carter called the "ridiculous assertion" that "man was first in creation and woman was first in the Edenic fall."[179] Carter's resultant decision to leave his Baptist faith was not without pain and loss: "For me, being a Southern Baptist has always been like being an American. I just never thought of making a change. My father and his father were deacons and Sunday school teachers. It's something that's just like breathing for us." But the president of the Southern Baptist Convention had no qualms about bidding Carter good riddance: "With all due respect to the president, he is a theological moderate. We are not a theologically moderate convention."[180]

The split between Carter and the Southern Baptists is but one small spat in the ongoing culture wars. On one side are those who recoil at the plethora of new families and relationships. In *It Takes a Family* (a rejoinder to Hillary Rodham Clinton's *It Takes a Village*), Santorum argues that family decay is the result of misguided social policies propagated by a "liberal elite" that have resulted in "an epidemic of promiscuity and sexually transmitted diseases among the young; . . . extreme violence and offensive sexual content on everything from video games to the Internet; 3,500 healthy expectant mothers carrying healthy children exercising a 'choice' to end the lives of their children every day; [and] the foundational institution of every civilization known to man—marriage—under siege."[181] But Popenoe writes that the "postnuclear" family trend is "closely linked to such well-known and seemingly entrenched phenomena of the modern era as affluence, secularism, and a strong emphasis on individualism. In other words, to reverse the family trend would require a massive shift in cultural values."[182]

During the 1960s and 1970s, the aphorism "The personal is political" assumed enhanced resonance. Blacks, heretofore denied basic rights, demanded that the federal government issue additional guarantees to fulfill the long-deferred promises contained in the Thirteenth, Fourteenth, and Fifteenth Amendments to the U.S. Constitution, which were grafted onto the document following the Civil War. Women, too, sought a greater measure of freedom outside the traditional realms of marriage and family life. Thus, in 1961, President Kennedy signed an executive order creating the President's Commission on the Status of Women.[183] Days before his death, Kennedy attached his name to another order, establishing an Interdepartmental Committee on the Status of Women that would "further the effort to achieve the full participation of women in American life."[184] After Kennedy's assassination, Lyndon B. Johnson moved aggressively to enact his Great Society programs, including the Civil Rights Act of 1964 and the Voting Rights Act of 1965, which forbade racial and gender bias and allowed blacks access to the polls.

"The personal is political" no longer carries quite the same meaning it held 40 years ago. In private, Americans remain loving individuals who are reluctant to condemn their personal moral choices. But in public, Americans have become more suspicious of the moral choices made by their compatriots. The chief justice of the Connecticut State Supreme Court describes a legal tussle that illustrates the tension between private morality and public values:

> We had a case of a couple who employed a surrogate mother. After fourteen years of marriage the couple decided to divorce. The father claimed it was his child, and not his wife's because a surrogate mother gave birth to the child. What do you do in an instance like this? Nobody ever thought of these issues and their legal aspects, but there will be more of them in the future.[185]

As the courts and other government institutions try to adjudicate these delicate disputes, the culture wars have added a poisonous passion to our politics, even as citizens remain passionate lovers at home.

The cultural battles that accompany present-day family relationships resemble the social polarization described by Benjamin Disraeli in his 1845 novel, *Sybil; or, The Two Nations.* An encounter between the novel's hero, Charles Egremont, and an unnamed stranger produces a dialogue that could easily be replicated in twenty-first-century America:

> "Well, society may be in its fancy," said Egremont slightly smiling; "but say what you like, our Queen reigns over the greatest nation that ever existed."
>
> "Which nation?" asked the younger stranger, "for she reigns over two. . . . Two nations; between whom there is no intercourse and no sympathy; who are as ignorant of each other's habits, thoughts, and feelings, as if they were dwellers in different zones or inhabitants of different planets; who are formed by a different breeding, are fed by a different food, are ordered by different manners, and are not governed by the same laws."[186]

As chapter 4 demonstrates, the division of the nation into two parallel universes—one private, one public—has been enhanced by the struggle over gay rights.

Four • The Gay-Rights Paradox

"I can't go that far—That's the year 2000."
—RICHARD M. NIXON, COMMENTING ON
GAY MARRIAGE, 1970

NEW YEAR'S DAY 2003 began almost like any other. As dawn broke, local hospitals reported news of the year's first babies. These press releases had all the oohs and aahs of the cooing parents, along with the vital statistics—size, weight, name. One story from Virginia began in the usual manner. After 15 hours of labor, an exhausted mother gave birth to a 5-pound, 20-ounce girl at precisely one minute after midnight. Amid the handmade signs heralding "First Baby of the Year," reporters gathered to hear the proud parents exclaim, "She's adorable. She's perfect. She's brilliant."[1]

But this time the story was different. This time, the newborn baby had two mommies: Helen Rubin, the birth mother, and her partner, Joanna Bare. After 12 years together, the two women decided to have a child through artificial insemination by a male family friend. Now, caught in the New Year's hoopla, neither the two lesbians nor the reporters covering the birth seemed sure how to act. When an eager photographer asked for a picture of the baby with her mother, the accommodating women responded in unison, "Sure—which mother would you like?" Photographs were taken with both women. Despite the confusion, family members stressed the "normalcy" of the newborn's circumstances. As Rubin told a crowded press conference, "Hopefully, we'll be like any family." Her father agreed: "She has a traditional family. There are grandparents on both sides. . . . We just consider ourselves to be grandparents just as much as our friends who have grandchildren."[2]

But this was not a traditional family, as indicated by the legal wrangling that had begun prior to the baby's birth. Virginia law forbade Bare from adopting the newborn, and both women sought legal counsel to help them wade through the state's adoption laws. Attorney Mina Ketchie advised her clients to pack up and move: "Virginia does not permit second-parent adoption. Quite frankly, in these matters of law, Virginia is being dragged kicking and screaming into the twentieth century—and we're in the twenty-first century. It is not a very gay-friendly state." Desperately wanting to keep their child, the couple decided to relocate: said Bare, "We're not interested in any legal battles—that's why we moved. I really like living in Virginia. But it's more important to be a parent." The couple left for the more gay-friendly environs of Bethesda, Maryland, where authorities permitted them to share full parental rights.[3]

Rubin and Bare are signs of yet another revolution involving twenty-first-century families: the high-profile emergence of gays and the families they are creating. Signs of this transformation are everywhere. In Wheaton, Illinois, Mark Demich and Kevin Hengst are known to their married neighbors, Mike and Sue Weinberg, as the couple across the street. When they moved into this conservative Christian community, the two men hung out a Gay Pride flag and were immediately invited by neighbors to a block party. Demich and Hengst are hardly alone. On one summer day in 2004, 30 gay men and lesbians played softball at a neighborhood park; on another, 60 homosexuals turned up for a wine-tasting party. Sue Weinberg says of her gay neighbors, "Growing up in a good Catholic family, I didn't even know about anything like this. It wasn't thrown in front of me. These kids, if they don't see it now, they're going to see it soon. Living on a block like this is more the real world." Weinberg's six-year-old son, Jack, is already absorbing the new world around him. When Jack declared his love for his mother and told her they would marry, she replied that was impossible since she was already married. Jack said, "Then I'll marry Daddy." When Weinberg told Jack, "You can't marry Daddy, he's a boy," her son replied, "But Mark and Kevin are boys."[4]

Demich and Hengst and other partnered gays are not just creating new families but spawning a novel type of politics. Today, elected leaders wrestle with some compelling questions their forebears never considered.

- Should health care and hospital visitation rights be granted to same-sex domestic partners?
- Should gay couples be permitted to adopt children, and if so, under what circumstances?
- Should the states and/or the federal government permit same-sex marriages, establish civil unions, or forbid same-sex relationships?
- Should same-sex marriages performed in a state or country where such marriages are legal be recognized by other states or nations?
- How should state and federal tax laws apply (if at all) to same-sex couples?
- What role should state and federal courts play in divorce and custody issues involving gay unions gone awry?

How governments will eventually resolve these questions remains undetermined, and the answers to date vary considerably. But the personal choices made by gay couples create political questions that often have their first public hearing in courtrooms. Take the case of Lisa Miller, her former lesbian partner, Janet Jenkins, and their six-year-old daughter, Isabella Miller-Jenkins. The couple lived together for several years before traveling to Vermont in 2000 to obtain a civil union. Two years later, their daughter was born in Virginia after Miller was impregnated with sperm from an anonymous donor. Knowing Virginia's hostility toward gay adoptions, the couple decided to relocate to the more gay-friendly environs of the Green Mountain State. But four months after Isabella's birth, the two women separated, and Miller and the baby returned to Virginia. Jenkins fought for custody rights and sought help from the courts. In 2006, the Vermont Supreme Court unanimously ruled that Isabella Miller-Jenkins has two mothers and granted Jenkins visitation rights. But that ruling contradicted a 2004 Virginia court decision that granted sole visitation rights to Miller based on the state's Marriage Affirmation Act, which makes same-sex unions issued by other states "void in all respects in Virginia."[5] Jenkins's attorney went back to court, claiming that Miller was in violation of the Federal Kidnapping Prevention Act, which prevents parents from taking their children to other states to avoid court rulings. In June 2007, the Virginia Supreme Court cited this law in a ruling in Jenkins's favor. Miller retains custody of Isabella, in violation of the court order, and many observers believe the U.S. Supreme Court might eventually rule in the matter.[6]

In many instances, gays' personal choices—for example, whether to live together—do not require governmental approval. And when sanction for their unions is sought, it often comes not from reluctant governments but from private businesses anxious to woo quality workers and customers. By 2006, 263 Fortune 500 companies offered health care benefits to same-sex couples.[7] One of those companies was Boeing, where Joyce E. Tucker, a vice president of global diversity and employee rights, observed that these were hardly altruistic decisions: "I think the corporations are recognizing that in order to be as innovative as we have to be and as competitive as we have to be, we have to avail ourselves of all the talent out there. Everyone has something to contribute. Wherever the talent is coming from, we want that."[8] Heyward Bell, Raytheon's chief diversity officer, agrees: "Over the next ten years we're going to need anywhere from 30,000 to 40,000 new employees. We can't afford to turn our back on anyone in the talent pool."[9]

Another cultural milestone of sorts was achieved in 2007, when the Walt Disney Company decided to permit gay-themed weddings at its resorts. For a starting price of $4,000, gay couples can exchange vows, have Disney characters in costume at receptions, and ride in a horse-drawn, glass-enclosed carriage. Disney spokesperson Donn Walker defended the new policy: "We believe this change is consistent with Disney's longstanding policy of welcoming guests in an inclusive environment." Critics were hardly mollified. Tony Perkins, president of the Family Research Council, was among the most vocal: "[F]or years, Disney has reflected the values of America. Now, I think it could be argued they are trying to shape those values in a very radical way."[10]

Perkins is right. The reshaping of society's values toward greater inclusiveness for homosexuals is taking place in the ordinary decisions made by individuals. These decisions often involve government approval, and more gays than ever before are willing to seek it. Some years ago, John Coon and Josh Turek approached authorities in Washington, D.C., and asked to adopt a black baby boy. Both were skeptical that the powers that be would approve. As Coon remembered, "There is no way they are going to choose us over the other people." Turek agreed: "Two white gay men? Not a chance." But they were chosen, and the two men changed their last names to the boy's name, Logan. John and Josh Logan later adopted another boy, and this time the process took only nine days.[11]

The Revolution Is Here

Rubin, Bare, Miller, Jenkins, the Logans, and their offspring are signs of a gay-rights revolution that shows no signs of abating.[12] At the dawn of the twenty-first century, gays and lesbians are emerging from the shadows of shame that once cloaked them behind closeted doors. In New Jersey, seven same-sex couples told their stories to the state supreme court in an effort to persuade the justices to legalize gay marriage. While the court did not grant the petitioners' requests per se, it was struck by the similarities between these homosexual couples and their heterosexual counterparts:

- Alicia Today and Saundra Heath, who reside in Newark, have lived together for 17 years and have children and grandchildren. Today is an ordained minister in a church, and her pastoral duties include coordinating her church's HIV prevention program. Heath works as a dispatcher for Federal Express.
- Mark Lewis and Dennis Winslow reside in Union City and have been together for 14 years. Both are pastors in the Episcopal Church. In their ministerial capacities, they have officiated at numerous weddings and signed marriage certificates, though their own relationship cannot be similarly sanctified under New Jersey law. When Winslow's father was suffering from a serious long-term illness, Lewis helped care for him in their home as a devoted son-in-law would.
- Diane Marini and Marilyn Maneely were committed partners for 14 years before Maneely's death in 2005. The couple lived in Haddonfield, where Marini helped raise Maneely's five children from an earlier marriage. Marini's mother considered Maneely her daughter-in-law and Maneely's children her grandchildren. The daily routine of their lives mirrored those of other suburban married couples their age. Maneely was a registered nurse. Marini is a businesswoman who serves on the planning board in Haddonfield, where she is also active in other community affairs.
- Chris Lodewyks and Craig Hutchison have been in a committed relationship with each other since their college days 35 years ago. They

have lived together in Pompton Lakes for the past 23 years. Hutchison works in Summit, where he is an investment asset manager and president of the Summit Downtown Association. He also serves as the vice chair of the board of trustees of a YMCA camp for children. Lodewyks, who is retired, helps Hutchison's elderly mother with daily chores, such as getting to the eye doctor.[13]

These stories are likely to become even more commonplace. Today, the average gay teenager publicly declares his/her homosexuality either just before or immediately after graduating from high school.[14] Coincidentally, more young people than ever before are likely to report having homosexual experiences. According to a recent U.S. government study, 14 percent of women aged 18 to 29 have had at least one homosexual experience; among men of the same age group, that figure is 7 percent.[15] In many instances, these sexual encounters became the genesis for creating new families. The 2000 Census reported a total of 594,391 same-sex partners residing in all but 255 of the nation's 3,141 counties (99.3 percent).[16] Five years later, a *New York Times* survey found the number of same-sex couples had grown to 776,000. Matt Foreman, executive director of the National Gay and Lesbian Task Force, believes that the rise in same-sex couples can be attributed to diminished inhibitions: "I would say the increase is due to people feeling more comfortable disclosing that they are gay or lesbian and living with a partner."[17]

Accompanying the rise in same-sex households is a dramatic increase in the number of children being raised in them. The 2000 Census reports that 22.3 percent of male same-sex partners and 34.3 percent of female same-sex partners have children residing with them.[18] Sociologist Stephanie Coontz contends that 5 million children are being raised by gay and lesbian parents; the American Civil Liberties Union believes that between 6 and 14 million children live either with a single gay parent or with a parent in a same-sex partnership.[19]

The stories of these family creations sometimes take on a decided 1950s-era ethos, albeit with a twist. For example, Mark is a gay neighbor to Candi and Jean, two lesbians. After some discussion, Mark agreed to father their children—one by Candi, another by Jean. When asked about the arrangement, Mark responded, "I guess in people's minds there's a kid's cartoon drawing of a family unit. Well, ours is the same thing. It's just that the characters have changed a bit. People make a lot out of it, but it's really quite simple: you've got four parents now instead of one." Candi contends that her family is hardly different from those of heterosexual couples:

> We're just as American as our next-door neighbors. You see all these families with stepdads and stepmoms and half-brothers and half-sisters. What do you say about marriages that 50 percent of the time end in divorce? Why are we so threatening?
>
> We want the same things that every other family wants! You know? We shop at Costco; we shop at Wal-Mart; we buy diapers. We're just average. We're downright boring![20]

Gay Marriage In Massachusetts

At the forefront of the gay family revolution is Massachusetts, where a 2003 decision from the state supreme court permitting gay marriage was especially controversial. The court ruled that denial of marriage made homosexuals second-class citizens, violating the equal protection and due process provisions of the Massachusetts constitution. Thus, the court ruled that marriage must be the "voluntary union of two persons as spouses," without regard for gender. Justice John M. Greaney noted that same-sex couples are "our neighbors, our friends who volunteer in the schools and worship beside us in our religious houses" and pleaded for residents to accept the court's verdict: "We share a common humanity and participate together in the social contract that is the foundation of our Commonwealth. Simple principles of decency dictate that we extend to plantiffs, and to their new status, full acceptance, tolerance, and respect. We should do so because it is the right thing to do."[21]

Not everyone agreed, to put it mildly. Following the court decision, both sides of the marriage debate took their battle to the state legislature and governor's office. Governor Mitt Romney ordered the state attorney general to enforce a 1913 statute (originally intended to prevent miscegenation) that forbade the issuance of marriage licenses to nonresidents whose unions would be "void" in their home states.[22]

Despite Romney's protests, gay marriages have proceeded apace. Immediately after the decision, Sue O'Connell, co-publisher of *Bay Windows*, a newspaper that serves Massachusetts's gay community, declared, "I absolutely plan to be married. I have a partner of seventeen years and a child, and we live in the suburbs and carpool. What could be more married?"[23]

Brian Lighty and Andrew Bigelow agreed. Lighty, returning from a trip to Canada after the court decision had been announced, thought he had "landed in the wrong country." After Lighty's plane touched down, Bigelow called him and asked, "Are you ready to do it?" Lighty responded, "Absolutely." A few months later, the two men married. Serving as their best men were their two sons, eight-year-old Mailik and six-year-old Fernelius. After the decision was promulgated, Jennifer Hess, a lesbian, declared, "This day to me means freedom and it means everything to me. I hear the words 'liberty and justice for all' and I feel like I'm part of that, and I'm not carved out of that anymore. [My] ten-year-old son Emmet can say, 'My parents are married, too,' and he hadn't the power of these words, ever."[24] From 2004 to 2008, 10,500 gay marriages were performed in Massachusetts, more than half of them within the first six months after the state Supreme Court ruling.[25]

And with these marriages have come children. In 2004, 61 children were born in Massachusetts to wedded gay couples. Their presence created yet another form of bureaucratic confusion. Because state birth certificates had places for the baby's mother and father (a designation that does not work for gay parents), hospital authorities were unsure about how to complete the required forms. The problem was finally resolved when a reluctant Romney advised hospitals to eliminate the word *father* and substitute the phrase *second parent*.[26]

In 2006, the controversy over gay marriage in the Bay State ended with a whimper when the state legislature failed to vote on a constitutional amendment to ban future gay marriages. Representative Byron Rushing, a Boston Democrat and assistant majority leader, expressed relief: "What members are expecting is that the majority of constituents are going to say, 'Thank you, we're glad it's over, we think it has been discussed enough.'" State senator Jarrett T. Barrios, who is gay and legally married his partner in 2004, pointed to his wedding ring and admonished his colleagues who continued to insist on a constitutional amendment: "It's time for a little straight talk. You don't have to live next to us. You don't have to like us. We are only asking you to end the debate [so that] we will at least have the right to enjoy the same rights that the rest of you have enjoyed from time immemorial."[27] Sealing the result, Romney's successor as governor, Democrat Deval Patrick, supports gay marriage, and all attempts to put the issue to the voters have been thwarted.

The Rise of Gay-Oriented Interest Groups

Another symbol of the gay-rights revolution is the proliferation of interest groups devoted to ending discrimination against homosexuals. Nowhere is this more apparent than in the nation's high schools. In 1997, there were approximately 100 gay-straight alliances (GSAs) for gay and gay-friendly high school students; today, there are more than 3,000.[28] During the 2004–5 academic year, GSAs were created at the rate of three per day. This increased visibility has resulted in more young people telling pollsters they know someone who is gay. One 2005 study of teenagers in the Washington, D.C., area found that 57 percent had gay friends.[29] Kevin Jennings, a leader in the GSA movement, says this exponential evolution portends a more gay-friendly future: "We're going to win because of what's happening in high schools right now. . . . This is the generation that gets it."[30]

Other organizations have achieved similar success. For example, the Parents, Families, and Friends of Lesbians and Gays (PFLAG), founded in 1981 by 25 parents of homosexual children, has 200,000 members and more than 500 local chapters. Founder Jeanne Manford has a story that explains the group's growth. In 1972, Manford stood at a parade holding a sign that read, "Parents of Gays: United in Support of Our Children" because her son, Morty, had been beaten during a previous march while police stood by and watched. Several bystanders began to applaud, and a crusade to end gay discrimination began. As Ron Schlittler, executive director of PFLAG, notes, "Every chapter has its own Jeanne Manford. They are honored and treasured people."[31]

Today, PFLAG lobbies local officials and school organizations on gay-related issues, especially when it comes to adopting policies to end bullying of young teenage gays. PFLAG has achieved notable success: many of the utopian aspirations contained in its 1981 mission statement have already been realized, far more quickly than the group's founders ever envisioned:

- Make our vision and our message accessible to the broadest range of ethnic and cultural communities, ending the isolation of families with gay, lesbian, bisexual, and transgender family members within those communities.

- Create a society in which all gay, lesbian, bisexual, and transgender persons may enjoy, in every aspect of their lives, full civil and legal equality and may participate fully in all the rights, privileges, and obligations of full citizenship in this country.[32]

Even the CIA Is Not Immune

The gay-rights revolution has even extended into unlikely places such as the Central Intelligence Agency (CIA). During the Cold War, fear that homosexuals could compromise the nation's security was so great that gays were routinely routed from the CIA, State Department, and National Security Agency. Dwight D. Eisenhower signed a 1953 executive order that automatically denied security clearances to gay people, defending his stance by noting that "many loyal Americans by reason of instability, alcoholism, homosexuality, or previous tendencies to associate with Communist-front groups, are unintentional security risks. In some instances, because of moral lapses, they become subjected to the threat of blackmail by enemy agents."[33] Forty years after Eisenhower approved Executive Order 10450, the U.S. Supreme Court upheld the CIA's decision to suspend a gay employee because his superiors believed his sexuality posed a security threat. In *Webster v. Doe*, the Court cited a provision of the 1947 National Security Act that allowed the CIA director to dismiss any employee "whenever he shall deem such termination necessary or advisable in the interests of the United States."[34]

Despite these setbacks, homosexuals continued to press the CIA to change its antigay policies. Those efforts began to make some headway. In 1991, the CIA decided not to automatically exclude prospective homosexual employees. Four years later, Bill Clinton rescinded Executive Order 10450, and in 1996 homosexuals at the CIA formed the Agency Network of Gay and Lesbian Employees.[35] In June 2000, the CIA held its first-ever Gay Pride celebration. Addressing the assembled agents was Massachusetts Democrat Barney Frank, one of the first members of Congress to openly declare his homosexuality.[36] Frank believes that the victories achieved by homosexuals at the CIA and elsewhere have resulted from the fact that the gay-rights crusade has become personal: "The key here is that so many people have acknowledged being gay and lesbian to their families. . . . You're not just beating up on gays and lesbian kids, you're beating up on all their relatives. That's why there has been a real change of opinion."[37]

The Private Becomes Public

The coming out of family members certainly knows no political bounds. Former Republican presidential candidate Alan Keyes, who once called Vice President Dick Cheney's homosexual daughter a "selfish hedonist,"[38] himself has a gay daughter, Maya Marcel-Keyes, who has rebelled against her father's homophobic stance and no longer speaks to him.[39] Marcel-Keyes has a girlfriend (but has dated two boys), likes the label "queer" (rather than lesbian), considers herself pro-life, and sometimes attends mass at a Chicago Catholic church.[40]

Another Republican, Randall Terry, is an ardent antiabortion activist and founder of Operation Rescue. Terry has an adopted gay son, Jamiel, who told the *Washington Post* that his homosexuality began to flourish when he read the gay literature his father kept at home for "research purposes."[41] Like Marcel-Keyes, Jamiel Terry is estranged from his father, who says of his son, "The truth is that his life is one long deception. May God have mercy. May Christ have mercy."[42] Campaigning for a Florida State Senate seat in 2006, Randall Terry featured a family photograph on his Web site that excluded his gay son and adopted daughter, Tila, from whom he became estranged when she found herself unmarried and pregnant. When asked about the exclusions, Jamiel Terry said that his father "is very big on image. In a large way, Tila and I mess up that image."[43] (Randall Terry lost to a Republican primary challenger by a two-to-one margin.)

Republicans are not alone in being squeamish about their homosexual relatives. In Massachusetts, Maryellen O'Neil and her partner of 18 years, Lisa-Annette DiStefano, announced their plans to marry shortly after the courts in that state permitted them to do so. But their marriage plans were hardly welcome news to O'Neil's first cousin, speaker of the Massachusetts House Thomas M. Finneran, a Democrat who was one of that state's most powerful opponents of same-sex marriage. Finneran backed a constitutional amendment that would overturn such marriages, a proposal O'Neil described as akin to "getting punched in the stomach." Finneran acknowledged the tension between his public and private roles: "This was an agonizing bit of turmoil for me. Maryellen and Lisa are dear, dear friends. They've been welcome in our home ever since they began their relationship, and they always will be." But Finneran also admitted that he and his cousin had "never actually had a long, detailed conversation" about her impending marriage, and he conceded that the lack of such a discussion "might be what has led to the anguish each side has felt." After the marriage ceremony, O'Neil sent her cousin a card reading, "Did the earth shake? Did the sky fall?"[44]

Tensions have been more muted in another family, that of former U.S. House minority leader Richard Gephardt, a Democrat who has a gay daughter, Chrissy. Campaigning for the presidency in 2004, Gephardt did not shy away from his homosexual daughter and even featured a picture of the two women, along with the rest of the Gephardt family, on his campaign Web site.[45] When asked about his daughter, Gephardt told reporters, "I'm sure there are people who don't like the decision that she's made and think that it's wrong, immoral, [or] whatever and will look badly on me. But I don't care. My family always comes first."[46] Such expressions of support are quite some distance from Gephardt's origins as the socially conservative son of a working-class family from a blue-collar St. Louis neighborhood. Seeking a congressional seat in 1976, Gephardt was a staunch opponent of gay rights.[47] But as a presidential candidate in 2004, Gephardt sensed that the ground had shifted. He backed civil unions for gays but retained his staunch opposition to gay marriage. On the latter point, Chrissy Gephardt says, "I want my dad to understand why this is so important to me. Why should I not be able to marry if my brother and sister can? I'm working on him with this issue. And I can assure you he's listening."[48]

Finally, Republican Newt Gingrich, a former speaker of the U.S. House, has a gay half-sister, Candace, whose relationships with her parents and famous sibling are complicated. When Candace Gingrich revealed her homosexuality in the mid-1980s, her mother said, "Well, you're going to have to give your Dad and I some time to get used to that because when we were growing up, they didn't have gay people." Candace Gingrich responded, "I explained to Mom that it wasn't like color television or microwaves—there were gay people when she was growing up; she just didn't know there were gay people."[49]

An Abundance of Paradoxes

However successful the gay-rights revolution has been (and it has), this crusade is still in progress, a fact underscored by the 2004 presidential campaign. That year, Republicans welcomed placement on several state ballots of constitutional initiatives banning homosexual marriages.[50] In each instance, antigay forces prevailed, with votes ranging from 56.6 percent against in Oregon to 86.0 percent against in Mississippi.[51] Of the 11 states that proposed gay marriage bans that year, George W. Bush won all but 2, including Ohio, which gave him a slender electoral college majority.[52] On Election Day 2006, 7 more states amended their constitutions to forbid gay marriages, bringing to 23 the total number of states that have prohibited this practice since Massachusetts legalized it in 2003.[53] Despite Barack Obama's victory in 2008, antigay measures continued to prevail at the polls. Californians passed Proposition 8, which overturned a state supreme court decision legalizing gay marriage. Florida voters banned both gay marriage and civil unions. Arizona voters also passed a measure banning gay marriage. And in Arkansas, a ballot measure prohibiting gays from adopting children won voter approval. Obama carried California and Florida, while John McCain won his home state of Arizona and Arkansas.

Yet to write about gay rights in the twenty-first century is to write about contradictions in public thinking. One year after Americans marched to the polling booths to ban gay marriages and reelect George W. Bush, the Hollywood film *Brokeback Mountain*, featuring two gay cowboys who consummated their homosexual relationship on annual outings, garnered record-setting audiences in pro-Bush states and won three prestigious awards at the 2005 Oscars.[54] In such diverse places such as Columbia, Missouri; Shreveport, Louisiana; and Sioux Falls, South Dakota, the film grossed a remarkable $10,000 each time it played.[55] Producer James Schamus marveled at his movie's successes in the heartland: "The culture is finding us."[56] But even *Brokeback Mountain* is fraught with internal tensions. After their first sexual encounter, both characters insist that they are not "queer." Each marries a loving woman and fathers children.[57] And at the movie's denouement, one cowboy is murdered in a way that echoes the real-life killing of Matthew Shepard in Wyoming in an antigay fusillade—a lesson, perhaps, to those who dare to engage in such forbidden love.

And that is just the beginning of the cognitive dissonance Americans experience when assessing homosexual relationships. The country is engaged in a furious debate about whether gay marriages should be institutionalized and if so, in what form. But the controversy is largely about semantics. As the Massachusetts State Supreme Court put it, "There is . . . an implacable determination to retain some distinction, however trivial, between the institution created for same-sex couples and the institution that is available to opposite sex couples. And . . . on the other side there is an equally implacable determination that no distinction, no matter how meaningless, be tolerated. As a result, we have a pitched battle over who gets to use the 'M-Word.'"[58]

That battle lies at the heart of today's gay-rights debate. When the New Jersey State Supreme Court ordered the state legislature to permit homosexuals to enter into either marriages or civil unions, the court acknowledged an essential reality underlying the conflict over gay rights: "Raised here is the perplexing question—'what's in a name?'—and is a name itself of constitutional magnitude after the State is required to provide full statutory rights and benefits to same-sex couples?"[59] So exactly what should gay unions be called? Are they marriages, civil unions, partnerships, or, as the Presbyterian Church prefers, "holy-union" ceremonies?[60] Should they have the same legal standing as heterosexual marriages? Can gay parents raise children as well (if not better) than heterosexual parents? And who gets to make these decisions: voters, state legislatures, Congress, federal or state courts, presidents, governors, or some combination of them all?

In 1999, Vermont provided some initial answers when it became the first state to enact a civil union law that bestowed on homosexual couples nearly all of the rights associated with marriage—except the word itself. At the time, 13,000 citizens contacted Governor Howard Dean to express their opinions, and hundreds attended town meetings to discuss the controversial change. Long-standing public values came into sharp contradiction. At one gathering, longtime resident Kenneth Wolvington wondered what all the fuss was about: "Mrs. Wolvington and I have been married for fifty-two years [and] for the life of us, we can't imagine how gay marriage would adversely affect anyone in our family."[61] Wolvington was immediately rebuked by Robert Charlesworth: "The government is responsible for protecting minorities. It is not responsible for imposing minority values on the majority."[62]

The eventual passage of Vermont's civil union law did not quell the public debate. Instead, the argument intensified and entered the 2000 presidential contest. Al Gore became the first Democratic presidential nominee to support civil unions, arguing that the rights of domestic partners should be legally protected. George W. Bush disagreed, maintaining that marriage must be "a sacred institution between a man and a woman."[63] But Bush running mate Dick Cheney dissented, telling a nationwide audience, "People should be free to enter into any kind of relationship they want to enter into."[64] Lurking behind Cheney's libertarianism was his lesbian daughter, Mary, who had a long-term relationship with a female partner and served as Coors beer's representative to the gay and lesbian community.

Four years later, Mary Cheney considered leaving the Bush-Cheney campaign when Bush made a proposed constitutional amendment banning gay marriage a centerpiece of his reelection effort. In his 2004 State of the Union Address, the president took dead aim at the Massachusetts State Supreme Court: "If judges insist on forcing their arbitrary will upon the people, the only alternative left to the people would be the constitutional process. Our nation must defend the sanctity of marriage."[65] Hearing these words, Republican members of Congress and Vice President Cheney applauded.[66] Mary Cheney recalled that the scene gave her "a knot in the pit of my stomach," and she described Bush's advocacy of the Federal Marriage Amendment as "a gross affront to gays and lesbians everywhere."[67] Still, the younger Cheney soldiered on, telling CNN's Larry King, "As strongly as I felt about same-sex marriage in 2004, I didn't have the luxury of being a single voter on that issue. . . . [W]hen push came to shove, I had to support the candidate who could do the best job of defending this country."[68]

That was hardly the end of the matter. When Kerry mentioned Mary Cheney's lesbianism in a nationally televised presidential debate, her mother, Lynne, took offense: "I did have a chance to assess John Kerry once more. And the only thing I could conclude is this is not a good man. This is not a good man. And, of course, I am speaking as a mom and a pretty indignant mom. This is not a good man. What a cheap and tawdry political trick."[69] Mary Cheney yelled at Kerry on the television set, "You son of a bitch."[70]

Yet behind these protestations was a family that has had enormous difficulty coming to grips with the issue of homosexuality. These difficulties have created an abundance of paradoxes that have penetrated the Cheney household—and many others. For example, when the teenage Mary came out to her parents in the mid-1980s, she recalled her mother crying and telling her, "Your life will be so hard."[71] But when Lynne Cheney was asked about her daughter's homosexuality at the 2000 Republican National Convention, she indignantly replied, "Mary has never declared such a thing."[72] Even more ironic is that 19 years earlier (long before *Brokeback Mountain* became a hit), Lynne Cheney penned a novel about a lesbian relationship, *Sisters*, that included several racy scenes:

Let us go away together, away from the anger and imperatives of men. There will only be the two of us, and we shall linger through long afternoons of sweet retirement. In the evenings I shall read to you while you work your cross-stitch in the firelight. And then we shall go to bed, our bed, my dearest girl.

The women who embraced in the wagon were Adam and Eve crossing a dark cathedral stage—no, Eve and Eve, loving one another as they would not be able to once they ate of the fruit and knew themselves as they truly were.[73]

Asked about the book shortly after her husband became vice president, Lynne Cheney snapped, "I'm not going to analyze a novel I wrote a long time ago. I don't remember the plot."[74] In 2004, she canceled plans to republish *Sisters*, saying it did not represent "her best work."[75] Radio talk show host Laura Flanders saw a dichotomy between Lynne Cheney's past and Bush's desire to ban gay marriage: "Here's a whole book where she gloried in lesbian love affairs. The hypocrisy is rank."[76] Elizabeth Edwards, wife of 2004 Democratic vice presidential nominee John Edwards, also saw a disconnect between Cheney's private expressions of support for her gay daughter and her public outrage at Kerry's highlighting her daughter's sexuality. According to Elizabeth Edwards, Lynne Cheney "overreacted" to Kerry's mention of Mary: "I think that's a very sad state of affairs—I think it indicates a certain degree of shame with respect to her daughter's sexual preferences—it makes me really sad that that's Lynne's response."[77]

The Cheney story took a dramatic turn when Mary Cheney gave birth to a son, Samuel David Cheney, on May 23, 2007. Dick Cheney's spokesperson noted that he was "pleased to be a grandfather for the sixth time." Leaving all thoughts of a federal marriage amendment aside, Bush told reporters that Mary Cheney will be "a loving soul to her child."[78] For her part, Mary Cheney described herself as "ecstatic" over the pregnancy and dismissed any claim that her choice was anything more than a personal one: "This is a baby. This is a blessing from God. It is not a political statement. It is not a prop to be used in a debate by people on either side of an issue. It is my child."[79]

But Mary Cheney's wish that she be left alone did not come true. The fact that the vice president's lesbian daughter was having a baby—and in Virginia where the legal rights of her partner were nonexistent—was reason enough for a vigorous political debate. Janice Crouse of Concerned Women for America, for one, was appalled at Cheney's pregnancy: "Her action repudiates traditional values and sets an appalling example for young people at a time when father absence is the most pressing social problem facing the nation."[80] Moreover, Crouse said, Cheney was not only doing a disservice to her child but "voiding all the effort her father put into the Bush administration."[81] Human Rights Campaign president Joe Solmonese sprang to Cheney's defense: "Mary and Heather's decision to have a child is an example that families in America come in all different shapes and sizes. The bottom line is that a family is made up of love and commitment."[82] Focus on the Family president James Dobson claimed that years of social research "indicates that children do best on every measure of well-being when raised by their married mother and father," adding, "birth and adoption are the purview of married heterosexual couples." Mary Cheney refuted Dobson: "Every piece of remotely responsible research that has been done in the last twenty years on this issue has shown there is no difference between children who are raised by same-sex parents and children who are raised by opposite sex parents. What matters is that children are being raised in a stable, loving environment."[83]

Eventually, Vice President Cheney was drawn into the fray. Asked by CNN's Wolf Blitzer about the impending birth of his grandchild, Cheney took umbrage at questions about the baby and his daughter's sexuality:

BLITZER: A couple of issues I want to raise with you: your daughter, Mary. She's pregnant. All of us are happy she's going to have a baby. You're going to have another grandchild. Some of the critics are suggesting—for example, a statement from someone representing Focus on the Family, "Mary Cheney's pregnancy raises the question of what's best for children. Just because it's possible to conceive a child outside of the relationship of a married mother and father doesn't mean that it's best for the child." Do you want to respond to that?

CHENEY: No.

BLITZER: She's obviously, a good daughter—

CHENEY: I'm delighted I'm about to have a sixth grandchild, Wolf. And obviously I think the world of both my daughters and all of my grandchildren. And I think, frankly, you're out of line with that question.[84]

The Cheneys are not alone when it comes to holding contradictory attitudes about homosexuality, especially when the subject drifts to the topic of gay marriage. Janice Shackelford, a single Oklahoma mother, explained why she voted to reelect Bush: "I have to agree with the president [on the constitutional ban on gay marriage]. We need to keep the family unit as intended." Yet this self-identified values voter is twice divorced, has a son struggling to cope with his homosexuality, and has an unmarried daughter who has an out-of-wedlock baby.[85] Joel Sidell and Dona Maloy are an unmarried couple living near Denver. They, too, are conflicted over gay marriage and providing civil unions. Sidell, a 62-year-old Republican, voted for a 2006 amendment to the Colorado Constitution banning gay marriage, telling the *New York Times*, "To me, it still does not seem right for a woman to be able to marry a woman and a male to marry a male. I don't think it's the sanctity of the term. It just doesn't seem proper." Maloy, a 61-year-old Democrat, voted against the amendment because "marriage is a personal thing, at least it is for me. Legally, I don't see why people can't have the same rights."[86] The cognitive dissonance does not occur only among heterosexuals. Even many gay voters (77 percent of whom opposed Bush) seem queasy about the idea of marriage.[87] In 2004, just 51 percent of homosexuals favored gay marriage, 31 percent supported civil unions, and 17 percent said there should be no legal recognition of gay marriages.[88]

Policymakers are similarly conflicted. In 1996, Congressman Bob Barr, a Georgia Republican who subsequently became the Libertarian Party's 2008 presidential candidate, sponsored the Defense of Marriage Act, which defined marriage as "a legal union between one man and one woman as husband and wife, and the word 'spouse' refers only to a person of the opposite sex who is a husband or a wife." Moreover, the legislation declared that no state was required to accept another state's definition of marriage (a provision inserted because Hawaii seemed on the verge of legalizing gay marriage). Barr defended the legislation by telling his colleagues, "The flames of hedonism, the flames of narcissim, the flames of self-centered morality are licking at the very foundation of our society, the family unit."[89] But Republican representative Constance Morella of Maryland pointed out the irony of Barr's position: "The Defense of Marriage Act is another issue that should have *never* come before us on the floor. It was offered by someone who had been divorced three times."[90]

The inconsistencies hardly stopped there. Former Arizona Republican congressman Jim Kolbe voted for the Defense of Marriage Act even though he is gay. Mark Foley, a Florida Republican whose scandalous e-mails to pages forced his resignation from the U.S. House of Representatives, also supported the Defense of Marriage Act, even though he, too, is homosexual. Another supporter was Larry Craig, the Idaho Republican senator who was arrested for disorderly conduct and pled guilty after an undercover male police officer accused him of soliciting sex in an airport bathroom.[91] President Bill Clinton's spokesperson, Michael McCurry, condemned the GOP-sponsored legislation as a "classic use of wedge politics designed to provoke anxieties and fears."[92] But fearing that he would be on the losing side of the culture wars and unwilling to risk his reelection on the issue, Clinton signed the Defense of Marriage Act into law at 12:50 A.M. on an otherwise quiet September night at the White House.

A decade later, the contradictions have only intensified. In 2006, Pennsylvania Republican Arlen Specter, chair of the Senate Judiciary Committee, voted for a ban on gay marriage in committee and against it on the Senate floor.[93] Republicans are not the only ones who are conflicted. Some Democrats who strongly support gay rights believe that their party should declare a moratorium on gay marriage. Dean, who as Vermont's governor approved that state's civil unions bill before becoming the Democratic Party's national chair, outraged homosexuals by abolishing the party's Gay and Lesbian Caucus. Former caucus chair Jeff Soref fumed, "Democrats are against gay marriage."[94] In New York, chief judge Judith Kaye saw contradictions aplenty in the state's marriage laws and sought to end them by endorsing gay marriage (a decision not supported by a majority of her colleagues). Noting that the petition seeking the right to marry had been brought by 44 same-sex couples that included a doctor, police officer, schoolteacher, nurse, artist, and state legislator, Kaye wrote,

> For most of us, leading a full life includes establishing a family. Indeed, most New Yorkers can look back on, or forward to, their wedding as among the most significant events of their lives. They, like the plaintiffs, grew up hoping to find that one person with whom they would share their future, eager to express their mutual lifetime pledge through civil marriage. Solely because of their sexual orientation, however—that is, because of who they love—plaintiffs are denied the rights and responsibilities of civil marriage. . . .
>
> Indeed, the true nature and extent of the discrimination suffered by gays and lesbians in this regard is perhaps best illustrated by the simple

truth that each one of the plaintiffs here could lawfully enter into a marriage of convenience with a complete stranger of the opposite sex tomorrow, and thereby immediately obtain all of the myriad benefits and protections incident to marriage. Plaintiffs are, however, denied these rights because they each desire instead to marry the person they love and with whom they have created their family.[95]

In 2006, the New Jersey State Supreme Court wrestled with a similar case but came to a very different conclusion. There, seven same-sex couples filed a lawsuit contending that the law treats them differently from heterosexual couples and that they are denied innumerable rights granted to heterosexual couples—including the right to change their surnames, property ownership and automatic transfer of such ownership when one partner dies, survivor benefits, free tuition at public universities for surviving spouses and children of certain members of the New Jersey National Guard, tuition assistance for spouses and children of volunteer firefighters and first responders, tax deductions for spousal medical expenses, and the testimonial privilege given to the spouse of an accused in a criminal action.[96] The court, however, sidestepped the question of same-sex marriage and civil unions, instead ordering the legislature to determine a designation for same-sex couples that would give them these rights and setting a deadline of 180 days for the legislators to act. In December 2006, the New Jersey legislature joined Vermont and Connecticut in permitting civil unions for same-sex couples. Signing the measure into law, Democratic governor Jon Corzine observed, "I think we're doing the right thing."[97]

Yet even as public officials hold contradictory attitudes about homosexuality, times are changing. While antigay ballot initiatives helped propel Mary Cheney's dad to victory in 2004, exit polls showed that civil unions, a once-radical idea, had become the moderate position in the gay marriage debate: 25 percent of those surveyed said that same-sex couples should have the right to legally marry, 35 percent favored civil unions, and 37 percent wanted no legal recognition. Put another way, 60 percent of voters preferred some form of legal recognition for same-sex couples. After his reelection, Bush no longer highlighted his amendment to ban gay marriage, and attempts to pass it in Congress failed in 2006 by a substantial margin. In fact, only 49 senators voted for the amendment, while 48 opposed it; passage would have required a two-thirds vote from all 100 senators. The vote echoed a drop in public support for the amendment. In a

2006 ABC News poll, only 42 percent of respondents supported such a measure.[98] In 2008, Al Gore became the first major public figure to endorse the idea of gay marriage. In an online post on his Current TV network, Gore declared, "I think that gay men and women ought to have the same rights as heterosexual men and women—to make contracts, to have hospital visiting rights, and to join together in marriage, and I don't understand why it is considered by some people to be a threat to heterosexual marriage to allow it by gays and lesbians. Shouldn't we be promoting the kind of faithfulness and loyalty to one's partner regardless of sexual orientation?"[99]

Gore may not be a lonely public crusader on this issue, as many state government officials are willing to grant homosexuals greater rights. In 2006, Connecticut legislators passed a civil union bill without being ordered to do so by a court. The vote was 27 to 3 in the State Senate and 85 to 63 in the State House.[100] Two years later, the Connecticut State Supreme Court struck down the law because it did not go far enough, legalizing gay marriage. Speaking for the court, Justice Richard N. Palmer wrote, "[O]ur conventional understanding of marriage must yield to a more contemporary appreciation of the rights entitled to constitutional protection."[101] Earlier in 2008, a similarly momentous decision emerged from the California State Supreme Court. Speaking for the majority, Chief Justice Ronald M. George declared, "In view of the substance and significance of the fundamental constitutional right to form a family relationship, the California Constitution properly must be interpreted to guarantee this basic civil right [to marry] to all Californians, whether gay or heterosexual, and to same-sex couples as well as to oppositive-sex couples."[102] The decision sparked immediate rejoicing from California's homosexual community. Longtime partners Stuart Gaffney and John Lewis announced immediate plans to marry, with an ecstatic Gaffney telling reporters, "We've waited for over twenty-one years for this day."[103] Robin Tyler, another plaintiff in the case, was equally overjoyed: "We now have equal rights under the law. We're going to get married. No Tupperware, please."[104] A month after the decision, 87-year-old Del Martin married her partner, 83-year-old Phyllis Lyon. The couple had lived together since 1955 and were pioneers in the gay-rights movement.[105] After Martin died just a few weeks later, Lyon eulogized, "I am devastated but I take some solace in knowing we were able to enjoy the ultimate right of love and commitment before she passed."[106]

Despite some states' actions affirming homosexual rights, the gay-rights debate remains characterized by competing public values that produce seemingly incalculable tensions and contradictions. Most Americans swear allegiance to the value of tolerance and seek to promote it. In a 2007 Gallup poll, 89 percent of respondents believed that homosexuals should have equal rights in terms of job opportunities, a 33 percent increase since the question was first asked 30 years earlier. Opposition to granting equal job opportunities fell by more than two-thirds during the same period.[107] Other polls also show early and consistent support for homosexuals when the question is phrased in terms of rights. For example, 66 percent of participants in a 1977 survey opposed legislation that permitted employers to fire people for being homosexual.[108]

But when the question of gay unions is tied to the ideas of marriage and family, Americans are deeply discomfited. Religious conservatives view the institution of marriage and their conceptual ideal of a "traditional" family as being threatened by a legal redefinition allowing for homosexual unions and with them greater possibilities of adoption and parenting rights. In 2003, Dobson sent an extraordinarily detailed letter to Focus on the Family members expressing his undying opposition to same-sex marriages: "The homosexual activist movement, which has achieved virtually every goal and objective it set out to accomplish more than fifty years ago, is poised to administer a devastating and potentially fatal blow to the traditional family. . . . The destruction of the traditional family will condemn millions of [children] to temporary relationships, involving multiple 'moms' or 'dads,' six or eight 'grandparents' and perhaps a dozen or more half-siblings who will come and go as those who care for them meander from one sexual relationship to another. . . . This effort to save the family is our D-Day, or Gettysburg or Stalingrad. This is the big one."[109]

The Roman Catholic bishops have also taken an especially vigorous stance in opposing same-sex marriages, declaring in 2006 that homosexuality is a "disordered" condition.[110] In Boston, the Massachusetts Conference of Bishops called that state's sanctioning of gay marriage "radical" and declared that it "must be reversed."[111] The bishops' stance was fueled by a decision to refuse a state license to the Archdiocese of Boston's Catholic Charities as a consequence of its refusal to place children with gay and lesbian couples.[112] In Maryland, Catholic leaders supported an amendment to that state's constitution banning gay marriage. In a pastoral letter that was required reading in every parish, the bishops asserted, "Marriage is essential to the continuation of the human race and to the dignity, stability, peace, and prosperity of the family and society. Any attempt to redefine marriage in a way that includes same-sex relationships should be viewed as an assault on these inherent characteristics and an assault on the common good."[113]

Despite these protests, the political and legal contradictions have only intensified. In 2003, the U.S. Supreme Court struck down state laws banning sodomy, reversing generations of prohibitions against homosexual behavior. Speaking in a quavering voice for the six-person majority in *Lawrence v. Texas*, Anthony Kennedy declared, "Liberty protects the person from unwarranted government intrusions into a dwelling or other private places. . . . It suffices for us to acknowledge that adults may choose to enter upon this [homosexual] relationship in the confines of their homes and their own private lives and still retain their dignity as free persons." But Kennedy also claimed that this historic decision could not be interpreted as a constitutional endorsement of gay marriage, though a careful reading suggested otehrwise as Antonin Scalia noted: "What justification could there possibly be for denying the benefits of marriage to homosexual couples exercising [t]he liberty protected by the Constitution?"[114]

The notion that private conduct can be excluded from public behavior has outraged gay activists. Many homosexuals no longer subscribe to the "live and let live" notion, believing instead that "The personal is political" and that there should be no distinctions between private behavior and public life. Steve May, a former Arizona state legislator and gay military officer, says that although he admires fellow Republican John McCain, the Arizona senator and 2008 presidential nominee does not understand that today's gay-rights movement is all about merging private and public behaviors:

> [McCain] doesn't understand why gay people can't remain in the closet. He doesn't understand how our government discriminates legally against gay people. For example, at the federal level his argument is that legislation is unnecessary because the Constitution fully protects people in employment. That's factually incorrect. We had a case in Arizona in 1994 where a guy was fired for being gay. The courts sided with the employer, and on appeal the court found that the lower court was correct in its ruling. So, we have had a case in Arizona where the courts have said very clearly you can be fired for being gay. John McCain thinks the

Constitution protects everybody. He's wrong. On "don't ask, don't tell," he doesn't understand why people have to tell. After we talked for a while, he saw where there was a problem in his understanding. He didn't understand (but he is starting to understand) the right to privacy for gay people.[115]

Many Americans—especially those who came of age in the 1950s and 1960s—have views similar to McCain's. While opinion is nearly universal that heterosexual couples should have a legal right to marry, endorsements of personal privacy and tolerance cause internal conflicts. In 2006, a majority of judges on the New York State Court of Appeals rejected the idea of a constitutional right to gay marriage: "Protecting the welfare of children is a legitimate governmental interest, and . . . there is a rational relationship between that interest and the limitation of marriage to opposite sex couples."[116] A 2006 ruling by the Washington State Supreme Court offered a similar conclusion. By a vote of five to four, the court decided that the legislature's decision to limit marriage to heterosexuals "furthers the State's interests in procreation and encouraging families with a mother and father and children biologically related to both."[117] And in 2008, Californians decided that they had the power to suspend a right that their supreme court said the state constitution granted to homosexuals. By a margin of 52 percent to 48 percent, voters voided the court's decision to legalize gay marriage.

These contradictions are not surprising. As the gay-rights revolution gains momentum, the pressure caused by contrary impulses to support tolerance and endorse marriage and family will only increase. That such visible public tensions exist is in itself remarkable and indicates the extent to which public attitudes have changed in the recent past. In August 1970, President Richard M. Nixon met with his closest aides to consider a high-level appointment for Rita E. Hauser, an administration appointee to the United Nations Commission on Human Rights. Hauser had impressed the president with her "responsible feminism," and he wanted to name her a White House assistant for women's affairs and have her appear extensively on television to appeal to the growing number of feminists.[118] However, Nixon discovered that in an address to the American Bar Association, Hauser had observed that passage of the Equal Rights Amendment "would void the legal requirement or practice of the states' limiting marriage, which is a legal right, to partners of different sexes."[119] Just three years after *Loving v. Virginia* had eliminated state bans on interracial marriage, Nixon was shocked to learn of Hauser's comment and concluded that he could not appoint her to a high-profile position: "I can't go that far—that's the year 2000. Negroes [and whites]—OK; but that's too far."[120]

Nixon was an astute politician. In 1970, when the idea of gay marriage entered the public debate for the first time, historian Allan Spear, himself gay, declared that only the "lunatic fringe" of the gay-rights movement "had any interest in marriage."[121] Nearly 40 years later when queried about the most controversial aspects of homosexuality—including gay marriage—Americans are willing to grant a far greater measure of tolerance. In 1999, for example, a survey found that 57 percent of respondents opposed the idea of gays adopting children and just 38 percent supported it. Today, the public is deadlocked at 46 percent in favor and 46 percent opposed. Conservatives–including 65 percent of Republicans, 75 percent of white Protestant evangelicals, and 60 percent of southerners—remain staunchly opposed. But core Democratic partisans are much more open-minded: 55 percent of partisan Democrats, 58 percent of those aged 18 to 29, 55 percent of college graduates, 57 percent of northeasterners, and 55 percent of Catholics support gay adoption rights.[122] Even the fiery opposition to gay marriage has cooled. In 2004, 63 percent of those polled opposed gay marriage; two years later, that figure had fallen to 51 percent. Between 2004 and 2006, the percentage of respondents who "strongly oppose" gay marriage dropped from 42 percent to 28 percent. This decline has been especially notable among key Bush supporters: from 59 to 41 percent among Republicans; from 58 to 33 percent among people aged 65 or older; and from 65 percent to 56 percent among white evangelical Protestants. By 2006, only 18 percent of white mainline Protestants and 19 percent of Catholics strongly opposed gay marriages.[123]

Even in the red state of Oklahoma, the fierce opposition to homosexuals has provoked a conservative backlash. In 2004, Bush captured 66 percent of Oklahoma's voters, thanks in part to a proposed state constitutional amendment banning same-sex marriages, which won 76 percent support. After a *Washington Post* reporter wrote a sympathetic article about 17-year-old Michael Shackelford's struggle to grow up gay in this socially conservative state, an ardent antigay pastor, the Reverend Fred Phelps, sponsored protests at Shackelford's Baptist church and high school. Declaring that Shackelford was a "doomed teenage fag" and carrying signs reading "Fags

Are Worthy of Death," "Fags Doom Nation," "Fag Church," and "Turn or Burn," the protesters provoked an outpouring of support for the besieged teenager. One burly man with a crew cut gave Shackelford a thumbs-up and told him, "Man, you be who you are. We got your back." A passerby quoted Jesus to the protesters: "Let he who is without sin cast the first stone." Shackelford's mother, Janice, was amazed at the reaction: Phelps's group "thought they could come to this town and break it apart. But it has brought the town together. It has opened some doors to talk."[124]

Such a reaction signals a change of heart. While a majority of Americans still consider homosexuality a sin, the message emanating from even the most conservative elements seems to be, "Hate the sin; love the sinner."[125] But even this common expression no longer carries its former power with regard to homosexuality. Back when Nixon was a important part of the American political psyche, homosexuality was anathema. Gay rights—let alone gay marriage—was such a taboo topic that even merely broaching it in polite company was considered a severe breach of etiquette.

The Verboten Word: Homosexuality

In 1950, the American Psychiatric Association listed homosexuality as a "mental disorder."[126] Such thinking was not uncommon. A 1950s educational film produced by the U.S. Navy depicts a gay man lying in a hospital bed as doctors strap him down and attach electrodes to his head, while a male voice in the background says, "We're going to make you better." Then the power is turned on, and the man jerks violently and begins to scream.[127] In a startling 1959 novel by Allen Drury, *Advice and Consent*, one of the leading characters, Brigham Anderson, is a dynamic U.S. senator on the rise who commits suicide after learning that a homosexual affair he had during World War II is about to be disclosed. Drury's novel neither mentions the word *homosexual* nor describes the love between the two men in any graphic detail. Rather, Anderson's homosexuality is characterized as "the snarl of the beast in the jungle that underlies the polite exchanges of society." Believing that he has gone "off track," Anderson aims a gun to his head, and his last thoughts turn to "a beach in Honolulu on a long, hot, lazy afternoon."[128] Homosexuality, the verboten word, was a "mental disorder," a love whose name could not be spoken.

Surveys confirm an overwhelmingly negative public reaction whenever the word *homosexuality* was mentioned. In 1965, 70 percent of respondents in one poll believed homosexuals were "harmful" to the American way of life. Seven years later, an equal percentage thought homosexual acts between consenting adults were "always wrong." Indeed, whenever pollsters asked about homosexuality during the freewheeling 1970s, the results were uniform (see table 6).

During the AIDS-ridden 1980s, attitudes toward homosexuality remained largely unchanged. In 1980, 52 percent of those surveyed disapproved of the idea of "homosexual rights," and in 1987, 50 percent of respondents said it would be "totally wrong" to characterize them as gay-rights supporters. In 1983, 82 percent said they would be unhappy if their child became involved in a homosexual or lesbian relationship, with 62 percent saying they would be "very upset" at such news. Six years later in 1989, 55 percent argued that television programs containing scenes that suggested (but did not depict) homosexual behavior should never be broadcast. That same year, 69 percent opposed giving homosexual couples the same rights as married couples, a sentiment that persisted in 1994, when 62 percent opposed sanctioning gay marriages (see table 6).

Today, some people still abhor the mere mention of homosexuality. In a 2003 poll, 55 percent of respondents believed that engaging in homosexual behavior was sinful. Moreover, 50 percent in the same study had an unfavorable impression of gay men, while 48 percent viewed lesbians unfavorably.[129] And in a 2006 poll, 91 percent of Americans said that the country "is not ready" to elect a gay or lesbian person as president. Gays placed dead last on a list of groups of people that the country was "not ready" to elect, trailing women (38 percent), African Americans (40 percent), Jews (42 percent), Hispanics (58 percent), Asians (64 percent); Mormons (66 percent), and atheists (84 percent).[130]

Members of some groups, especially those with strong religious beliefs, continue to find homosexuality anathema. For example, a 2004 survey showed that 96 percent of Christian fundamentalists believed that same-sex relationships were against God's will.[131] In another 2004 survey, 49 percent of respondents thought homosexuality was unacceptable for themselves (though it might be acceptable for others), while an additional 38 percent found it unacceptable either for themselves or others.[132] Ziad Nimri, a 41-year-old salesperson and Democrat who lives in Spokane, told the *New York Times* that he strongly supported a constitutional amendment banning gay marriage: "I don't want my children to start getting ideas. They see it's out in the open and you see men kissing on television these

TABLE 6. The Verboten Word: Homosexuality, 1965–94

Text of Question	
"America has many different types of people in it. But we would like to know whether you think each of these different types of people is more helpful or harmful to American life, or don't they help or harm things one way or the other?. . . Homosexuals." (1965)[a]	
Percentage answering "more harmful"	70
"What about sexual relations between two adults of the same sex—do you think it is always wrong, almost always wrong, wrong only sometimes, or not wrong at all?" (1972–82)[b]	
Percentage answering "always wrong"	70
"If you heard there was a new movie out which had an interesting plot and in which many of the characters portrayed were homosexuals, do you think you would want to see this movie?" (1976)[c]	
Percentage answering "no"	66
"Do you think homosexuals should or should not be allowed to adopt children?" (1977)[d]	
Percentage answering "should not be allowed to adopt children"	77
"Would you agree that homosexuals should be allowed to hold any job for which they are qualified, or do you think they should be barred from certain kinds of jobs?" (1977)[e]	
Percentage answering "should be barred from certain kinds of jobs"	48
"Today there are many different kinds of lifestyles which people find acceptable such as homosexual relationships. How do you feel about this? Do you find it acceptable for other people but not yourself, acceptable for other people and yourself, or not acceptable at all?" (1978)[f]	
Percentage answering "not acceptable at all"	59
"If your party nominated a generally well-qualified man for President, would you vote for him if he happened to be a homosexual?" (1978)[g]	
Percentage answering "no"	66
"Would you favor or oppose permitting homosexual school teachers to work in your public school?" (1978)[h]	
Percentage answering "oppose permitting homosexual teachers to work in your school"	66
"Do you think homosexuals should be ordained priests, ministers, or rabbis, or don't you think so?" (1979)[i]	
Percentage answering "no, should not be ordained"	61
"Do you approve or disapprove of homosexual rights?" (1980)[j]	
Percentage "disapprove of homosexual rights"	52
"Would you tell me whether you generally favor or generally oppose each of these proposals. Allowing homosexuals to teach in the public schools?" (1980)[k]	
Percentage answering "generally oppose to teach in the public schools"	66
"Please tell me how you would respond to each of the following possibilities concerning your children. (If you don't have children, just imagine that you do and answer accordingly.) If your child became involved in a homosexual or lesbian relationship." (1980)[l]	
Percentage answering either "unhappy" or "very unhappy" "if your child became involved in a homosexual or lesbian relationship"	82
"Compared to non-homosexuals do you feel that homosexuals are more likely to lead happy, well-adjusted lives?" (1982)[m]	
Percentage answering "homosexuals are less likely to lead happy, well-adjusted lives"	66
"If you had a child who told you he or she was a homosexual, what do you think your reaction would be? Would you be very upset, not very upset, or not upset at all?" (1983)[n]	
Percentage answering "very upset if their child was a homosexual"	62

TABLE 6.—*Continued*

"On a scale from 1 to 10 where '10' represents a description that is perfect for you and '1' a description that is totally wrong for you, how well do each of the following describe you? To what extent do you regard yourself as a supporter of the Gay Rights Movement?" (1987)[o]

Percentage answering 1 (description "totally wrong") to "regard yourself as a supporter of the Gay Rights Movement"	50

"Should homosexual couples have the same legal rights as married couples?" (1989)[p]

Percentage answering "no, homosexual couples should not have the same legal rights as married couples"	69

"Here are some things that may or may not be objectionable on TV. For each thing I mention, please tell me if you think it should not be allowed on TV, if it is OK only if shown late at night after children have gone to bed, or if it is acceptable on TV any time. . . . Scenes that suggest, but do not actually show, homosexuality." (1989)[q]

Percentage answering "scenes that suggest, but do not actually show, homosexuality should not be allowed on TV"	55

"Do you think there should or should not be legally-sanctioned gay marriage?" (1994)[r]

Percentage answering "should not be legally-sanctioned gay marriage"	62

[a]Louis Harris and Associates poll, September 1965. Responses: More helpful, 1 percent; more harmful, 70 percent; doesn't matter, 29 percent.

[b]National Opinion Research Center, General Social Surveys, 1972–82. Responses: Always wrong, 70 percent; Almost always wrong, 5 percent; wrong only sometimes, 6 percent; not wrong at all, 14 percent; don't know (volunteered), 4 percent.

[c]Cambridge Reports Research International poll, July 1976. Responses: Yes, 18 percent; no, 66 percent; not sure, 17 percent.

[d]Gallup poll, June 17–20, 1977. Responses: Should, 14 percent; should not, 77 percent; no opinion, 9 percent.

[e]Louis Harris and Associates poll, June 13–18, 1977. Responses: Allowed to hold any job, 41 percent; should be barred from certain kinds of jobs, 48 percent; not sure, 11 percent.

[f]Yankelovich, Skelly and White poll, March 14–30, 1978. Responses: Acceptable for others, 35 percent; acceptable for others and self, 6 percent; not acceptable, 59 percent.

[g]Gallup poll, July 21–24, 1978. Responses: Yes, 26 percent; no, 66 percent; no opinion, 9 percent.

[h]*CBS News* poll, November 7, 1978. Responses: Favor, 34 percent; oppose, 66 percent.

[i]*NBC News*/Associated Press poll, September 24–25, 1979. Responses: Yes, should be ordained, 29 percent; no, should not be ordained, 61 percent; not sure, 10 percent.

[j]*Los Angeles Times* poll, November 9–13, 1980. Responses: Approve, 36 percent; disapprove, 52 percent; not sure, 11 percent; refused, 1 percent.

[k]Gallup poll, September 12–15, 1980. Responses: Generally favor, 34 percent; generally oppose, 66 percent.

[l]Research and Forecasts poll, September 1–11, 1980. Responses: Very happy, less than .5 percent; happy, 1 percent; neutral, 17 percent; unhappy, 30 percent; very unhappy, 52 percent.

[m]Gallup poll, June 25–28, 1982. Responses: More, 13 percent; less, 66 percent; don't know, 21 percent.

[n]*Los Angeles Times* poll, September 18–22, 1983. Responses: Very upset, 63 percent; somewhat upset, 27 percent; not very upset, 4 percent; not at all upset, 3 percent; not sure, 2 percent; refused, 1 percent.

[o]Gallup poll, April 25–May 10, 1987. Responses: 1 (description totally wrong), 50 percent; 2, 9 percent; 3, 7 percent; 4, 5 percent; 5, 10 percent; 6, 4 percent; 7, 3 percent; 8, 3 percent; 9, 2 percent; 10 (description perfect), 4 percent; don't know, 3 percent.

[p]Gallup poll, October 1–4, 1989. Responses: Yes, 23 percent; no, 69 percent; don't know, 8 percent.

[q]Kane, Parsons, and Associates poll, 1989. Responses: Should not be allowed, 55 percent; OK only if shown late at night, 35 percent; acceptable any time, 9 percent; not sure, 1 percent.

[r]Princeton Survey Research Associates poll, February 3–4, 1994. Responses: Should, 29 percent; should not, 62 percent; don't know, 9 percent.

days. Because they're in a minority, they're going to start actually giving them more privileges than normal people would have. Minorities always tend to get more than your average person." Theresa Eaton, a 49-year-old Republican financial analyst from Corona, California, agreed: "If I knew that we had a neighbor who was gay, I would not let my nieces and nephews go close by there. I don't want to accept their lifestyle. It can be acquired and it is not right."[133] Supreme Court justice Antonin Scalia concurred, declaring in a powerful dissent to *Lawrence v. Texas*, "Many Americans do not want persons who openly engage in homosexual conduct as partners in their business, as scoutmasters for their children, as teachers in their children's schools, or as boarders in their home. They view this as protecting themselves and their families from a lifestyle that they believe to be immoral and destructive."[134] Former U.S. senator Rick Santorum, a Pennsylvania Republican, is even more emphatic: "And if the Supreme Court says that you have the right to consensual (gay) sex within your home, then you have the right to bigamy, you have the right to polygamy, you have the right to incest, you have the right to adultery. You have the right to do anything."[135]

Mixing Tolerance with Rights

Yet even as many Americans still profess their public dislike of homosexuals and their private behaviors, some signs indicate that opinions have shifted in favor of more tolerance. In 1973, the American Psychiatric Association removed homosexuality from its list of mental illnesses, and in 1994, the group went further, declaring, "Homosexuality is neither mental illness nor moral depravity. It is simply the way a minority of our population expresses human love and sexuality."[136] That same year, the association proposed making it unethical for psychiatrists to attempt to alter patients' sexual orientations. And a decade later, the group endorsed gay marriage.[137] Cornell University psychology professor Daryl Bem explains why his colleagues have changed their minds: "If your notion of a gay man was someone lurking in the park looking for sex—now it's your son. It's hard to regard [gays] as sinners or as second-class citizens, because we want our children to be happy."[138]

Other signs also point toward increased public tolerance. In survey results from the National Opinion Research Center from 1972–82, 70 percent of respondents described homosexual relations as "always wrong," while just 14 percent answered "not wrong at all." In 2006, the percentage who believed homosexual acts were "always wrong" fell to 54 percent, while the number who said such acts were "not wrong at all" more than doubled, to 31 percent.[139] These attitudes have resulted in a stunning reversal of opinion. For example, during the height of the "Don't ask, don't tell" controversy, 47 percent of the public favored the idea, while 43 percent opposed it. By 2005, a stunning 76 percent favored allowing gays to serve in the military, and 79 percent favored allowing gays to serve openly.[140] And that's not all. In a 2004 poll, 68 percent of those asked would not be bothered to learn that their child's schoolteacher was gay. When asked in 2007 whether school boards should have the right to fire teachers because they were homosexual, 63 percent disagreed (including 39 percent who "completely disagreed" with the idea), while just 28 percent were in favor.[141]

One reason for the greater degree of tolerance is the increasing number of Americans who have close friends who are homosexual. In 1986, only 24 percent of those surveyed reported having such friends.[142] Today, more than 8 in 10 respondents say they know someone who is gay, and 6 in 10 report having homosexual friends, colleagues, or family members.[143] Brad Sears, director of the Williams Project on Sexual Orientation Law at the University of California at Los Angeles Law School, says, "The act of coming out has probably been the single most important determinant in the change in public opinion polls. People learn that this isn't some kind of abstract, foreign, exotic creature. This is somebody who lives down the street."[144]

Generations at Odds

More than 30 years ago, Leonard Matlovich was a young gay man who had served three tours in Vietnam with the U.S. Air Force. While there, he won the Bronze Star and the Purple Heart. But in Vietnam, the sergeant wrestled with his sexuality, and in 1975 he wrote to the secretary of the air force, "After some years of uncertainty, I have arrived at the conclusion that my sexual preferences are homosexual as opposed to heterosexual."[145] With that, Matlovich became a leader of the gay-rights movement. Like Margaret Rusk and Guy Gibson Smith, he appeared on the cover of *Time:* the banner headline read, "Gays on the March."[146] Up to that point, no openly gay person had ever appeared on the prestigious magazine's cover.

Matlovich's realization that he was a homosexual was long and painful, especially because he was a Roman Catholic, and his religion taught that homosexuality was a sin. In addition, he was a conservative Republican who had strongly backed Barry Goldwater in 1964.[147] Shortly after making his sexual preference public, Matlovich spoke before a gay-rights demonstration in what became a life-changing experience: "I found myself, little nobody me, standing up in front of tens of thousands of gay people. And just two years ago I thought I was the only gay person in the world. It was a mixture of joy and sadness. It was just great pride to be an American, to know I'm oppressed but able to stand up there and say so. They were very beautiful people out there."[148]

Despite his stellar military record, Matlovich was dismissed from the air force, which at the time had a regulation prohibiting homosexuals from service: "Participation in a homosexual act, or proposing or attempting to do so, is considered serious misbehavior regardless of whether the role of a person in a particular act was active or passive." But the air force also had an exemption to its policy that became the basis for a legal challenge: "Exceptions to permit retention may be authorized only where the most unusual circumstances exist and provided the airman's ability to perform military service has not been compromised."[149] Matlovich's personal conduct had been above reproach, and his military record was impeccable.

After numerous court battles, federal district judge Gerhard Gesell concluded that the Air Force had not complied with an appeals court order to clarify its exemption policy, and on September 9, 1980, he reinstated Matlovich with full back pay. Not wanting a gay person in the ranks, the Air Force gave Matlovich $160,000 to leave. David Addlestone, an American Civil Liberties Union lawyer, remembered the outcome as a victory for the gay-rights movement: "It brought people out of the closet who were in positions of authority in the Air Force. It affected the way the [Veterans Administration] treated people with undesirable discharges for homosexuality. And it forced the services to change their regulations as to what types of discharges they were giving people who committed homosexual acts." On June 22, 1988, Matlovich died of AIDS, but he still had the last word. After his burial in Congressional Cemetery with full military honors, a tombstone was erected on his grave with the epitaph he wrote: "When I was in the military, they gave me a medal for killing two men and a discharge for loving one."[150]

Since Matlovich's death, the contradictions surrounding the gay-rights movement have abounded. But those paradoxes will gradually become less extreme. Commentator Andrew Sullivan, a gay conservative, believes that we are rapidly approaching a moment when being called gay "will cease to tell you very much about any individual": "The distinction between gay and straight culture will become so blurred, so fractured, and so intermingled that it may become more helpful not to examine them separately at all."[151] Sullivan's prediction has already become a reality in Chicago's Boystown, the nation's first city-designated gay business district. There, the gay bookstore sells more children's books than gay-themed ones, and Baby Gap and Walgreen's have opened stores to capitalize on the diversified market.[152]

Signs of a new future are evident in the attitudes of the people who will spend the majority of their lives in the twenty-first century. Those currently aged 18 to 24 strongly support gay rights, while those 65 or older are unsympathetic (see table 7). But support from the nation's youth for gay equality is not just political but also personal: 70 percent are sympathetic to homosexuals, an equal number would permit their children to play at homosexuals' residences, 56 percent would allow gay babysitters to watch their children, and 74 percent believe that homosexuals can be good role models. In addition, 74 percent of those aged 18 to 24 no longer see homosexual relations as a moral issue, and 71 percent say they can accept two people of the same sex living together. Finally, 65 percent say it is possible for two people of the same sex to be in love the same way a man and woman can be in love. One gay teenager explained his peers' blasé attitudes: "When everyone discovers that the kid they were saying is gay actually *is* gay, and he *knows* he's gay, then people don't want to talk about it anymore. It's old news. It's not interesting gossip."[153]

By embracing the moral freedom to make more personal choices (including homosexual ones), 71 percent of young Americans have easily reconciled themselves to believe that gay marriages are inevitable (see table 7). So, too, have an overwhelming majority of their fellow citizens. In 1998, 74 percent of those polled—including overwhelming majorities in all age groups, 73 percent of Republicans, 74 percent of Democrats, and 81 percent of independents—believed that gay marriages would be commonplace by 2025.[154]

Even though the gay-rights revolution generates a lot of political controversy, the outcome seems inevitable. A decade ago, Paul Weyrich, an ardent conservative and a spear-carrier in the culture wars, made a startling

TABLE 7. Generations at Odds

Text of Question	Aged 18–29 Years Old	Aged 65 or More
"Generally speaking, do you approve or disapprove of homosexual or gay rights—or haven't you heard enough to say?"		
Percentage "approve"	54	23
"Generally speaking, how sympathetic would you say you are to the gay community? Would you say you are very sympathetic, somewhat sympathetic, somewhat unsympathetic, or very unsympathetic?"		
Percentage "very/somewhat sympathetic to the gay community"	70	43
"Do you think homosexuals have too little political power, or about the right amount, or do you think that homosexuals have too much political power?"		
Percentage answering "too much political power"	23	45
"Would you be willing or not willing to vote for a well-qualified candidate running for an elected office if that person was openly gay?"		
Percentage "willing to vote for a gay candidate"	69	42
"If you had a child who told you he or she was gay or lesbian, what do you think your reaction would be? Would you be upset or not?"		
Percentage "upset"	48	82
"Do you think it is possible for two people of the same-sex to be in love with one another the way that a man and woman can be in love?"		
Percentage answering "two people of the same sex can be in love the way a man and woman can be in love"	65	31
"Do you favor or oppose gay couples legally adopting children?"		
Percentage "favor"	54	22
"If you had a child of elementary school age, would you object to having a gay person as your child's school teacher, or would that not bother you?"		
Percentage "object"	19	44
"If you had a child, would you permit or not permit your child to play at the home of a friend who lives with a gay parent?"		
Percentage "permit"	70	39
"If you had a child, would you permit or not permit a gay person to baby-sit your child?"		
Percentage "permit"	56	22
"If you had a child, would you permit your child to read a book that contains a story about a same-sex couple?"		
Percentage "permit"	55	31
"Do you think that a gay person can be a good role model for a child, or do you not think so?"		
Percentage answering "good role model"	74	39
"Do you personally believe that same-sex relationships between consenting adults are morally wrong, or is that not a moral issue?"		
Percentage answering "not a moral issue"	62	34

TABLE 7.—*Continued*

Text of Question	Aged 18–29 Years Old	Aged 65 or More
"No matter if you think it is morally right or wrong, can you accept two men or two women living together like a married couple, or can you not accept that kind of living arrangement?"		
Percentage "accept"	71	47
(Agree/Disagree) "Homosexuality is wrong because people were put on this earth to reproduce."		
Percentage "agree"	36	68
(Agree/Disagree) "As long as two people are in love and are committed to each other it doesn't matter if they are a same-sex couple or a heterosexual couple."		
Percentage "agree"	70	38
(Agree/Disagree) "Regardless of your opinion about same-sex marriage, do you think legal recognition of it is inevitable, or not?"		
Percentage answering "inevitable"	71	45
"Do you favor or oppose an amendment to the U.S. Constitution that legally defines marriage as a union between a man and a woman only, and would prevent states from legally recognizing same-sex marriages?"		
Percentage "favor"	32	63
(Agree/Disagree) "If gays are allowed to marry, the institution of marriage will be degraded."		
Percentage "agree"	44	67
(Agree/Disagree) "If gays are allowed to marry, then it is only a matter of time before things like incest and polygamy are legalized."		
Percentage "agree"	33	46

Source: Los Angeles Times poll, March 27–30, 2004.

admission: "I believe that we probably have lost the culture war. That does not mean the war is not going to continue, and that it isn't going to be fought on other fronts. But in terms of society in general, we have lost. This is why, even when we win in politics, our victories fail to translate into the kind of policies we believe are important."[155] At first, Weyrich's admission seems to have been premature. After Weyrich made that statement, Republicans twice won the presidency, expanded their control of Congress until the 2006 debacle, and prevailed in any number of antigay state ballot initiatives. Moreover, George W. Bush appointed federal judges who are very unsympathetic to gays' use of the courts to win rights. But the pitched battles between the two major parties over the extension of gay rights masks a settling of this controversy within the hearts of most twenty-first-century Americans. With personal acceptance has come greater tolerance. In a 2001 survey, 64 percent of respondents believed that their fellow citizens should be "more tolerant of people who choose to live by their own moral standards, even if we think they are wrong."[156] Harvard law professor Elizabeth Bartholet states that there is no return to the status quo ante: "Our society believes so powerfully in reproductive freedom, we have allowed, and are not going to stop allowing, gays to parent—to have children, both naturally and through reproductive technology, and to hold onto those children. We also believe in relational freedom. We have allowed, and are not going to stop allowing, gays to live together."[157]

This moral libertarianism is deeply felt. Changing demography suggests that the proliferation of varied family lifestyles (both homosexual and heterosexual), along with an accompanying acceptance of those lifestyles and of people of different races, will persist. With respect to gay marriage, for every step backward taken by states that have adopted gay marriage bans to their constitutions, there are others willing to advance the issue. In April 2009, Iowa's Supreme Court justices ruled that the state ban on same-sex marriages is unconstitutional. Richard Socarides, an attorney and former senior advisor to President Clinton, maintained that the Iowa ruling represents the "mainstreaming of gay marriage."[158] He may be right. Just a few days after this observation, Vermont became the first state to legalize gay marriage by legislative fiat, even overriding the veto of the state's Republican governor. Maine and New Hampshire shortly followed, and by 2012, gay rights activists hope that all six of the New England states (Rhode Island being the only exception) will have legalized gay marriage.

In 2008, the emergence of a new and different America became evident in the election of Barack Obama. While gays still suffered defeats at the polls even as they won victories in the courts, Obama's election provided one indication that our politics was about to match the moment. Yet even as the race, family-, and gay-rights revolutions were gathering steam, one more significant alteration was reshaping American society—how we think about and practice our religious faiths. That is the subject of the next chapter.

Five • Shrunken Congregations,
Soulful Citizens

"This is a Christian Nation."
—HARRY TRUMAN, 1947

"Christianity will go."
—JOHN LENNON, 1966

CHRISTMAS DAY 2007. At precisely 10 A.M. the White/Pre-
vost family made its usual trek to the century-old St. Anne's Shrine in Fall
River, Massachusetts. But as we took our seats and admired the familiar
Christmas decorations, something was clearly amiss. Unlike the crowded
pews of past Christmases, this particular mass had no more than 75 worshipers, most of them elderly. Only two children were present, including
our daughter, Jeannette. The pastor took note of the empty seats, telling
the few gathered that many others had gone to mass either the day before
or at midnight.

Still, the vacant pews were a shock, especially to me. I was reared in the
1950s, when Sunday mass attendance (and in particular, Christmas Day
mass) was virtually compulsory. I am hardly alone in having such recollec-
tions. In *The Lost City*, Alan Ehrenhalt remembers that in 1957, the
Catholic church in his Chicago neighborhood had 1,100 seats filled to capacity every Sunday at nearly "every hour on the hour": "at seven o'clock,

when the nuns attended and Monsignor Fennessy sometimes presided; at nine, when the parish children filed in and arranged themselves next to their school classmates; at noon, when the stragglers got their final chance to avoid starting the new week on a sinful note."[1] A 1958 poll confirms these remembrances: 75 percent of Catholics surveyed said they attended mass every week.[2] As Bishop Kenneth Untener of Saginaw, Michigan, put it, "When I grew up you had two choices: go to Mass . . . or go to hell. Most of us chose Mass."[3] Such devotion (however compulsory) certainly enhanced one's sense of religious identification: in 1952, 83 percent of Catholics told pollsters that their religion was a very important part of their daily lives.[4]

But in the twenty-first century, shrunken congregations in Catholic parishes and other houses of worship are commonplace. According to a 2005 survey, only 40 percent of Catholics attend mass on any given Sunday, while the number of young Catholic churchgoers has dropped to a mere one in five.[5] Charles Morris notes that starting in the late 1960s, "skipping Sunday Mass was quietly, if unofficially, dropped from the Catholic catalog of mortal sins." "Rightly or wrongly," he argues, "most Catholics apparently feel that once-or-twice-a-month Mass attendance keeps them in sufficient touch with their religion."[6] Even among religiously active Catholics, the once-familiar church practices are falling by the wayside: 61 percent never pray with a rosary, 76 percent never engage in the novena (nine consecutive evenings of prayer), 44 percent never participate in the stations of the cross, and 53 percent never attend benediction.[7]

Catholics are hardly alone in loosening ties to established faiths. Princeton sociologist Robert Wuthnow reports that although 58 percent of those surveyed believe that "Christianity is the best way to understand God," only 25 percent think it is "best for everybody." Today Wuthnow finds that most Americans see elements of truth in many religions: 59 percent would welcome Buddhists becoming a stronger presence in the United States, while 58 percent feel the same about Hinduism, and 51 percent feel the same about Islam.[8]

The alarums sounding the end of traditional religious worship have been heard for several decades. In 1966, *Time* magazine printed its infamous "Is God Dead?" issue, declaring, "In the traditional citadels of Christendom, grey Gothic cathedrals stand empty, mute witnesses to a rejected faith."[9] Nearly forty years later, Sister Kathleen Hughes, a professor of word and worship, observed that at too many churches, "dwindling numbers gather for lifeless, dispirited worship."[10] One weekly churchgoer sadly noted, "I'm watching the church, watching priests get older, priests disappearing, nobody coming in, and then I started observing that there seemed to be less young people and I said, 'Geez, we've got ceremonies, but we don't have community."[11] According to a 2008 survey, 62 percent of Catholics say their church is out of touch.[12] Given these results, it is not surprising that the U.S. Roman Catholic Church is in trouble. In 2008, the Pew Research Center reported that while nearly one in three Americans were raised as Catholics, fewer than one in four identified themselves as such. Ten percent of all Americans describe themselves as "former Catholics," yet another warning bell for a church that is home to millions of immigrants and still finds itself with shrinking numbers.[13]

Other troubling signs for the U.S. Catholic Church include fewer priests—a decline from 58,132 clergy in 1965 to just 45,713 in 2002.[14] According to Father Allan Figueroa Deck of the U.S. Conference of Catholic Bishops, "We don't have enough foot soldiers."[15] New York Times religion columnist Peter Steinfels believes that unless drastic action is taken, "a soft slide into a kind of nominal Catholicism is quite foreseeable. [Catholics'] faith will become an increasingly marginal or superficial part of their identity, bearing less and less on the important choices of their lives. . . . At the outside, there is even the possibility of a sudden collapse, in a single generation or two—such as has been seen in Ireland and, earlier, in French Canada—of what appeared to be a virtually impregnable Catholicism."[16]

Two years before Catholics in eastern Massachusetts (and elsewhere) faced their personal anomie on that lonely Christmas Day in 2007, pews at an evangelical Protestant church halfway across the continent stood empty, albeit for a very different reason. The Willow Creek Community Church, established in 1975 and located in South Barrington, Illinois, normally has 20,000 worshipers each week.[17] But in 2005, Christmas fell on a Sunday, prompting senior pastor Bill Hybels to shutter his doors and tell the members of his flock to spend the religious holiday with their family and friends. Rather than seek compulsory Christmas attendance, Hybels distributed a free DVD that recounted the familiar story of Jesus's birth. Willow Creek communications director Cathy Parkinson explained the church's decision: "What we're encouraging people to do is take that DVD and in the comfort of their living room, with friends and family, pop it into the player and hopefully hear a different and more personal and maybe more intimate Christian message, that God is with us wherever we are."[18]

Willow Creek was not the only church to close on Christmas 2005. At least eight other megachurches also canceled services, while others limited their worship to just one or two gatherings. Bishop Eddie L. Long, pastor of the New Birth Missionary Baptist Church in Lithonia, Georgia, was particularly innovative. Long held two services and broadcast them on the church's Web site, thereby giving his 25,000 members "an option if they want to join their family around the computer and worship with us." But crowding around a computer screen was not the only choice, as Long explained: "We're encouraging our members to do a family worship. They could wake up and read Scripture and pray and sometimes sing a song, and go over the true meaning of what Christmas is, before opening their gifts. It keeps them together and not running off to get dressed up to go off to church."[19]

The cancellation of Christmas Day services sparked scathing criticisms from more traditional religious spokespersons. Robert J. Miller, director of research and planning at the Roman Catholic archdiocese of Philadelphia, said, "From the Catholic perspective, the whole purpose of the holiday is to celebrate it as a religious holiday in the company of the community, and for Catholics that means at Mass." Ben Witherington III, a professor at Asbury Theological Seminary in Wilmore, Kentucky, was equally dismissive: "I see this in many ways as a capitulation to narcissism, the self-centered, me-first, I'm going to put me and my immediate family first agenda of the larger culture. If Christianity is an evangelistic religion, then what kind of message is this sending to the larger culture—that worship is an optional extra?" But Willow Creek's Rev. Mark Ashton countered that adherence to outdated twentieth-century customs (such as mandatory church attendance, even when Christmas fell on a Sunday) was passé: "We've always been a church that's been on the edge of innovation. We've been willing to try and experiment, so this is another one of those innovations." Boston University sociologist Nancy Ammerman concurred: "This attachment to a particular day on the calendar is just not something that mega-churches have been known for. They're known for being flexible and creative, and not for taking these traditions, seasons, dates, and symbols really seriously."[20]

In many ways, the tales of these empty pews—some Catholic, others Protestant—capture conflicting yet consistent realities about present-day worship. To some, the belief that God is dead is symbolized by the sparse crowd at St. Anne's Parish. In 1966, Beatle John Lennon famously predicted, "Christianity will go. It will vanish and shrink. I needn't argue about that. I'm right and will be proven right. We're more popular than Jesus now. I don't know which will go first—rock 'n roll or Christianity. Jesus was alright, but his disciples were thick and ordinary. It's them twisting it that ruins it for me." Amplifying the controversial remarks, Beatle manager Brian Epstein noted that Lennon "was astonished that in the last fifty years the Church of England, and therefore Christ, had suffered a decline in interest. He did not mean to boast about the Beatles' fame. He meant to point out that the Beatles' effect appeared to be, to him, a more immediate one upon certain of the younger generation."[21] Across the Atlantic Ocean, Princeton University theologian Paul Ramsey echoed Lennon's critique, arguing that the United States was quickly shedding its forebears' religious beliefs: "Ours is the first attempt in recorded history to build a culture upon the premise that God is dead."[22]

But to other observers, today's shrunken congregations hardly represent the death of religion or a lack of a belief in God; rather, they demonstrate an institutional capacity on the part of today's churches to adapt to individual needs. For every empty St. Anne's, there is an equally crowded Willow Creek Community Church. One example illustrates the truism that empty pews can still become crowded ones, even if the programming is somewhat unfamiliar. In 2004, Mel Gibson's movie *The Passion of the Christ* garnered $23.6 million on its opening day, Ash Wednesday, making it the fifth-best Wednesday box-office opening in history. Yet the monies generated came not only from ticket counters at traditional theaters but from crowded churches where the movie was a blockbuster hit. Taking note of the dollars made and the unusual church venues, *Daily Variety*'s Todd McCarthy commented, "It's pretty astounding, no doubt about it. The prospect of something like this happening for a film that when it was announced sounded like a small little personal art film, not intended as a blockbuster, is an amazing transformation. I've never seen anything like that." Paul Dergarabedian, president of the company that compiles studio grosses, was equally flummoxed: "This number [$23.6 million] would be a good number for a mainstream blockbuster. This is a subtitled historical epic." Grey Kilday, a film editor for the *Hollywood Reporter*, exclaimed that *The Passion of the Christ* has "gone well beyond being a movie and become a cultural touchstone."[23]

In many ways, both the argument proclaiming the impending death of religion and the argument proclaiming its prospective revival contain kernels of truth. But gaining an understanding of how shrunken congregations do not necessarily result in soulless citizens first requires an examination of just how empty many traditional churches have become.

Shrunken Congregations, Soulful Citizens

As with race and the composition of the American family, the religious portrait of the United States has undergone dramatic alterations since the mid–twentieth century. These changes are especially important for a country whose originators expressed a belief that God had a divine plan for the United States. In 1630, for example, Massachusetts governor John Winthrop exhorted his fellow Pilgrims to follow God's precepts in the new land:

> The eyes of all people are upon us; so that if we shall deal falsely with our God in this work we have undertaken and so cause Him to withdraw His present help from us, we shall be made a story and a byword through the world, we shall open the mouths of enemies to speak evil of the ways of God . . . ; we shall shame the faces of many of God's worthy servants, and cause their prayers to be turned into curses upon us till we be consumed out of the good land whether we are going. . . . Beloved there is now set before us life and good, death and evil in that we are commanded this day to love the Lord our God, and to love one another to walk in His ways and to keep His commandments and his ordinances, and His laws, and the articles of our covenant with him that we may live and be multiplied, and that the Lord our God may bless us in the land whether we go to possess it. . . . Therefore, let us choose life, that we, and our seed may live. By obeying His voice, and cleaving to Him, for He is our life and our prosperity.[24]

Throughout the centuries, U.S. presidents have voiced similar sentiments. In a July 4, 1837, peroration to the citizens of Newburyport, Massachusetts, John Quincy Adams argued that the nation's founders were keenly attuned to the teachings of Jesus Christ and sought to incorporate them in the new government: "Is it not that the Declaration of Independence first organized the social compact on the foundation of the Redeemer's mission upon Earth? That it laid the cornerstone of human government upon the first precepts of Christianity, and gave to the world the first irrevocable pledge of the fulfilment of the prophecies announced directly from Heaven at the birth of the Saviour and predicted by the greatest of the Hebrew prophets six-hundred years before?"[25] Adams answered each of these questions in the affirmative. In 1911, Woodrow Wilson voiced similar thoughts: "America was born a Christian nation. America was born to exemplify that devotion to the elements of righteousness which are derived from the revelations of Holy Scripture. . . . I ask of every man and woman [to] realize that part of the destiny of America lies in their daily perusal of this great book of revelations—that if they would see America free and pure they will make their own spirits free and pure by this baptism of the Holy Scripture."[26] Forty-six years later, Harry S. Truman cast the founding of his homeland in explicitly religious terms in a letter to Pope Pius XII: "Your Holiness, this is a Christian Nation. More than a half century ago that declaration was written into the decrees of the highest court in this land. It is not without significance that the valiant pioneers who left Europe to establish settlements here, at the very beginning of their colonial enterprises, declared their faith in the Christian religion and made ample provision for its practice and for its support. The story of the Christian missionaries who in earliest days endured perils, hardship—even death itself in carrying the message of Jesus Christ to untutored savages is one that still moves the hearts of men."[27]

Truman's successors continue to act as high priests for a public espousal of religious values, although none so publicly insulted Native Americans as Truman did. Campaigning in 1976, Jimmy Carter sounded more like a pastor than a presidential candidate in his plea for a more religiously centered public morality: "We have a responsibility to try to shape government so that it does exemplify the will of God."[28] Ronald Reagan believed that God not only had a hand in creating the nation but also guided it in a way that exemplified a larger plan for salvation: "Think for a moment how special it is to be an American. Can we doubt that only a Divine Providence placed this land, this island of freedom, here as a refuge for all those people in the world who yearn to breathe free?"[29] In 2000, George W. Bush proclaimed Jesus Christ his favorite philosopher "because he changed my heart."[30] As president, Bush told the congregation at the Austin Presbyterian Church, "I have a sense of calm because I do believe in the Bible when it implores: 'Thy will be done.' I guess it is the Presbyterian in me that says if it is meant to be, it is meant to be. There is something very assuring in the belief that there is a higher being and a divine plan."[31]

Prospective presidents are likewise expected to be faithful Christian believers and worshipers. Back in 1958, 83 percent of respondents to one poll told the Gallup Organization that the "ideal president" was someone who attended church regularly.[32] Fifty years later, little has changed. John McCain believed faith was a necessary qualification for the presidency: "Since this nation was founded primarily on Christian principles . . . personally, I prefer someone [for president] who has a solid grounding in my faith."[33] Reflecting on the journey that led him to join the Trinity United Church of Christ, Barack Obama admitted that without a firm religious grounding, he would forever stand apart from the citizens he hoped to lead: "I came to realize that without a vessel for my beliefs, without an unequivocal commitment to a particular community of faith, I would be consigned at some level to always remain apart, free in the way that my mother [who was a secularist] was free, but also alone in the same ways she was ultimately alone."[34] As McCain and Obama illustrated, a public profession of faith remains a virtual prerequisite for becoming president. One 2007 survey found that more than three-quarters of registered voters thought their fellow citizens would be uncomfortable with an atheist president, and nearly two-thirds would not vote for any candidate who was an atheist.[35] Republicans were even more adamant in imposing a religious test: 70 percent said it was important for them to have a prospective president who believed that the Bible is the actual word of God.[36]

While Americans like their presidents to be faithful (and conventional) in their expressions of faith, the means by which citizens express their religious views have substantially changed. Nowhere is this more evident than in the decline of those who regularly attend religious services. In 1959, when attendance peaked, 59 percent of Americans attended churches or synagogues every week.[37] By 2007, the number of frequent attendees had fallen to just 42 percent.[38] Other surveys show an even more dramatic decline. When pollsters phrase their questions to allow for different gradations of churchgoers, the results suggest a continued weakening of religious identification. In 2008, for example, the Gallup Organization found that only 31 percent of people surveyed attended a church or synagogue "once a week"; 10 percent answered "almost every week"; 12 percent said "about once a month"; 26 percent replied "seldom"; and 19 percent claimed to "never" go. Put another way, those who often stayed away from a house of worship outnumbered those sitting in the pews, 45 percent to 41 percent.[39]

But shrunken attendance does not mean that Americans have become a soulless people. Back in 1966, evangelist Billy Graham declared, "I know that God exists because of my personal experience. I know that I know him. I've talked with Him and walked with Him. He cares about me and acts in my everyday life."[40] A vast majority of U.S. citizens still agree with Graham: they believe in God; say that heaven and hell are real places; think that the Bible is the inspired Word of God; hold true to the old-fashioned notion that prayer should be part of the nation's civic life; and adhere to the maxim that prayers can make a powerful difference in their personal lives. According to one inventory,

- 92 percent of Americans believe in God or a universal spirit, including 21 percent of atheists and 55 percent of agnostics;[41]

- 86 percent support a constitutional amendment permitting prayer in the public schools;[42]

- 82 percent believe in the healing power of prayer;[43]

- 81 percent believe in heaven;[44]

- 79 percent say religion has played a role in making them the person they have become;[45]

- 78 percent think the Bible is the inspired Word of God;[46]

- 78 percent say prayer is an important part of their daily lives;[47]

- 78 percent believe there is a life after death;[48]

- 76 percent express the view that through the life, death, and resurrection of Jesus, God provided the way for forgiveness of sins;[49]

- 69 percent believe in hell;[50]

- 55 percent claim to have received a definite answer to a prayer request.[51]

Taking note of similar data, Samuel P. Huntington concludes, "At the start of the twenty-first century, Americans were no less committed and quite possibly were more committed to their Christian identity than at any time in their history."[52] Alan Wolfe agrees: "Let a court try to decide, as one did in San Francisco, that the words 'under God' should not be in the Pledge of Allegiance, and the reaction will be both swift and furious."[53]

But Americans no longer believe that belonging to a particular church and faithfully attending its services is necessary to make them a moral people. In *After Heaven: Spirituality in America since the 1950s,* Wuthnow contends that "a traditional spirituality of inhabiting sacred places has given way to a new spirituality of seeking—that people have been losing faith in a metaphysic that can make them feel at home in the university and that they increasingly negotiate among competing glimpses of the sacred, seeking partial knowledge and practical wisdom."[54] Today, 58 percent of Americans say it is not necessary to believe in God to be moral citizens with good values.[55] More than two-thirds agree that someone can be both a moral person and an atheist.[56] And only 20 percent cite religion as "the most important factor" in the formation of one's own personal values.[57]

This separation of faith from the buildings that house it is a relatively new phenomenon. By the end of the twentieth century, an overwhelming 82 percent of Americans thought that a person could be a good Christian or Jew without attending a church or synagogue;[58] 56 percent agreed that it was important "to follow one's conscience, even if that meant going against what the churches or synagogues say and do";[59] and 53 percent did not believe it is necessary to strengthen religion to improve the nation's moral values.[60] As Alexis de Tocqueville noted nearly 150 years ago, "The Americans combine the notions of Christianity and of liberty so intimately in their minds that it is impossible to make them conceive the one without the other."[61] The results have included a multitude of expressions of private faith (even within a single household) and a decline in the public practice of it. Nowhere is this development more evident than among baby boomers. This plethora of faiths (even within individuals) has not only altered the U.S. religious landscape but changed the relationship between institutional religions on the one hand and soul-filled citizens on the other.

The Death of Doctrine

Given that soulful Americans are detaching themselves from the institutional churches of their childhoods, it is not surprising that more Americans than ever before are unwilling to either condemn many behaviors as sinful or adhere to a rigid doctrine as prescribed by a particular faith. Although 84 percent of respondents tell pollsters that they still believe in the idea of sin, many are increasingly reluctant to employ the term.[62] David Brooks invented the word *flexidoxy* (a combination of the words *flexibility* and *orthodoxy*) to characterize present-day thinking about sin and religious doctrine. Instead of a Last Judgment, Brooks envisions doctrinaire-free Americans preferring a "Last Discussion" with the Almighty.[63]

The tendency to eschew doctrinaire language is reflected in a profound reluctance to identify many behaviors or situations as sinful. Thus, 72 percent of those surveyed reject the notion that AIDS might be "God's punishment for immoral sexual behavior," with 52 percent expressing their "complete disagreement" with the idea.[64] Similarly, 69 percent reject the idea that divorce is a sin, with 48 percent "strongly disagreeing" with that contention.[65] The result, according to social scientist Os Guinness, is that Christianity is "strong numerically" and "weak culturally" because of "the watering down of the message."[66] Sociologist David Popenoe makes a similar connection between the absence of sin and the rise of secular individualism, whose chief attributes include "the gradual abandonment of religious attendance and beliefs, a strong leaning toward 'expressive values' that are preoccupied with personal autonomy and self-fulfillment, and a political emphasis on egalitarianism and the tolerance of diverse lifestyles."[67]

The National Cultural Values Survey lends credence to these scholarly observations, finding that just 36 percent of participants believed that "people should live by God's teachings and principles." An additional 15 percent thought that "people should always live their lives by their own personal set of morals and values, even when they contradict God's teachings and principles," and another 45 percent believed that "people should live their lives by a combination of God's teachings and a personal set of moral values." Only 30 percent of respondents in the same study believed that a strong religious grounding "is the most important ingredient to living a good and moral life"; 49 percent say that religious beliefs "are only one of many essential ingredients to living a good and moral life," and 19 percent contend that "having deep religious beliefs is not an essential ingredient at all to living a good and moral life." Looking at these figures, the directors of the Culture and Media Institute, which sponsored the study, concluded, "America no longer enjoys a cultural consensus on God, religion, and what constitutes right and wrong."[68]

This lack of consensus makes many Americans uncomfortable. In one survey, 71 percent of respondents thought that their fellow citizens were "too tolerant and accepting of behaviors that in the past were considered immoral or wrong."[69] Another poll found that 62 percent of those surveyed agreed that "immoral actions by one person can corrupt society in general."[70] According to Brooks, the "toppling of old authorities has not led to a glorious new dawn but instead to an alarming loss of faith in institutions and to spiritual confusion and social breakdown."[71] But the present discomfiture at having no absolute sense of what constitutes right or wrong does not mean that religious orthodoxy is making a comeback. Far from it. Indeed, the refusal to live by established religious doctrine is altering the ways in which Americans practice their faith and how churches respond to it.

The Catholic Conundrum

One illustration of this trend is contemporary Catholics' attitudes toward the sacrament of confession. Fifty years ago, Monsignor Thomas Kane, pastor of St. Patrick's Church in Rockville, Maryland, would spend Saturday afternoons sitting in a confessional booth and listening to a litany of sins, with would-be confessors "lined up and down the aisle to the front doors of the church." But on a typical Saturday afternoon in 2003, Kane heard no more than six confessions and completed his priestly duties in a mere 45 minutes. Surveys reflect the dwindling numbers of confessors: fewer than 25 percent of Catholics say that they have gone to confession in the past 12 months; an additional 57 percent say they "never" or "almost never" go to confession.[72]

Surveying the empty confessional booths, Washington, D.C., archbishop Donald W. Wuerl began a media campaign, The Light Is on for You, to get Catholics to go to confession. To reach out to those who had not gone to confession in years, Wuerl took to the airwaves to beckon wayward Catholics to come back to their local churches on Wednesday evenings and have priests hear confessions. Such pleas from Wuerl and other church leaders often fall on deaf ears, however. Kane blames the decline of confession on many Catholics' unwillingness to acknowledge that sin even exists: "This may be a little philosophical, but I don't think there's a sense that there's intrinsic evil. A kind of moral relativism has taken over. . . . Nothing is really wrong. If I have a good reason to do it, it's not a sin."[73] Pope Benedict XVI agrees that Catholics are "losing the notion of sin," adding, "Any tendency to treat religion as a private matter must be resisted."[74] Catholic University of America sociologist William V. D'Antonio argues that changing conceptions of sin have created "a different attitude toward conscience—both a greater respect for it on the part of the church hierarchy and a greater sense among the laity that they have a right to their own conscience. And that leads them to think they haven't done anything wrong."[75]

Polling among Catholics lends support to the ongoing privatization of belief: 86 percent say it is possible to disagree with the Pope on articles of faith and still be a "good Catholic," and 83 percent believe a person can have sexual relations before marriage and remain a "good Catholic."[76] Addressing the bishops at the Catholic University of America during a papal visit to the United States, Pope Benedict XVI denounced such thinking: "Is it consistent to profess our beliefs in church on Sunday, and then during the week to promote business practices or medical procedures contrary to those beliefs? Is it consistent for practicing Catholics to ignore or exploit the poor and the marginalized, to promote sexual behavior contrary to Catholic moral teaching, or to adopt positions that contradict the right to life of every human being from conception to natural death?"[77] Despite these pontifical warnings, the inevitable conclusion from survey research is that American Catholics believe that what constitutes a "good Catholic" is not for church leaders to decide but is a matter of individual conscience. As one young Catholic put it, "I just feel as long as you live a life without harming others or yourself . . . , then you really are living the way God intended you to live."[78]

This diminution of sin makes it much harder for church leaders to have their authority accepted with the deference to which they were previously accustomed. The sex abuse scandal that rocked the U.S. Catholic Church in 2002 has certainly taken its toll. According to a 2008 poll, 73 percent of respondents disapproved of how church leaders handled the sexual abuse of minors by priests; 58 percent "strongly disapproved."[79] The scandal's toll on church leadership has been incalculable. No longer is the hierarchy given the benefit of the doubt or seen as the authoritative voice on most church doctrine. Thus, when one Catholic priest told his congregants that revelation came from God through the church hierarchy and that only it "was in a position to translate revelation to lay people," one parishioner, already upset by the priest abuse scandal, vociferously objected: "I believe God reveals himself to all of us in different ways. God reveals himself in family experiences and work experiences and as laity we have a special wisdom that comes from being a layperson."[80]

Reflecting on the origins of Voice of the Faithful, an organization of

Catholic laity formed after the revelations of priestly sexual abuse, one member described his change of heart toward the church hierarchy: "As Catholics we have been the abused, not sexually, but by being treated like children. I think a lot of us felt this; it was bottled up and then all of a sudden it came flying out and there was no way to stuff it back."[81] D'Antonio reports that there is today "not one age group or gender where there is a majority saying they look to church leaders as the automatic source of authority."[82] Overall, D'Antonio and his colleagues find that Catholics increasingly rely on themselves as a source of moral authority on the important issues they and their church face (see table 8).

Many Catholics' willingness to dissent from church doctrine began with the 1968 publication of *Humanae Vitae*, Pope Paul VI's declaration that using birth control pills was sinful. Steinfels wrote that the document "spurred questioning by the clergy as well as by the laity of the church's moral competence in matters of sexuality. Theologians publicly dissented from official teaching; priests quietly or not so quietly resigned from the priesthood to marry; nuns shed not only their peculiar head-to-foot garb

TABLE 8. Sources of Moral Authority, U.S. Catholics on Moral Issues, 1987–2005 (in percentages)

	1987	1993	1999	2005
Church Leaders				
Divorce and remarriage without an annulment	23	23	19	22
Practicing contraceptive birth control	12	14	10	13
Advocating choice regarding abortion	29	21	20	25
Engaging in homosexual behavior	32	26	20	24
Engaging in nonmarital sex	34	23	23	22
Individuals (themselves)				
Divorce and remarriage without an annulment	31	38	45	42
Practicing contraceptive birth control	62	57	62	61
Advocating choice regarding abortion	45	44	47	44
Engaging in homosexual behavior	39	39	49	46
Engaging in nonmarital sex	42	44	47	47
Both				
Divorce and remarriage without an annulment	43	37	32	35
Practicing contraceptive birth control	23	26	23	27
Advocating choice regarding abortion	22	33	29	30
Engaging in homosexual behavior	19	30	25	28
Engaging in nonmarital sex	21	30	26	30

Source: William V. D'Antonio, James D. Davidson, Dean R. Hoge, and Mary L. Gautier, *American Catholics Today: New Realities of Their Faith and Their Church* (Lanham, Md.: Rowman and Littlefield, 2007), 96.

but, in many cases, their traditional roles as schoolteachers and nurses, and not a few left their strife-ridden religious orders altogether." Steinfels likens *Humanae Vitae* to the Vietnam War, noting that both created large rifts in society. But, he adds, there was one crucial difference: the United States exited Vietnam, while the papacy has intensified its commitment to opposing artificial birth control.[83]

As more and more Catholics began to deviate from established doctrine, church leaders became increasingly exasperated. In 1987, Pope John Paul II chastised those Catholics who believed that they could choose which of the church's moral teachings to comply with and which to reject: "It is sometimes reported that a large number of Catholics today do not adhere to the teaching of the Catholic Church on a number of questions, notably sexual and conjugal morality, divorce, and remarriage. Some are reported as not accepting the clear position [of the church] on abortion. It has to be noted that there is a tendency on the part of some Catholics to be selective in their adherence to the Church's moral teaching. It is sometimes claimed that dissent from the magisterium is totally compatible with being a 'good Catholic,' and poses no obstacle to the reception of the Sacraments. This is a grave error that challenges the teaching of the Bishops in the United States and elsewhere."[84] On the eve of his selection as Pope in 2005, Cardinal Joseph Ratzinger issued a similar warning. Presiding over the funeral of Pope John Paul II, Ratzinger took dead aim at those who selectively accept church doctrine: "We are building a dictatorship of relativism that does not recognize anything as definitive and whose ultimate goal consists solely of one's own ego and desires."[85] Listening to the homily, the members of the assembled College of Cardinals were impressed, naming Ratzinger to succeed John Paul II. The new Pope took the name Benedict XVI.

Despite the popularity of Pope John Paul II's and Benedict XVI's promulgations against "moral relativism" within the Vatican walls, these papal declarations have created a schism among the Catholic laity. Today, "Orthodox Catholics" long for a bygone era when church teachings were unquestioningly accepted, while a growing number of "Cafeteria Catholics" pick and choose which doctrines to accept. In this new environment, church leaders must either use the bully pulpit of their altars (along with other media forums) to make their arguments or risk facing more empty pews. The rise of Cafeteria Catholics does not mean that all Catholic teachings are rejected. According to a 2008 survey, 73 percent of Catholics believe abortion is a sin. Moreover, 76 percent agreed with the Vatican that "willfully harming the environment is a sin," a figure that jumped to 83 percent among Catholics born after 1960.[86] Still, the unwillingness of Catholics and many other religiously minded citizens to condemn most behaviors as sinful illustrates their desire to have their morality writ small. According to D'Antonio, Catholics have become "quite tolerant about the truth claims of other religions—tending to believe that all religions have at least some truth. Their commitment no longer includes claims of being the one, true church."[87]

The trend among Catholics to eschew the idea of sin is broadly reflected in the public at large. According to one survey, 73 percent of respondents believe that "all people are inherently good when they are born," an explicit refutation of the doctrine of original sin. The same poll found that 51 percent agreed with the statement, "Immoral thoughts are okay as long as they don't become immoral actions."[88] In another poll, only 45 percent of participants believed that premarital sex was sinful, and just 30 percent condemned gambling. In fact, only a few actions are judged to be sinful, including adultery (81 percent) and racism (74 percent).[89]

This general refusal to label most individual actions as either moral or immoral is especially prevalent among the young. Pollster Dick Morris asked respondents of many faiths whether they were governed by a strict code of morality or whether they let individual common sense dictate their actions. Those aged 35 or younger were split between adherence to a strict moral code and individual common sense, whereas those older than 65 were much more inclined to be governed by a larger moral code (see table 9). An Eleventh Commandment seems to have taken hold among the nation's young: "Thou shalt not make moral judgments about other people's behavior." As one Yale coed told the school's chaplain some years ago, "I don't know whether I'll ever believe in God, but [the all-knowing yet all-forgiving] Jesus is my kind of guy."[90]

A Heinz 57 Church

This change in attitude has caused many churches to make very different appeals to would-be worshipers. Rather than stressing adherence to particular doctrines or rules, pastors often strike a welcoming and forgiving tone from their pulpits. One Oregon minister, for example, told Wolfe that his was a "Heinz 57" church, meaning that his congregants believed in a wide variety of doctrines. Another declared, "It's alright to be different, as long as you're not different from the Lord." Faith in Jesus, this particular pastor reasoned, was essential, but "everything else concerning doctrine is negotiable."[91] The result is a kind of fungible Christianity. According to a 2008 Pew Forum Report on Religion and Public Life, 70 percent of Americans believe that many religions can lead to eternal life.[92] Gregory Smith, a Pew research fellow, summarized the findings: "Even though Americans tend to take religion quite seriously and are a highly religious people, there is a certain degree of openness and a lack of dogmatism in their approach to faith and the teachings of their faith."[93]

Given this nearly doctrine-free environment, it is not surprising that many people see Christian evangelization as becoming passé. Wuthnow reports that very few Christians have attempted to persuade non-Christians to join their faith: only 4 percent have tried to persuade a Muslim; just 2 percent have evangelized to a Hindu.[94] Exactly what it means to be a Christian is often left to congregants' imagination, thanks to leaders' willingness to allow considerable discretion in the pews. And congregants, for their part, appreciate pastors' willingness to deemphasize fire-and-brimstone sermons. Presbyterian Betty Taylor told Wolfe that she likes her church because there is "so much leeway" concerning doctrine; her minister encourages "questioning and arriving at your own conclusions about beliefs."[95] At Taylor's church and many others, sin is frequently discussed

TABLE 9.   Morality and the Generation Gap (in percentages)

Age Group	Statement A: Governed by a Strict Code of Morality	Statement B: Governed by Common Sense
Under 35 years	40	45
36–55 years	52	38
56–65 years	54	32
Over 65	54	32

Source: Dick Morris, *Vote.com* (New York: Renaissance Books, 1999), 78–79. Text of question: "Agree/Disagree. Statement A: I believe in a strict code of morality and right and wrong which comes from God's word and the Bible. I try to live by it. Drugs and illicit sex are wrong, so I don't engage in them. To do so would violate my personal, moral, and religious beliefs. Statement B: My conduct is governed more by common sense and practicality than by abstract morality. It is more factors, like the dangers of AIDS, the possibility of pregnancy, and the importance of a good marriage than morality or religion that stops me from illicit sex. The bad experiences people have had with drugs and the way I have seen it mess up lives is the reason I abstain from them, not some moral judgment that drugs are wrong."

in terms of how it harms the individual, not how it offends God. The prevalence of such thinking has led Wuthnow to declare, "In the United States, all religions are true."[96]

The resulting conflict between those who like their morality writ large (and view sin as part of an eternal narrative between good and evil) and those who prefer their morality writ small (and reject any suggestion of dogma) marks an emerging distinction between what Wolfe describes as a "nurturing" Christianity (emphasizing individual needs) and an "authoritative" Christianity (stressing eternal truths). As a more nurturing Christianity gains favor with religiously minded citizens, the result, Wolfe claims, is a kind of doctrinal death:

> Americans, who shun overly intellectual ideas on radio and television, are also likely to avoid faiths that ask them to take doctrine seriously. They define themselves and each other by their religion, yet they are willing to shape and reshape the traditions that offer religions their distinctive identities. They pay homage to a force larger than themselves. Americans know that faith offers fellowship, but then they treat the institutions capable of offering fellowship with a decided suspicion. They believe that religion is a precondition for morality but are not at all surprised when religious figures prove themselves immoral. They understand that God judges some of what they do as sinful, but they do not believe him to be too demanding and they avoid trying to judge each other. And those who feel a special obligation to spread their faith acknowledge that, for the sake of neighborliness, they are reluctant to shove anything down anyone else's throat.[97]

The Triumph of Individualism

In 1968, journalist and television personality David Frost asked a Democratic and a Republican presidential candidate, "What do you think we are on Earth for?" The Republican responded,

> Well, of course, the biologist I suppose would say that like all breeds of animals, the basic instinct is to reproduce our kind, but I believe it's inherent in the concept that created our country—and in the Judeo-Christian religion—that man is for individual fulfillment; for our religion is based on the idea not of any mass movement but of individual

salvation. Each man must find his own salvation; I would think that our national purpose in this country—and we have lost sight of it too much in the last three decades—is to be free—to the limit possible with law and order, every man to be what God intended him to be.[98]

The Democrat's answer had a very different emphasis:

I think you have to break it down to people who have some advantages, and those who are just trying to survive and have their family survive. If you have enough to eat, for instance, I think basically it's to make a contribution to those who are less well off. "I complained because I had no shoes until I met a man who had no feet." You can always find someone that has had a more difficult time than you do, has suffered more, and has faced some more difficult time one way or another. If you've made some contribution to someone else, to improve their life, and make their life a bit more livable, a little bit more happy, I think that's what you should be doing.[99]

Both Ronald Reagan and Robert F. Kennedy saw the meaning of life as connected to the individual's relationship to God. But Reagan's answer placed great emphasis on the one-to-one relationship between human beings and the Almighty, while Kennedy stressed collective action with God as its center. Charlie Peters, editor of the *Washington Monthly*, quipped that Reagan's answer was the religious version of John F. Kennedy's famous inaugural address: "Ask not what you can do for God, but what God can do for you."[100] More seriously, for Reagan the connection between God and the individual was a personal choice (one that often eschewed doctrine) that left little room for the institutional church. As president, Reagan did not often attend church services, citing security concerns. Yet the real reason might well have been his long-standing belief that the connection between God and human beings transcended the institutional church. In contrast, RFK's response emphasized the Social Gospel, with its stress on a communitarian approach and on fulfilling the words of Jesus to reach out to the least among us. For Kennedy, the institutional church had a prominent role in fulfilling social needs, since collective public action required a focal point, and churches are a logical place to house and give direction to such compassionate outreach.

Reagan and Kennedy provide crucial insights into two strains of religious thought, the ongoing debate between those who focus on the individual's relationship to God, with its emphasis on the present and hereafter, and those who think faith must beget collective action to promote the social needs of the here and now. This tension has been repeated throughout American history. Tocqueville noted that in the United States, religious expression emphasized equality by allowing individuals to commune with God, while public assemblies focused on the need for social action that stressed the common good:

> It must be acknowledged that equality, which brings great benefits into the world, nevertheless suggests to men . . . some very dangerous propensities. It tends to isolate them from one another, to concentrate every man's attention upon himself; and it lays open the soul to an inordinate love of material gratification.
>
> The greatest advantage of religion is to inspire diametrically contrary principles. There is no religion that does not place the object of man's desires above and beyond the treasures of earth and that does not naturally raise his soul to regions far above those of the senses. Nor is there any which does not impose on man some duties toward his kind and thus draw him at times from the contemplation of himself. This is found in the most false and dangerous religions.
>
> Religious nations are therefore naturally strong on the very point on which most democratic nations are weak; this shows of what importance it is for men to preserve their religion as their conditions become more equal.[101]

Today, many observers believe that Tocqueville's vision of equality and religion have lost their equilibrium. The decline of institutional churches and the self-centeredness of religious practice have resulted in a failure of some churches to meet their obligations to the larger society. Kathleen Kennedy Townsend, the daughter of Robert F. Kennedy, is among this group: "Not so long ago, our churches helped engage their congregations in the fight for social justice in the world. But today I am unhappy and dissatisfied with my [Roman Catholic] Church and its failure to honor its best traditions."[102] Even Pope Benedict XVI sees an American Catholic overemphasis on the individual at the expense of the collective good: "In a society which values personal freedom and autonomy, it is easy to lose sight of our dependence on others as well as the responsibilities we bear towards them. . . . We were created as social beings who find fulfillment only in love—for God and for our neighbor."[103] The Reverend Bob Edgar, general secretary of the National Council of Churches and a former member of Congress, is adamant that churches must do more. In *Middle Church*, Edgar cites the late Hubert H. Humphrey as setting the standard for socially minded religious Americans: "It was once said that the moral test of Government is how that Government treats those who are in the dawn of life, the children; those who are in the twilight of life, the elderly; and those who are in the shadows of life, the sick, the needy, and the handicapped." According to Edgar, the United States is "flunking the test."[104]

For many observers of American religious expression, the current personalization of faith is akin to the personalization of politics. Eschewing doctrine—indeed, deriding it as being pointless—has given way to a faith that emphasizes the personal (i.e., the entertainment value of a sermon and liturgy, a sense of belonging to a particular community but not necessarily committing to something larger beyond it). Townsend was "stunned" when Pastor Rick Warren, head of the Saddleback Community Church, a megachurch, informed her that in twenty-five years of ministry, "he had never, until recently, considered religion's role in helping the poor at all."[105]

Yet for every shrunken congregation and for every diminished commitment to social justice, there are people like Chris and Gabrielle Wagener (she's Jewish, he's Roman Catholic), who are determined to find their individual pathways to God. Rather than regularly attending either a church or synagogue, the Wageners blend their religious customs and teach them to their children at home. Says Gabrielle, "I'm going to start my own tradition, and it may be different from my parents, but that's okay."[106] Wuthnow believes the Wageners's experience is typical: "A person is no longer limited simply to deciding whether to be a Baptist, a Lutheran, or a Catholic. . . . With dozens of small groups meeting in their neighborhoods, individuals trying to identify a comfortable spiritual niche can shop around more easily."[107]

Baby boomers are especially emblematic of the religious predilections expressed by the Wageners. According to sociologist Wade Clark Roof, baby boomers are "spiritual seekers, shopping around for bits and pieces of religious wisdom from various traditions."[108] Wolfe agrees that baby boomers are relentless in searching for religious combinations that suit their individualistic tastes: "Seeking but not always finding, impatient for results, anxious for authenticity, ever sensitive to hypocrisy, the religious life of the American people may not yet have experienced the turbulence of professional sports, where free agents search around for the team that will offer them the best contract, or the cut-your-own-best-deal retirement plans that increasingly characterize the benefits offered by American business firms. But it does seem to be heading in that direction."[109] Or, as one disabilities counselor and daughter of a Methodist minister has found, sometimes the best deal is not with one church but with many. She described herself to David Brooks as a "Methodist Taoist Native American Quaker Russian Orthodox Buddhist Jew."[110]

Interfaith marriages are certainly one reason for today's religious individualism. In a 1955 Gallup poll, a mere 4 percent of respondents did not adhere to the religion of their childhoods.[111] By the 1980s, that figure had risen to one in three, and by 2008, 44 percent of adults had switched their religious affiliations, moved from being unaffiliated with any religion to belonging to a particular faith, or dropped any connection to a specific religious tradition.[112] Not surprisingly, only 42 percent of all single adults believe it important to find a mate who shares their church membership.[113] Says Brooks, "The American tendency to switch religions—sometimes several times over the course of a lifetime—is probably unprecedented in world history."[114]

Yet switching religions does not make God any less personal, as Wolfe notes: "When they worship, Americans revere a God who is anything but distant, inscrutable, or angry. They are more likely to honor a God to whom they can pray in their own, self-chosen way." The result, Wolfe claims, is that "all of America's religions face the same imperative: Personalize or die." As one person put it, congregants should not be "weak and co-dependent on a structure or a man to tell us how to think or what to say or to DEFINE WHO WE ARE IN CHRIST."[115]

For many Americans, finding God happens not within an institutional church but in the doctrinaire-free privacy of their own homes. Pollster George Barna reports that 9 percent of adults presently attend a house church on a weekly basis (a ninefold increase in just 10 years), while another 70 million have experienced a religious service in someone's home. By 2025, Barna predicts that the market for the megachurches will be cut in half by growth in the home-church market.[116]

For others, religious individualism comes from either shedding or modifying the practices of their immigrant forebears. One young Korean

Christian described his journey away from his parents' church: "I felt like I had a grasp of what the Korean church had to offer. I just wanted a new direction, wanted to see what else was available."[117] This college student's experimentation was hardly novel; in fact, some estimates show that more than half of second-generation Koreans have participated in a silent exodus from the church of their fathers. Chinese immigrants have experienced a similar phenomenon. At the Chinese Christian Church in Washington, D.C., English-language services are the norm and the presiding pastor was hired because, according to one parishioner, "he cites no Chinese stories [and] refers to no Chinese cultural values or customs."[118]

Some Hispanic immigrants have also experienced a migration away from the Roman Catholic Church of their forebears. Many observers note the tremendous growth in the number of Hispanics who have switched to evangelical churches. While precise figures are hard to obtain, Ron Unz, chair of Wall Street Analytics, believes that "a quarter or more of Hispanics have shifted from their traditional Catholic faith to Protestant evangelical churches, a religious transformation of unprecedented speed, and one obviously connected partly to their absorption into American society."[119] One Jesuit priest believes that Hispanic evangelicals are seeking a "more self-conscious, individualized faith," which evangelical Protestantism offers.[120] Vineyard Church in Monrovia, California, offers Hispanics an opportunity to engage in Pentecostal worship without converting from their Catholic faith. According to the church, "faith," not "religion," counts. Even the school that trains new ministers for this church boasts that it is "a multiethnic school that helps each group develop its own approach to reaching its people for Christ."[121] Immigrant individualism in religious practice is a bold step from which others follow. As Wolfe aptly observes, "A Buddhist from China or a Catholic from Mexico who becomes Protestant upon arrival in the United States has made one giant step, and after it is made, follow-up choices are never quite as momentous."[122]

The End of the White Anglo-Saxon Protestant Majority

In 1962, political journalist Richard Rovere observed, "It is now, of course, conceded by most fair-minded and objective authorities that there is an Establishment in America—a more or less closed and self-sustaining institution that holds a preponderance of power in our more or less open society." Rovere noted that the Establishment "maintains effective control over the

Executive and Judicial branches of government; . . . dominates most of American education and intellectual life; . . . has very nearly unchallenged power in deciding what is and what is not respectable opinion in this country. Its authority is enormous in organized religion (Roman Catholics and fundamentalist Protestants to one side), in science, and indeed, in all the learned professions except medicine."[123] In short, Rovere believed that membership in a mainline Protestant church was essential for gaining admission into the Establishment.

Today, that power is rapidly disappearing. For a country once so closely associated with the term *white Anglo-Saxon Protestant*, the number of WASPs is rapidly declining. From 1993 to 2008, the proportion of Americans who identified themselves as Protestants fell from 63 percent to 51 percent.[124] Purdue University sociologist James Davidson notes, "We're right at the point where Protestants have become the minority for the first time in history. That fact alone is making some folks in the Protestant community quite nervous."[125] Indeed, the losses among some elements of Protestantism are nothing short of monumental. According to the Pew Research Center, mainline Protestant churches constitute just 18 percent of America's faithful, far fewer than the 26 percent who identify with evangelical churches.[126] For some sects, the decline in membership has been momentous: the Episcopal Church lost more than 25 percent of its members from 1965 to 1990; Presbyterians, 33 percent; United Church of Christ, 23 percent; the Disciples of Christ, 46 percent; Methodists, 20 percent.[127] Today, mainline Protestants are in third place among religious identifiers, behind Roman Catholics and evangelicals. According to political scientist John C. Green, "We didn't have a religious establishment in the United States, but we did have large, prominent denominations with power and influence. That has fallen apart." Green adds, "If you're well-connected, you don't need to be a Presbyterian elder" to ascend to a local leadership position.[128]

One reason for the declining numbers is the postponement of marriage. More Americans are delaying marriage and children, and singles tend to stay away from church. With the passage of time, these religious sabbaticals tend to become permanent. During his 2008 U.S. visit, Pope Benedict XVI told the Catholic bishops, "How can we not be dismayed as we observe the sharp decline of the family as a basic element of Church and society? Divorce and infidelity have increased, and many young men and women are choosing to postpone marriage or to forgo it altogether."[129] As many observers have noted, the redesign of the family away from the traditional model of married parents residing with their children has meant that even when adults do remarry, fewer attend church, and they do so less frequently. Even Protestant evangelicals are subject to the same trends, as the number of evangelicals who are married and have children has declined, causing membership to dwindle. Membership in the Southern Baptist Convention, which soared during the 1970s, is now barely keeping up with population growth.[130]

At the same time, other religions—particularly non-Christian denominations—have showed a marked growth. For example, the number of Muslims in the United States grew 109 percent from 1990 to 2008. Over that same period, the number of Buddhists grew 170 percent; Hindus, 237 percent; adherents of Native American religion, 119 percent; Baha'is, 200 percent; Sikhs, 338 percent; and Taoists, 74 percent.[131] These faiths remain dwarfed by the more than 159 million Americans who subscribe to some form of Christianity and the 2.8 million who are Jewish. Nonetheless, as Diana Eck notes, such rising numbers have "shattered the paradigm of America" as an overwhelmingly Judeo-Christian country with a white Anglo-Saxon Protestant majority. Add the more than 27 million people who subscribe to no religious faith, and it is evident why the once mighty WASP majority is no more.[132]

The Rise of the Megachurch

While changing relationships between Americans and the churches they have traditionally known have produced fewer people in the pews, the major exception has been the growth of so-called megachurches. These large edifices gather between 2,000 and 30,000 worshipers on any given Sunday. Today there are more than 1,200 megachurches throughout the United States, far more than the mere 74 that existed in 1983. They include Robert Schuller's Crystal Cathedral in Orange Grove, California; Joel Osteen's Lakewood Church in Houston; Rick Warren's Saddleback Valley Community Church in Lake Forest, California; and Bill Hybels's Willow Creek Community Church in South Barrington, Illinois. Osteen usually attracts 30,000 to Sunday services, held in a former basketball arena; Warren routinely gets 22,000, and Hybels, 20,000. The Crystal Cathedral congregation exceeds 10,000 members, while its *Hour of Power* television program claims to reach nearly 20 million people in 180 countries.[133]

These churches are especially popular not just because of their dynamic and entertaining liturgies but also because they seek to be one-stop shopping centers that cater to both the spiritual and the physical. Houston's Second Baptist Church is typical: it fields 64 softball teams, 48 basketball teams, and an orchestra and chorus. In addition, it houses six bowling lanes, an indoor jogging track, and weight and aerobics rooms.[134] James B. Twitchell, author of *Shopping for God*, claims that megachurches "have done for churching what Wal-Mart did to merchandising. They are the low-cost deliverer of salvation." Barry Harvey, a professor of contemporary theology at Baylor University, agrees: "The church is essentially becoming indistinguishable from its biggest competitor, the mall. To allow the commercial enterprise to come into the church is to allow the desire for accumulating things, buying things, to dominate even the relationship with God."[135]

But to credit the success of the megachurch to its Wal-Mart-style product pitch is to miss the spiritual hunger such churches seek to address. Barack Obama maintains that the megachurches' success is directly proportional to their meeting the needs of so many spiritually hungry Americans:

> Each day, it seems, thousands of Americans are going about their daily rounds—dropping off the kids at school, driving to the office, flying to a business meeting, shopping at the mall, trying to stay on their diets— and coming to the realization that something is missing. They are deciding that their work, their possessions, their diversions, their sheer busyness are not enough. They want a sense of purpose, a narrative arc to their lives, something that will relieve a chronic loneliness or lift them above the exhausting, relentless toll of daily life. They need an assurance that somebody out there cares about them, is listening to them—that they are not just destined to travel down a long highway toward nothingness.[136]

Nowhere is the appeal of the megachurch more apparent than in Lake Forest, California, home to Saddleback Community Church. According to *Washington Post* columnist E. J. Dionne Jr., Warren canvassed the community for twelve weeks before starting his church, telling those he met, "I'm not here to sell you anything, I'm not here to convert you, I'm not here to witness to you. I just want to ask you three or four questions." Warren's "ingenious" queries included:

Question number one: "Are you an active member of a local church—of any kind of religion—synagogue, mosque, whatever?" If they said yes, I said, "Great, God bless you, keep going," and I politely excused myself and went to the next home. When I'd find somebody who'd say, "No, I don't go anywhere," I'd say, "Perfect; you're just the kind of guy I want to talk to. This is great, you don't go anywhere. So let me ask you a question. Why do you think most people don't attend church?" And I just wrote the answers down. I asked, "If you were looking for a church, what kind of things would you look for?" And I'd just list them. "What advice would you give to me as the pastor of a new church? How can I help you?" So they'd say, "I think churches exist for the community; not vice versa," and I'd write that down.

Now the four biggest reasons in my area why people didn't go to church—here's what they were: Number one, they said, "Sermons are boring and they don't relate to my life." So I decided I had to say something on Sunday that would help people on Monday. Number two, they said, "Members are unfriendly to visitors; I feel like it's a clique." Number three, they said, "Most churches seem more interested in your money than you as a person." And number four, they said, "We want quality children's programs for our children."

Now it's interesting to me that out of the four biggest reasons why people said they didn't go to church, none of them were theological. They were all sociological. And I had people say, "Oh, it's not that I don't like God. I like God; I just can't stand church." I go, okay; we'll build a whole new kind of church.[137]

Many of these megachurches, including Warren's, eschew any emphasis on religious doctrine. Like clergy in many more traditional churches, successful megapastors deemphasize the notion of sin. According to Osteen, "I never thought about [whether I use the word *sinners*], but I probably don't. Most people already know what they're doing wrong. When I get them to church, I want to tell them that you can change."[138] Instead of conjuring vivid images of hell, many megapastors prefer to preach their own version of Americanism, the Prosperity Gospel. In Surprise, Arizona, Pastor Lee McFarland oversaw a congregation's growth from just a few members to more than 5,000 weekly churchgoers with his "successful principles for living" message. Says McFarland of his emphasis on personal finances, "If Oprah and Dr. Phil are doing it, why shouldn't we? We should be better at it because we have the power of God to offer."[139] As Wolfe puts it, "Jesus will save your soul and your marriage, make you happy, heal your body, and even make you rich. Who wouldn't look twice at that offer?"[140]

The successes enjoyed by so many megachurches has left other, more traditional congregations scrambling. When St. James Episcopal Church in Bowie, Maryland, found itself attracting only 40 worshipers each Sunday, leaders decided to hire a consultant to devise a plan for increasing the congregation's size. The Reverend Anne-Marie Jeffrey admits that her challenge is great: "We live in a megachurch world. It's going to be interesting to see if we can [grow]."[141] Dean Hoge, a sociologist and professor at the Catholic University of America, was pessimistic about American Protestantism's ability to meet the challenge, telling the *San Diego Tribune* in 1994 that the question was not whether mainline Protestantism would survive but for how long: "To bring back the church the way it used to be, I just don't think that's going to happen."[142]

Revival of the Culture Wars

During the 1960s, when the Catholic Church was undergoing profound changes in its thinking and approaches to the faithful, the church hierarchy noted in its Vatican II documents that altering church practices would not undermine essential doctrine: "The body of the faithful as a whole, anointed as they are by the Holy One . . . cannot err in matters of belief. Thanks to a supernatural sense of the faith which characterizes the People as a whole, it manifests this unerring quality when, from the bishops down to the last member of the laity, it shows universal agreement in matters of faith and morals."[143] More than a century earlier, Tocqueville arrived at a similar conclusion: "The sects that exist in the United States are innumerable. They all differ in respect to the worship which is due to the Creator; but they all agree in respect to the duties which are due from man to man. Each sect adores the Deity in its own peculiar manner, but all sects preach the same moral law in the name of God."[144] Vaclav Havel expressed similar sentiments at the turn of the twenty-first century: "[I]t seems to me that the major faiths have much more in common than they are willing to admit. They share a basic point of departure—that this world and our existence are not freaks of chance but rather part of a mysterious, yet integral, act whose sources, direction and purpose are difficult for us to perceive in their entirety. And they share a large complex of moral imperatives that this mysterious act implies. In my view, whatever differences these religions might have are not as important as these fundamental similarities."[145]

Yet despite these common areas of agreement—a consensus that continues to hold sway among the public—Americans are engaged in a culture war that includes not just the politics of persona (as described in previous chapters) but also matters of faith. Writing to the editors of *Time* magazine in response to its 1966 cover, "Is God Dead?" Jesuit priest Stephen R. DeAngeles noted, "It must be frankly admitted by Catholics that the 'new theology' that preaches an atheistic secularism cannot be casually dismissed as a fad. It is too prominent, too widespread, and seeks to rock the essentials of a Christian faith that must articulate a position in the face of such a challenge."[146] DeAngeles's recognition of an "atheistic secularism" was prescient.

As secularism has become more prevalent, hurt feelings on both sides of the religious culture wars have intensified because, in the words of Jon Meacham, author of *American Gospel*, "both sides feel they're losing."[147] The infusion of religion into the culture wars has created a set of conditions whereby those on the political right and left stake out extreme positions in the debate. Wuerl recently asserted that Catholics and other religiously minded Americans have been excluded from the public square, an exclusion that he believes has coarsened public debate:

> [U]ntil very recently in our public civic life mention of God was taken for granted and prayer inspired by God was a routine part of public, government-sponsored programs and activities. What was expected of the one offering the prayer was that it be generic enough so as not to exclude the specific denominational sensitivities of the vast majority of those present. Hence, one did not use a formula of prayer that clearly spoke to only one religious tradition.
>
> The current non-acceptability of reference in public civil life to any religious point of transcendence has become a matter of preoccupation.[148]

Other Catholics adopt an even harsher tone, especially in the wake of the 2008 election, in which their side in the culture wars, the Republican ticket of John McCain and Sarah Palin, was defeated by Barack Obama and Joseph Biden. In a speech at the Catholic University of America, Cardinal Joseph Francis Stafford called Obama's election "a cultural earthquake" and likened his presidency to Jesus's agony in the Garden of Gethsemane: "For the next few years, Gethsemane will not be marginal. We will know that garden."[149] Stafford and others in the Catholic hierarchy cited Obama and Biden's pro-choice views on abortion, and some Catholic prelates refused to offer Biden communion, a refusal that is particularly noteworthy because as vice president, Biden is the highest-ranking Catholic in government since John F. Kennedy. The bishop in Biden's hometown, Scranton, Pennsylvania, was particularly forceful: "No Catholic politician who supports the culture of death should approach Holy Communion. I will be truly vigilant on this point."[150]

On the other side of the culture wars is author Christopher Hitchens. In *God Is Not Great* (2007), Hitchens argues that "religion poisons everything" and maintains that all traces of religion should be expunged from the public square in favor of a renewed (and secular) Enlightenment:

> The study of literature and poetry, both for its own sake and for the eternal questions with which it deals, can now easily depose the scrutiny of sacred texts that have been found to be corrupt and confected. The pursuit of unfettered scientific inquiry, and the availability of new findings to masses of people by easy electronic means, will revolutionize our concepts of research and development. Very importantly, the divorce between the sexual life and fear, the sexual life and disease, and the sexual life and tyranny, can at last be attempted, on the sole condition that we banish all religions from the discourse. And all this and more is, for the first time in our history, within the reach if not the grasp of everyone.[151]

Elites' prevailing sense that they are losing the culture war has spread to the public at large. According to the National Cultural Values Survey, the gulf between the 31 percent of Americans who are "Orthodox" (those who are religiously observant, seek to live by God's teachings, and consider religious faith essential to living a moral life) and the 17 percent of citizens who are "Progressives" (those who advocate a secularized approach to private and public life and do not think that religion is essential for living a moral life) has grown into a chasm. Even "Independents" (46 percent), who reject both the Orthodox and Progressive viewpoints and believe that religion is just one of many ingredients needed to live a moral life, are caught up in the culture wars (see table 10). As opinions polarize, both

TABLE 10.   The Culture Wars Revisited

Issue	Orthodox	Independents	Progressives
Having deep religious beliefs is the most important ingredient to living a good and moral life.			
Percentage "agree"	82	6	0
Religious beliefs are one of many essential ingredients to living a good and moral life.			
Percentage "agree"	17	84	13
Having deep religious beliefs is not an essential ingredient at all to living a good and moral life.			
Percentage "agree"	1	9	86
People should always live by God's teachings and principles.			
Percentage "agree"	92	10	2
People should live their lives by a combination of God's teachings and a personal set of moral values.			
Percentage "agree"	8	82	17
People should always live their lives by their own personal set of morals and values even when they contradict God's teachings and principles.			
Percentage "agree"	0	4	77
Every situation has a clear set of right and wrong behaviors and people should behave accordingly.			
Percentage "agree"	63	36	20
Some situations don't have a clear set of right and wrong behaviors and people should act accordingly.			
Percentage "agree"	33	58	66
In every situation, people should behave however they feel comfortable and not be tied down by subjective judgments of right and wrong.			
Percentage "agree"	2	5	13

Source: Culture and Media Institute, *The National Cultural Values Survey* (Alexandria, Va.: Culture and Media Institute, 2007), 2–4.

sides have come to believe that the other side does not respect their views, and they find themselves increasingly alienated from each another.

The four revolutions depicted in this book—racial, family, gay-rights, and religious—have upended our outdated twentieth-century understandings of politics. Applying old nostrums to present-day politics often results in misreading the forces that are reshaping the American electorate. Many years ago, sociologist Daniel Bell reminded us of the Latin phrase "nomen est numen" (to name is to know). Bell wrote that "*nomen* are not merely names but concepts, or prisms. A conceptual schema selects particular attributes to discern similarities and differences. As a logical ordering device, a conceptual schema is not true or false but either useful or not. . . . Conceptual prisms are logical orders imposed by the analyst on the factual order."[152]

As the politics of the twenty-first century unfolds in the midst of these four revolutions (any one of which would be enough to transform politics as previously understood), it is good to be reminded of that old Latin phrase. Too often, we misname and therefore do not know what is happening in our contemporary politics. The revolutions in race, family, sexual identity, and religious life clearly show no signs of abating. As a result, the once-familiar in American politics—that which we have named and have known so well no longer applies and a new, still unnamed, and not yet fully realized politics is emerging.

Six • The Death of the Reagan Coalition

"We are dying at the box office."
—ARNOLD SCHWARZENEGGER, 2007

IN 1959, RONALD REAGAN received an unsolicited fan letter. While it was not unusual for the famous actor to get mail from his many admirers, the author of this particular missive was the vice president of the United States, Richard M. Nixon. Preparing to seek the presidency the following year, Nixon admired Reagan's ventures into politics, telling the actor, "You have the ability of putting complicated technical ideas into words everyone can understand. Those of us who have spent many years in Washington too often lack the ability to express ourselves in this way."[1] Nixon urged Reagan to "continue your very effective speeches," hoping that the Hollywood celebrity would abandon his Democratic roots and back the vice president in his forthcoming race against John F. Kennedy.[2] Replying from his Southern California home, Reagan prophesied the coming conservative revolution, darkly warning, "It is our responsibility to see that our freedom is not sacrificed from within—lost by default." He added, "[W]e are told that it is we who have asked for and received each of our services from the government. But how many of the current government programs have resulted from the demands of the people? Isn't it true that government itself has dangled many programs before us with no mention of the ultimate cost or the loss in personal freedoms? In many cases the people in government were well-meaning, but aren't we justified in suspecting that there are those who have fostered the growth of government by deliberate intent and design?"[3]

Nixon's letter to Reagan was prophetic. Nixon recognized Reagan's raw political talent, his grace and stage presence—both of which Nixon lacked. Thirty years later, Reagan left the White House a beloved president known as the Great Communicator, while Nixon retained the aura of shame that had accompanied his resignation from the nation's highest office.[4] On the eve of becoming president, Reagan revealed his knack for politics when a reporter asked what voters could possibly see in the actor turned politician: "Would you laugh if I told you that I think, maybe, they see themselves and that I'm one of them? I've never been able to detach myself or think that I, somehow, am apart from them."[5]

As president, Reagan never forgot his audience. Shortly before leaving the presidency, he acknowledged that his acting skills lay behind many of his successes: "There have been times in this office when I've wondered how you can do this job if you hadn't been an actor."[6] Reagan's command of the stage was such that he often expressed amazement at his ability to woo a crowd. In a diary entry written early in his presidency, for example, Reagan described a particularly enthusiastic response from a New York City audience:

> The streets were lined with people as if for a parade all the way to the Waldorf [Hotel]. They cheered & clapped and I wore my arms out waving back to them.
>
> I keep thinking this can't continue and yet their warmth & affection seems so genuine I get a lump in my throat. I pray constantly that I won't let them down.[7]

Reagan won the hearts of his countrymen not because he articulated conservative ideas but because he grasped and conveyed a vision of a country during happier and simpler times. Reagan biographer Richard Reeves captures the essence of Reagan's political acumen, noting that he was a dreamer who wanted to take the nation "back into remembrances of his own boyhood and a *Reader's Digest* version of the 1950s."[8] Indeed, whenever Reagan recollected his childhood, he painted idyllic portraits: "There were woods and mysteries, life and death among the small creatures, hunting and fishing. . . . Waiting and hoping for the winter freeze without snow so that we could go skating on the Rock River . . . swimming and picnics in the summer, the long thoughts of spring, the pain with the coloring of the falling leaves of autumn."[9] Creating these pictures meant overlooking major blemishes, including his father's alcoholism and the family's frequent relocations during the Great Depression as a consequence of his dad's inability to hold a job.

Reagan's presidency was, as Reeves eloquently states, a triumph of our collective imaginations. Addressing cultural leaders in Moscow, he revealed one of the most important secrets of success both as an actor and as president: "You must see and feel what you are thinking. . . . You must hold and fix it in your memory and senses. To grasp and hold a vision, to fix it in your senses—that is the very essence, I believe, of successful leadership."[10] For Reagan, that meant clinging to his imagined vision of an America during the 1950s. In his 1989 Farewell Address, Reagan made one final plea for the resuscitation of the traditional family values that his fellow citizens had once so uniformly accepted:

> Those of us who are over thirty-five or so years of age grew up in a different America. We were taught, very directly, what it means to be an American, and we absorbed almost in the air a love of country and an appreciation of its institutions. If you didn't get these things from your family, you got them from the neighborhood, from the father down the street who fought in Korea, or the family who lost someone at Anzio. Or you could get a sense of patriotism from school. And if all else failed, you could get a sense of patriotism from the popular culture. The movies celebrated democratic values and implicitly reinforced the idea that America was special. TV was like that, too, through the mid-sixties.[11]

Reagan's vision carried weight because the voters' collective memories encompassed the idyllic pictures he painted. And Reagan frequently referred to those festive times, not only in the vivid word portraits contained in his speeches but in the imagery created in his campaign commercials. The most memorable of those commercials was "Morning in America" (1984), which used a series of iconic images to depict an idealized version of American life much as Reagan himself envisioned it: a briefcase-toting dad climbing into a station wagon and heading for work while a kid on a bike tosses the morning paper onto his front porch; a pair of young newlyweds leaving church and kissing as a set of grandparents looks on approvingly; a mom, dad, and kids bringing the latest acquisition (a carpet) into their home (complete with white picket fence); a family outside a log cabin hoisting an American flag; a police officer doing the same. The advertisement concluded with an announcer making the pitch that Reagan had restored pride and patriotism to their rightful places in the civic culture:

> It's morning again in America. Today more men and women will go to work than ever before in our country's history. With interest rates at about half the record highs of 1980, nearly 2,000 families today will buy new homes, more than at any time in the past four years. This afternoon 6,500 young men and women will be married, and with inflation at less than half of what it was just four years ago, they can look forward with confidence to the future. It's morning again in America, and under the leadership of President Reagan, our country is prouder and stronger and better. Why would we ever want to return to where we were less than four short years ago?[12]

Reviewing the commercial today, one is struck that all of the characters depicted are white (though one child at the end may be biracial). The emotive images of newly married couples moving into new homes—along with proud, patriotic communities celebrating traditional family values—certainly resonated with white voters, who gave Reagan 56 percent of their votes in 1980 and 64 percent in 1984.[13]

In his 1980 campaign, Reagan presented himself as having just the right tonic for what ailed the country, promising to usher in "an era of national renewal [that would] revitalize the values of family, work, and neighborhood."[14] For years, Reagan had worried about the effects of the women's rights and sexual revolutions on his idealized 1950s-era vision of the family. As he wrote while serving as governor of California, "I am deeply concerned with the wave of hedonism—the humanist philosophy so prevalent today—and believe this nation must have a spiritual rebirth, a rededication to the moral precepts which guided us for so much of our past, and we must have such a rebirth very soon."[15] In 1979, Reagan pollster Richard Wirthlin discovered that Americans were not joining the Reagan cause because of the issues per se; rather, people had a prevailing unease that a rapid erosion of the country's values was creating an era of personal anomie. Revealingly, Wirthlin learned,

- two-thirds of Americans agreed with the statement that "everything changes so quickly these days that I often have trouble deciding which are the right rules to follow";

- a majority said that the country was "better off in the old days when everyone knew just how they were expected to act";

- 71 percent believed that "many things our parents stood for are going to ruin right before our eyes";

- nearly 8 in 10 believed that "what is lacking in the world today is the old kind of friendship that lasted for a lifetime";

- one in two described themselves as "left out of things going on around me."[16]

Into this breach stepped the veteran actor. In his personal appearance, Reagan was a prototypical 1950s organization man, complete with neatly folded handkerchief in his breast pocket, white shirt, knotted tie, dark blue suit, and polished black shoes. Reagan the salesman not only pitched himself as a reincarnation of Robert Young in *Father Knows Best* but also sold the electorate on a Republican Party that would, in his words, "build a new consensus with all those across the land who share a community of values embodied in these words: family, work, neighborhood, peace, and freedom."[17] The party's 1980 platform elaborated on its standard-bearer's themes:

> We will reemphasize those vital communities like the family, the neighborhood, the workplace, and others which are found at the center of our society between government and the individual.[18]

Reagan's rhetoric never deviated from that plank. Thus, he extolled "parents who sacrifice long and hard so their children will know a better life than they've known; church and civic leaders who help to feed, clothe, nurse, and teach the needy; millions who've made our nation and our nation's destiny so very special—unsung heroes who may not have realized their own dream themselves but then who reinvest those dreams in their children."[19] Reagan later commemorated Mother's Day by calling the nation's moms "quiet, everyday heroes [from whom] we first learn about values and caring and the difference between right and wrong."[20] Listeners could have easily imagined that Reagan was describing the real Harriet Nelson, as portrayed in *The Adventures of Ozzie and Harriet*, or the mythical June Cleaver and Betty Anderson of *Leave It to Beaver* and *Father Knows Best*.

Reagan also resorted to telling stories, as, for example, in 1987, when the besieged president left the nation's capital to escape the fury of the Iran-Contra affair. Just after Air Force One landed in the relatively friendly environs of West Lafayette, Indiana, the president told a large crowd about a letter he received concerning a boy named Billy. Reagan vividly described the scene: Billy nagged his father to oblige him in his sole pastime of playing baseball, while Billy's dad wanted to relax and read the Sunday newspaper. To stall the boy, the father cut a newspaper map of the world into tiny pieces and asked Billy to tape it back together. The two agreed that when Billy had completed the task, they would play ball. In just seven minutes, Billy put the map together. When asked how he had accomplished this seemingly impossible task so quickly, the boy proudly responded, "On the other side of the map there was a picture of the family, and I found that if you put the family together the world took care of itself."[21] At that, the crowd burst into applause. Nancy Reagan, who understood her husband's knack for reading audiences, said, "There's a certain cynicism in politics. You look back [on] a statement for what a man really means. But it takes people a while to realize that with Ronnie you don't have to look in back of anything."[22]

This simplicity in the president's thinking helped him make a powerful connection with voters who shared both his sense of order and his reverence for tradition. Indeed, the longing for order was particularly apparent in the place that gave birth to Reaganism, Southern California. Recalling his childhood there, political scientist James Q. Wilson observed that an obsessiveness with normalcy was constantly on display: "Each family had a house: there it was for all to see and inspect. With a practiced glance, one could tell how much it cost, how well it was cared for, how good a lawn had been coaxed into uncertain life, and how tastefully plants and shrubs had been set out." On their Sunday afternoon drives, families would call on friends, visit distant relatives, and see the sights—and examine other people's homes and evaluate the neatness of their neighborhoods.[23]

An old adage holds that success in politics requires the person and the moment to meet. Such was the case for Reagan in 1980. The longing for order following defeat in Vietnam, the Watergate scandals and Nixon's resignation, and the societal revolutions of the 1960s and 1970s were crucial to Reagan's enormous electoral victories.[24] In his campaign biography, *The Audacity of Hope*, Barack Obama captured the spell that Ronald Reagan cast on the electorate:

> [A]s disturbed as I might have been by Ronald Reagan's election in 1980, as unconvinced as I might have been by his John Wayne, *Father Knows Best* pose, his policy by anecdote, and his gratuitous assaults on the poor, I understood his appeal. It was the same appeal that the military bases back in Hawaii always held for me as a young boy, with their tidy streets and well-oiled machinery, the crisp uniforms and crisper salutes. It was related to the pleasure I still get from watching a well-played baseball game, or my wife gets from watching reruns of *The Dick Van Dyke Show*. Reagan spoke to America's longing for order, our need to believe that we are not simply subject to blind, impersonal forces but that we can shape our individual and collective destinies, so long as we rediscover the traditional virtues of hard work, patriotism, personal responsibility, optimism, and faith.[25]

From first to last, Reagan never deviated from emphasizing the nostrums of family, work, neighborhood, peace, and freedom. By creating such vivid mental images, Reagan, in the words of former ABC News anchor Peter Jennings, "held us spellbound."[26]

"We Will Act as If He Were Here"

Shortly after the unsuccessful attempt on Ronald Reagan's life in 1981, Vice President George H. W. Bush flew to the nation's capital from Houston, where he had been attending a dedication ceremony. Arriving at a panic-stricken White House, Bush told Reagan's shaken Cabinet, "We will act as if he were here."[27]

In many ways, the Republican Party has followed Bush's advice ever since. The vice president essentially won Reagan's third term in 1988 by promising to pursue the fortieth president's conservative values; twelve years later, Bush's son, George W. Bush, promised to outdo Reagan in cutting taxes and reaching out to evangelicals with his faith-based initiatives. The younger Bush demonstrated a remarkable penchant for making Reagan's values his own. Seeking reelection as Texas governor in 1998, a Bush television advertisement had the candidate echoing Reagan: "Whether for government or individuals, I believe in accountability and responsibility. For too long, we've encouraged a culture that says if it feels good, do it, and blame somebody else if you've got a problem. We've got to change our culture to one based on responsibility." Two years later, Bush told a New Hampshire audience that while winning the presidency would be a great honor, it would not be his most important accomplishment: "After power vanishes and pride passes, this is what remains: The promises we kept. The oath we fulfilled. The example we set. The honor we earned. . . . We are united in a common task: to give our children a spirit of moral courage."[28] *Washington Post* columnist E. J. Dionne Jr. noted that Bush's rhetoric resonated with those discomfited by alterations both in family life and in the popular culture: "If you hate the 1960s, you love this stuff."[29]

By explicitly rejecting the sexual freedom espoused during the "Make love, not war" heyday of the 1960s, George W. Bush offered himself as a reincarnated Reaganesque father figure, someone who, unlike the morally challenged Bill Clinton, would set a personal example as president that complemented his publicly stated commitment to traditional family values. Conservative commentator Andrew Sullivan once likened the governing style followed by Bush and his vice president, Dick Cheney, to a 1950s-era Hallmark card: "The model of their masculinity is definitely retro—stern dads in suits and ties, undemonstrative, matter-of-fact, but with alleged hearts of gold."[30] First Lady Laura Bush similarly presented herself as someone who lacked any aspirations other than being a helpmeet to her husband. Laura Welch quit her job as a librarian to marry George W. and became a stay-at-home mom after her twins were born.[31] In 2004, President Bush's values strategy reached its zenith: 22 percent of voters cited "moral values" as their most important concern, and 80 percent of that group backed him.[32]

But unlike his father, George W. wanted to do more than be a pale imitation of Reagan.[33] Both Bush and his political strategist, Karl Rove, believed that a combination of new issues and changing demography would destroy the rough equilibrium in which the two major parties found themselves after the Bush-Gore tie of 2000 and give the Republicans a solid majority. Accordingly, the younger Bush championed tax reductions at a greater and faster pace than Reagan, proudly signing a major tax cut into law just five months into his first term, three months faster than the venerable Reagan had done so.

Bush also sought to take away the Democratic advantage on education by championing the No Child Left Behind law, even overcoming the GOP's state's-rights-based resistance. In 2007, Michigan Republican Peter Hoekstra capitalized on his party's feelings of buyer's remorse and collected signatures from 65 GOP House members on a measure that would allow states to opt out of the law's requirements. Says Hoekstra, "I always had misgivings [about No Child Left Behind]. But I did vote for it on the basis that maybe [Bush] was right and this was his big domestic initiative and let's give him a chance. But all my concerns . . . have proven to be justified."[34] Bush similarly suppressed intraparty opposition when he demanded that the Republican-controlled Congress enact a $140 billion Medicare prescription drug benefit, the largest federal entitlement program since Medicare itself was enacted in 1965.[35] Florida congressman Tom Feeney was one of several GOP members who berated the new entitlement as a betrayal of the party's historic commitment to fiscal conservatism: "It was probably the greatest failure in my adult lifetime."[36] But these Bush-engineered legislative victories achieved an important strategic goal: neutralizing the Democratic advantage on education and Medicare. Both Bush and Rove knew that Clinton had won an unexpected victory in 1996 by using the formula M2E2—shorthand for Medicare, Medicaid, education, and the environment—and emphasizing how a Democratic-controlled White House would preserve these programs from a Republican-led onslaught. Now Bush and his fellow Republicans could claim credit for the preservation and expansion of two crucial Clinton-era ideas.

To satisfy evangelical voters who had moved en masse into the Republican tent during the Reagan years but who were becoming increasingly dissatisfied with the Republican Party's inability to satisfy their demands (especially with regard to stopping abortion), Bush proposed government-sponsored faith-based initiatives. The idea had arisen during Bush's governorship, when he championed programs such as Second Chance, which provided group homes for unwed teenage mothers; some of the homes were run by faith-based groups. As president, Bush promised that his administration would restore religious organizations to "an honored place in our plans and in our laws," adding a biblical reference: "When we see that wounded traveler on the road to Jericho, we will not pass to the other side."[37]

Finally, as noted in chapter 2, Bush made a major play for Hispanic voters by championing immigration reform.[38] Bush's rhetoric resonated with

Hispanics, and he held Democrat John F. Kerry to just 58 percent of their votes in 2004.[39] Yet despite these herculean efforts to engender a Republican realignment, former National Committee chair Ken Mehlman conceded on the eve of the 2008 contest that "conditions remain where they were" in 2000.[40] The realignment for which Republicans had hoped had not taken place. In fact, an emerging new demography had changed everything, leaving the GOP in an especially weakened condition.

"We Are Dying at the Box Office"

After the turn of the twenty-first century, Reagan's appeal to a 1950s-era America with its traditional families and tightly structured moral codes lost its aura. The Pew Research Center found that between 1987 and 2007, public support for "old fashioned values and family and marriage" dropped from 87 percent to 76 percent.[41] A year before John McCain and the Republicans were beaten at the presidential polls, another actor turned politician, California governor Arnold Schwarzenegger, sounded an alarm. Noting that his party had shed 370,000 registered voters in his state in just two years, Schwarzenegger analogized the Republicans' perilous plight to that of a failed motion picture: "In movie terms, we are dying at the box office. We are not filling the seats."[42] Virginia Republican Tom Davis told his House colleagues that the party's brand was "in the trash can": "[I]f we were a dog food, they would take us off the shelf."[43]

One reason why Republicans are losing support is that they appear to be a party of naysayers. Even though the world has profoundly changed since the Reagan-dominated 1980s, Schwarzenegger, for one, believes his party has not changed with it: "In business if you lose market share, you do something about it. But I wonder if we've been so beaten down by our minority status that we've developed a bunker mentality? I wonder if we've come to believe that our only remaining power is to say no?"[44]

Indeed, saying no is not enough to build a winning campaign. In 2006, Pennsylvania Republican Rick Santorum structured his reelection effort around the notion that his no-nonsense prescriptions about the importance of adhering to traditional values merited his return to the U.S. Senate. Denouncing the demise of the 1950s-era family, Santorum claimed that individual selfishness had tempted women to surrender their stay-at-home mom roles: "Many women have told me, and surveys have shown, that they find it easier, more 'professionally' gratifying, and certainly more socially affirming, to work outside the home than to give up their careers to take care of their children. Think about that for a moment. What happened in America so that mothers and fathers who leave their children in the care of someone else—or worse yet, home alone after school between three and six in the afternoon—find themselves more *affirmed* by society?"[45]

Santorum's assault on the social and cultural liberalism of the 1960s and 1970s generated outright skepticism, even from members of his own party. Donna Wright, a Republican township supervisor, said of Santorum's bromides, "Women are entitled to their choice, whether they become professionals or stay home. I don't appreciate anyone, public figure or not, telling anyone what they can and cannot do." Vicki Lightcap, another Republican, explained that she cast her senatorial vote for Democrat Bob Casey because "Women do have a future in politics, we have a future in our business professions, and it's up to us to become role models for our daughters—and our sons."[46] Sixty-one percent of Pennsylvania's women felt similarly, and Santorum suffered a landslide defeat, losing by a margin of 59 percent to 41 percent.[47]

Santorum's loss was emblematic of a troubled GOP future. His defeat did not happen simply because George W. Bush and the Iraq War were wildly unpopular. Rather, Santorum's evocation of Reagan's "family, work, neighborhood, peace, and freedom" values mantra appealed to a much smaller slice of the electorate. According to exit polls, Santorum's best sources of support were the same groups that had formed the heart of the Reagan coalition: Republicans (86 percent), conservatives (80 percent), white evangelical born-again voters (71 percent), more-than-weekly churchgoers (65 percent), and those who believed abortion should be illegal (64 percent).[48] But the electoral coalition that was vibrant enough to elect Santorum in 1994 and 2000 had lost voters and could not replace them with others. Moreover, Pennsylvania has voted Democratic in five straight presidential contests: Clinton in 1992 and 1996, Gore in 2000, Kerry in 2004, and Obama in 2008. In 2009, Santorum's former Republican seatmate in the Senate, Arlen Specter, saw the writing on the wall and bolted to the Democrats.

Despite the overwhelming Republican victory in the 1980 presidential election, one ambitious Democratic politician saw vulnerability in the Reagan coalition. Speaking before the Mecklenburg County Democratic Men's Club in Charlotte, North Carolina, in 1981, Bill Clinton told listeners that while Reagan had accomplished a good deal in a few months, he and the Republican Party were courting eventual trouble: "Reagan is pandering to the people who want to tell the rest of us how to live. The Republican party is trying to tell the rest of us whether we are moral or not. We will never make heaven on Earth; that is what heaven's for."[49] Today, conservative scholar Bruce Bartlett has reached a similar conclusion: "There are cycles in history where one party or one movement ascends for a while and then it sows the seeds of its own self-destruction. It's clear we have come to an end of a Republican conservative era."[50]

By the first decade of the twenty-first century, personal experimentation with the definition of the family, along with demographic changes that have turned the face of America bronze, have brought the Reagan juggernaut to a halt. Put bluntly, the Reagan coalition, like the old actor himself, has died of natural causes.

An Exhausted Philosophy

Seeking reelection to the presidency in 1932, Herbert Hoover declared that on Election Day, voters would choose "between two philosophies of government": "You cannot extend the mastery of government over the daily life of a people without somewhere making it master of people's souls and thought."[51] Franklin D. Roosevelt disagreed, noting that under Hoover, the nation was afflicted with "hear-nothing, see-nothing, do-nothing government" operating under a "doctrine that the government is best which is most indifferent."[52] Although Hoover lost decisively, the philosophy he articulated survived and was resurrected by former New Dealer Ronald Reagan. Hoover's laissez-faire, minimalist approach to governance has always appealed to a free, prosperous, and middle-class nation—the latter two qualities sorely lacking in 1932. The perennial challenges to would-be conservative presidents include (1) how to say no to new government initiatives without being perceived as naysayers and (2) how to set forth an action agenda to address urgent problems that require a federal response.

These problems did not hamper the conservative movement when Reagan took the helm in 1980. After five decades of big government, many Americans had come to agree with Reagan when he said, "In the present crisis, government is not the solution to our problem; government is the problem."[53] By making the bloated bureaucracy a target, Reagan's proposed surgery became part of a new, action-oriented conservative agenda. Before Reagan, activist presidents had been liberals—for example, Woodrow Wilson, Franklin D. Roosevelt, Harry S. Truman, John F.

Kennedy, and Lyndon B. Johnson. Beginning with Reagan, activist presidents were conservatives—Reagan and George W. Bush.

But Reagan's denunciations of big government did not represent a rejection of the past; rather, Americans deemed the New Deal and Great Society unqualified successes. In 1937, Roosevelt bleakly outlined the problems besetting a nation still crippled by the Great Depression:

> I see millions of families trying to live on incomes so meager that the pall of family disaster hangs over them day by day.
>
> I see millions whose daily lives in city and on farm continue under conditions labeled indecent by a so-called polite society half a century ago.
>
> I see millions denied education, recreation, and the opportunity to better their lot and the lot of their children.
>
> I see millions lacking the means to buy the products of farm and factory and by their poverty denying work and productiveness to many other millions.
>
> I see one-third of a nation ill-housed, ill-clad, ill-nourished.[54]

By 1980, FDR's "ill-housed, ill-clad, ill-nourished" nation had become decidedly middle class, despite the inflationary pressures so often associated with prosperity. The result was not a populace that wanted more government but a nation of taxpayers that viewed government through the green eyeshades of penny-pinching accountants. Yet instead of shrinking government, Reagan made it cheaper. Daniel Patrick Moynihan noted that during the Reagan years, "For seventy-five cents worth of taxes, you got a dollar's worth of return."[55] Reducing the rate of government growth—and the taxation that accompanied it—were central goals of the Reagan administration. And they were accomplished. Former Reagan campaign manager Ed Rollins believes that Reagan's successes have rendered his once-potent coalition inert: "[W]hat was the Reagan coalition—social conservatives, defense conservatives, anti-tax conservatives—it doesn't mean a whole lot to people anymore."[56] Conservative columnist Brendan Miniter agrees. Writing in the *Wall Street Journal*, Miniter claims that the political windfall once associated with the Reagan (and later Bush) tax cuts has passed its zenith: "On both the national and state level, some Republicans are starting to bet that they know where the point of diminishing political returns is, and that for tax cuts, we've already reached it."[57]

In foreign affairs, Reagan took on the mantra of "peace through strength," and he and his fellow Republicans claimed a significant victory in this arena. In 1991, the Soviet Union collapsed, fulfilling Reagan's 1983 prophesy: "I believe that communism is another sad, bizarre chapter in human history whose last pages even now are being written."[58] But the fall of communism created new problems for the GOP. By 1992, Reagan's successor, George H. W. Bush, was a Cold War president without the Cold War. Bush tried to turn voter attention to his foreign policy successes, plaintively telling CNN's Frank Sesno, "I hope every mother and dad out there says, 'Hey, we ought to give this president a little credit out there for the fact that our little kids don't worry so much about nuclear war.' Isn't that important?"[59] It was important, but the Reagan coalition was already entering its death throes—again, as a consequence of its architect's singular successes.

Reagan's domestic and foreign policy triumphs, like those of FDR and LBJ, created a unique set of challenges for the Republican Party. After having turned Reagan's conservative platitudes into law, what remained for the Republicans to do except continuously to seek and hold power? The problem became especially acute by 1988, when reporters repeatedly asked George H. W. Bush what he would do as president. Bush derided the queries, dubbing them "the vision thing." Not only did Bush avoid answering, but his campaign staff encouraged him to do so. Policy adviser Deborah Steelman noted that if Reagan's heir were to declare himself on a few big issues, "we'd have less of a chance to win than we do."[60]

During the Clinton years, Republicans continued to avoid setting forth a futuristic agenda. Instead, they emphasized the largely procedural items contained in their 1994 Contract with America and continued to stress their cultural differences with Clinton. Rather than thinking philosophically, Republicans concentrated on the mechanics associated with building a formidable political machine. As journalist Thomas B. Edsall explains in his insightful *Building Red America*,

Over the past forty years, the Republican Party and the conservative movement have together created a juggernaut—a loosely connected but highly coordinated network of individuals and organizations—with a shared stake in a strong, centralized political machine. This machine includes the national party itself, a collection of campaign contributors large and small, a majority of the country's business and trade associations, the bulk of the corporate lobbying community, and an interlocking alliance of muscular conservative "values" organizations and churches (The Family Research Council, the Coalition for Traditional Values, Focus on the Family, the Southern Baptist Convention, thriving Pentecostal, evangelical, and right-leaning Catholic communities, and so forth). It includes a powerful array of conservative foundations with focused social and economic agendas (Scaife, Bradley, Loin, Koch, Smith Richardson, Carthage, Earhart, etc.), as well as prosperous right-of-center think tanks such as the American Enterprise Institute, the Cato Institute, the Free Congress Foundation, the Heritage Foundation, and the Manhattan Institute. This interlocking alliance—a "new conservative labyrinth"—has proven deft at redefining key American concepts of social justice, at marketing conservative ideologies in both domestic and international affairs, and at successfully integrating these redefined ideals—in the eyes of many voters—with goals of economic efficiency.[61]

Newt Gingrich led Republicans on the final phase of their 40-year odyssey to reclaim control of the House of Representatives. But after taking power in 1994, Republicans came to see it as an end in itself. As former Federal Reserve chair Alan Greenspan ruefully observed, the GOP has "fundamentally been focusing on how to maintain political power, and my question is, for what purpose?" Greenspan noted that under George W. Bush, a party that had stood for fiscal accountability became a big spender, leading the economist to conclude, "The Republican Party, which ruled the House, the Senate, and the presidency, I no longer recognize."[62] Greenspan has a point: in 1940, the GOP had a 17-point advantage over the Democrats as the party more likely to balance the federal budget; six years later, the GOP beat the Democrats by 31 points as the party best able to "cut down government expense."[63] More than a half century ago, when the Gallup Organization asked respondents why they identified with the Republican Party, the most common answers were

- policies: more conservative, 100 percent American—28 percent;
- more economical with money, cut taxes—16 percent;
- favor business, encourage free enterprise—13 percent;
- tradition: family Republican, always been Republican—13 percent;
- oppose welfare state, socialism, government regulation—5 percent.[64]

But in the George W. Bush years, many of these GOP strengths disappeared. A 2004 American Enterprise Institute study found that during Bush's first term, federal discretionary spending rose by an astounding 30.2 percent. Only Lyndon B. Johnson's Great Society ("We're in favor of a lot of things and we're against mighty few") had outspent Bush.[65] The party of fiscal responsibility suddenly lost credibility on this core issue, even among its own faithful. Bartlett claimed that Bush was a "pretend conservative."[66] New York City mayor Michael Bloomberg maintained that the level of federal indebtedness that future taxpayers will have to absorb constituted "lunacy."[67] Bloomberg was so upset at the Republican Party's lack of fiscal discipline that he abandoned the party in 2007 to become an independent.

If liberal Republicans such as Bloomberg were upset with Bush's record spending, conservatives were apoplectic. Paul Weyrich of the Free Congress Foundation rebuked Bush for his free-spending fiscal policies: Bush "says, 'Well, I had a Republican Congress and I didn't want to go against a Republican Congress.' Well, why not? He could've vetoed all those bills. People would've been happy about it." Richard Cooper, a Reaganite Republican and former chair of Weight Watchers, argues that "Democrats are the new conservatives" thanks to their alarms about deficit spending and calls to end the Bush tax cuts.[68] Even David Frum, author of a sympathetic 2003 pro-Bush book, has recanted.[69] In a provocative 2008 work, *Comeback: Conservatism That Can Win Again*, Frum wrote that Bush's presidency was a conservative catastrophe: "On the debit side: So many mistakes! And such stubborn refusal to correct them when there was still time! So many lives needlessly sacrificed, so much money wasted, so many friends alienated, so many enemies strengthened."[70]

Libertarian-minded Republicans were equally unhappy, deeply disturbed by Bush's eavesdropping on millions of private telephone conversations and ordering phone companies to provide the federal government with records of calls made, all without court approval. House minority leader John Boehner voiced skepticism about Bush's actions: "I am not sure why it would be necessary to keep and have that kind of information."[71] Former Republican congressman and MSNBC commentator Joe Scarborough issued a scathing indictment: "Memo to the President and congressional leaders who signed up on this lousy program: We don't trust you anymore. We don't trust you with our phone bills. We don't trust you with our bank records. We don't trust you with our medical histories. From now on, if you want to look at Americans' private records, get a damn search warrant!"[72]

Just as southerners deserted the Democratic Party in droves during Reagan's heyday, record numbers of liberal Republicans are abandoning the party of their forebears. In 2007, former Rhode Island senator Lincoln Chafee, the son of John H. Chafee, Rhode Island's governor from 1963 to 1969 and a U.S. senator from 1976 until his death in 1999, left his father's party to become an independent. Lincoln Chafee opposed Bush on such key issues as the Iraq War, the environment, and the administration's creation of "permanent deficits," believing that Bush had taken the Republican Party far from its origins. Declaring that the GOP was "not my party anymore," Chafee denounced Bush as a "rogue president" who had started an "unnecessary war."[73] Leaving the GOP, he said, "felt good."[74] In 2008, Chafee took the final step away from the Republicans by endorsing the presidential bid of Democrat Barack Obama, a staunch opponent of the Iraq War, which Chafee described as "a colossal error in judgment. For Americans who feel like I do, we deserve a choice on this issue."[75]

Chafee is not the only New England Republican to defect. In 2001, Vermont Republican Jim Jeffords became an independent, thereby handing control of the U.S. Senate to the Democrats. Like Chafee, Jeffords disagreed with Bush on a host of issues—"choice, the direction of the judiciary, tax and spending decisions, missile defense, energy and the environment." Jeffords concluded that Bush's Republican Party no longer stood for "moderation; tolerance; fiscal responsibility."[76] A decade earlier, former U.S. senator and Connecticut governor Lowell Weicker claimed that the GOP had lost its way when it came to standing "for the rights of the individual, for equal opportunity for the individual, for private initiative, private enterprise."[77] Christine Todd Whitman, a former New Jersey governor and Environmental Protection Agency director under George W. Bush, remains a Republican but believes that her party faces "a clear and present danger" that it "will move so far to the right that it ends up alienating centrist voters and marginalizing itself."[78]

Demography Is Destiny

In May 2004, George W. Bush convened a meeting of his top reelection advisors. After thanking everyone for their hard work, Bush told them,

"Our numbers are right at where Reagan's were at this point in 1984. So that means we're headed for a big victory." At this, a bewildered look came over pollster Matthew Dowd's face, and he conveyed the bad news: "Our numbers are nowhere near Reagan's. We're like twelve to fourteen points off his. I mean, we're ahead slightly. But we're in the margin of error. And if we win, it won't be a big victory. It'll be like two or three points."[79] Dowd was right: Bush defeated Kerry by a margin of 51 percent to 48 percent. But even if Bush had equaled Reagan's popularity among the groups that had supported the fortieth president, there would have been no guarantee of victory. In the 20 years since Reagan had swamped Mondale, the Reagan coalition itself had been swamped by vast transformations in the nation's demography.

When political revolutions happen, old rules of politics are upended. Thus, when Nixon won the presidency in 1968, a rule of thumb held that Democrats needed to carry urban areas by substantial margins to offset Republican majorities everywhere else. But journalist Samuel Lubell noted at the time that Democrat Hubert H. Humphrey had overwhelmingly won urban areas yet had lost the presidency because the nation's demography had changed. For example, Humphrey decisively carried Richmond, Virginia, where the political maxim dictated that he should have won the entire state. Yet he did not.[80] Changing demography—in this case, growing suburbs dominated by whites who fled the inner cities, leaving them with black majorities—made Nixon the victor. Henceforth, Republicans could win the White House by dominating among angry suburban whites upset by school integration, inner-city crime, and race riots. In effect, the GOP became the white party, a pattern that continued under Reagan.

Today the political demography that gave Nixon, Reagan, and both Bushes the presidency—that is, near-lockstep southern support and backing among suburban whites who were married, divided their religious loyalties between some variant of Protestantism and Roman Catholicism, and had kids living at home—has changed dramatically. With each passing year, the Republican share of the presidential vote has declined to the point where old rules are again about to be broken. Nowhere is the evidence more powerful than among whites. At the onset of the twenty-first century, 69 percent of Americans were white, 12 percent were Hispanic, another 12 percent were black, 4 percent were classified as Asian and Pacific Islander, and 3 percent were listed in "some other category."[81] This is quite unlike 1970, when Richard M. Scammon and Ben J. Wattenberg described the "real majority" as being "unyoung," "unpoor," and "unblack."[82] At the time, 87.5 percent of the population was white, and only 11.1 percent was black.[83] Whites still dominate the voting population, as evidenced by the fact that 77 percent of 2004 voters were white. But only 65 percent of voters aged 18 to 24 were white. And in 2008, white voters fell to just 74 percent of the total, the smallest ever recorded.[84]

Here Come the Hispanics

As noted in chapter 2, Hispanics have become a new and potent political force. Nowhere is this more apparent than in the state that launched Reagan's political star, California. The twentieth-century version of the state that elected Reagan its governor in 1966 and 1970 and gave him its presidential electors in 1980 and 1984 no longer exists, except perhaps on the commemorative state license plates honoring the late president. By 2000, Democrats had assumed a dominant position: that year, Al Gore spent zero campaign dollars for television advertisements there, while George W. Bush laid out a hefty $20 million. Nonetheless, Gore handily beat Bush (53 percent to 42 percent), largely accounting for Gore's 500,000 edge in the national popular vote. Key to Gore's Golden State landslide was the fact that Hispanics constituted 14 percent of the electorate and gave him 68 percent of those votes.[85]

Four years later (and despite the September 11 attacks), Bush's California tallies did not significantly improve, as he received 45 percent of the vote to Kerry's 54 percent. Once again, the Democrat's Golden State victory can be attributed to the 63 percent backing he received among Hispanics. Hispanics constituted a record 21 percent of the California electorate in 2004, while whites fell to just 44 percent of those aged 18 to 24.[86] Four years later, Barack Obama won an impressive 61 percent of California's votes and took 74 percent of California's Hispanic votes, a victory made even more powerful because the Hispanic percentage of all votes cast stood at 18 percent. At the same time, the percentage of whites continued its decline, reaching 63 percent of the state's total vote.[87]

Two former Republican National Committee chairs believe that their party has too many whites. According to Mehlman, "America is every day, less of a white country. We rely too hard on white guys for votes."[88] Ed Gillespie concurs: "Our majority already rests too heavily on white voters, given that current demographic voting percentages will not allow us to hold our majority in the future."[89] According to Mehlman and Gillespie, the Republican Party's base does not reflect the café au lait face of the twenty-first-century American. If that does not change, the GOP could lose valuable votes, even in places it once took for granted.

One of the best places to see the crash of the GOP sailing ship is Orange County, California. Site of John Wayne Airport, Disneyland, and the Crystal Cathedral (home to Dutch Reform televangelist Robert Schuller), Orange County was once a bastion of right-wing Republican conservatism. For years, the profoundly anticommunist and conspiracy-minded John Birch Society called it home. A 1961 report on the group's activities compiled by California attorney general Stanley Mosk noted that the Birchers were "wealthy businessmen, retired military leaders, and little old ladies in tennis shoes."[90] Mosk's description also applied to the typical Orange County resident.

That bygone era of white faces and sunny beaches, memorialized in the 1964 hit "The Little Old Lady from Pasadena," has been replaced by an Orange County that is both multiracial and multicultural. During the 1990s, the number of Hispanics residing there rose to 31 percent, while the number of whites declined by 6 percent. The Hispanic influx was augmented by an increase in those of Asian background, who presently constitute 14 percent of the county's population.[91] A 2004 Census study found that whites had become a minority there (49 percent).[92]

The addition of Orange County to a growing list of "majority-minority" suburbs runs counter to the long-standing stereotype of the area's pristine beaches populated by sun-drenched conservative white Republicans. Such imagery still appears in popular culture, most notably on MTV's *Laguna Beach: The Real Orange County*. The only problem with this "reality" program's all-white cast of high school students is that it fails to mirror the present-day demographic realities.

Orange County's racial revolution has been accompanied by a political upheaval that has seen its white, conservative Republican officeholders replaced with Hispanic Democrats. In 1996, Loretta Sanchez beat Bob Dornan for the area's congressional seat. Dornan, a conservative Republican nicknamed "B-1 Bob" for his support of the B-1 bomber and other military hardware, began his tenth campaign supremely confident of victory: Sanchez "can't beat me," he announced. "Bob Dornan is a father of five, grandfather of ten, military man, been married forty-one years. She has no kids, no military, no track record. [Therefore,] I win."[93] But voters disagreed, and Sanchez edged Dornan by 984 votes.[94] Today, Sanchez is an entrenched incumbent, drubbing her Republican opponents every two years. In 2008, for example, Sanchez dispatched a Hispanic Republican rival by a gargantuan 44 percentage points.

When the 110th Congress convened in the nation's capital in January 2007, 30 Hispanic representatives took seats in the U.S. House, among them Loretta Sanchez and her sister, Linda, who represents the nearby town of Whittier, where Nixon grew up and began his long political odyssey.[95] The Sanchez sisters are but 2 of 24 Hispanic Democrats in the 110th Congress, a group that also includes two committee chairs and thirteen subcommittee chairs. A similar pattern emerged in the U.S. Senate, where Florida Republican Mel Martinez, Colorado Democrat Ken Salazar, and New Jersey Democrat Robert Menendez became the first Hispanic trio to serve.[96] Nationwide, there are more than 6,000 elected Hispanic officials, including officeholders in such seemingly unlikely places as Wichita, Kansas (mayor), Idaho (state senator), Minnesota (state senator), New Hampshire (state representative), and Carrboro, North Carolina (city council member).[97] Arturo Vargas, executive director of the National Association of Latino Elected and Appointed Officials Educational Fund, says, "If you want to run a winning campaign, you must have a strategy to reach and engage Latino voters."[98]

But Republicans are both unable and unwilling to do so. In 2008, McCain received a mere 31 percent of the Hispanic vote, a 13-point drop from Bush's support in 2004.[99] Throughout the 2008 campaign, Republicans alienated nonwhites in order to satisfy the party's base. For example, a Republican debate sponsored by the Spanish network Univision was canceled because McCain was the only one of the ten GOP presidential candidates who would commit to participating. One, Representative Tom Tancredo, objected on principle: "We should not be doing things that encourage people to stay separate in a separate language."[100] The GOP's problem with nonwhites became even more pronounced when only a handful of its candidates—a group that did not include front-runners McCain, Fred Thompson, Mitt Romney, or Rudy Giuliani, appeared at a public television debate to discuss issues affecting black Americans. Former GOP congressman J. C. Watts, who is black, harshly criticized the no-shows: "I think the best that comes out of stupid decisions like this is that African-Americans might say, 'Was it because of my skin color?' Now, maybe it wasn't, but African-Americans do say, 'It crossed my mind.'"[101]

The situation was further aggravated at the 2008 Republican National Convention, where only 36 of the 2,380 delegates were black, the lowest number in 40 years.[102] The absence of persons of color in the GOP led former Bush speechwriter Michael Gerson to conclude that his party may be on the verge of committing political suicide:

> In politics, some acts are so emblematic and potent that they cannot be undone for decades—as when Republican presidential candidate Barry Goldwater voted against the Civil Rights Act of 1964. Goldwater was no racist; his constitutional objections were sincere. Members of the Republican party actually voted for the Civil Rights Act in higher percentages than Democrats. But all of this was overwhelmed by the symbolism of the moment. In his autobiography, former secretary of state Colin Powell says that after the Goldwater vote, he went to his car and affixed a Lyndon Johnson bumper sticker, as did many other African-Americans.
>
> Now Republicans seem to be repeating history with Hispanic-Americans. Some in the party seem pleased. They should be terrified.[103]

Gerson was right. If Hispanics (and other nonwhites) view Republicans as the anti-immigrant party, it is disastrous for their prospects beyond 2008. Recent history makes the point. In 1994, California Republican governor Pete Wilson supported Proposition 187, a measure that banned state aid to illegal immigrants. That year, television sets across the Golden State flickered with pictures of illegal Mexicans swarming across the border as an announcer ominously intoned, "They just keep coming."[104] Thanks to these ads, Wilson and Proposition 187 won handily, with the ballot initiative passing by a margin of 59 percent to 41 percent. But while 64 percent of whites backed Proposition 187, 69 percent of Hispanics disapproved.[105] Alfredo Alvarez, a legal immigrant from Honduras, declared, "I love this country, but I feel unwanted. I feel like unless I am a true American, the government could one day knock on my door and tell me, 'Alfredo, go back to Honduras!'"[106] In 1996, the Republican presidential ticket of Bob Dole and Jack Kemp received just 21 percent of Hispanic votes, the worst Republican showing since 1972. Sal Mendoza, an insurance broker and member of one of California's local school boards, explains the GOP dilemma: "I think Republicans are so obsessed with their traditional conservatism . . . that they've lost track of the bigger picture. They're sitting on a pot of gold [the Hispanic vote] but they don't know how to mine it. And if you can't mine it, you will lose."[107]

Signs already show that California's Hispanic voting history is repeating itself on a grander scale. A 2007 Pew Research Center study found that 57 percent of Hispanics nationwide call themselves Democrats, while only 23 percent see themselves as Republicans. Among voters aged 18 to 29, the Democrats hold an overwhelming advantage of 64 percent to 18 percent. Immigration is a primary reason: 79 percent name it as a top voting issue. George W. Bush is another. He receives particularly poor marks from Hispanics, just 16 percent of whom believed that he had helped them; 41 percent claimed he hurt their cause, while 33 percent said his policies had no particular effect. Forty-one percent of the poll's participants believed that the Democratic Party did a better job of handling illegal immigration, compared to only 14 percent who chose the Republicans and 26 percent who chose neither party. Finally, when asked which party cared more about people like them, 44 percent of Hispanics chose the Democrats, 8 percent chose the Republicans, and 41 percent said neither party.[108]

A New Generation of Democrats

Today, the age group with the largest number of Republicans is persons between 43 and 54—that is, those who came of age during the Reagan years. These voters, born between 1955 and 1966, had not experienced a successful presidency until Reagan's: Kennedy was assassinated in 1963; Johnson and Nixon left the White House as discredited public figures; Ford provided a brief but not very consequential interlude; and Carter was a disappointment. Only Reagan conveyed a sense of optimism combined with accomplishment. Thus, in 1984, candidate Reagan frequented college campuses, something neither Johnson or Nixon could do in light of the protests that marked the Vietnam War. Reagan expressed amazement at the reception he received, noting during an appearance at Bowling Green State University, "There is certainly a new generation on hand. The crowd both in & out were wildly enthusiastic and supportive. I thought I was at a Republican convention."[109] Polls reflected Reagan's observations, as 61 percent of voters aged 18 to 24 backed him that year.[110] The Reagan generation has subsequently tilted consistently toward the GOP. Among those who came of age between 1978 and 1981, Republicans enjoyed a 6-point edge over the Democrats in party identification, and among those who voted for the first time between 1982 and 1985, the Republican lead swelled to 14 points.[111] Today, the Reagan generation still makes its influence felt. According to a study by Mason-Dixon Polling and Research, the Reagan generation was key to Bush's 2004 victories in Florida, Ohio, Iowa, Nevada, and New Mexico, giving him between 54 and 59 percent of their votes; Kerry prevailed in every other age category.[112] And the Reagan generation remained inclined toward McCain in 2008 (see chapter 7).

Bush's unpopularity among today's young voters, coupled with a corresponding Democratic advantage in party identifiers, has the potential to be historically significant. In 2007, 56 percent of those aged 18–29 identified with the Democratic Party; only 36 percent associated with the Republican Party.[113] These figures are highly significant: in 2008, 50 million young people voted, a number higher than the post–World War II baby-boom generation. By 2015, estimates show that this new generational cohort will comprise one-third of the electorate.[114]

How young voters will frame the politics of the future is unclear. But Bush and the Republicans have given Democrats a historic opportunity. Dowd believes that Bush squandered a generational opportunity for the GOP: "If you look at Ronald Reagan and how he performed among youth, he created a generation of Republicans that was able to sustain itself. What Bush has done in his presidency is almost the opposite: He has won elections and lost a generation."[115] Numerous surveys bear out Dowd's observations: young voters opposed the Iraq War, disliked GOP positions on gay marriage and abortion, believed Republicans were incompetent, and favored a bigger government that would provide them with more services. According to a 2007 survey among voters aged 18 to 31, Democrats enjoyed substantial advantages in some key areas: 39 points when it came to "paying attention to issues that affect younger people"; 38 points on the environment; 35 points on health care; 33 points on handling the situation in Iraq; 32 points on becoming energy independent; 25 points on handling the federal budget; 24 points on dealing with the economy and jobs; 21 points on managing the war on terrorism; 15 points on "sharing your values"; and 13 points on taxes.[116]

The support Democrats generate among the young may result from the importance they accord to tolerance. One 2007 survey found that 87 percent of the nation's youth said that they were tolerant, and 73 percent thought that description best applied to the Democrats.[117] In a nation of changing racial and family compositions, tolerance is an especially important public value. On that point, it is hardly coincidental that the Democratic Party's advantages among the young come entirely from nonwhites, the fastest-growing segment of the population. Put another way, Democrats are on the losing end of the party identification scale among young white voters.[118]

Destroying a Brand Name

During the 1930s, Republicans had a hard time selling voters on their brand name. At the opening of the 75th Congress in January 1937, the Republicans held a mere 89 of 435 seats in the House of Representatives and had just 17 of 96 senators.[119] So engorged were the Democratic ranks that several of the new members had to sit on the Republican side of the aisle in both houses. A few days before the 1936 election, Franklin D. Roosevelt spoke before a throng of supporters at New York City's Madison Square Garden, artfully practicing the politics of emotion: "I should like to have it said of my first Administration that in it the forces of selfishness and of lust for power met their match. I should like to have it said of my second Administration that *in it these forces have met their master*." Roosevelt biographer James MacGregor Burns described the audience response as a "raucous, almost animal-like roar [that] burst from the crowd, died away, and then rose again in wave after wave."[120]

Following Roosevelt's script, the Democrats henceforth cast themselves as the "party that cares more about people like yourself," and Republicans were demonized as the "party of privilege." Class became a tool Democrats used to win presidential contests. As *The Economist* observed following FDR's 1936 landslide, "The poor won the election from the well-to-do."[121] This class-based politics—with its powerful images of Democrats named Mike, Sammy, Mary, and Jane, while Republican men had Roman numerals after their names, attended elite universities, and dated women named Muffie and Buffy—lasted until 1980. Carter's inability to control inflation, keep unemployment low, and return the Iranian hostages to U.S. soil created a "misery index" that gave Reagan an opportunity to toss FDR's portrait into the dustbin of history and replace it with a bright new picture of a Republican Party whose 1950s-era values of family, work, neighborhood, peace, and freedom had more in common with ordinary citizens than the boutique liberalism espoused by many Democrats.

At the same time, the 40-year-long Cold War gave beleaguered Republicans a new lease on life. From 1952 to 1988, Republicans won 7 of the 10 presidential contests, although the party lost Congress, most governorships, and most state legislative seats. The victories of Kennedy in 1960, Johnson in 1964, and Carter in 1976 represented exceptions to the pro-Republican trend. Specifically, Kennedy outhawked Nixon in 1960; following his assassination, the country was not willing to have three presidents in fifteen months; and after the criminality associated with Watergate, the nation was ready for a pious president, a role Carter fulfilled.

Eisenhower, Nixon, Reagan, and George H. W. Bush maintained their hold on the presidency because Republicans created a powerful post–New Deal image for themselves: tough-minded patriots who drove hard bargains with the Soviet Union, kept the military strong, exercised prudence in sending U.S. troops to battle (even as they rhetorically railed against communism), and responsible economic stewards who would safeguard the military-industrial complex.[122] Although FDR's New Deal–era image held sway for most other offices, this new Republican picture with its bold anticommunist hues predominated in presidential contests. Put another way, Americans did not use foreign policy as a calculus in selecting members of Congress, governors, or state legislators but did so when casting presidential ballots.

As Republican presidents became the norm, the GOP accrued another advantage, becoming the party of competence. Rather than appointing political hacks to important posts, Republicans cultivated a stable of bureaucratic infighters who served their presidents in several capacities yet always remained careful to cultivate an image of administrative ability, even if that meant foregoing (as it often did) electoral politics. Thus, George H. W. Bush, Dick Cheney, George Shultz, Caspar Weinberger, James A. Baker III, and Donald Rumsfeld occupied a variety of cabinet-level positions and executive appointments. By 1980, 42 percent of voters believed that Republicans were "better able to manage the government," while only 29 percent preferred Democrats.[123] After five years of the Reagan presidency, 32 percent of respondents associated the Republican Party with "able and competent leadership," while an additional 25 percent named the GOP as "effective at getting things done."[124] *New York Times* columnist Tom Wicker noted that the Democrats' absence from the presidency had transformed it into "a *party of access* in which the voiceless find a voice," while the Republicans "maintain enough coherence and unity to become *a party of government.*"[125] Even when George H. W. Bush ran into strong political headwinds in late 1991, two-thirds of voters still associated *Republican* with *competence*.[126]

Seeking the presidency in 2000, George W. Bush sought to allay concerns about his thin résumé by promising to surround himself with the same administrative managers who had populated previous Republican administrations. According to one poll taken that year, only 2 percent of respondents thought Bush was either qualified or competent to be president.[127] Therefore, Bush's selection of Cheney as vice president and his all-but-announced intention to make Powell secretary of state sent powerful signals to voters that his incoming administration would be ready to run the government on its first day in office. Recounting his decision to choose Cheney, Bush said, "I don't know what's going to come on my desk, but I'm going to need somebody who's seen things before, who can give me advice to make good decisions."[128]

By 2006, the Republican image of competence was in tatters, thanks to a mismanaged war in Iraq and a tardy, incoherent response to Hurricane Katrina's devastation of New Orleans. A year later, 46 percent of the public thought Bush was competent, while 49 percent disagreed.[129] As one Republican professional noted after the Katrina disaster, "We're supposed to be the party of competence. When we look incompetent, it's a real problem."[130] Peggy Noonan, a former speechwriter for Reagan and George H. W. Bush, believes that George W. Bush "destroyed the Republican party, by which I mean he sundered it, broke its constituent pieces apart, and set them against each other. He did this on spending, the size of government, war, the ability to prosecute war, immigration and other issues."[131]

The destruction of the Republican brand, coupled with the enormous demographic changes in the American polity, has left both major political parties in a state of transition. On the eve of the 2008 election, the old was dying and the new was waiting to be born. That birth took place on November 4, 2008.

Seven · Barack Obama's America

"We are the ones we've been waiting for."
—BARACK OBAMA

ELECTION NIGHT 2008. At 11:00 P.M. Eastern Standard Time, the television networks universally declared that Barack Hussein Obama had acquired more than the 270 electoral votes necessary to become the 44th president of the United States. Obama had won 52.63 percent of the popular vote, the first Democrat to win a majority since Jimmy Carter's minimalist 50.08 percent victory over Gerald R. Ford in 1976.[1] And unlike 2000, when George W. Bush lost the popular vote but beat Al Gore by four votes in the Electoral College, this time the electors reflected Obama's strong popular showing: 365 electoral votes for Obama to 173 for John McCain.[2] The red state–blue state stasis that bedeviled the country during the George W. Bush years was finally broken, as former red states that had twice backed Bush—Virginia, North Carolina, Ohio, Florida, Indiana, Colorado, and Nevada—switched to Obama.[3] In the immediate aftermath of Obama's victory, MSNBC host David Gregory marveled, "The son of an African father, a Kenyan, and a white mother from Kansas, in a country that was stained by slavery, is now President of the United States. The ultimate color line has been crossed."[4]

Voters in 2008 clearly were searching for someone very different from the president they had come to know (and dislike). The editors of *The New Republic* captured this prevailing sentiment when they implicitly observed that Obama had become the antithesis of the incumbent he sought to replace: "On the whole, he has turned in one of the most impressive performances in recent political history—demonstrating an ability to explain complex ideas in plainspoken English, impeccable managerial skills, evenness of temper, avoidance of sloppy errors, and pragmatism, not to mention that he can really deliver a speech."[5] Most Americans agreed, and they largely set aside the cultural and values differences that created the partisan paralysis that had begun a decade earlier with Bill Clinton's impeachment.[6]

"Party Like It's 1964"

The un-Bush-like qualities discerned by voters (and *The New Republic*) in Obama prompted most Democrats to rhapsodize about the new president. Introducing Obama to adoring audiences, talk show host Oprah Winfrey recalled reading *The Autobiography of Miss Jane Pittman*, which describes how the enslaved Pittman searched for "the one" who would lead her to freedom. Winfrey told rapt audiences that she had discovered "the one" in Obama: "Well, I believe, in '08, I have found the answer to Ms. Pittman's question. I have fo-o-u-und the answer! It is the same question that our nation is asking: 'Are you the one? Are you the one?' I'm here to tell y'all, he is the one. He is the one. *Barack Obama!*"[7]

It had been a long time since Democrats had been so giddy about a presidential contest. Not since Lyndon B. Johnson's 1964 landslide had they so throughly routed Republicans in a presidential election.[8] Several weeks before the 2008 denouement, *Washington Post* columnist Richard Cohen forecast that when all the votes were counted, jubilant Democrats would "party like it's 1964."[9] In fact, the comfortable victories achieved by Obama and the rest of his ticket made the night seem like political déjà vu. In the Senate, Democrats added 7 new members, adding a comfortable (and potentially filibuster-proof) cushion to their former 1-seat majority.[10] The Democrats added 21 seats in the House; with the 30 the party had added two years earlier, the gains nearly equaled the 54 seats that House Republicans added in the 1994 elections to take the speaker's gavel for the first time in 40 years.

Conservative columnist George F. Will observed that the 2006 and 2008 congressional results were the worst for the Grand Old Party since the Great Depression–era elections of 1930 and 1932, when Republicans also suffered back-to-back Election Night losses.[11] Particularly stinging was the defeat of Connecticut Republican Christopher Shays, a loss that reduced the number of New England House Republicans to 0. New York state elected only 3 Republicans to the 111th Congress, and only 8 of the 64 congressional districts in the entire Northeast were represented by Republicans. Democrats even took the New York City borough of Staten Island, long controlled by a Republican machine. As a consequence, no Republican in the new House represented an urban area of more than 500,000 inhabitants. The picture was equally dismal for Republicans at the state legislative level: north of Virginia, Republicans do not hold a majority in any legislative body except for the Pennsylvania State Senate.[12]

These tallies reflected the toxic political environment in which McCain and his fellow Republicans found themselves. Democrats won because voters officially pronounced the Bush presidency dead and wanted a new direction, a message that the electorate had attempted to deliver in 2006, and one that Bush had ignored, to the everlasting ire of Democrats and independents alike.[13] As the campaign approached its conclusion, Democrats became competitive in congressional, state, and local districts, like Staten Island, that had previously been the exclusive province of the Republicans. Consequently, Republicans were reduced to their southern base, where McCain beat Obama by a solid margin, 54 percent to 45 percent. McCain's southern support was buoyed by the 68 percent backing he received from the southern whites who remain a GOP mainstay.[14] Republicans also maintained their grip on Dixie's congressional seats. In the 111th Congress, 65 percent of senators and 52 percent of the representatives from the former Confederate states will be Republicans. Obama thus has become the first Democratic president to assemble a governing coalition that does not include the South. Obama's cabinet and closest advisers include few who speak with southern accents, with the notable exception of secretary of defense Robert Gates, a holdover from the Bush administration. The conservative Dixiecrats who used to vote with the GOP in Congress are gone.

A Southern Lock Becomes a Southern Cage

For decades, a southern lock ensured GOP dominance of the presidency. In the wake of Nixon's Faustian bargain with South Carolina's J. Strom Thurmond in 1968—a promise to go slow on civil rights and to appoint "strict constructionists" to the federal courts in return for support from

Thurmond and other southerners—Nixon and Reagan won near-unanimous southern support for their presidential bids.[15] Indeed, the Republican lock on the Confederacy strengthened each time Democrats placed a northerner at the top of their ticket (Hubert H. Humphrey in 1968, George S. McGovern in 1972, Walter F. Mondale in 1984, and Michael S. Dukakis in 1988). Clinton was the only Democrat who could pick the Republicans' southern lock, and even that took some luck (a poor economy in 1992) and a lot of effort (choosing Tennessee's Al Gore as vice president).[16]

But in 2008, the southern lock turned into a southern cage. McCain's best showings included the Deep South states of Alabama (60 percent), Louisiana (59 percent), Mississippi (56 percent), and South Carolina (54 percent). In all of these states, Obama's overwhelming black vote was offset by a deluge of white votes: 88 percent for McCain in Alabama and Louisiana, and 84 percent in Mississippi.[17] Similarly, McCain performed well in the southern reaches of Appalachia, where he won 366 of its 410 counties, and he prevailed in Arkansas (59 percent), Kentucky (57 percent), Tennessee (57 percent), and West Virginia (56 percent).[18] McCain's victories there also resulted from his strong base among whites: he got 68 percent of the white vote in Arkansas, 63 percent in Kentucky and Tennessee, and 57 percent in West Virginia. Ironically, the home states of the most recent successful Democratic ticket, Arkansas and Tennessee, were solidly in McCain's corner, and they remain firmly ensconced in the Republican camp when it comes to presidential contests.[19]

Yet the more McCain and his fellow Republicans experienced solid victories in the Confederacy and Appalachia, the worse it became for the GOP everywhere else. The Republican Party now largely occupies territory controlled by the Democrats following William McKinley's party-realigning triumph in 1896. Back then, Republicans dominated in the electoral-rich Northeast and Midwest, while Democrats retained their Civil War–era legacy of strength in the South along with populist support in the interior West. McCain's chief strategist, Steve Schmidt, decries the shrinking of the GOP: "The party in the Northeast is all but extinct; the party on the West Coast is all but extinct; the party has lost the mid-South states—Virginia, North Carolina—and the party is in deep trouble in the Rocky Mountain West, and there has to be a message and a vision that is compelling to people in order for them to come back and to give consideration to the Republican party again."[20] Minnesota governor Tim Pawlenty, a prospective 2012 presidential candidate, concurs: "We cannot be a majority governing party when we essentially cannot compete in the Northeast, we are losing our ability to compete in Great Lakes States, we cannot complete on the West Coast, we are increasingly in danger of [not] competing in the Mid-Atlantic States, and the Democrats are now winning some of the Western States. This is not a formula for being a majority governing party in this nation."[21]

The financial crisis that blossomed in October only sealed the Republicans' fate. That month, the Dow Jones Industrial Average fell 6,000 points from its peak at 14,000 a year earlier. More than $8 trillion in stock value was lost in just a few weeks. On October 10 alone, the market swung 1,000 points, the first time it had ever experienced such violent gyrations. In the ensuing days, the market remained extremely jittery, rising 900 points one day and losing 700 the next. To ensure financial stability, the Bush administration proposed a massive $700 billion Wall Street rescue plan, the largest government intervention in the private markets since Franklin D. Roosevelt's National Recovery Administration efforts of the 1930s. Despite rapid congressional passage of the federal bailout (after an initial false start), Wall Street's financial crisis hit Main Street. Unemployment rose to 6.5 percent in October, with 2 million people described as being "long-term unemployed," or not having jobs for 27 months or more.[22] From January to October 2008, 1 million jobs evaporated.[23]

And these were not the only bad economic tidings. Millions of otherwise employed citizens who joined what pollster John Zogby once called the "investor class" (and had been staunch supporters of George W. Bush) were shocked to open their 401(k) statements and discover that their retirement savings had dropped sharply.[24] Home foreclosures reached record levels as the combination of unemployment and bad credit meant that millions had to surrender their personal palaces to the banks. Between July and September 2008, foreclosures totaled 765,000, with six states (Nevada, California, Florida, Ohio, Michigan, and Arizona) accounting for 60 percent of the lost homes.[25] Obama won five of these states, losing only in McCain's adopted home state of Arizona.

The result was a consumer crisis of confidence. In October, retail sales fell 2.8 percent, as would-be customers pared their spending in the wake of gloomy financial headlines.[26] The prevailing mood was captured in the Consumer Confidence Index, which fell from 61.4 in September 2008 to just 38.0 one month later, its lowest level since 1967.[27] Jerry Mills, an Ohio welder and former Bush supporter, was among those fearing foreclosure and blaming the president: "I voted for Bush, and I can't believe it. I don't want to admit to it, I'm not happy with where he put us."[28] In 2008, Mills backed Obama, as did 51 percent of his fellow Ohioans.

Not since 1933 had a new president assumed office under such dire circumstances—an economic implosion combined with two wars. Economic anxiety remained palpable, and further government action was required; Iraq was a source of danger, and a political solution to the war had yet to be established; and a growing consensus held that Afghanistan was slipping away and that more U.S. troops would be needed to succeed there. A *New York Times* editorial endorsing Obama captured the urgency of the moment: "It will be an enormous challenge just to get the nation back to where it was before Mr. Bush, to restore its self-confidence and its self-respect."[29] Voters agreed, concluding that they could no longer afford the luxury of having an election dominated by social and cultural issues such as guns, gay marriage, abortion, Willie Horton, William Ayers, or even the Reverend Jeremiah Wright. According to the exit polls, only 30 percent of voters cited "shares my values" as the most important candidate quality (and 65 percent of those who did so backed McCain), whereas 34 percent mentioned "can bring about needed change" as the most important attribute they sought (and 89 percent of this group supported Obama).[30] For the moment, the clanging culture wars had reached a tentative truce.

Other straws in the October wind also pointed toward a Democratic victory.

- Bush recorded a 21 percent job approval rating, 3 points lower than Nixon's rating on the eve of his 1974 resignation and 1 point below the previous record, set by Harry S. Truman in February 1952, when the United States was beset by stalemate in the Korean War and a host of other Cold War–era challenges.[31]

- Only 9 percent of respondents to one survey pronounced themselves satisfied with the direction of the United States, the lowest recorded response to that question in the history of the Gallup Poll.[32]

- September fund-raising totals (reported in mid-October) showed that Obama had raised a record $150 million. Overall, the Democratic candidate had 3.1 million contributors (with 630,000 added in September alone) and an average contribution of $86. This treasure chest allowed Obama to blanket the airwaves with paid advertisements (including a 30-minute infomercial) and financed an enormous get-out-the-vote campaign.[33]

- In mid-October, when the *New York Times* asked Tommy Thompson, a former Republican governor of Wisconsin, whether he was satisfied with the McCain campaign, he answered, "No, and I don't know anyone who is."[34] A dozen years earlier, on the eve of Bob Dole's defeat, Thompson had told the *Times*, "I thought George Bush's [1992] campaign was probably the poorest run Presidential campaign—and I think [Dole's campaign] is a close second."[35] On both occasions, Thompson expressed what many Republicans privately thought about their ticket's chances in November.

Despite all the good news for Obama and his Democratic ticketmates, many questions remained unanswered until Americans gathered around their Election Night television campfires. Most of these questions involved race and whether the old shibboleths of politics still retained enough power to determine the outcome.

- Would October's bad economic news be enough to induce voters to elect a black man president of the United States? Even the idea of an African American president was relatively new. In 1958, the Gallup Poll first asked its respondents whether they would support a "well-qualified" African American for President. Only 37 percent of respondents answered yes; 53 percent said no.[36]
- Would the so-called Bradley effect create an Election Night surprise? In the 1982 California gubernatorial race, Los Angeles mayor Tom Bradley, who was black, lost to Republican George Deukmejian, who was white, despite the fact that preelection polls showed Bradley with a significant lead.[37]
- Would any Bradley effect be offset by increased nonwhite (especially African American) turnout?
- Would enough blue-collar, Joe the Plumber whites come home to the Democratic Party after years of supporting Reagan and the Bushes?
- Would younger, twenty-first-century voters show up at the polls and vote for Obama? And would these first-time voters form part of a new and enduring Democratic majority?

Obama's comfortable win provided answers to all of these questions. Sixty-three percent of voters named the economy as the most important issue, and 53 percent of them supported Obama. Other concerns received scant mention: Iraq, 10 percent; terrorism, 9 percent; health care, 9 percent; energy, 7 percent. Second, Americans were more than willing to accept an African American as president. In fact, only 9 percent of respondents said that race was an important factor in their voting decisions, and 53 percent of these voters supported Obama. In fact, McCain's age proved a more significant factor than did race: 15 percent of those polled said that age mattered, and 77 percent of these voters backed Obama.[38] Third, there was no significant Bradley effect, as preelection polls consistently gave Obama a lead of between 6 and 7 points, exactly the scenario that played out on Election Night.[39] The disappearance of the Bradley effect heartened historians, who noted that the long arc of the civil rights movement that began in the 1960s had finally come to rest with the election of an African American president.[40]

Republicans reeled. In many ways, their present-day funk is reminiscent of their despair in 1964. After the Johnson landslide, political scientist Nelson Polsby noted that efforts to revive the GOP "may be insufficient to prevent an effective shift in this country to a one-and-one-half party system."[41] But few Democrats compared Obama to Johnson. Instead, many Democrats believed (and hoped) that in Obama they had found their own modern-day version of an iconic Republican—Reagan.[42]

Reagan and Obama share many similarities: both were gifted writers and effective communicators, and both somehow managed to avoid having attacks stick to them.[43] (Years ago, Colorado congresswoman Pat Schroeder dubbed Reagan the "Teflon president" because of his ability to shrug off Democratic efforts to make him appear uncaring or callous toward the poor and to paint his tax and budget cuts as unfair.)[44] More than two decades later, Republican vice presidential nominee Sarah Palin evoked fears about an impending Obama presidency, telling audiences, "This is not a man who sees America the way you and I see America."[45] The GOP ticket accused Obama of being unpatriotic and having "palled around with" Ayers, an "old washed up terrorist."[46] But the repeated references to Ayers, a founding member of the Weather Underground who attempted to bomb the Pentagon in protest of the Vietnam War, actually cost the Republican ticket votes. According to an October survey, 23 percent of registered voters thought less of McCain than they did at the start of the campaign.[47] The exit polls confirmed this result: nearly two-thirds of voters thought McCain had unfairly attacked Obama, while only a minority believed that Obama had unfairly attacked McCain.[48]

1980 and 2008: History Repeats Itself

The comparisons between Reagan's 1980 victory and Obama's triumph in 2008 are striking. Twenty-eight years ago, Reagan deplored the incumbent president, Carter, telling Republican delegates, "Can anyone look at the record of this administration and say, 'Well done?' . . . Can anyone look at our reduced standing in the world and say, 'Let's have four more years of this?'"[49] In 2008, Democrats quoted Reagan's words back at another Bush and made sure that voters saw McCain as Bush's stand-in. At one Democratic debate, Bush's name was invoked 47 times, all of them negatively, while at a comparable Republican debate, Bush was mentioned just twice (and Representative Ron Paul, an antiwar candidate, did so a negative context).[50] Obama seemed almost uninterested in running against McCain, a war hero, making "Bush-McCain" his opponent of choice.

Writing about Reagan's 1980 victory, political scientist Gerald M. Pomper summoned the ghost of Oliver Cromwell, who told the British Parliament, "You have sat too long here for any good you have been doing. Depart, I say, and let us have done with you. In the name of God, go!" According to Pomper, Americans delivered the same message to Carter and the Democrats.[51] In 2008, voters again channeled Cromwell, but this time they were speaking to Bush and his fellow Republicans. Indeed, after all the gains in party identification during the efflorescence of the Reagan years, Republicans unhappily discovered that their advances had evaporated. In 1980, 51 percent of voters called themselves Democrats, 30 percent were Republicans, and 19 percent were independents.[52] By 1994, a high point of the Reagan Revolution, the number of partisan identifiers was nearly equal, with 34 percent of Americans calling themselves Democrats and 31 percent labeling themselves Republicans.[53] The tug-of-war persisted for the rest of the Clinton regime and into the George W. Bush years. But by 2008, the number of Republican partisans was at 37 percent of likely voters, virtually the same as in 1980, while the number of Democratic identifiers had soared to 51 percent.[54] Exit polls also found a 7-point Democratic advantage, the largest disparity between the parties since 1980.[55] Simply put, the shifts toward the Democrats during Bush's second term were so powerful that it was as if Reagan's two terms had never happened.

Nowhere was the Republican collapse more evident than among independents. In 2007, only 33 percent of those with no party preference expressed favorable views of the GOP, while 55 percent held unfavorable opinions.[56] Former Reagan pollster Richard B. Wirthlin likened the GOP attempts to woo disillusioned independents to "raking water up a hill."[57] A year later, only 44 percent of independents voted for McCain, an especially noteworthy figure given that McCain ran well among independents in the 2000 and 2008 Republican primaries; in fact, independents gave him the margin of victory in those contests.[58] Other Republican notables—including Elizabeth Dole, John Sununu, Gordon Smith, and Ted Stevens—bid adieu to their Senate colleagues as a consequence of the one-two punch of overwhelming Democratic and independent opposition, and the 111th Congress is the first since 1952 that does not include either a Bush or a Dole.

At the heart of the problem lay the strong link between the Grand Old Party and George W. Bush. That association proved fatal to Republican hopes, and Republicans must break that connection to begin a recovery. In 2007, CBS News and the *New York Times* conducted a survey that showed just how tarnished the Republican brand had become. When respondents were asked to name the first word that came to their minds when thinking about the Republican Party, they answered,

> personal word—negative (12 percent);
>
> conservative (10 percent);
>
> liars/illegal/corruption (9 percent);
>
> good/positive word (5 percent);
>
> rich/upper class (7 percent);
>
> George W. Bush (5 percent);
>
> confused/disorganized (5 percent);
>
> bad/the bad people (4 percent);
>
> business/big business (3 percent);
>
> personal word (3 percent);
>
> strong/fights for its beliefs (2 percent);
>
> taxes/tax cuts/spending (2 percent);

reasonable/unreasonable (2 percent);

Iraq/war/wars/military (2 percent);

other policies (2 percent);

other words (10 percent);

don't know/no answer (17 percent).[59]

Republicans preferred to counter the bad polling news by summoning the glory days of the Reagan years. But Reagan had exited the White House two decades earlier. In many ways, the GOP's reaction to bad news has resembled that of the Democrats following their 1980 rejection at the polls. That year, political scientist Wilson Carey McWilliams wrote that Reagan's election signified the end of the New Deal era: "[T]he Roosevelt coalition has come to an end, as it was bound to. There are middle-aged voters today who were not born when Franklin Roosevelt died, and the youngest voters in 1980 were only a year old when John Kennedy was shot. We will remember Roosevelt and the Great Depression less and less, and—just as Truman has suddenly acquired cachet—Kennedy will increasingly be the symbol whose memory excites Democratic partisans."[60] Today, something similar is happening as memories of Reagan steadily fade into history, taking with them his potent political coalition. The recent unhappy experiences of the Bush years remain fresh, especially with the young—that is, 18-year-old voters born in 1990—whose political attitudes were shaped almost exclusively by the Bush years.

A Twenty-first-Century Hoover?

Near the end of Reagan's time in the White House, Wirthlin sent a memo to the president, taking stock of his accomplishments and outlining three "conditions for greatness" that "have long served to underpin the 'can-do spirit' that has made America a leader among nations":

- there must be strong public confidence and pride in America—belief in "the great experiment";
- there must be trust in the government and a confidence that elected officials can deal effectively with problems;
- the public view of the future must be hopeful and optimistic.[61]

In each category, Wirthlin argued that Reagan met these criteria and therefore had earned a positive assessment of his presidency in the history books. And time has proven Wirthlin right.

By Wirthlin's measures, however, George W. Bush has failed miserably. Confidence in the U.S. experiment and in the institutions of government that keep the American Dream alive fell to all-time lows. In 2007, the Gallup Organization found that public disenchantment had reached a level not seen since the dark days of Watergate:

- 51 percent of respondents trusted the federal government to handle international problems, the lowest percentage recorded since 1972;
- 47 percent had faith in the federal government to handle domestic problems, the lowest number since 1976;
- 43 percent believed in the executive branch of government, just above the 40 percent expressing support in April 1974, four months before Nixon resigned;
- 50 percent trusted the legislative branch, a decline from 62 percent in 2005;
- 55 percent trusted "the men and women in political life who are seeking office," matching the low point reached in 2001.[62]

It is no surprise, therefore, that voters turned on Bush. Two-thirds were dissatisfied with the way he was running the country; 70 percent said that he had no clear plan for getting U.S. troops out of Iraq; and 75 percent maintained that he had acquired more power than his predecessors and that this development had been bad for the country.[63] Most tellingly, when asked whether George W. Bush or Ronald Reagan had been a better chief executive, more than three-quarters chose Reagan, reaffirming Wirthlin's conditions.[64] For nearly all of his second term, Bush's approval rating remained far below 50 percent, a record for longevity in the annals of presidential polling. Given this lack of public consent, it is fair to say that the United States did not have a fully functional president before Obama took the oath of office.

Several academics and even a former president have echoed these harsh judgments. Princeton history professor Sean Wilentz believes that Bush is "headed for a colossal historical disgrace."[65] George Mason University political scientist James P. Pfiffner maintains that Bush's excesses—for example, suspending the Geneva Conventions and interrogating prisoners using harsh methods; creating military tribunals to try terrorist suspects; permitting warrantless wiretapping; and deciding which laws to enforce and which ones to bypass—endangered democracy itself: "Even if President Bush was a noble defender of freedom, the authority that he claims to be able to ignore the law, if allowed to stand, would constitute a dangerous precedent that future presidents might use to abuse their power."[66] Columbia political scientist Eric Foner maintains that Bush "has managed to combine the lapses of leadership, misguided policies and abuse of power of his failed predecessors," concluding that "there is no alternative but to rank [Bush] as the worst president in history."[67] Yale political scientist Stephen Skowronek believes Bush's abuses of power helped institutionalize an imperial presidency.[68] And in a breach of presidential protocol, former president Carter publicly denounced Bush: "I think as far as the adverse impact on the nation around the world, this administration has been the worst in history."[69] Not to be outdone, Republican senator Chuck Hagel told the Council on Foreign Relations that the Bush presidency was "one of the most arrogant, incompetent administrations I've ever seen personally or ever read about."[70]

Perhaps there was no greater commentary on Bush's shortcomings than a McCain television advertisement aired just three weeks prior to Election Day in which the candidate stated the obvious: "The last eight years haven't worked very well, have they?"[71] But even that admission proved to be too little, too late. In his final debate with Obama, an exasperated McCain tried to shed the "Bush-McCain" label that Obama had pinned to the Republican's chest: "Senator Obama, I am not President Bush. If you wanted to run against President Bush, you should have run four years ago. I'm going to give a new direction to this economy in this country."[72] But McCain's protestations suffered yet another setback the weekend before the balloting when he received Vice President Dick Cheney's hearty endorsement: "I believe the right leader for this moment in history is Senator John McCain. John is a man who understands the danger facing America. He's a man who has looked into the face of evil and not flinched. He's a man who's comfortable with responsibility, and has been since he joined the armed forces at the age of seventeen. He's earned our support and confidence, and the time is now to make him commander-in-chief."[73] Obama seized on Cheney's words, cutting a commercial quoting Cheney and sarcastically adding that McCain had worked hard for the vice president's support, voting with the Bush-Cheney administration 90 percent of the time.

There is one particularly obvious reason why McCain sought to keep his distance from Bush and why Obama never failed to mention Bush and McCain in the same breath: Bush's job approval ratings descended into the 20 percent range, especially as the financial crisis transformed discontented voters into scared voters. As Bush prepared to depart the White House, 79 percent of those surveyed said that they would not miss him, and 48 percent of respondents picked him as among the worst of our recent presidents.[74] Clare Boothe Luce once said that every president gets one line in the history books. Thus, George Washington "was the Father of the Country"; Abraham Lincoln "saved the Union and freed the slaves"; Franklin Roosevelt "launched the New Deal and fought World War II"; and Reagan "helped end the Cold War." Bush's assessment has not yet been written, but it seems likely to include words such as *terrorism, September 11, Iraq, Afghanistan, Katrina,* and *financial crisis.*

In his 1933 Inaugural Address, Roosevelt delivered a harsh assessment of his predecessor, Herbert Hoover: "Only a foolish optimist can deny the dark realities of the moment."[75] Obama echoed Roosevelt, noting in his Election Night victory speech, "For even as we celebrate tonight, we know the challenges that tomorrow will bring are the greatest of our lifetime—two wars, a planet in peril, the worst financial crisis in a century. . . . The road ahead will be long. Our climb will be steep. We may not get there in one year or even in one term. But, America, I have never been more hopeful than I am tonight that we will get there. I promise you, we as a people will get there."[76] During the next four years, the hope is that the financial crisis, the wars in Iraq and Afghanistan, and the "dark realities of the moment" will give way not just to brighter days but to a sense of order in both foreign and domestic affairs, something Americans deeply craved at the start of the Obama administration.

Elections that transform U.S. politics often happen because voters want a restoration of order. So it was in 1968. In his masterful *Nixonland,* historian Rick Perlstein wrote that the nightly televised chaos was crucial to Nixon's victory: "Turn on the TV: burning huts in Vietnam. Turn on the TV: burning buildings in Watts. Turn on the TV: one set of young people were comparing another set of young people to Nazis, and Da Nang was equated with Nagasaki."[77] Similarly, Wirthlin advised Reagan in 1980 to "convey the clearest possible message that Reagan stands for leadership and control. The prevailing view in America is that no one is in control; the prevailing impression given by the [Carter] White House is that no one can be in control; and the prevailing view abroad is that the will to be in control is gone."[78] For both Nixon and Reagan, promises to restore order provided a powerful mandate.

A similar desire for order was evident in 2008. Writing a few weeks before the election, *New York Times* columnist David Brooks described how the proverbial "Patio Man"—a suburban male beset by falling home prices, job insecurity, credit card debt, and investments gone sour—was searching for order amid the financial chaos. Patio Man, who liked Nixon and adored Reagan, was shifting his thinking "from risk to caution, from disorder to consolidation." According to Brooks, the cool, self-contained, and reassuring Obama was poised to win lots of votes from Patio Men (and Patio Women) because he seemed like "the safer choice—socially moderate, pragmatic, and fiscally hawkish."[79] Exit polls proved Brooks right, as suburban voters backed Obama by a margin of 50 percent to 48 percent.[80]

But it was more than the votes of discontented Patio People that made Obama president. A new demography had reshaped the political landscape and transformed old ways of thinking about politics.

The Real Majority Becomes a Real Minority

In 1970, Richard M. Scammon and Ben J. Wattenberg published *The Real Majority*, a tour de force that concluded the real majority consisted of those voters who were "*un-young, un-poor,* and *un-black.*"[81] These voters, who were suburban, married, white, middle aged, and middle income, who had kids under age 18 residing at home, and who attended church regularly, had drifted away from Roosevelt's Democratic Party and were about to enter a Republican Party led by Nixon and Reagan, who conjured memories of a happier, more orderly era.

These newly minted real majority Republicans were decidedly middle class and relatively prosperous, thanks to the successes of Roosevelt's New Deal, which transformed a generation of have-nots into haves. According to Scammon and Wattenberg, the members of the real majority were concerned about an emerging social issue—a first explication of the culture wars. Scammon and Wattenberg listed crime, drug use, pornography, law and order, and race as voter priorities.[82] Nixon speechwriter Patrick J. Buchanan was an avid fan of the book, and he sent it along to Nixon, who, in turn, encouraged his fellow Republicans to employ the social issue in their upcoming campaigns.[83] In 1971, Buchanan fired off a memo to Nixon on "Dividing the Democrats." In it, Buchanan argued that race was the ultimate social issue that could separate white Democrats from the party of Roosevelt. Buchanan urged the Nixon White House to act: "Bumper stickers calling for black Presidential and especially Vice-Presidential candidates should be spread out in the ghettoes of the country. We should do what is within our power to have a black nominated for Number Two, at least at the Democratic National Convention." Such gambits, he added, could "cut the Democratic Party and the country in half; my view is we would have far the larger half."[84]

Although Buchanan's bumper stickers were never printed, the emergence of the real majority, with its emphasis on social and cultural issues, transformed many Democrats from economic voters into values voters. That transmutation helped Nixon to a narrow victory in 1968 and to a sweeping landslide in 1972, when his coalition was augmented by supporters of a third-party candidate, former Alabama governor George C. Wallace. Watergate was only a temporary detour in the building of a new Republican coalition that encompassed large swaths of Scammon and Wattenberg's real majority. As chapter 6 notes, Reagan completed the work when he appealed to the real majority's conservative values of family, work, neighborhood, peace, and freedom and its desire for order in an age where these old verities had come under siege from the baby boomers.[85]

In 2008, the real majority remained strongly tilted toward the Republican Party. McCain won majorities of the white vote and held onto a plurality of middle-aged voters—those who had come of age during the Reagan years. McCain also performed well among the older whites who formed Scammon and Wattenberg's real majority in 1970. While middle-income voters (those making between $50,000 and $75,000) barely supported McCain (shaken as they were by the financial crises on Wall Street and Main Street), other elements of Scammon and Wattenberg's real majority remained loyal to the GOP—married voters, those with children under the age of 18 living in their households, white Catholics, white Protestants, and regular churchgoers (see table 11).

Especially noteworthy is the largely white hue of the 2008 Republican coalition. Exit polls revealed that nearly 90 percent of McCain's total vote came from whites.[86] This finding was reflected in the crowds that came to see McCain and Palin in their joint appearances. According to *New York*

Times columnist Frank Rich, "There are indeed so few people of color at McCain events that a black senior writer from *The Tallahassee Democrat* was mistakenly ejected by the Secret Service from a campaign rally in Panama City in August, even though he was standing with other reporters and showed his credentials. His only apparent infraction was to look glaringly out of place."[87]

But the influence of white voters is quickly waning. In 1976, when Carter became the first southern white elected president since Zachary Taylor in 1848, whites constituted 90 percent of the electorate. By 2004, that figure had fallen to 77 percent.[88] And in 2008, the white percentage of the electorate fell further, to 74 percent, the lowest in the history of exit polling.[89] The U.S. Census Bureau recently estimated that by 2042, whites will be a minority throughout the United States, a prediction that supports the idea that the total percentage of white voters will continue to drop.[90] Obama was prescient in thinking his race would be an asset in 2008: "I think that if you can tell people, 'We have a president in the White House who still has a grandmother living in a hut on the shores of Lake Victoria and has a sister who's half-Indonesian, married to a Chinese-Canadian,' then they're going to think that he may have a better sense of what's going on in our lives and in our country. And they'd be right."[91]

Other portions of Scammon and Wattenberg's real majority are also on the wane. In 1970, the United States was still an industrialized nation with

TABLE 11.   McCain vs. Obama: The "Real Majority" Decides (in percentages)

Demographic Group	McCain	Obama
Whites	55	43
Whites, aged 45–59	56	42
Whites, aged 60 and older	57	41
Aged 45–59	49	49
White Catholics	52	47
White Protestants/Other Christian	65	34
Southern whites	68	30
$50,000–$75,000 income	49	48
Live in suburbs	50	48
Weekly churchgoers	55	43
Married	52	47
Married with children	51	48
Nonworking women	48	50
Those who want candidate that shares my values	65	32

Source: Edison Media Research and Mitofsky International exit polls, November 4, 2008.

only hints of the emerging Information Age. Industrialization placed a premium on working with one's hands; the Information Age requires an active mind that is the means of production. Thus, a college education has become today's union card for employment. Many Americans find themselves not just attending four-year colleges but also earning graduate degrees to advance their employment prospects. In many respects, McCain and Obama were twentieth- and twenty-first-century candidates, respectively. In the 10 states with the fewest number of residents aged 25 years or older who had earned a bachelor's degree or more, McCain prevailed in 8 (often by solid margins). Moreover, in all of these states except Nevada, Mississippi, and Indiana, McCain won solid majorities of those who either held only high school diplomas or had not finished high school (see table 12).

That portion of the electorate that can be best described as un-young, un-poor, and un-black is truly waning. Scammon and Wattenberg's real majority could only muster 48 percent of the vote for Bush in 2000. Four years later, Bush garnered just 51 percent of all ballots cast, and he reached that level largely as a consequence of the fear still emanating from the September 11 attacks and the 44 percent support he received among Hispanics. In 2008, McCain won only 46 percent of the votes cast. Each year, the

TABLE 12. McCain Vote in Top Ten States with Fewest Numbers of College Graduates

State	Percentage of Population with B.A. Degree or More	Statewide Percentage of McCain Vote	McCain Percentage among High School Graduate or Less
West Virginia	15.9	56 (won)	58
Arkansas	19.0	59 (won)	51
Kentucky	20.2	57 (won)	55
Wyoming	20.8	65 (won)	78
Alabama	20.8	60 (won)	58
Nevada	20.8	43 (lost)	38
Mississippi	21.1	56 (won)	48
Louisiana	21.2	59 (won)	54
Indiana	21.9	49 (lost)	47
Tennessee	22.0	57 (won)	58

Source: Data from http://www.census.gov/compendia/statab/tables/08s0221 .pdf (accessed October 1, 2008); Edison Media Research and Mitofsky International exit polls, November 4, 2008.

un-young, un-poor, and un-black portion of the electorate becomes smaller. The real majority of 1970 is today's new real minority.

"We Are the Ones We've Been Waiting For"

After wrestling Hillary Clinton to a draw in the 24 Democratic primaries and caucuses held on Super Tuesday, Barack Obama took to the stage and repeated his mantra of change. But this time he added a twist: "Change will not come if we wait for some other person, or if we wait for some other time. We are the ones we've been waiting for."[92] In this speech, as in so many others, Obama implied that his supporters were just the sort of twenty-first-century citizens who could make change happen. Throughout the campaign, Obama attracted crowds that were both racially diverse and young. These demographics proved crucial to his victory.

In 2008, youth mattered. Simply put, voters who had lived a majority of their lives in the twentieth century tilted toward McCain. But voters who were likely to spend more than half their lives in the twenty-first century were strongly inclined toward Obama. Two-thirds of young people aged 18 to 29 voted for Obama, a dramatic shift toward the Democratic Party. In 2000, Al Gore carried 18- to 29-year-olds by just 2 points; four years later, Kerry took that group by 9 points; Obama beat McCain within this group by 34 points.

History teaches that after a political party captures a generation, its members often remain loyal. During the 1930s, for example, Roosevelt's popularity among the very young was so strong that demographers began to speak of a New Deal generation. Accordingly, Americans who came of age between 1930 and 1937 gave the Democrats a 14-point advantage over the Republicans in party identification; among those who voted for the first time between 1938 and 1941, the Democratic lead swelled to 20 points.[93] Likewise, voters who backed Reagan when they were young largely have remained loyal to the GOP. In 2008, those voters (now aged between 45 and 59) split down the middle, giving 49 percent of their votes to each of the major-party candidates. The only cohort in which McCain did better was older voters, among whom he took 51 percent of votes while Obama received 47 percent.[94]

College-educated voters backed Obama. Just as states with few college-educated voters were more likely to back McCain, those with higher proportions of college-educated voters supported Obama. Of the 15 states with the highest percentage of their populations aged 25 and older who possessed bachelor's or other advanced degrees, all except Kansas voted for Obama (see table 13). Many of these states—Massachusetts, Colorado, Connecticut, Vermont, Virginia, Washington, and Illinois—have Information Age economies. Among people with postgraduate degrees, Obama received two-thirds of the vote (see table 13). The collapse of Republican support among the most highly educated has made the backing Democrats receive from today's new "creative class" a dominant feature of the electoral landscape.[95]

Another important component of the Obama coalition was nonwhites, who now comprise a quarter of the electorate. In 2004, Bush took 11 percent of the African American vote; McCain captured just 4 percent of that group, a historic low for the Republican Party.[96] As recently as the 1940s, the Party of Lincoln collected a substantial share of the African American vote. For example, in 1940, Republicans won 32 percent of the black vote, and 42 percent of African Americans called themselves Republicans.[97] Even in 1960, Nixon received one out of every four black votes.[98] But after Johnson signed the Voting Rights Act into law in 1965 and Republican

TABLE 13.   Obama Vote in Top 15 College-Educated States with Greatest Numbers of College Graduates

State	Percentage of Population with B.A. Degree or More	Statewide Percentage of Obama Vote	Obama Percentage of College Graduates	Obama Percentage among Post-college Graduates
District of Columbia	49.1	93 (won)	92	87
Massachusetts	40.4	62 (won)	59	68
Colorado	36.4	54 (won)	51	63
Connecticut	36.0	61 (won)	55	62
Maryland	35.7	62 (won)	54	70
New Jersey	35.6	57 (won)	54	61
Vermont	34.0	67 (won)	67	80
Minnesota	33.5	54 (won)	49	67
Hawaii	32.3	72 (won)	71	78
New York	32.2	62 (won)	63	66
New Hampshire	32.1	54 (won)	52	68
Virginia	32.1	53 (won)	50	52
Kansas	31.6	41 (lost)	40	51
Washington	31.4	57 (won)	62	64
Illinois	31.2	62 (won)	55	58

Source: Data from http://www.census.gov/compendia/statab/tables/08s0221.pdf (accessed October 1, 2008); Edison Media Research and Mitofsky International exit polls, November 4, 2008.

lawmakers subsequently promised to go slow on civil rights and school busing, African American support for the GOP fell into the low double-digits. Thus in 1972, Nixon won just 18 percent of the black vote in what was otherwise a historic landslide.[99]

Republican support among African Americans in the low single digits is a prescription for disaster that is compounded by the poor GOP showing among Hispanics. In 2008, two-thirds of Hispanics voted for Obama, a sharp contrast from Bush's showing among members of that group in 2004. Bush won a substantial number of Hispanic votes for three reasons. First, he provided strong leadership following September 11 attacks. Second, he strongly condemned anti-Hispanic ballot measures. During his 1994 campaign for the Texas governorship, for example, Bush opposed Proposition 187, a California initiative that would have made it illegal for state agencies to provide assistance to illegal immigrants. As president, he continued to oppose anti-Hispanic measures, including state-sponsored English-only laws. As he wrote in his campaign autobiography, *A Charge to Keep*, "Those who advocate 'English-only' poke a stick in the eye of people of Hispanic heritage. 'English-only' says me, not you. It says I count, but you do not. This is not the message of America."[100] Finally, Bush's strident opposition to gay marriage played well among Hispanics, who have been largely unsympathetic to gay-rights claims.

But in 2008, the Hispanic vote tilted strongly to Obama. One obvious reason was continued Republican opposition to immigration reform. Obama won 8 of the 10 states with the greatest proportions of Hispanics (see table 14). These states combined to give Obama 168 electoral votes, nearly half of his total.[101] The combination of overwhelming black and Hispanic support for the Democratic ticket led Republican consultant Steve Lombardo to conclude, "Given the demographic trends in the country, the GOP is unlikely to win any future presidential election if it is losing 95 percent of the black vote and 67 percent of the Hispanic vote."[102]

Stepping off a Bridge

Accepting renomination at the 1996 Democratic National Convention, President Bill Clinton observed that during his second term, his administration would construct a "bridge to the twenty-first century."[103] But Clinton's bridge took several detours: the 1998 Monica Lewinsky scandal that resulted in his impeachment; the September 11 attacks; and the wars in

Afghanistan and Iraq, to name but a few. Obama's election seems to have completed Clinton's bridge, and Americans have finally stepped off on the other side and marched into the future. Nearly two centuries ago, Alexis de Tocqueville wrote, "People often manage public affairs very badly." But, he added, becoming genuinely engaged "is bound to extend their mental horizon and shake them out of the rut of ordinary routine."[104] The lethargy and fear that prevented the public from marching forward during the Clinton and Bush years has given way to a newfound sense of urgency that the United States must either fully embrace the twenty-first century or risk becoming a former superpower enervated by memories of yesteryear.

The 2008 election surely represented a final public judgment on George W. Bush. But it was much more than that, for it represented a moment when a new demography caught up to a new politics. Speaking in the afterglow of Obama's victory, MSNBC commentator and *Washington Post* columnist Eugene Robinson declared, "This is a moment of demarcation. There was a before and an after. We don't know what happens in the after. But we know it's different from the before. It feels different to me to be an American tonight."[105] Robinson spoke as an African American, but he could have just been as easily speaking for all those who find themselves part of the nation's new demographic majority.

TABLE 14. Obama Vote in Top Ten Hispanic States

State	Percentage of Hispanics Eligible to Vote as a Total of the State Population	Statewide Percentage for Obama	Hispanic Percentage for Obama
New Mexico	44.0	57 (won)	69
California	35.9	61 (won)	74
Texas	35.7	44 (lost)	63
Arizona	29.2	45 (lost)	56
Nevada	24.4	55 (won)	76
Florida	20.1	51 (won)	57
Colorado	19.7	54 (won)	61
New York	16.3	62 (won)	N/A[a]
New Jersey	15.6	57 (won)	78
Illinois	14.7	62 (won)	72

Source: Paul Taylor and Richard Fry, "Hispanics and the 2008 Election: A Swing Vote?" Pew Hispanic Center press report, December 6, 2007, 18; Edison Media Research and Mitofsky International exit polls, November 4, 2008.

[a]It appears as though the question was not asked in New York.

The racial, family, women's rights, and gay-rights revolutions, combined with an unusually engaged public disturbed about the direction the United States was taking, gave Obama and his fellow Democratic officeholders an enormous opportunity to make policy changes and consolidate political gains. The immediate aftermath of Obama's victory included a tremendous sense of optimism. In a December 2008 poll, 56 percent of respondents believed that Obama's victory bode well for the nation's future.[106] George McGovern, the Democrats' 1972 presidential nominee, agreed that the United States was heading into a period of reconciliation: "I believe we have a chance to heal the wounds the nation has suffered in the opening decade of the twenty-first century. This recovery may take a generation and will depend on the election of a series of rational presidents and Congresses. At age 85, I won't be around to witness the completion of the difficult rebuilding of our sorely damaged country, but I'd like to hold on long enough to see the healing begin."[107]

Any healing will depend largely on whether Americans are willing to cast aside the familiar and comfortable conflicts. In that regard, 2008 sent mixed messages: while Obama's election indicated just such a willingness, the passage of California's Proposition 8 implied just the opposite. In fact, we seem to be at the cusp of a moment when our social experiences are about to be woven into a new political culture. Translating these new experiences regarding race, family, gender roles, sexuality, and how we express our religious faiths will create new areas of political discomfort and conflict. Ideology has not ended, but the Reagan era has come to a close and the Obama era has begun. What this new period holds for us both politically and as Americans is unclear. But this much is apparent: after traipsing off Bill Clinton's bridge, however slowly and tentatively Americans have done so, we are entering a period of consequence.

Notes

Introduction

1. Sam Roberts, "A 300 Millionth American: Don't Ask Who," *New York Times*, October 18, 2006, A15.

2. See, for example, Gallup/*USA Today* poll, April 18–20, 2008.

3. Gregg Easterbrook, "America at 300 Million," *Los Angeles Times*, October 8, 2006, 1; Blaine Harden, "America's Population Set to Top 300 Million," *Washington Post*, October 12, 2006, A1.

4. Lyndon B. Johnson, "Remarks at a Ceremony Marking the Birth of the 200 Millionth American," Washington, D.C., November 20, 1967 (available at www.presidency.ucsb.edu/ws/index.php?pid=28558).

5. "Win, Place, Show in the Population Sweeps," *Life*, December 1, 1967, 26.

6. "200 Million: Not Far from a Madding Crowd," *Newsweek*, November 27, 1967, 89.

7. Richard M. Scammon, "What a Baby Can Look Forward To," *Life*, December 1, 1967, 29, 28.

8. Quoted in "200 Million," 89.

9. Quoted in Harden, "America's Population," 1.

10. "U.S. Population Reaches 300 Million Mark," Associated Press, October 17, 2006.

11. Quoted in Harden, "America's Population," A1.

12. Easterbrook, "America at 300 Million," 1.

13. Paul Theroux, "America the Overfull," *New York Times*, December 31, 2006, WK8.

14. Roberts, "300 Millionth American," A15.

15. Ibid.

16. Ibid.

17. Ibid.

18. Darryl Fears, "Ethnic Pageants Restyle the American Beauty Contest," *Washington Post*, October 19, 2005, A1.

19. Patrick J. Buchanan, *State of Emergency: The Third World Invasion and the Conquest of America* (New York: Dunne/St. Martin's, 2006), 5, 7.

20. Quoted in Evan Thomas, "Americans Wary of 300-Million Population," Newsweek.com, October 10, 2006.

21. Buchanan, *State of Emergency*, 5.

22. Johnson, "Remarks."

23. Gallup Organization poll, March 10–15, 1939.

24. Neil Strauss, "After the Horror, Radio Stations Pull Some Songs," *New York Times*, September 19, 2001, E1.

25. David Segal, "All Together Now," *Washington Post*, September 24, 2001, C1.

26. Gallup poll, September 7–10, 2001.

27. Ibid., September 21–22, 2001.

28. Chris Matthews, *Now Let Me Tell You What I Really Think* (New York: Free Press, 2001), 37.

29. Zogby International poll, September 17–18, 2001.

30. Zogby International poll, October 8–10, 2001.

31. *Los Angeles Times* poll, January 30–February 2, 2003.

32. "As Marriage and Parenthood Drift Apart, Public Is Concerned about Social Impact," Pew Research Center press release, July 1, 2007, 5.

33. Christopher Lydon, "Carter Issues an Apology on 'Ethnic Purity' Phrase," *New York Times*, April 9, 1976, 1.

34. Quoted in Robert Reinhold, "Carter Elaborates on His 'Ethnic' View," *New York Times*, April 10, 1976, 10.

35. Abraham Lincoln, First Inaugural Address, Washington, D.C., March 4, 1861. This presidential address, along with many others quoted throughout this book, is available at the American Presidency Project (www.presidency.ucsb.edu).

36. Gertrude Himmelfarb, *One Nation, Two Cultures* (New York: Knopf, 1999), 98.

37. Rahm Emanuel and Bruce Reed, *The Plan: Big Ideas for America* (New York: Public Affairs, 2006), xvii.

38. Barack Obama, *The Audacity of Hope: Thoughts on Reclaiming the American Dream* (New York: Crown, 2006), 8.

39. Barack Obama, Keynote Address, Democratic National Convention, Boston, July 27, 2004 (available at www.americanrhetoric.com/speeches/conven tion2004/barackobama2004dnc.htm).

40. Quoted in Andrew Delbanco, "The Educations," *The New Republic*, October 17, 2005, 33.

41. Edison Media Research and Mitofsky International California exit poll, November 4, 2008. Of the 52 percent who supported Proposition 8, 37 percent came from Obama supporters, and 61 percent came from McCain backers.

42. African Americans gave Obama 94 percent of their votes; Hispanics, 74 percent (ibid.).

43. Rick Perlstein, *Nixonland: The Rise of a President and the Fracturing of America* (New York: Scribner, 2008), 748.

44. Seymour Martin Lipset, *American Exceptionalism: A Double-Edged Sword* (New York: Norton, 1996), 26.

Chapter One

1. United Press wire report, "South Korean Unit, Bayoneting Reds, Regains Key Peak," *New York Times*, October 10, 1952, 1; Thomas J. Hamilton, "Work Completed on U.N. Buildings," *New York Times*, October 10, 1952, 1; James Reston, "Stevenson Taunts Rival for Backing McCarthy, Dirksen," *New York Times*, October 10, 1952, 1; Felix Belair Jr., "U.S. to Give France $525,000,000 in Aid and Hints at More," *New York Times*, October 10, 1952, 1.

2. Quoted in Richard Bernstein, "Long Conflict Deeply Marked the Self-Image of Americans," *New York Times*, February 2, 1992, 11.

3. Ronald Reagan, "Remarks at the Annual Convention of the National Association of Evangelicals," Orlando, Fla., March 8, 1983.

4. Arthur Larson, *A Republican Looks at His Party* (New York: Harper, 1956), 14, 15.

5. Daniel Bell, *The End of Ideology: On the Exhaustion of Political Ideas in the Fifties* (Glencoe, Ill.: Free Press, 1960), 369–70.

6. Robert Lane, *Political Ideology: Why the Common Man Believes What He Does* (New York: Free Press, 1962), 24, 69.

7. Hillary Rodham Clinton, *Living History* (New York: Simon and Schuster, 2003), 9.

8. Elaine Tyler May, "Explosive Issues: Sex, Women, and the Bomb," in *Recasting America: Culture and Politics in the Age of Cold War*, ed. Lary May (Chicago: University of Chicago Press, 1989), 163.

9. Ibid.

10. U.S. Department of Health, Education, and Welfare, *Vital Statistics of the United States, 1950* (Washington, D.C.: Public Health Service, National Vital Statistics Division, 1962), 33.

11. William H. Whyte Jr., *The Organization Man* (New York: Simon and Schuster, 1956), 7.

12. Hillary Rodham Clinton, *Living History*, 9.

13. Quoted in David Halberstam, *The Fifties* (New York: Villard, 1993), 163.

14. John M. Broder, "Lakewood Journal: Fifty Years Later, a Still-Proud Suburb Is Starting to Fray," *New York Times*, July 14, 2004, A16.

15. Halberstam, *Fifties*, 132.

16. Whyte, *Organization Man*, 10.

17. Ibid., 591.

18. Carl Solberg, *Hubert Humphrey: A Biography* (New York: Norton, 1984), 67–68. After receiving a promotion to full time, Muriel Humphrey resumed wearing her wedding ring.

19. Quoted in Stephanie Coontz, *The Way We Never Were: American Families and the Nostalgia Trap* (New York: Basic Books, 1992), 32.

20. Halberstam, *Fifties*, 588.

21. Ibid., 591–92.

22. Quoted in William V. D'Antonio, James D. Davidson, Dean R. Hoge, and Katherine Meyer, *American Catholics: Gender, Generation, and Commitment* (Walnut Creek, Calif.: AltaMira, 2001), 58.

23. Ben Gaffin and Associates poll, June–July 1952.

24. Alexis de Tocqueville, *Democracy in America*, ed. J. P. Mayer (New York: Harper and Row, 1966), 450.

25. Peter Steinfels, *A People Adrift: The Crisis of the Roman Catholic Church in America* (New York: Simon and Schuster, 2003), 7, 257.

26. David Kocieniewski, "In New Jersey, an Archbishop Conservative and Controversial," *New York Times*, May 30, 2004, 27.

27. U.S. Conference of Catholic Bishops, "Catholics in Political Life," June 21, 2004.

28. Coontz, *Way We Never Were*, 27–28.

29. Halberstam, *Fifties*, 509.

30. Ibid., 197.

31. Ibid., 200.

32. Ibid., 514.

33. Quoted in Douglas B. Sosnik, Matthew J. Dowd, and Ron Fournier, *Applebee's America: How Successful Political, Business, and Religious Leaders Connect with the New American Community* (New York: Simon and Schuster, 2006), 30.

34. Brink Lindsey, "Liberaltarians," *The New Republic*, December 11, 2006, 16.

35. Quoted in Coontz, *Way We Never Were*, 36.

36. Betty Friedan, *The Feminine Mystique* (New York: Norton, 1963), 19, 15. Friedan's book began as a study of Smith College graduates. She initially sought to publish her findings as a magazine article but wrote a book instead when she could not find any takers.

37. Quoted in Patricia Sullivan, "Voice of Feminism's 'Second Wave': Betty Friedan, 1921–2006," *Washington Post*, February 5, 2006, A1.

38. "Port Huron Statement of Students for a Democratic Society," June 11–15, 1962 (available at www2.iath.virginia.edu/sixties/HTML_docs/Resources/Primary/Manifestos/SDS_Port_Huron.html).

39. Quoted in Coontz, *Way We Never Were*, 32.

40. Ibid.

41. Ibid., 33.

42. Ibid.

43. Cited in Benoit Denizet-Lewis, "Friends, Friends with Benefits, and the Benefits of the Local Mall," *New York Times Magazine*, May 30, 2004, 33.

44. Quoted in May, "Explosive Issues," 159.

45. Ibid.

46. Kathryn Shattuck, "Norma Fritz and Michael O'Brien," *New York Times*, February 29, 2004, ST15.

47. Ibid.

48. David Brooks, *Bobos in Paradise: The New Upper Class and How They Got There* (New York: Simon and Schuster, 2000), 19.

49. Friedan, *Feminine Mystique*, 18.

50. *"Times* Will Begin Reporting Gay Couples' Ceremonies," *New York Times,* August 18, 2002, 30.

51. The couple decided to adopt the name Goodridge after Hillary's grandmother.

52. Quoted in Pam Belluck and Katie Zezima, "Hearts Beat Fast to Opening Strains of the Gay-Wedding March," *New York Times,* May 16, 2004, 22.

53. "Hillary Goodridge, Julie Goodridge," *New York Times,* May 23, 2004, ST15.

54. Michael Levenson, "After Two Years, Same-Sex Marriage Icons Split Up," *Boston Globe,* July 21, 2006, A1.

55. Dave Anderson, "Tiger Woods in a Blaze, Rewrites Masters' History," *New York Times,* April 14, 1997, 1; Celestine Bohlen, "Pope in Sarajevo, Calls for Forgiveness," *New York Times,* April 14, 1997, 1; B. Drummond Ayres Jr., "Women in Washington State House Lead U.S. Tide," *New York Times,* April 14, 1997, 1; David Barboza, "Smaller Investors Keeping Faith, Despite Stock Market Troubles," *New York Times,* April 14, 1997, 1.

56. Quoted in Al Gore and Tipper Gore, *Joined at the Heart: The Transformation of the American Family* (New York: Holt, 2002), 9.

57. Linda Perlstein, "Montgomery Schools at Diversity Landmark," *Washington Post,* October 14, 2003, A1.

58. Quoted in Linda Perlstein, "Class of Diversity Awarded Diplomas," *Washington Post,* June 6, 2004, C1.

59. Ibid.

60. Montgomery County, Md., Public Schools Web site, http://www.mcps.k12.md.us/schools/regulatoryaccountability/glance/currentyear/schools/02558.pdf.

61. D'Vera Cohn, "Area Soon to Be Mostly Minority," *Washington Post,* March 25, 2006, A1.

62. Barbara Dafoe Whitehead and David Popenoe, *The State of Our Unions, 2006* (New Brunswick, N.J.: Rutgers University National Marriage Project, 2006), 30.

63. William J. Bennett, *The Broken Hearth: Reversing the Moral Collapse of the American Family* (New York: Doubleday, 2001), 12.

64. Whitehead and Popenoe, *State of Our Unions, 2006,* 31; Tom W. Smith, "The Emerging 21st Century American Family," paper presented at the National Opinion Research Center, University of Chicago, November 24, 1999, 3.

65. Whitehead and Popenoe, *State of Our Unions, 2006,* 29–30.

66. Ibid., 24; Smith, "Emerging 21st Century American Family," 23.

67. Fern Shen, "Defining Marriage," *Washington Post,* March 17, 2004, C16.

68. Quoted in D'Vera Cohn, "Census Shows Big Increase in Gay Households," *Washington Post,* June 20, 2001, A1.

69. Bernard Weinraub and Jim Rutenberg, "Gay-Themed TV Gains a Wider Audience," *New York Times,* July 29, 2003, A1.

70. Alessandra Stanley, "Say, Darling, Is It Frigid in Here? Television, in a Darkening Mood, Looks at Marriage and Finds Despair," *New York Times,* August 19, 2007, AR1.

71. Quoted in Thomas B. Edsall, *Building Red America: The New Conservative Coalition and the Drive for Permanent Power* (New York: Perseus, 2006), 89.

72. Weinraub and Rutenberg, "Gay-Themed TV."

73. "Gay Issues, Characters, Join Prime Time," CNN, October 16, 2000.

74. Teresa Wiltz, "TV's Rare Bird," *Washington Post*, May 21, 2006, N1.

75. "Gay Issues, Characters, Join Prime Time."

76. Ryan Lee, "Southern Stations shun 'Queer Eye,'" *Washington Blade*, August 8, 2003, 1.

77. Quoted in Sharon Waxman, "*Simpsons* Animates Gay Nuptials, and a Debate," *New York Times*, February 21, 2005, A1.

78. Quoted in Weinraub and Rutenberg, "Gay-Themed TV."

79. Henry J. Kaiser Family Foundation poll, February 7–September 4, 2000.

80. Halberstam, *Fifties*, 199.

81. Tocqueville, *Democracy in America*, 453.

82. U.S. Department of Commerce, Bureau of the Census, *Historical Statistics of the United States: Colonial Times to 1970* (Washington, D.C., 1975), 105–6.

83. Daniel Chauncey Brewer, *The Conquest of New England by the Immigrant* (New York: Putnam, 1926).

84. Steinfels, *People Adrift*, 104.

85. Quoted in A. James Reichley, "Party Politics in a Federal Polity," in *Challenges to Party Government*, ed. John Kenneth White and Jerome M. Mileur (Carbondale: Southern Illinois University Press, 1992), 48.

86. Quoted in Robert D. Putnam, *Bowling Alone: The Collapse and Revival of American Community* (New York: Simon and Schuster, 2000), 19.

87. "Proceedings of the State Conference on Immigration in Massachusetts Industries," *Bulletin of the Department of Education* (Massachusetts), November 5, 1920.

88. For an accounting of these incidents, see Coontz, *Way We Never Were*, 30–31.

89. Quoted in Dwight D. Eisenhower, *Waging Peace: The White House Years, 1956–1961* (Garden City, N.Y.: Doubleday, 1965), 163.

90. Ibid., 170.

91. Quoted in Robert A. Caro, *The Years of Lyndon Johnson: Master of the Senate* (New York: Knopf, 2002), 959.

92. E. E. Schattschneider, *The Semi-Sovereign People: A Realist's View of Democracy in America* (1960; Hinsdale, Ill.: Dryden, 1975), 124.

93. Dwight D. Eisenhower, "Farewell Address," Washington, D.C., January 17, 1961.

94. Gore and Gore, *Joined at the Heart*, 14.

95. "Democratic Platform, 1952," in Kirk H. Porter and Donald Bruce Johnson, *National Party Platforms: 1840–1968* (Urbana: University of Illinois Press, 1970), 480.

96. Eisenhower, "Farewell Address."

97. John F. Kennedy, "Acceptance Speech," Democratic National Convention, Los Angeles, July 15, 1960.

98. Quoted in Deborah Solomon, "The Way We Live Now: A New Moral Majority? Questions for Roberta Combs," *New York Times Magazine*, November 16, 2003, 26.

99. Associated Press, "San Diego Council Bans the Word 'Minority,'" CNN, April 3, 2001.

100. The vote was 801,725 in favor and 545,933 against. See also Peter Wallenstein, *Tell the Court I Love My Wife: Race, Marriage, and Law: An American History* (New York: Palgrave Macmillan, 2002), 247.

101. Kim M. Williams, *Mark One or More: Civil Rights in Multiracial America* (Ann Arbor: University of Michigan Press, 2006), 85.

102. Quoted in Wallenstein, *Tell the Court I Love My Wife*, 182.

103. Anne Hull, "How 'Don't Tell' Translates: The Military Needs Linguists, but It Doesn't Want This One," *Washington Post*, December 3, 2003, A1.

104. "History of the Defense Language Institute" (available at www.dliflc.edu/Academics/academic_affairs/dli_catalog/hist.htm).

105. Hull, "How 'Don't Tell' Translates," A1.

106. Ibid.

107. Stephen Benjamin, "Don't Ask, Don't Translate," *New York Times*, June 8, 2007, A29.

108. Nathaniel Frank, "Stonewalled," *The New Republic*, January 24, 2005, 10.

109. Ibid.

110. Quoted in Lolita C. Baldor, "Hearing Sought over Linguists' Discharge," Associated Press, May 23, 2007.

111. Quoted in Bill Clinton, *My Life* (New York: Knopf, 2004), 483.

112. Ibid., 485.

113. Ibid., 483.

114. Quoted in Hillary Rodham Clinton, *Living History*, 242.

115. Bill Clinton, *My Life*, 485.

116. Hull, "How 'Don't Tell' Translates," A1.

117. Lizette Alvarez, "Gay Groups Renew Drive against 'Don't Ask, Don't Tell,'" *New York Times*, September 14, 2006, A1. See also John Files, "Military's Discharges for Being Gay Rose in '05," *New York Times*, August 15, 2006, 17. In 2001, 1,227 gay service members were dismissed; in 2002, 885; in 2003, 770; and in 2004, 653.

118. Hillary Rodham Clinton, *Living History*, 241.

119. Everett Carll Ladd Jr., foreword to John Kenneth White, *The Fractured Electorate: Political Parties and Social Change in Southern New England* (Hanover, N.H.: University Press of New England, 1983), ix–x.

120. *Report of the National Advisory Commission on Civil Disorders* (New York: New York Times, 1968), 1.

121. F. James Davis, *Who Is Black? One Nation's Definition* (University Park: Pennsylvania State University Press, 1991).

122. Quoted in D'Vera Cohn and Darryl Fears, "Multiracial Growth Seen in Census," *Washington Post*, March 13, 2001, A1.

123. Schattschneider, *Semi-Sovereign People*, 66.

124. Quoted in Michael Barone, *Our Country: The Shaping of America from Roosevelt to Reagan* (New York: Free Press, 1990), 310.

125. Theodore H. White, *The Making of the President, 1960* (New York: New American Library, 1961), 125.

126. Quoted in Richard M. Nixon, *Six Crises* (New York: Warner, 1979), 364.

127. John Kenneth White, *Fractured Electorate*, 10–11.

128. Monika L. McDermott, "Can Kerry Carry the Catholic Vote?" KCBS, May 24, 2004 (available at cbsnews.com/stories/2004/05/21/politics/main618886 .shtml).

129. Nixon, *Six Crises*, 436.

130. John F. Kennedy, Speech Before the Greater Houston Ministerial Association, Houston, September 12, 1960.

131. Ibid.

132. Quoted in Nixon, *Six Crises*, 389.

133. Ibid., 433–34.

134. Quoted in Laurie Goodstein, "How the Evangelicals and Catholics Joined Forces," *New York Times*, May 30, 2004, WK4.

135. Cited in Barone, *Our Country*, xii.

136. Nixon, *Six Crises*, 465.

137. Robert Dallek, *An Unfinished Life: John F. Kennedy, 1917–1963* (Boston: Little, Brown, 2003), 691.

138. *Emerging Trends*, 1993:5, cited in William V. D'Antonio, James D. Davidson, Dean R. Hoge, and Ruth A. Wallace, *Laity American and Catholic: Transforming the Church* (Kansas City: Sheed and Ward, 1996).

139. "Bob Jones University Responds," http://www.sullivan-county.com/ news/bob_jones/bju.htm, August 1, 2006.

140. David Van Biema, "Catholic Bashing?" CNN.com/AllPolitics, February 28, 2000 (available at www.cnn.com/AllPOLITICS/time/2000/02/28/catholic .html).

141. Voter News Service exit poll, November 7, 2000.

142. John C. Green, James L. Guth, Lyman A. Kellstedt, and Corwin B. Smidt, "How the Faithful Voted: Religion and the 2000 Presidential Election," BeliefNet.com, n.d.

143. Matt Malone, "Catholics and Candidates," *America*, May 17, 2004, 8.

144. Ibid.

145. Alan Wolfe, *One Nation after All* (New York: Viking, 1998), esp. 275–322.

146. Barbara Bradley Hagerty, "Kerry and the Catholic Vote," *Morning Edition*, National Public Radio, April 30, 2004.

147. Goodstein, "How the Evangelicals and Catholics Joined Forces," WK 4.

148. Susan Page, "Churchgoing Closely Tied to Voting Patterns," *USA Today*, June 3, 2004, A1.

149. John Kerry, Speech at the National Prayer Breakfast, February 4, 1993, personal copy sent to author.

150. Quoted in Karen Tumulty and Perry Bacon Jr., "A Test of Kerry's Faith," *Time*, April 5, 2004, 42.

151. Daniel J. Wakin, "A Divisive Issue for Catholics: Bishops, Politicians, and Communion," *New York Times*, May 31, 2004, 12.

152. Maureen Dowd, "Vote and Be Damned," *New York Times*, October 17, 2004, WK11.

153. National Election Pool exit poll, November 2, 2004.

154. Kennedy, "Address to Southern Baptist Leaders."

155. Schattschneider, *Semi-Sovereign People*, 71.

156. National Election Pool exit poll, November 2, 2004.

157. David D. Kirkpatrick, "Bush Campaign Seeks Help from Congregations," *New York Times*, June 3, 2004, 1.

158. Schattschneider, *Semi-Sovereign People*, 71.

159. Richard M. Scammon and Ben J. Wattenberg, *The Real Majority* (New York: Coward-McCann, 1970).

Chapter Two

1. Wallace Turner, "Rusk's Daughter, 18, Is Wed to Negro," *New York Times*, September 22, 1967, 1.

2. Dean Rusk as told to Richard Rusk, *As I Saw It* (New York: Norton, 1990), 581.

3. Turner, "Rusk's Daughter," 1.

4. Douglas Martin, "Mildred Loving, Who Fought Marriage Ban, Dies," *New York Times*, May 6, 2008, A1; Peter Wallenstein, *Tell the Court I Love My Wife: Race, Marriage, and Law: An American History* (New York: Palgrave Macmillan, 2002), 216, 217, 219; Neely Tucker, "Loving Day Recalls a Time When the Union of a Man and a Woman Was Banned," *Washington Post*, June 13, 2006, C1; Neely Tucker, "Mildred Loving Followed Her Heart and Made History," *Washington Post*, May 6, 2008, C1. Mildred Loving's mother was part Rappahannock Indian and her father was part Cherokee, leading Mildred to think of herself as being an American Indian, not black. The first American laws against miscegenation had been enacted in Maryland in 1661, and miscegenation not only voided a marriage but declared the children of interracial marriages to be illegitimate. Further, spouses had no inheritance rights, and heirs could not receive death benefits.

5. *Loving v. Virginia*, 388 U.S. 1 (1967). The Lovings had traveled to Virginia in 1964 to visit her mother and were arrested again. Richard Loving wrote to Attorney General Robert F. Kennedy, who referred the case to the American Civil Liberties Union, which brought the case to the Supreme Court. Richard Loving built a home for his family in Caroline County, where his three children were raised. He was killed in an automobile accident in 1975. Mildred Loving never remarried and died in 2008.

6. Wallenstein, *Tell the Court I Love My Wife*, 223, 224, 227.

7. Ibid., 228. In some places, violations of the law could result in a 10-year jail sentence.

8. Ibid., 185.

9. National Opinion Research Center poll, April 1968; Louis Harris and Associates poll, February 1971.

10. Barack Obama, *Dreams from My Father: A Story of Race and Inheritance* (New York: Times Books, 1995), 11.

11. United Press International, "Rusk's Daughter, Husband Felicitated by Mrs. Johnson," *New York Times*, September 23, 1967, 14.

12. Rusk, *As I Saw It*, 581.

13. "A Marriage of Enlightenment," *Time*, September 29, 1967, 30.

14. Rusk, *As I Saw It*, 605. Harris's racism has been well documented: he is quoted as having said, "Niggers are niggers and no amount of crossbreeding is going to help them any. The tiniest drop of nigger blood will spoil a man. History shows that. Everybody knows that, and those who don't know that have probably got some nigger blood in them, that's all" (quoted in James Wooten, *Dasher: The Roots and the Rising of Jimmy Carter* [New York: Summit, 1978], 267).

15. Rusk, *As I Saw It*, 605, 627. Rusk is buried at Oconee Hill Cemetery, next to the University of Georgia's football stadium.

16. Darryl Fears and Claudia Deane, "Biracial Couples Report Tolerance," *Washington Post*, July 5, 2001, A1.

17. Richard Morin, "What Teens Really Think," *Washington Post Magazine*, October 23, 2005, 16–17.

18. Ibid., 18.

19. Quoted in Jose Antonio Vargas, "In Living Colors," *Washington Post Magazine*, October 23, 2005, 28, 48, 49.

20. Ibid., 49. According to the 2000 Census, 9.7 percent of black men married someone of another race, twice the rate of black women and higher than any other race and sex except Asian women (Krissah Williams, "Singled Out: In Seeking a Mate, Men and Women Find Delicate Imbalance," *Washington Post*, October 8, 2006, A1).

21. Obama, *Dreams*, 10.

22. Jimmy Carter, Inaugural Address, Atlanta, January 12, 1971. On January 14, 1963, George Wallace famously declared in his inaugural address as Alabama's new governor, "In the name of the greatest people that have ever trod the earth, I draw the line in the dust and toss the gauntlet before the feet of tyranny . . . and I say . . . segregation today . . . segregation tomorrow . . . segregation forever."

23. "New Day A'Coming in the South," *Time*, May 31, 1971, 19.

24. Quoted in Bill Clinton, *My Life* (New York: Knopf, 2004), 263.

25. Peter G. Bourne, *Jimmy Carter: A Comprehensive Biography from Plains to Post-Presidency* (New York: Scribner, 1997), 183.

26. Georgia law requires that the winner of statewide elections receive a majority of the popular vote. Because the Republican candidate also failed to win more than 50 percent of the vote, the election outcome was decided by the legislature.

27. "Mississippi Will Retain Its 107-Year-Old Flag," CNN.com, April 18, 2001. Mississippi is the last state whose flag retains Confederate symbols.

28. One year later, Perdue designed a flag without the Confederate Stars and Bars and asked voters to approve it; they did so by an overwhelming margin.

29. "Hundreds Protest as Confederate Battle Flag Comes Down in South Car-

olina," CNN.com, July 1, 2000. South Carolina began to fly the flag in 1962, ostensibly to commemorate the centennial of the Civil War, though many observers saw the display as a response to the burgeoning civil rights movement.

30. "South Carolina House Approves Final Measure to Relocate Confederate Flag," CNN.com, May 11, 2000.

31. Barack Obama, "A More Perfect Union," speech at the National Constitution Center, Philadelphia, March 18, 2008.

32. "Hartsfield-Jackson History" (available at www.atlanta-airport.com/Air port/ATL/GM_letter.aspx).

33. Anne Hull, "Two Jobs and a Sense of Hope," *Washington Post*, December 11, 2002, A1.

34. Ibid.

35. Ibid.

36. Gayle White, "Atlanta's Faithful Gather in Increasing Numbers," *Atlanta Journal-Constitution*, July 24, 2003, 1.

37. Quoted in John Blake and Bo Emerson, "William Gregory Brings Charisma," *Atlanta Journal-Constitution*, December 10, 2004, 1.

38. Anne Hull, "Old South Goes with the Wind," *Washington Post*, December 8, 2002, A1.

39. Hull, "Two Jobs," A1.

40. Hull, "Old South," A1.

41. Quoted in *Immigrant Nation: Divided Country*, CNN, October 23, 2004.

42. Anne Hull, "Dreaming against the Odds," *Washington Post*, December 9, 2002, A1.

43. Ibid.

44. Rachel L. Swarns, "Hispanic Teenagers with Outside Roots Are Finding a Way In," *New York Times*, December 31, 2006, 16; Rachel L. Swarns, "In Georgia, Newest Immigrants Unsettle an Old Sense of Place," *New York Times*, August 4, 2006, A1.

45. Hull, "Dreaming," A1.

46. Hull, "Old South," A1.

47. Ibid.

48. Ronald Fernandez, *America beyond Black and White: How Immigrants and Fusions are Helping Us Overcome the Racial Divide* (Ann Arbor: University of Michigan Press, 2007), 148.

49. Quoted in "Perspectives," *Newsweek*, July 17, 2006, 21.

50. Quoted in Peter Slevin, "Town's Eye View of Immigration Debate," *Washington Post*, April 3, 2006, A1.

51. Swarns, "In Georgia," A1.

52. Hull, "Old South," A1.

53. The categories were white, black, African American or Negro, American Indian or Alaska Native, Mexican, Mexican American, Chicano, Puerto Rican, Cuban, Other Spanish/Hispanic/Latino, Asian Indian, Chinese, Filipino, Japanese, Korean, Vietnamese, Other Asian, Native Hawaiian, Guamanian or Chamorro, Samoan, and Other Pacific Islander.

54. Kim M. Williams, *Mark One or More: Civil Rights in Multiracial America* (Ann Arbor: University of Michigan Press, 2006), 55, 2.

55. Quoted in ibid.

56. Under existing regulations, schools and colleges must report how many of their students fall into each of five categories: black, white, Hispanic, Asian/Pacific Islander and Native American/Alaska Native. The proposed regulations would first ask a student if he/she is Hispanic. Students could then select one or more descriptions from the following groups: American Indian or Alaska Native, Asian, black, Native Hawaiian or other Pacific Islander, and white (Elissa Gootman, "U.S. Proposal Offers Students Wider Way of Racial Identity," *New York Times*, August 9, 2006, A12).

57. Hull, "Old South," A1.

58. Bill Clinton, "Remarks by the President at Portland State University Commencement," Portland, Ore., June 13, 1998. Clinton often cited the importance of the country's changing racial complexion. He called attention to it in a 1997 address at the University of California at San Diego and returned to this theme again in his 2000 State of the Union Address.

59. See Patrick J. Buchanan, *The Death of the West: How Dying Populations and Immigrant Invasions Imperil Our Country and Civilization* (New York: Dunne/St. Martins, 2002), 2.

60. Samuel P. Huntington, *Who Are We? The Challenges to America's National Identity* (New York: Simon and Schuster, 2004), 196.

61. Buchanan, *The Death of the West*, 2.

62. Zogby International poll, December 6–8, 2005.

63. Gallup poll, April 4–7, 2006.

64. John Pomfret and Sonya Geis, "Immigrants' Voice Reaches the Hill," *Washington Post*, March 28, 2006, A1.

65. Sheryl Gay Stolberg, "Three Wounded Soldiers Take Another Oath," *New York Times*, July 25, 2006, A19; Adrian Sainz, "Senate Committee Hears Testimony on Immigrants in Military," Associated Press, July 10, 2006.

66. Carol Morello, "Granting a Wish to a Slain Marine," *Washington Post*, January 28, 2005, B4.

67. Sharon Cohen and Pauline Arrillaga, "U.S. War Death Toll Hits 1,000," Associated Press, September 8, 2004.

68. Morello, "Granting a Wish," B4.

69. Cohen and Arrillaga, "U.S. War Death Toll Hits 1,000."

70. Stan Grossfeld, "'It's a Good Life,'" *Boston Globe*, May 6, 2001, E1.

71. Peggy Levitt, *The Transnational Villagers* (Berkeley: University of California Press, 2001), 3.

72. Lisa Wangsness, "Tapping New Voters in City Races," *Boston Globe*, July 12, 2005, B1.

73. Quoted in Lisa Wangsness, "Only Modest Changes Expected in Council Focus," *Boston Globe*, November 9, 2005, B5.

74. Ibid.

75. D'Vera Cohn, "Hispanic Growth Surge Fueled by Births in U.S.," *Washington Post*, June 9, 2005, A1.

76. Huntington, *Who Are We?* 226.

77. "About Hartford's Mayor," <http://www.hartford.gov/government/mayor/biography.asp>.

78. David Brooks, *On Paradise Drive: How We Live Now (and Always Have) in the Future Tense* (New York: Simon and Schuster, 2004), 35.

79. Sam Dillon, "In Schools across U.S., the Melting Pot Overflows," *New York Times*, August 27, 2006, A1.

80. Huntington, *Who Are We?* 207.

81. Haya El Nasser, "Jump in Hispanics Energizes Economy in Kansas County," *USA Today*, June 30, 2008, 7A.

82. Rick Lyman, "New Data Show Immigrants' Growth and Reach," *New York Times*, August 15, 2006, A1.

83. The "melting pot" image was both conjured and dispelled by Nathan Glazer and Daniel Patrick Moynihan in their seminal book, *Beyond the Melting Pot: The Negroes, Puerto Ricans, Jews, Italians, and Irish of New York City* (Cambridge: MIT Press, 1963).

84. U.S. Department of Commerce, "Number of Foreign-Born Up 57 Percent since 1990, According to Census 2000," June 4, 2002; Huntington, *Who Are We?* 231.

85. Huntington, *Who Are We?* 223.

86. "Growing Values Gap between Poor and Middle Class," Pew Research Center press release, November 13, 2007, 11. See also Gary Younge, "Black Americans Move Back to Southern States," *Guardian*, May 25, 2004, 13.

87. Jeffrey S. Passel and D'Vera Cohn, "U.S. Population Projections: 2005–2050," Pew Research Center, February 11, 2008, 9; Sam Roberts, "A Generation Away, Minorities May Become the Majority in U.S.," *New York Times*, August 14, 2008, A1.

88. D'Vera Cohn and Tara Bahrampour, "Of U.S. Children under 5, Nearly Half Are Minorities," *Washington Post*, May 10, 2006, A1.

89. Huntington, *Who Are We?* 227, 224.

90. Samuel Huntington, "José, Can You See?" *Foreign Policy*, March–April 2004, 44.

91. Passel and Cohn, "U.S. Population Projections"; Amitai Etzioni, *The Monochrome Society* (Princeton: Princeton University Press, 2001), 31.

92. Ben J. Wattenberg, *The Birth Dearth* (New York: Pharos, 1987).

93. Cited in Buchanan, *Death of the West*, 129.

94. Ibid., 139.

95. Michael Barone and Richard E. Cohen, *The Almanac of American Politics, 2004* (Washington, D.C.: National Journal, 2003), 154.

96. Edison Media Research and Mitofsky International California exit poll, November 4, 2008.

97. U.S. Department of Commerce, Bureau of the Census, "American Fact Finder: Los Angeles County, California: Profile of General Demographic Characteristics, 2000," (available at http://factfinder.census.gov/servlet/QTTable?_bm=n&_lang=en&qr_name=DEC_2000_SF1_U_DP1&ds_name=DEC_2000_SF1_U&geo_id=05000US06037).

98. Peter Dreier, "Villaraigosa's Challenge: Governing Los Angeles in the Bush and Schwarzenegger Era," CommonDreams.org, May 28, 2005.

99. Huntington, *Who Are We?* 253.

100. Michael Finnegan and Mark Z. Barabak, "Villaraigosa Landslide: Voter Discontent Helps Propel Challenger to a Historic Victory," *Los Angeles Times*, May 18, 2005, A1.

101. Dreier, "Villaraigosa's Challenge."

102. *Los Angeles Times* exit poll, May 17, 2005.

103. Quoted in John M. Broder, "Latino Defeats Incumbent in L.A. Mayor's Race," *New York Times*, May 18, 2005, A1.

104. Quoted in Antonio Villaraigosa, Inaugural Address, Los Angeles, July 1, 2005 (available at www.lacity.org/mayor).

105. Eric Schmitt, "Whites in Minority in Largest Cities, the Census Shows," *New York Times*, April 30, 2001, A1.

106. Dale Russakoff, "Census Finds Diversity Spreading to Suburbs," *Washington Post*, March 9, 2001, A14; Genaro C. Armas, "Census Highlights Varied Racial Mix," *Boston Globe*, March 9, 2001, A3; Tim Craig, "Minorities in GOP Rally for Allen in Virginia," *Washington Post*, September 10, 2006, C6.

107. Craig, "Minorities in GOP," C6.

108. Teresa Wiltz and Paul Farhi, "WHFS Changes Its Tune to Spanish," *Washington Post*, January 13, 2005, A1.

109. Quoted in Frank Ahrens, "Radio: WHFS Off the Air," Washington Post.com, January 12, 2005.

110. Teresa Wiltz, "Warming Trend: El Zol Radio's Latino Mix Gains Listeners," *Washington Post*, April 20, 3005, C1; Paul Farhi, "Shock Jock's Audience Is Beating Him to the Door," *Washington Post*, October 20, 2005, C1.

111. Wiltz and Farhi, "WHFS Changes Its Tune," A1.

112. Wiltz, "Warming Trend," C1.

113. Quoted in Karin Brulliard, "Spanish Radio Tunes in to Immigration Quandaries," *Washington Post*, April 3, 2006, B1.

114. Betsy Streisand, "Latino Power: Big Media Tune in to the Nation's Largest Minority," *U.S. News and World Report*, March 17, 2003, 34.

115. Heidi Vogt, "TeleFutura, One Year Old, Finds Its Legs," *Media Life Magazine*, January 3, 2003.

116. Maria Matzer Rose, "Univision Net Soars 62% on Record Viewership," HollywoodReporter.com, February 20, 2004.

117. Streisand, "Latino Power," 35.

118. Taco Bell Web site (www.tacobell.com).

119. Amanda Hesser, "Tex Macs: McDonald's Is Creating Its Own Worst Enemy: A Healthy Burrito," *New York Times Magazine*, February 27, 2005, 85.

120. Quoted in Huntington, *Who Are We?* 250.

121. Ibid., 249.

122. "Miami Herald Publisher to Resign in July," Associated Press, January 28, 2005; "Working at Knight-Ridder: Profiles of *el Nuevo Herald*" (www.knightrid der.com/working/profiles/nuevo_miami.html; accessed January 28, 2005).

123. Quoted in Huntington, *Who Are We?* 210.

124. Quoted in Huntington, "José, Can You See?" 43.

125. Quoted in Etzioni, *Monochrome Society*, 4–5.

126. Buchanan, *Death of the West*, 1.

127. Slevin, "Town's Eye View," A1.

128. Opinion Dynamics poll, April 6–7, 2004.

129. "Bush's Speech on Immigration Closely Follows Public Opinion," Gallup poll, press release, May 17, 2006.

130. Gallup poll, May 5–7, 2006.

131. Ibid., June 8–25, 2006.

132. Ibid., June 4–24, 2007.

133. NBC News/*Wall Street Journal* poll, March 6–8, 2004.

134. Ibid., December 14–17, 2007.

135. Gallup poll, June 4–24, 2007.

136. Ibid.

137. Abby Goodnough, "A Florida Mayor Turns to an Immigration Curb to Fix a Fading City," *New York Times*, July 10, 2006, A12. In 2007, a federal judge voided the Hazelton ordinance, noting that the statute interfered with federal law and violated the due-process rights of employers, landlords, and illegal immigrants (Julia Preston, "Judge Voids Ordinance on Illegal Immigrants," *New York Times*, July 27, 2007, A12).

138. Quoted in Holly Bailey, "A Border War," *Newsweek*, April 3, 2006, 22.

139. Alec MacGillis, "Tancredo's Politics of Fear," *Washington Post*, November 14, 2007, A7.

140. Tamar Jacoby, "A Line Has Been Drawn in the Arizona Sand," *Washington Post*, November 14, 2004, B3.

141. Amanda J. Crawford, Elvia Diaz, and Yvonne Wingett, "Initiative Raises Questions," *Arizona Republic*, November 4, 2004, 1.

142. Quoted in Dan Balz and Darryl Fears, "'We Decided Not to Be Invisible Anymore,'" *Washington Post*, April 11, 2006, A1.

143. Alan Wolfe, *One Nation after All* (New York: Viking, 1998), 133.

144. Zogby International poll, January 15–28, 2004.

145. Samuel P. Huntington, "Reconsidering Immigration: Is Mexico a Special Case?" *Center for Immigration Studies Backgrounder*, November 2000, 5.

146. Swarns, "In Georgia," A1.

147. George W. Bush, Address to Congress, Washington, D.C., February 27, 2001.

148. Mike Allen, "Bush: Respect Mexican Immigrants," *Washington Post*, May 6, 2001, A7.

149. D'Vera Cohn, "Area Immigration Booming," *Washington Post*, November 23, 2004, A1.

150. George W. Bush, Acceptance Speech, Republican National Convention, New York, September 2, 2004.

151. George W. Bush, Address to the Nation on Immigration Reform, Washington, D.C., May 15, 2006.

152. Quoted in Pomfret and Geis, "Immigrants' Voice Reaches the Hill," A1.

153. Joseph Lelyveld, "The Leading Edge of a New American Nativism," *New York Times Magazine*, October 15, 2006, 46.

154. Quoted in N. C. Aizenman and David Finkel, "Shared Bond Stretched to the Limit," *Washington Post*, April 11, 2006, B1.

155. "Rally Voices," *Washington Post*, April 11, 2006, A11.

156. Quoted in Balz and Fears, "'We Decided Not to Be Invisible,'" A1.

157. Ibid.; Sonya Geis and Michael Powell, "Hundreds of Thousands Rally in Cities Large and Small," *Washington Post*, April 11, 2006, A8.

158. Sue Anne Pressley and Karin Brulliard, "Marchers Flood Mall with Passion, Pride," *Washington Post*, April 11, 2006, A1.

159. Jonathan Weisman, "With Senate Vote, Congress Passes Border Fence Bill," *Washington Post*, September 30, 2006, A1; Carl Hulse and Rachel L. Swarns, "Senate Passes Bill on Building Border Fence," *New York Times*, September 30, 2006, A1.

160. Quoted in Alan Wolfe, "Getting In," *The New Republic*, May 8, 2006, 30.

161. Quoted in Lelyveld, "Leading Edge," 42.

162. Ellis Cose, *Color-Blind: Seeing beyond Race in a Race-Obsessed World* (New York: HarperCollins, 1997), 3.

163. Tucker, "Loving Day," C1.

164. Williams, *Mark One or More*, 1.

165. Tucker, "Loving Day," C1.

166. Wallenstein, *Tell the Court I Love My Wife*, 251. Donald Loving died in 2000. Mildred Loving died in 2008.

167. Quoted in Mireya Navarro, "Going Beyond Black and White, Hispanics in Census Pick 'Other,'" *New York Times*, November 9, 2003, 1.

168. Ibid. Six percent of Hispanics said they were members of two or more races, and 2 percent identified themselves as black. In 2004, the Census Bureau announced that it intended to eliminate the "some other race" category because so many Hispanics checked it (Fernandez, *America Beyond Black and White*, 162).

169. Quoted in Fernandez, *America Beyond Black and White*, 162.

170. International Communications Research poll, April 4–June 11, 2002. This question was asked of Hispanics who identified themselves as white/black/Asian but preferred another option when asked about race.

171. Quoted in Etzioni, *Monochrome Society*, 20.

172. Cose, *Color-Blind*, 25.

173. Navarro, "Going Beyond Black and White," 1.

174. Quoted in Cohn, "Hispanic Growth Surge," A1.

175. Al Gore and Tipper Gore, *Joined at the Heart: The Transformation of the American Family* (New York: Holt, 2002), 33.

176. Huntington, *Who Are We?* 240.

177. Benedict Carey, "In-Laws in the Age of the Outsider," *New York Times*, December 18, 2005, section 4, 1.

178. Quoted in Fernandez, *America Beyond Black and White*, 218.

179. *Washington Post*/Henry J. Kaiser Family Foundation/Harvard University poll, March 8–April 22, 2001.

180. Quoted in Cose, *Color-Blind*, 19, 20.

181. Gore and Gore, *Joined at the Heart*, 113.

182. Michael Lind, "Far from Heaven," *The Nation*, June 16, 2003, 3.

183. Gore and Gore, *Joined at the Heart*, 113.

184. Ibid., 113–14.

185. Lisa De Pasquale, "Miss America Chiefs Turn Politically Correct, Downplay Winner's Conservative Views," *Human Events*, October 7, 2002. In 2004, the Miss America title was awarded to another black contestant, Ericka Dunlap.

186. Quoted in Tom Callahan, *In Search of Tiger: A Journey through Golf with Tiger Woods* (New York: Crown, 2003), 150.

187. Wallenstein, *Tell the Court I Love My Wife*, 249. Colin Powell, for one, strongly disagrees with Woods's self-invented racial identification: "In America . . . when you look like me, you're black" (quoted in Etzioni, *Monochrome Society*, 30).

188. "Tiger Tied," *Time*, October 18, 2004, 97.

189. Chris Matthews, *Hardball*, MSNBC, April 2, 2008.

190. Halle Berry Acceptance Speech, BBC News, March 24, 2002.

191. Quoted in William Booth, "Oscar's Golden Gloves," *Washington Post*, February 28, 2005, C1.

192. Quoted in "Picture Perfect: 2005 Oscar Roundtable," *Newsweek*, January 31, 2005, 53.

193. Stephen M. Silverman and Sarah Elkins, "Bachelor Bush to Change His Ways Soon," People.com, June 30, 2003.

194. Anne E. Kornblut, "Little Talk of Dynasty as a Bush Weds," *Boston Globe*, August 8, 2004, A24; Mike Allen, "In Maine, One Bush Wedding and a Fish Story," *Washington Post*, August 8, 2004, D3; Justin Ellis and Tom Bell, "Town Bustles with Bush Family," *Portland Press Herald*, August 7, 2004, A1.

195. David Margolick, "Brother Dearest," *Vanity Fair*, July 2001, 96.

196. George P. Bush, Address to the Republican National Convention, Philadelphia, August 2, 2000.

197. Mike Ferullo, "At GOP Convention, Bush Nephew Appeals to Young Voters, Hispanics," CNN, August 4, 2000.

198. Russell Contreras, "Voters' Vida Loca," *Houston Press*, June 29, 2000, 1.

199. Quoted in Brendan Farrington, "Governor's Son—and Political Hunk—to Wed in Maine," Associated Press, August 5, 2004.

200. Quoted in Deborah Sharp, "George P. Bush at Center of Campaign Buzz," *USA Today*, June 19, 2000, 6A.

201. Helen Anders, "Cute Bush Is Altar-Bound," *Austin American-Statesman*, August 16, 2004, 1.

202. Associated Press, wire report, August 7, 2004.

203. Quoted in Silverman and Elkins, "Bachelor Bush."

204. Maria Elena Salinas, "Bush: The Latino Connection," *Passaic County (New Jersey) Herald News*, September 5, 2004, B9.

205. National Election Pool exit poll, November 2, 2004.

206. Quoted in Fernandez, *America beyond Black and White*, 40.

207. Greenberg Quinlan Rosner Research poll, March 8–11, 2004.

208. Quoted in D'Vera Cohn, "Area Soon to Be Mostly Minority," *Washington Post*, March 25, 2006, A1.

209. Cited in Navarro, "Going Beyond Black and White," 1.

210. Jennifer S. Lee, "In New York's Most Diverse Police Class, Blue Comes in Many Colors," *New York Times*, July 8, 2005, A22. Although whites remain a strong presence on the New York City police force, many are immigrants from Eastern Europe.

211. Sam Roberts, "Immigrants Swell Numbers Near New York," *New York Times*, August 15, 2006, A17.

212. Lee, "In New York's Most Diverse Police Class," A22.

Chapter Three

1. Richard Reeves, *President Kennedy* (New York: Simon and Schuster, 1993), 354.

2. John F. Kennedy, Inaugural Address, Washington, D.C., January 20, 1961.

3. George W. Bush, Inaugural Address, Washington, D.C., January 20, 2005.

4. George W. Bush, State of the Union Address, Washington, D.C., January 28, 2008.

5. Alan Wolfe, *Moral Freedom: The Impossible Idea That Defines the Way We Live Now* (New York: Norton, 2001), 199.

6. Francis Fukuyama, *The Great Disruption: Human Nature and the Reconstitution of Social Order* (New York: Free Press, 1999), 47.

7. Liberty-Tree.ca Web site, at http://quotes.liberty-tree.ca/quotes/morals.

8. Quoted in Arthur M. Schlesinger, *A Thousand Days: John F. Kennedy in the White House* (New York: Greenwich, 1983), 105–6.

9. John Kenneth White, *The New Politics of Old Values* (Hanover, N.H.: University Press of New England, 1988), 31.

10. Quoted in Rick Santorum, *It Takes a Family: Conservatism and the Common Good* (Wilmington, Del.: ISI, 2005), 300.

11. Ibid., 280.

12. Claudia Deane, "Trend Lines: America's Moral Compass," *Washington Post*, June 8, 2006, A2.

13. Ayers, McHenry, and Associates poll, March 6–9, 2005.

14. Cited in Norval Glenn and Elizabeth Marquardt, *Hooking Up, Hanging Out, and Hoping for Mr. Right: College Women on Dating and Mating Today* (New York: Institute for American Values, 2001), 52.

15. Ibid., 13. Fifty-nine percent strongly agreed with this statement.

16. MSNBC/Zogby International online opt-in survey, September 2005.

17. William D. Mosher, Anjani Chandra, and Jo Jones, *Sexual Behavior and Selected Health Measures: Men and Women 15–44 Years of Age, United States, 2002* (Washington, D.C.: U.S. Department of Health and Human Services, Centers for Disease Control and Prevention, National Center for Health Statistics, 2005), 3.

18. Cited in Monica A. Longmore, Wendy D. Manning, and Peggy C. Gior-

dano, "Adolescents' Self-Identities and Sexual Debut," paper presented at the 2005 International Union for the Scientific Study of Population, Tours, France.

19. Sabrina Weill, *The Real Truth about Teens and Sex* (New York: Penguin, 2005), 17.

20. Katy Kelly, "Just Don't Do It!" *U.S. News and World Report*, October 17, 2005.

21. Shannon Ethridge, "Sex and Young America: Ministering to Sexually Addicted Youth," *Enrichment Journal*, Fall 2005.

22. Kelly, "Just Don't Do It!"

23. Weill, *Real Truth*, 18.

24. Princeton Survey Research Associates International poll, September 4–November 7, 2004. This poll surveyed 1,000 adults nationwide who were parents of teens aged 13 to 16.

25. Quoted in Ethridge, "Sex and Young America."

26. Princeton Survey Research Associates International poll, September 4–November 7, 2004.

27. Princeton Survey Research Associates poll, September 29–October 23, 2003.

28. Quoted in Kelly, "Just Don't Do It!"

29. "Faith and Family in America," Greenberg Quinlan Rosner Research press release, October 19, 2005; David Popenoe, *The Future of Marriage in America* (New Brunswick, N.J.: Rutgers University National Marriage Project, 2007), 23.

30. Barbara Dafoe Whitehead and David Popenoe, "Life without Children," in Barbara Dafoe Whitehead and David Popenoe, *The State of Our Unions, 2006* (New Brunswick, N.J.: Rutgers University National Marriage Project, 2006), 1.

31. "As Marriage and Parenthood Drift Apart, Public Is Concerned about Social Impact," Pew Research Center press release, July 1, 2007, 15.

32. Ibid., i.

33. Greenberg Quinlan Rosner poll, July 25–August 7, 2005.

34. William A. Galston and Elaine C. Kamarck, "Five Realities That Will Shape 21st Century U.S. Politics," in *The Global Third Way Debate*, ed. Anthony Giddens (Malden, Mass.: Blackwell, 2001), 106.

35. Ibid.

36. Associated Press, "Manhattan Leads Single-Living Trend," *Washington Post*, September 3, 2005, A4.

37. Galston and Kamarck, "Five Realities," 106.

38. Quoted in William J. Bennett, *The Broken Hearth: Reversing the Moral Collapse of the American Family* (New York: Doubleday, 2001), 1.

39. Quoted in Ellis Cose, "Long after the Alarm Went Off," *Newsweek*, March 14, 2005, 37.

40. Popenoe, *Future of Marriage*, 10–11.

41. Dan Quayle, "Address to the Commonwealth Club of California," San Francisco, May 19, 1992.

42. Dan Quayle, *Standing Firm: A Vice Presidential Memoir* (New York: Harper-Collins, 1994), 318, 326.

43. Amy Argetsinger and Roxanne Roberts, "Oh, Baby! Big News for Sanchez," *Washington Post*, November 21, 2008, C3.

44. Stephanie Coontz, *Marriage, a History: From Obedience to Intimacy; or, How Love Conquered Marriage* (New York: Viking, 2005), 247.

45. Al Gore and Tipper Gore, *Joined at the Heart: The Transformation of the American Family* (New York: Holt, 2002), 11.

46. Ibid., 13–14, 11.

47. Quoted in James Davison Hunter, *Culture Wars: The Struggle to Define America* (New York: Basic Books, 1991), 181.

48. Quoted in Coontz, *Marriage*, 253.

49. Ibid., 248.

50. Ibid., 298.

51. Margalit Fox, "Molly Yard, Advocate for Liberal Causes, Dies at 93," *New York Times*, September 22, 2005, C1. Only in 1975 did it become illegal to require a married woman to have her husband's written permission to obtain a loan or a credit card (Coontz, *Marriage*, 255).

52. Stephanie Coontz, *The Way We Never Were: American Families and the Nostalgia Trap* (New York: Basic Books, 1992), 25.

53. Coontz, *Marriage*, 230.

54. Gallup Poll, June–July 1962.

55. Quoted in Coontz, *Marriage*, 236–37.

56. Ibid., 236.

57. Ibid., 234.

58. Robert Strauss, "Miss America, Atlantic City Move on after Breakup," *Washington Post*, January 20, 2006, A3.

59. Ibid.

60. Libby Copeland, "In Las Vegas, It's Miss Oklahoma's Lucky Night," *Washington Post*, January 22, 2006, D1.

61. Maureen Dowd, "What's a Modern Girl to Do?" *New York Times Magazine*, October 30, 2005, 52.

62. Eduardo Porter and Michelle O'Donnell, "Facing Middle Age with No Degree, and No Wife," *New York Times*, August 6, 2006, A1.

63. Peg Tyre and Daniel McGinn, "She Works, He Doesn't," *Newsweek*, May 12, 2003, 46.

64. Brian Braiker, "Just Don't Call Me Mr. Mom," *Newsweek*, October 8, 2007, 54.

65. Whitehead and Popenoe, *State of Our Unions*, 2006, 17.

66. Laura Kipnis, "Should This Marriage Be Saved?" *New York Times*, January 25, 2004, WK15.

67. For the Civil War statistic, see Fukuyama, *Great Disruption*, 41. The 1950s and 1960s divorce rates are reported in Barbara Dafoe Whitehead, "Dan Quayle Was Right," *Atlantic Monthly*, April 1993, 47. Sociologist David Popenoe believes that divorce has declined as a consequence of the greater rates of cohabitation (*Future of Marriage*, 6).

68. Whitehead, "Dan Quayle Was Right," 50.

69. Harbour Fraser Hodder, "The Future of Marriage: Changing Demographics, Economics, and Laws Alter the Meaning of Marriage in America," *Harvard Magazine*, November–December 2004, 42.

70. The New England colonies allowed divorce on just two grounds—adultery and desertion. Virginia, North Carolina, South Carolina, Georgia, and Maryland had no provisions for divorce (Bennett, *Broken Hearth*, 144).

71. Fukuyama, *Great Disruption*, 46.

72. Quoted in Barbara Dafoe Whitehead and David Popenoe, "Why Men Won't Commit: Exploring Young Men's Attitudes about Sex, Dating, and Marriage," in Barbara Dafoe Whitehead and David Popenoe, *The State of Our Unions, 2002* (New Brunswick, N.J.: Rutgers University National Marriage Project, 2002), 13.

73. Fukuyama, *Great Disruption*, 58.

74. Ibid., 26.

75. Mary Eberstadt, "Eminem Is Right: The Primal Scream of Teenage Music," *Policy Review*, December 2004–January 2005, 21, 22, 23.

76. Ibid., 22.

77. Quoted in J. Freedom Du Lac, "A Loser Fairy Tale," *Washington Post Magazine*, March 18, 2007, 17.

78. Ibid., 24.

79. Eberstadt, "Eminem Is Right," 24.

80. Ibid., 32.

81. Tamar Lewin, "Poll Says Even Quiet Divorces Affect Children's Paths," *New York Times*, November 5, 2005, A1.

82. Elizabeth Marquardt, "Just Whom Is This Divorce 'Good' For?" *Washington Post*, November 6, 2005, B1.

83. Mireya Navarro, "More Options to Answer 'What about the Kids?'" *New York Times*, November 27, 2005, ST1. Sociologists Judith S. Wallerstein and Joan B. Kelly also describe the trauma divorce often causes children, including feelings of loneliness, helplessness, and rejection ("How Children React to Divorce," in *Marriage and Family in a Changing Society*, ed. James M. Henslin [New York: Free Press, 1992], 397–409).

84. Gallup poll, May 8–11, 2006.

85. Ibid., April 13–18, 1936.

86. Quoted in Whitehead, "Dan Quayle Was Right," 52.

87. Quoted in Bennett, *Broken Hearth*, 151.

88. Tiffany Sharples, "Bye Bye, Love," *Time*, February 11, 2008, 60.

89. Quoted in Whitehead, "Dan Quayle Was Right," 52.

90. Sharples, "Bye Bye, Love," 60.

91. Greenberg Quinlan Rosner Research poll, August 10–17, 2005.

92. Quoted in Glenn and Marquardt, *Hooking Up*, 44.

93. Goldie Hawn interview, *Larry King Live*, CNN, February 24, 2006.

94. "U.S. Divorce Rates," ReligiousTolerance.com, January 6, 2008 (available at www.religioustolerance.org/chr_dira.htm). The eleven southern states are Alabama, Arkansas, Arizona, Florida, Georgia, Mississippi, North Carolina, New

Mexico, Oklahoma, South Carolina, and Texas. The Texas data is for 1997. No data from Louisiana were available. The nine states in the Northeast are Connecticut, Massachusetts, Maine, New Hampshire, New Jersey, New York, Pennsylvania, Rhode Island, and Vermont.

95. Pam Belluck, "Ideas and Trends: To Avoid Divorce, Move to Massachusetts," *New York Times,* November 14, 2004, WK12.

96. Sam Roberts, "It's Official: To Be Married Means to Be Outnumbered," *New York Times,* October 15, 2006, 14; Alice V. McGillivray, Richard M. Scammon, and Rhodes Cook, *America at the Polls, 1960–2004* (Washington, D.C.: CQ Press, 2005), 383, 677, 893.

97. "U.S. Divorce Rates"; Jimmy Carter, *Our Endangered Values: America's Moral Crisis* (New York: Simon and Schuster, 2005), 69.

98. "Faith and Family in America."

99. "U.S. Divorce Rates."

100. Ibid.

101. Barbara Dafoe Whitehead and David Popenoe, *The State of Our Unions, 2004* (New Brunswick, N.J.: Rutgers University National Marriage Project, 2004), 4.

102. Quoted in Alan Wolfe, *One Nation after All* (New York: Viking, 1998), 99.

103. Greenberg Quinlan Rosner Research poll, August 10–17, 2005.

104. Stephanie Coontz, "For Better, for Worse; Marriage Means Something Different Now," *Washington Post,* May 1, 2005, B1; Coontz, *Marriage,* 278.

105. Roberts, "It's Official."

106. "As Marriage and Parenthood Drift Apart," 29, 2.

107. Barbara Dafoe Whitehead and David Popenoe, *The State of Our Unions, 2003* (New Brunswick, N.J.: Rutgers University National Marriage Project, 2003), 15.

108. Quoted in Bennett, *Broken Hearth,* 11.

109. Quoted in Blaine Harden, "Numbers Drop for Married with Children," *Washington Post,* March 4, 2007, A3.

110. Greenberg Quinlan Rosner Research poll, August 10–17, 2005.

111. "Coming of Age in America, Part II," Greenberg Quinlan Rosner press release, September 2005.

112. Coontz, "For Better, for Worse," B1.

113. Quoted in Debra Rosenberg and Pat Wingert, "First Comes Junior in a Baby Carriage," *Newsweek,* December 4, 2006, 57.

114. David Fein and Theodora Ooms, *What Do We Know about Couples and Marriage in Disadvantaged Populations?* (Washington, D.C.: Center for Law and Social Policy, 2006), 2 (see www.clasp.org).

115. George W. Bush, "Marriage Protection Week, 2003," press release, October 3, 2003.

116. George W. Bush, "State of the Union Address," Washington, D.C., February 2, 2005.

117. Laura Bush, "President and Mrs. Bush Discuss Helping America's Youth at White House Conference," Howard University, Washington, D.C., press release, October 27, 2005.

118. Rosenberg and Wingert, "First Comes Junior," 57.

119. Quoted in Joy Jones, "'Marriage Is for White People,'" *Washington Post*, March 26, 2006, B1.

120. Hodder, "Future of Marriage," 40.

121. "GI Bill of Rights" (available at http://en.wikipedia.org/wiki/G.I._Bill).

122. Betty Friedan, *The Feminine Mystique* (New York: Norton, 1963), 17.

123. Michael Gurian, "Where Have the Men Gone? No Place Good," *Washington Post*, December 4, 2005, B1.

124. David Brooks, "Mind over Muscle," *New York Times*, October 16, 2005, WK12.

125. Quoted in Tamar Levin, "At Colleges, Women Are Leaving Men in the Dust," *New York Times*, July 19, 2006, A1.

126. Quoted in Glenn and Marquardt, *Hooking Up*, 48.

127. Quoted in Ellis Cose, "The Black Gender Gap," *Newsweek*, March 3, 2003, 50.

128. Jones, "'Marriage Is for White People,'" B1.

129. Edison Media Research and Mitofsky International exit poll, November 4, 2008.

130. Associated Press, "Manhattan Leads Single-Living Trend."

131. Ibid.

132. Popenoe, *Future of Marriage*, 7.

133. Greenberg Quinlan Rosner Research poll, August 10–17, 2005.

134. Rosenberg and Wingert, "First Comes Junior," 56.

135. Quoted in Whitehead, "Dan Quayle Was Right," 58.

136. Quoted in Glenn and Marquardt, *Hooking Up*, 46.

137. Barbara Dafoe Whitehead and Marline Pearson, *Making a Love Connection: Teen Relationships, Pregnancy, and Marriage* (Washington, D.C.: National Campaign to Prevent Teen Pregnancy, 2006), 7.

138. Quoted in Porter and O'Donnell, "Facing Middle Age," A1.

139. Ibid.

140. Quoted in Jones, "'Marriage Is for White People,'" B1.

141. Coontz, *Marriage*, 270.

142. "As Marriage and Parenthood Drift Apart," 24.

143. Quoted in Harden, "Numbers Drop," A3.

144. National Opinion Research Center poll, February 6–June 26, 2002.

145. Quoted in Kathryn Edin and Maria Keflas, "Unmarried Because They Value Marriage," *Washington Post*, May 1, 2005, B4.

146. Quoted in Whitehead, "Dan Quayle Was Right," 74–75.

147. The trend is even more pronounced in Europe. In France, couples can acquire a *pacte civil de solidarité* that allows couples to share property rights and after three years grants them the same tax breaks as married couples. Either partner can dissolve the relationship after three months. In Scandinavia, heterosexual couples can register with the government to give their children the same protections offered to the offspring of married couples (Sarah Lyall, "In Europe, Lovers Now Propose: Marry Me a Little," *New York Times*, February 15, 2004, 3).

148. Popenoe, *Future of Marriage*, 20; Roberts, "It's Official."

149. "As Marriage and Parenthood Drift Apart," 3.

150. David Popenoe and Barbara Dafoe Whitehead, *Should We Live Together? What Young Adults Need to Know about Cohabitation before Marriage*, 2nd ed. (New Brunswick, N.J.: Rutgers University National Marriage Project, 2002), 1. One-quarter of unmarried women aged 25 to 39 currently live with partners; about half have lived at some time with unmarried partners (Popenoe and Whitehead, *Should We Live Together?* 3).

151. Quoted in Roberts, "It's Official," 14.

152. Quoted in Sue Browder, "Is Living Together Such a Good Idea?" in *Marriage and Family*, ed. Henslin, 77.

153. Coontz, *Marriage*, 279.

154. Quoted in Roberts, "It's Official," 14.

155. British demographer Kathleen Kiernan posits a four-stage process that has made cohabitation the equivalent of marriage. In the first stage, most people marry without having lived together. Only a small bohemian minority and some of the very poor live together outside marriage. In the second stage, more people from more walks of life live together for a time, but they usually marry, especially when they have children. In the third stage, cohabitation becomes a socially acceptable alternative to marriage. The couple is open to their families and coworkers about their relationship. They even have children, although many subsequently marry. In the fourth stage, cohabitation and marriage become inseparable. The couple does not marry, even when they have children. Kiernan believes that the United States was moving from stage 1 to stage 3 at the end of the twentieth century (Coontz, *Marriage*, 272).

156. "Town Cracks Down on Unwed Couples," CBSNews.com, May 17, 2006.

157. Gallup/*USA Today* poll, September 7–8, 2007.

158. Popenoe and Whitehead, *Should We Live Together?* 3.

159. Gallup poll, July 22–24, 2002.

160. Gore and Gore, *Joined at the Heart*, 60.

161. D'Vera Cohn, "Live-Ins Almost as Likely as Marrieds to Be Parents," *Washington Post*, March 13, 2003, A1. It is estimated that 70 percent of these children are the offspring of only one cohabitating partner (Popenoe, *Future of Marriage*, 25).

162. Cohn, "Live-Ins," A1.

163. Popenoe and Whitehead, *Should We Live Together?* 8.

164. Greenberg Quinlan Rosner Research poll, August 10–17, 2005.

165. Quoted in Glenn and Marquardt, *Hooking Up*, 22.

166. Quoted in Laura Sessions Stepp, *Unhooked: How Young Women Pursue Sex, Delay Love, and Lose at Both* (New York: Riverhead, 2007), 41.

167. Quoted in Glenn and Marquardt, *Hooking Up*, 47.

168. Ibid., 26, 27, 46.

169. Amy Kass, "A Case for Courtship," Keynote Address to the Institute for American Values Annual Symposium, September 22, 1999.

170. Elizabeth L. Paul, Brian McManus, and Allison Hayes. "'Hookups':

Characteristics and Correlates of College Students' Spontaneous and Anonymous Sexual Experiences," *Journal of Sex Research*, June 2000, 76–88.

171. Glenn and Marquardt, *Hooking Up*, 14, 20.

172. Quoted in Stepp, *Unhooked*, 21.

173. Quoted in Ethridge, "Sex and Young America."

174. Quoted in Glenn and Marquardt, *Hooking Up*, 31.

175. Quoted in Weill, *Real Truth*, 18.

176. Whitehead and Popenoe, *State of Our Unions, 2004*, 9.

177. Fukuyama, *Great Disruption*, 49.

178. Alan Wolfe, "The Pursuit of Autonomy," *New York Times Magazine*, May 7, 2000, 54.

179. Carter, *Our Endangered Values*, 41, 90. See also Coontz, *Marriage*, 298.

180. Kristen Wyatt, "Carter Cuts Southern Baptist Tie," *Washington Post*, October 21, 2000, A1.

181. Santorum, *It Takes a Family*, 5.

182. David Popenoe, *On the Future of Marriage* (New Brunswick, N.J.: Rutgers University National Marriage Project, 2001), 1.

183. Executive Order 10980, signed December 14, 1961.

184. Executive Order 11126, signed November 1, 1963.

185. Quoted in Gary L. Rose, *Connecticut Government at the Millennium* (Fairfield, Conn.: Sacred Heart University Press, 2001), 81.

186. Benjamin Disraeli, *Sybil; or, The Two Nations* (New York: Penguin, 1984), 12.

Chapter Four

1. Peter Whoriskey, "A New Year's Baby with an Additional Difference: Two Moms," *Washington Post*, January 2, 2003, A1.

2. Ibid.

3. Ibid.

4. Quoted in Kate Zernike, "The New Couples Next Door, Gay and Straight," *New York Times*, August 24, 2003, A16.

5. Adam Liptak, "Parental Rights Upheld for Lesbian Ex-Partner," *New York Times*, August 5, 2006, A10.

6. Lorraine Ali, "Mrs. Kramer vs. Mrs. Kramer," *Newsweek*, December 15, 2008, 36.

7. Marc Gunther, "Queer Inc.," *Fortune*, December 11, 2006, 95. A decade earlier, only 28 companies on the Fortune 500 offered health care benefits to domestic partners.

8. Quoted in Amy Joyce, "For Gays, Some Doors Open Wider," *Washington Post*, September 24, 2006, F1.

9. Quoted in Gunther, "Queer Inc.," 95.

10. Quoted in Frank Ahrens, "Disney's Theme Weddings Come True for Gay Couples," *Washington Post*, April 7, 2007, A1.

11. Al Gore and Tipper Gore, *Joined at the Heart: The Transformation of the American Family* (New York: Holt, 2002), 65, 67.

12. Most observers date the beginning of the gay rights revolution to a 1969 police raid on the Stonewall bar in New York City.

13. *Mark Lewis and Dennis Winslow, et al. v. Gwendolyn L. Harris, etc., et al. (A-68-05)*, Superior Court of New Jersey Appellate Division, Docket No. A-224-03T5, 9–10.

14. John Cloud, "The Battle over Gay Teens," *Time*, October 10, 2005, 44.

15. William D. Mosher, Anjani Chandra, and Jo Jones, *Sexual Behavior and Selected Health Measures: Men and Women 15–44 Years of Age, United States, 2002* (Washington, D.C.: U.S. Department of Health and Human Services, Centers for Disease Control and Prevention, National Center for Health Statistics, 2005), 15. Altogether, 6.9 million women aged 18 to 44 report having homosexual contact; for men, the figure is 3.7 million.

16. U.S. Department of Commerce, Bureau of the Census, "Married-Couple and Unmarried Partner Households: 2000," February 2003, 2; Zernike, "New Couples Next Door." Of the 594,391 same-sex couples, 301,026 were men and 293,365 were women.

17. Sam Roberts, "It's Official: To Be Married Means to Be Outnumbered," *New York Times*, October 15, 2006, 14. Of the 776,000 same-sex households, 413,000 were male couples and 363,000 were female couples.

18. U.S. Department of Commerce, Bureau of the Census, "Married-Couple and Unmarried Partner Households," 6, 9. See also D'Vera Cohn, "Live-Ins Almost as Likely as Married to Be Parents," *Washington Post*, March 13, 2003, A1. This figure includes children who reside with a homosexual parent. The census found that there are 160,000 children being raised by same-sex partners (Jonathan Rauch, "Family's Value," *The New Republic*, May 30, 2005, 15).

19. Stephanie Coontz, "For Better, for Worse; Marriage Means Something Different Now," *Washington Post*, May 1, 2005, B1; Gore and Gore, *Joined at the Heart*, 38.

20. Quoted in John Bowe, "Gay Donor or Gay Dad? Gay Men and Lesbians Are Having Babies and Redefining Fatherhood, Commitment, and What a Family Can Be," *New York Times Magazine*, November 19, 2006, 70, 121.

21. Kathleen Burge, "Gays Have Right to Marry, Supreme Judicial Court Says in Historic Ruling," *Boston Globe*, November 19, 2003, A1.

22. Jeninne Lee–St. John, "Viewpoint: Civil Rights and Gay Rights," Time.com, October 25, 2005. The Massachusetts state legislature repealed the 1913 law in 2008.

23. Quoted in Charles Lane, "Massachusetts Court Backs Gay Marriage," *Washington Post*, February 5, 2004, A1.

24. Yvonne Abraham, "Among Same-Sex Couples, Proposals, Tears Flow," *Boston Globe*, February 4, 2004, A1.

25. Pam Belluck, "Gay Couples Find Marriage Is a Mixed Bag," *New York Times*, June 15, 2008, A1.

26. Michael Levenson, "Birth Certificate Policy Draws Fire," *Boston Globe*, July 22, 2005, B1.

27. Quoted in Pam Belluck, "Gain for Same-Sex Marriage in Massachusetts," *New York Times*, November 10, 2006, A16.

28. Cloud, "Battle over Gay Teens," 44. According to the *Washington Post*, there are 110 GSAs in U.S. middle schools (Theresa Vargas, "Owning His Gay Identity—at 15 Years Old," *Washington Post*, July 14, 2008, A1).

29. Richard Morin, "What Teens Really Think," *Washington Post Magazine*, October 23, 2005, 16.

30. Ibid., 45.

31. Quoted in Tom Owens, "One Mother's Voice: PFLAG Cofounder Recalls Group's Beginnings," Tolerance.org, July 14, 2005.

32. Parents, Families, and Friends of Lesbians and Gays Web site, see http://www.pflag.org.

33. Dwight D. Eisenhower, *Mandate for Change: 1953–1956* (Garden City, N.Y.: Doubleday, 1963), 309.

34. Stuart Taylor, "Dismissal of Gay C.I.A. Worker Is Subject to Review, Court Holds," *New York Times*, June 16, 1988, A1.

35. Christopher Marquis, "Gay Pride Day Is Observed by about 60 C.I.A. Workers," *New York Times*, June 9, 2000, A24.

36. Michael Barone and Richard E. Cohen with Charles E. Cook Jr., *The Almanac of American Politics, 2002* (Washington, D.C.: National Journal, 2001), 751.

37. Barney Frank, interview by author, Washington, D.C., December 20, 2000.

38. Mary Cheney, *Now It's My Turn: A Daughter's Chronicle of Political Life* (New York: Simon and Schuster, Threshold, 2006), 194.

39. Mary Cheney, interview, *Larry King Live*, CNN, May 10, 2006.

40. Cloud, "Battle over Gay Teens," 47.

41. Frank Rich, "Mr. Bush Won't Be at the Tonys," *New York Times*, June 6, 2004, section 2, 1.

42. Quoted in Michael Powell, "Family Values: Randall Terry Fights Gay Unions; His Son No Longer Will," *Washington Post*, April 22, 2004, C1.

43. Quoted in David Royse, "In Senate Race, Family Values Campaign Tested by Real Life," Associated Press, August 21, 2006.

44. Pam Belluck and Katie Zezima, "Hearts Beat Fast to Opening Strains of the Gay-Wedding March," *New York Times*, May 16, 2004, 22.

45. "Gephardt's Gay Daughter: Chrissy Gephardt Is Revving Up to Solicit Gay and Lesbian Votes for Her Dad's Presidential Bid," *Advocate*, June 10, 2003.

46. Quoted in Rachel L. Swarns, "Daughter Spurs Gephardt's Changed Views on Gays," *New York Times*, November 1, 2003, A1.

47. Linda Feldmann, "Dick Gephardt: An Insider Looking Out," *Christian Science Monitor*, November 12, 2003, 1.

48. Quoted in Swarns, "Daughter Spurs Gephardt's Changed Views," A1.

49. Quoted in Pamela Stallsmith, "Gay Rights Activist Urges Education," *Richmond Times-Dispatch*, July 23, 2006, 1.

50. In Ohio, 62 percent of voters supported the ban on gay marriage, while 38 percent opposed it. The presidential race there was much closer, with Bush winning 51 percent of the vote to Kerry's 49 percent.

51. Rhodes Cook, "Gay Marriage Ban and the Bush Vote in 2004," *Rhodes Cook Letter*, May 2005, 8.

52. These states were Mississippi, Georgia, Oklahoma, Arkansas, Kentucky, North Dakota, Montana, Utah, Ohio, Michigan, and Oregon. Of those, Kerry won only Michigan and Oregon.

53. Only Arizona bucked the trend, with 51 percent of its voters opposing an anti-gay-marriage constitutional amendment (Monica Davey, "Liberals Find Rays of Hope on Ballot Measures," *New York Times*, November 9, 2006, P16).

54. They were for best director, best adapted screenplay, and original score. In Plano, Texas, a multiplex theater sold more advance tickets for *Brokeback Mountain* than for *King Kong* (Frank Rich, "Two Gay Cowboys Hit a Home Run," *New York Times*, December 18, 2005, see 4, 13).

55. Ben Fritz, "Cowboys Galloping Along," Variety.com, January 15, 2006.

56. Rich, "Two Gay Cowboys," 13.

57. Gary J. Gates, a demographer at the Williams Institute, reports that of the 27,000,000 Americans currently married, 436,000 (1.6 percent) identify themselves as gay or bisexual (Jane Gross, "When the Beard Is Too Painful to Remove," *New York Times*, August 3, 2006, E1).

58. "Opinions of the Justices to the Senate," *Boston Globe*, February 4, 2004, 1.

59. *Mark Lewis and Dennis Winslow, et al. v. Gwendolyn L. Harris, etc., et al.*, 58.

60. David Van Biema, "Mainline Churches: Not Quite as Liberal as They Look," *Time*, February 16, 2004, 64.

61. Quoted in Carey Goldberg, "A Kaleidoscope Look at Attitudes on Gay Marriage," *New York Times*, February 6, 2000, 16.

62. Quoted in Tammerlin Drummond, "The Marrying Kind," *Time*, May 24, 2001, 52.

63. "Transcript of the Second Bush-Gore Presidential Debate," CNN, October 11, 2000.

64. "Transcript of the Cheney-Lieberman Vice Presidential Debate," CNN, October 5, 2000.

65. George W. Bush, State of the Union Address, Washington, D.C., January 20, 2004.

66. Ruth Marcus, "Finally, Something from Mary." *Washington Post*, May 9, 2006, A23.

67. Mary Cheney, *Now It's My Turn*, 179, 175.

68. Mary Cheney, interview.

69. Quoted in David Stout, "The 2004 Campaign: The Vice President: Cheney Criticizes Kerry for Mentioning Daughter," *New York Times*, October 15, 2004, A21.

70. Mary Cheney, *Now It's My Turn*, 223.

71. Ibid., 34. Dick Cheney's response to his daughter's confession: "You're my daughter and I love you and I just want you to be happy."

72. Quoted in Marcus, "Finally, Something from Mary."

73. Lynne Cheney, *Sisters* (New York: Signet, New American Library, 1981), 101, 124.

74. Melinda Henneberger, "This Second Lady Is Keeping Her Day Job," *New York Times*, February 6, 2001, A1.

75. "Publisher Cancels Reissue of Racy Novel by Lynne Cheney," Associated Press, April 3, 2004.

76. Quoted in Lloyd Grove, "Gay Time with Cheney Book," *New York Post*, March 10, 2004.

77. Quoted in Mary Cheney, *Now It's My Turn*, 228.

78. Quoted in "Cheney's Daughter Gives Birth to Son," ABC News, May 23, 2007.

79. Quoted in Amy Argetsinger and Roxanne Roberts, "Mary Cheney and Partner Are about to Be Moms," *Washington Post*, December 6, 2006, C1; Amy Argetsinger and Roxanne Roberts, "Baby Cheney, Weighed on Political Scale, Too," *Washington Post*, May 24, 2007, C1.

80. Quoted in Ruth Marcus, "It's a Cheney!" *Washington Post*, December 8, 2006, A39.

81. Quoted in Johanna Neuman, "A Pregnant Pause in Right Wing," *Los Angeles Times*, December 7, 2006, 1.

82. Quoted in David Crery, "Groups Mixed on Mary Cheney's Pregnancy," Associated Press, December 6, 2006.

83. Quoted in Katherine Q. Seelye, "Decision to Have Baby Isn't Political, Mary Cheney Says," *New York Times*, February 1, 2007, A20.

84. *The Situation Room with Wolf Blitzer*, CNN, January 24, 2007.

85. Anne Hull, "A Slow Journey from Isolation," *Washington Post*, September 27, 2004, A1.

86. Quoted in Kirk Johnson, "Gay Marriage Losing Punch as Ballot Issue," *New York Times*, October 14, 2006, A1.

87. Edison Media Research and Mitofsky International exit poll, November 2, 2004.

88. Patrick J. Egan and Kenneth Sherrill, "Marriage and the Shifting Priorities of a New Generation of Lesbians and Gays," *PS*, April 2005, 231.

89. "House Votes to Bar Gay Marriages under Federal Law," CNN/AllPolitics, July 12, 1996.

90. Constance Morella, interview by author, Washington, D.C., June 13, 2000.

91. On his Web site, Craig listed as his third-most-important goal, "Defend and strengthen the traditional values of the American family" (see http://www.craig.senate.gov).

92. "House Says No to Same-Sex Marriages," CNN/AllPolitics, July 12, 1996.

93. Andy Sullivan, "Senate Panel OKs Gay-Marriage Ban," *Reuters*, May 18, 2006.

94. "Democrats Are against Gay Marriage," *San Francisco Bay Times*, March 23, 2006, 1; Lou Chibarro Jr., "Dems Abolish Gay Outreach Post," *Washington Blade*, February 3, 2006, 2.

95. *Daniel Hernandez, et al. v. Victor L. Robles*, 855 N.E. 2d 1, 16 (N.Y. 2006).

96. *Mark Lewis and Dennis Winslow, et al., v. Gwendolyn L. Harris, etc., et al.*, 43–44.

97. Laura Mansnerus, "Legislators Vote for Gay Unions in New Jersey," *New York Times*, December 15, 2006, A1.

98. Edison Media Research and Mitofsky International exit poll, November 2, 2004.

99. Al Gore, Current TV posting, January 23, 2008.

100. William Yardley, "Connecticut Approves Civil Unions for Gays," *New York Times*, April 21, 2005, B5; William Yardley, "Senate Passes Civil Unions for Gays in Connecticut," *New York Times*, April 7, 2005, B5.

101. Quoted in Robert D. McFadden, "Gay Marriage Is Ruled Legal in Connecticut," *New York Times*, October 11, 2008, A1.

102. *In re Marriage Cases* (2008), S147999, 7.

103. Quoted in Robert Barnes and Ashley Surdin, "California Supreme Court Strikes Bans on Same-Sex Marriage," *Washington Post*, May 16, 2008, A1.

104. Quoted in Lisa Leff, "Gay Marriage Ban Overturned by California Supreme Court," Associated Press, May 15, 2008.

105. Howard Mintz, Mary Anne Ostrom, and Mike Swift, "Path to the Altar: Stories of People in Same-Sex Marriage Fight," *San Jose Mercury News*, June 16, 2008, 1.

106. Amy Cavanaugh, "Del Martin Remembered as 'A Real Hero,'" *Washington Blade*, September 5, 2008, 1.

107. Gallup poll, May 10–13, 2007.

108. Ibid., June 17–20, 1977. Nonetheless, in 2006 thirty-four states still permitted employers to fire people because they were gay (Gunter, "Queer Inc.," 96).

109. Quoted in Thomas B. Edsall, *Building Red America: The New Conservative Coalition and the Drive for Permanent Power* (New York: Perseus, 2006), 89–90.

110. "Bishops Pass Guidelines on Gay Outreach," Associated Press, November 14, 2006.

111. Quoted in Michael Paulson, "Strong Divided Opinions Mark Clergy Response," *Boston Globe*, November 19, 2003, A1.

112. Michael Paulson, "Group to Rally Opposition to Gay Marriage," *Boston Globe*, October 15, 2006, A1.

113. Maryland Catholic Bishops, "Preserving Marriage: The Union of One Man and One Woman," Maryland Catholic Conference, November 8, 2005.

114. *Lawrence et al. v. Texas*, 539 U.S. 558 (2003), 1, 21.

115. John Kenneth White, telephone interview with Steve May, March 19, 2000.

116. Judge Robert S. Smith in *Daniel Hernandez, et al., v. Victor L. Robles*, 12.

117. *Andersen, et al. v. King County*, Supreme Court of the State of Washington, No. 04-2-04964-4 SEA 48, available at http://www.courts.wa.gov/news info/content/pdf/759341opn.pdf. See also Tracy Johnson and Phuong Cat Le, "State's High Court Upholds Ban on Gay Marriage," *Seattle Post-Intelligencer*, July 26, 2006, 1.

118. Quoted in Dean J. Kotlowski, *Nixon's Civil Rights: Politics, Principle, and Policy* (Cambridge: Harvard University Press, 2001), 247.

119. Quoted in Phyllis Schlafly, "The Effects of the Equal Rights Amendments in State Constitutions," *Policy Review*, 1979, 78.

120. Quoted in Kotlowski, *Nixon's Civil Rights*, 247.

121. Quoted in David von Drehle, "Same-Sex Unions Move Center Stage," *Washington Post*, November 23, 2003, A1.

122. "Less Opposition to Gay Marriage, Adoption, and Military Service," Pew Research Center press release, March 22, 2006.

123. Ibid.

124. Quoted in Anne Hull, "Coming Out for One of Their Own," *Washington Post*, November 14, 2004, D1.

125. Princeton Survey Research Associates poll, October 15–19, 2003.

126. "Gays on the March," *Time*, September 8, 1975, 36.

127. Chandler Burr, "Homosexuality and Biology," *Atlantic Monthly*, June 1997.

128. Allen Drury, *Advise and Consent* (Garden City, N.Y.: Doubleday, 1959), 431, 432, 447.

129. Pew Research Center poll, October 15–19, 2003.

130. Gallup poll, September 21–24, 2006.

131. *Los Angeles Times* poll, March 27–30, 2004.

132. *Time*/CNN/Harris Interactive poll, February 5–6, 2004.

133. Quoted in Kathryn Q. Seelye and Janet Elder, "Strong Support Is Found for Ban on Gay Marriage," *New York Times*, December 21, 2003, A1.

134. Antonin Scalia, dissent, *Lawrence v. Texas*, 18.

135. Rick Santorum, *It Takes a Family: Conservatism and the Common Good* (Wilmington, Del.: ISI, 2005), 235–36.

136. "Professional Associations' Statements about Homosexuality," February 5, 1998, ReligiousTolerance.org, <http://www.religioustolerance.org/hom_prof.htm>.

137. Stephanie Coontz, *Marriage, a History: From Obedience to Intimacy; or, How Love Conquered Marriage* (New York: Viking, 2005), 275.

138. Quoted in James Ricci and Patricia Ward Biederman, "Acceptance of Gays on Rise," *Los Angeles Times*, March 30, 2004, A1.

139. National Opinion Research Center, General Social Surveys.

140. NBC News/*Wall Street Journal* poll, June 4–8, 1993; *Boston Globe*/University of New Hampshire poll, May 4–9, 2005.

141. *Los Angeles Times* poll, March 27–30, 2004; Pew Research Center poll, December 12, 2006–January 9, 2007.

142. Frank Rich, "Joy of Gay Marriage," *New York Times*, February 29, 2004, A1.

143. Los Angeles Times poll, March 27–30, 2004; Pew Research Center survey, October 15–19, 2003.

144. Quoted in Ricci and Biederman, "Acceptance of Gays on Rise," A1.

145. Mike Hippler, *Matlovich: The Good Soldier* (Boston: Alyson, 1989), 9, 7. Matlovich also won the Air Force Airman of the Month Award in 1965, the Air Force Commendation Medal in 1971, and the Meritorious Service Medal in 1974.

146. "Gays on the March," 34.

147. Hippler, *Matlovich*, 20, 26. Matlovich later converted to Mormonism but was excommunicated from the church because of his homosexuality.

148. "Gays on the March," 34.

149. Quoted in Hippler, *Matlovich*, 45, 46.

150. Ibid., 106–10, 155.

151. Andrew Sullivan, "The End of Gay Culture," *The New Republic*, October 24, 2005, 16.

152. Zernike, "New Couples Next Door," A16.

153. Quoted in Claudia Deane, "Everybody Loves Andy," *Washington Post Magazine*, October 23, 2005, 43.

154. Gallup/*USA Today* poll, September 30–October 1, 1998.

155. Paul Weyrich, letter to Free Congress Foundation supporters, Washington, D.C., February 16, 1999.

156. Democracy Corps poll, December 2–4, 2001.

157. Quoted in Harbour Fraser Hodder, "The Future of Marriage: Changing Demographics, Economics, and Laws Alter the Meaning of Marriage in America," *Harvard Magazine*, November–December, 2004, 41.

158. Quoted in Amy Lorentzen, "Iowa Gay Marriage Ban Ruled Unconstitutional," Associated Press, April 3, 2009.

Chapter Five

1. Alan Ehrenhalt, *The Lost City: Discovering the Forgotten Virtues of Community in the Chicago of the 1950s* (New York: Basic Books, 1995), 112.

2. William V. D'Antonio, James Davidson, Dean Hoge, and Ruth Wallace, *American Catholic Laity in a Changing Church* (Kansas City: Sheed and Ward, 1989), 44.

3. Quoted in Peter Steinfels, *A People Adrift: The Crisis of the Roman Catholic Church in America* (New York: Simon and Schuster, 2003), 172.

4. Samuel P. Huntington, *Who Are We? American National Identity and the Challenges It Faces* (New York: Simon and Schuster, 2004), 101–2.

5. William V. D'Antonio and Anthony Pogerelc, *Voices of the Faithful: Loyal Catholics Striving for Change* (New York: Crossroad, 2007), 79.

6. Quoted in Alan Wolfe, *The Transformation of American Religion: How We Actually Live Our Faith* (New York: Free Press, 2003), 13.

7. Ibid., 120.

8. Robert Wuthnow, *American Mythos: Why Our Best Efforts to Be a Better Nation Fall Short* (Princeton: Princeton University Press, 2006), 146, 132.

9. John T. Elson, "Toward a Hidden God," *Time*, April 8, 1966, 82.

10. Quoted in Steinfels, *People Adrift*, 179.

11. Quoted in D'Antonio and Pogerelc, *Voices*, 25.

12. *Washington Post*/ABC News poll, April 10–13, 2008.

13. "U.S. Religious Landscape Survey: 2008," Pew Forum on Religion and Public Life, February 25, 2008, 5–6, 26.

14. Steinfels, *People Adrift*, 29.

15. Quoted in Greg Trotter, "Catholics Lose More Members Than Any Other Group," *National Catholic Reporter*, March 7, 2008, 1.

16. Quoted in Peter Katel, "Future of the Catholic Church," *CQ Researcher*, January 19, 2007, 52.

17. Alan Greenblatt and Tracie Powell, "Rise of Megachurches: Are They Straying Too Far from Their Religious Mission?" *CQ Researcher*, September 21, 2007, 779.

18. Quoted in Laurie Goodstein, "When Christmas Falls on a Sunday, Megachurches Take the Day Off," *New York Times*, December 9, 2005, A1.

19. Ibid. Those canceling included Southland Christian Church in Nicholasville, Kentucky; Crossroads Christian Church in Lexington, Kentucky; Fellowship Church in Grapevine, Texas; Redemption World Outreach Center in Greenville, South Carolina; North Point Community Church in Alpharetta, Georgia; First Baptist Church in Atlanta; and Mars Hill Bible Church in Grandville, Michigan.

20. Ibid.

21. Quoted in Bob Spitz, *The Beatles: The Biography* (New York: Little, Brown, 2005), 615, 629. Forty-six years later, the Vatican newspaper forgave Lennon, declaring the remark to be a youthful "boast" ("Church Forgives John Lennon 'Boast,'" *New York Times*, November 23, 2008, 18).

22. Elson, "Toward a Hidden God," 82.

23. Quoted in Bridget Byrne, "'Passion' Fills Movie Theaters on Blockbuster Opening Day," *Washington Post*, February 27, 2004, C1.

24. See John Winthrop, "A Model of Christian Charity," *Winthrop Papers*, ed. Stewart Mitchell (Boston: Massachusetts Historical Society, 1931), 2: 294–95.

25. John Quincy Adams, *An Oration Delivered before the Inhabitants of the Town of Newburyport, at Their Request on the Sixty-first Anniversary of the Declaration of Independence, July 4th, 1837* (Newburyport, Mass.: Morss and Brewster, 1837), 5–6.

26. Woodrow Wilson, "Address of Honorable Woodrow Wilson on the Occasion of the Tercentenary Celebration of the Translation of the Bible into the English Language," Denver, Colo., May 7, 1911, available at http://wwl2.datafor mat.com/Document.aspx?doc=30360.

27. Harry S. Truman, letter to Pope Pius XII, August 6, 1947.

28. Quoted in Gary DeMar, *America's Christian History: The Untold Story* (Atlanta: American Vision, 2000), 3.

29. Ronald Reagan and Nancy Reagan, Remarks by the President and First Lady in a National Television Address on Drug Abuse and Prevention, Washington, D.C., September 14, 1986.

30. Quoted in Rich Lowry, "It's Not Personal, Mr. Bush," *Washington Post*, July 1, 2001, B1.

31. Quoted in Robert Draper, *Dead Certain: The Presidency of George W. Bush* (New York: Free Press, 2007), 190.

32. Gallup Organization poll, February 14–19, 1958.

33. Dan Gilgoff, "John McCain: Constitution Established a 'Christian Nation,'" BeliefNet.com, n.d., available at www.beliefnet.com/News/Politics/2007/ 06/John-Mccain-Constitution-Established-A-Christian-Nation.aspx.

34. Barack Obama, *The Audacity of Hope: Thoughts on Reclaiming the American Dream* (New York: Crown, 2006), 206.

35. Fox News/Opinion Dynamics poll, October 9–10, 2007; Princeton Survey Research Associates International poll, March 28–29, 2007.

36. Princeton Survey Research Associates International poll, February 6–7, 2008.

37. Gallup Organization poll, April 2–7, 1959.

38. Ibid., December 6–9, 2007.

39. Gallup/*USA Today* poll, January 10–13, 2008. Those who attend at least once a week or almost every week total 41 percent; those who seldom or never attend total 45 percent.

40. Quoted in Elson, "Toward a Hidden God," 83.

41. "U.S. Religious Landscape Survey," 26.

42. Princeton Survey Research Associates International poll, November 2–3, 2006.

43. Yankelovich Partners poll, June 12–13, 1996.

44. Gallup poll, May 10–13, 2007.

45. Blum and Weprin Associates poll, March 13–16, 2000.

46. Virginia Commonwealth University Life Sciences poll, November 26–December 9, 2007.

47. Princeton Survey Research Associates International poll, December 12–January 9, 2007.

48. CBS News poll, October 3–5, 2005.

49. Ipsos–Public Affairs poll, April 11–12, 2006.

50. Gallup poll, May 10–13, 2007.

51. Princeton Survey Research Associates International poll, July 20–September 7, 2006.

52. Huntington, *Who Are We?* 103.

53. Wolfe, *Transformation*, 247.

54. Robert Wuthnow, *After Heaven: Spirituality in America since the 1950s* (Berkeley: University of California Press, 1998), 3.

55. Public Agenda Foundation poll, November 4–25, 2000.

56. Princeton Survey Research Associates International poll, March 28–29, 2007.

57. Brian Fitzpatrick, *National Cultural Values Survey* (Alexandria, Va.: Culture and Media Institute, 2007), 21.

58. *U.S. News and World Report* poll, March 5–7, 1994.

59. National Opinion Research Center poll, February 1–June 19, 1998.

60. Henry J. Kaiser Family Foundation/*Washington Post*/Harvard University poll, September 7–17, 2000.

61. Alexis de Tocqueville, *Democracy in America* (New York: Vintage, 1945), 317.

62. Gallup/CNN/*USA Today* poll, March 14–15, 2003.

63. David Brooks, *Bobos in Paradise: The New Upper Class and How They Got There* (New York: Simon and Schuster, 2000), 224, 250.

64. Princeton Survey Research Associates International poll, December 12–January 9, 2007.

65. Greenberg Quinlan Rosner Research poll, July 25–August 7, 2005.

66. Quoted in Greenblatt and Powell, "Rise of Megachurches," 772.

67. David Popenoe, *The Future of Marriage in America* (New Brunswick, N.J.: Rutgers University National Marriage Project, 2007), 1.

68. Fitzpatrick, *National Cultural Values Survey*, 2, 3, iii.

69. Henry J. Kaiser Family Foundation/*Washington Post*/Harvard University poll, September 7–17, 2000.

70. National Opinion Research Center General Social Survey, March 10–August 7, 2006.

71. Brooks, *Bobos in Paradise*, 227.

72. Quoted in Caryle Murphy, "Confession Rite Evolves to Meet Changing Need," *Washington Post*, October 5, 2003, B1.

73. Ibid.

74. Quoted in Nancy Gibbs, "The New Road to Hell," *Time*, March 24, 2008, 78; Laurie Goodstein and Sheryl Gay Stolberg, "Pope Praises U.S., but Warns of Secular Challenges," *New York Times*, April 17, 2008, A1.

75. Quoted in Murphy, "Confession Rite Evolves," B1.

76. *Time*/CNN/Yankelovich Partners poll, January 20–21, 1999; ABC News/*Washington Post* poll, September 28–October 1, 1995.

77. "The Subtle Influence of Secularism," *Washington Post*, April 17, 2008, A10.

78. Quoted in Wolfe, *Transformation*, 90.

79. *Washington Post*/ABC News poll, April 10–13, 2008.

80. Quoted in Mary E. Hines, "Voice of the Faithful Survey: An Ecclesiological Reflection," in D'Antonio and Pogerelc, *Voices*, 125.

81. Quoted in D'Antonio and Pogerelc, *Voices*, 26–27.

82. Quoted in Sherry Fisher, "Sociologist's New Book Shows Catholics Changing with Times," *UCONN Advance*, February 4, 2008, 5.

83. Steinfels, *People Adrift*, 7, 257.

84. Statement of Pope John Paul II to the American Bishops, Los Angeles, September 1987. See Associated Press, "Pope Counsels Bishops to Hold to Christ's Teachings in the Face of Dissent." Associated Press, September 17, 1987.

85. Joseph Ratzinger, "Homily of His Eminence Cardinal Joseph Ratzinger, Dean of the College of Cardinals," Vatican Basilica, April 18, 2005.

86. "Interest Is High for Papal U.S. Visit; Republican McCain Favored in Presidential Race; 73% Say Abortion Is a Sin," Zogby International press release, April 9, 2008.

87. Quoted in Fisher, "Sociologist's New Book," 5.

88. Blum and Weprin Associates poll, March 13–16, 2000.

89. Cathy Lynn Grossman, "Has the 'Notion of Sin' Been Lost?" *USA Today*, March 19, 2008, 1.

90. Quoted in Elson, "Toward a Hidden God," 85.

91. Quoted in Wolfe, *Transformation*, 71, 82.

92. "U.S. Religious Landscape Survey," 4.

93. Quoted in Jacqueline L. Salmon, "Most Americans Believe in Higher Power, Poll Finds," *Washington Post*, June 24, 2008, A2.

94. Wuthnow, *American Mythos,* 147.

95. Quoted in Wolfe, *Transformation,* 93.

96. Wuthnow, *American Mythos,* 128–62.

97. Wolfe, *Transformation,* 166, 246.

98. Quoted in Kathleen Kennedy Townsend, *Failing America's Faithful: How Today's Churches Are Mixing God with Politics and Losing Their Way* (New York: Warner, 2007), 16.

99. Ibid., 15.

100. Ibid., 17.

101. Alexis de Tocqueville, *Democracy in America* (New York: Knopf, 1953), 22.

102. Townsend, *Failing America's Faithful,* 5.

103. Quoted in E. J. Dionne Jr., "Disquieting Words for the Faithful," *Washington Post,* April 18, 2008, A27.

104. Bob Edgar, *Middle Church: Reclaiming the Moral Values of the Faithful Majority from the Religious Right* (New York: Simon and Schuster, 2006), 141–42.

105. Townsend, *Failing America's Faithful,* 170–71.

106. Quoted in Al Gore and Tipper Gore, *Joined at the Heart: The Transformation of the American Family* (New York: Holt, 2002), 115.

107. Quoted in Wolfe, *Transformation,* 46.

108. Cited in Wuthnow, *American Mythos,* 144.

109. Wolfe, *Transformation,* 65.

110. Quoted in Brooks, *Bobos in Paradise,* 242.

111. Wolfe, *Transformation,* 41.

112. "U.S. Religious Landscape Survey," 5.

113. Gore and Gore, *Joined at the Heart,* 39.

114. David Brooks, *On Paradise Drive: How We Live Now (and Always Have) in the Future Tense* (New York: Simon and Schuster, 2004), 76.

115. Wolfe, *Transformation,* 9–10, 35, 50.

116. Greenblatt and Powell, "Rise of Megachurches," 788.

117. Quoted in Wolfe, *Transformation,* 216.

118. Ibid., 220.

119. Quoted in Huntington, *Who Are We?* 241.

120. Wolfe, *Transformation,* 224.

121. Ibid., 225.

122. Ibid., 243.

123. Richard Rovere, *The American Establishment and Other Reports, Opinions, and Speculations* (New York: Harcourt, Brace and World, 1962), 3, 9.

124. George F. Will, "Events Sprint Past Politics," *Newsweek,* August 2, 2004, 70; "U.S. Religious Landscape Study," 18.

125. Quoted in Marcia Clemmitt, "Protestants Today," *CQ Researcher,* December 7, 2007, 1011.

126. "U.S. Religious Landscape Study," 24.

127. Clemmitt, "Protestants Today," 1011.

128. Ibid., 1013.

129. "Subtle Influence of Secularism."

130. Clemmitt, "Protestants Today, " 1026.

131. Ibid., 1022. In this country, there are presently 1,104,000 Muslims, 1,082,000 Buddhists, 766,000 Hindus, 103,000 people who describe themselves as professing Native American religion, 84,000 Baha'is, 57,000 Sikhs, and 40,000 Taoists.

132. Huntington, *Who Are We?* 99.

133. Greenblatt and Powell, "Rise of Megachurches," 771, 775, 776. See also Crystal Cathedral Web site at www.crystalcathedral.org/about/.

134. Wolfe, *Transformation*, 195.

135. Quoted in Greenblatt and Powell, "Rise of Megachurches," 773, 778.

136. Obama, *Audacity of Hope*, 202.

137. E. J. Dionne Jr., *Souled Out: Reclaiming Faith and Politics after the Religious Right* (Princeton: Princeton University Press, 2008), 6–7.

138. Quoted in Grossman, "Has the 'Notion of Sin' Been Lost?"

139. Quoted in Greenblatt and Powell, "Rise of Megachurches," 773.

140. Wolfe, *Transformation*, 32.

141. Quoted in Jacqueline L. Salmon, "Big Churches Not Always Impersonal, Study Finds," *Washington Post*, September 19, 2008, A6.

142. Quoted in Joe Holley, "Dean Hoge; Wrote Key Studies on Religion," *Washington Post*, September 19, 2008, B7.

143. Quoted in D'Antonio and Pogerelc, *Voices*, 184.

144. Tocqueville, *Democracy in America* (1945), 314.

145. Quoted in Brooks, *Bobos in Paradise*, 244.

146. "Letters," *Time*, April 15, 1966, 13.

147. Jon Meacham on *Meet the Press*, NBC News, December 24, 2006. See also Jon Meacham, *American Gospel: God, the Founding Fathers, and the Making of a Nation* (New York: Random House, 2006).

148. Donald W. Wuerl, "The Role of Religion in a Pluralistic Society: Religious Faith and Public Policy," Cardinal John Dearden Lecture, Catholic University of America, Washington, D.C., October 23, 2007.

149. Quoted in Elizabeth Grden, "Cardinal at CUA: Obama Is 'Aggressive, Disruptive and Apocalyptic,' " *The Tower*, November 14, 2008, 1.

150. Quoted in Chris Dickson, "Catholic Bishop Refusing Holy Communion for Joseph Biden," September 3, 2008, <http://chrisdickson.blogspot.com/2008/09/catholic-bishop-refusing-holy-communion.html>.

151. Christopher Hitchens, *God Is Not Great: How Religion Poisons Everything* (New York: Twelve, Hachette, 2007), 13, 283.

152. Cited in Everett Carll Ladd Jr. with Charles D. Hadley, *Transformations of the American Party System* (New York: Norton, 1975), 183 n.3.

Chapter Six

1. Quoted in Stephen E. Ambrose, *Nixon: The Education of a Politician, 1913–1962* (New York: Simon and Schuster, 1987), 541–42.

2. Reagan supported Democrat Harry Truman in 1948 but backed Republican Dwight Eisenhower in 1952 and 1956. Reagan did not become a registered Republican until 1962. For more on these letters, see Ronald Reagan, *Reagan: A Life in Letters*, ed. Kiron K. Skinner, Annelise Anderson, and Martin Anderson (New York: Free Press, 2003), 702.

3. Ronald Reagan, "Business, Ballots, and Bureaus," May 1959, in *Ronald Reagan, Actor, Ideologue, Politician: The Public Speeches of Ronald Reagan*, ed. Davis W. Houck and Amos Kiewe (Westport, Conn.: Greenwood, 1993), 19, 20. New York postmaster Robert K. Christenberry sent Reagan's speech to Nixon.

4. See, among others, Dick Wirthlin with Wynton C. Hall, *The Greatest Communicator: What Ronald Reagan Taught Me about Politics, Leadership, and Life* (Hoboken, N.J.: Wiley, 2004).

5. Quoted in Lou Cannon, "Why the Band Has Stopped Playing for Ronald Reagan," *Washington Post*, December 21, 1986, D1.

6. *Ronald Reagan and David Brinkley: A Farewell Interview*, ABC News, December 22, 1988.

7. Ronald Reagan, *The Reagan Diaries*, ed. Douglas Brinkley (New York: HarperCollins, 2007), 8.

8. Richard Reeves, *President Reagan: The Triumph of Imagination* (New York: Simon and Schuster, 2005), xiv.

9. Ronald Reagan with Richard G. Huebler, *Where's the Rest of Me?* (New York: Duell, Sloan and Pearce, 1965), 13.

10. Ronald Reagan, remarks at a luncheon hosted by leaders of the cultural and art community in Moscow, May 11, 1988.

11. Ronald Reagan, Farewell Address, Washington, D.C., January 11, 1989.

12. Ronald Reagan, "It's Morning Again in America" (commercial), 1984.

13. "Portrait of the Electorate," *New York Times*, November 10, 1996, 28.

14. Ronald Reagan, "A Vision for America," November 3, 1980.

15. Quoted in Helene von Damm, *Sincerely, Ronald Reagan* (Ottawa, Ill.: Green Hill, 1976), 84.

16. Richard B. Wirthlin, "Reagan for President: Campaign Action Plan," June 29, 1980, 35–36. I am grateful to Wirthlin for providing me this document. For more on Reagan and his connection to the American electorate, see John Kenneth White, *The New Politics of Old Values* (Hanover, N.H.: University Press of New England, 1988).

17. Ronald Reagan, Acceptance Speech, Republican National Convention, Detroit, July 17, 1980.

18. 1980 Republican National Platform.

19. Ronald Reagan, State of the Union Address, Washington, D.C., January 26, 1982.

20. Ronald Reagan, Radio Address to the Nation on the Observance of Mother's Day, Washington, D.C., May 7, 1983.

21. Ronald Reagan, remarks on arrival at West Lafayette, Ind., April 9, 1987 (available at www.reagan.utexas.edu/archives/speeches/1987/040987h.htm).

22. Quoted in Michael Rogin, *Ronald Reagan, the Movie and Other Episodes in Political Demonology* (Berkeley: University of California Press, 1987), 7.

23. James Q. Wilson, "A Guide to Reagan Country: The Political Culture of Southern California," *Commentary*, May 1967, 40.

24. In two outings as a presidential candidate, Reagan won 93 of 100 states and 1,014 of 1,078 electoral votes.

25. Barack Obama, *The Audacity of Hope: Thoughts on Reclaiming the American Dream* (New York: Crown, 2006), 31.

26. *Ronald Reagan: Memo to the Future*, ABC News, April 23, 1987.

27. Quoted in Reeves, *President Reagan*, xvii.

28. Quoted in E. J. Dionne Jr., "The George W. Phenomenon," *Washington Post*, October 27, 1998, A23.

29. Ibid.

30. Andrew Sullivan, "Who's Your Daddy?" *Time*, June 18, 2001, 92.

31. Beatrice Gormley, *Laura Bush: America's First Lady* (New York: Aladdin, 2003), 47.

32. Edison Media Research and Mitofsky International exit poll, November 2, 2004.

33. For more on this point, see Lou Cannon and Carl M. Cannon, *Reagan's Disciple: George W. Bush's Troubled Quest for a Presidential Legacy* (New York: Public Affairs, 2008).

34. Quoted in Peter Baker, "An Unlikely Partnership Left Behind," *Washington Post*, November 5, 2007, A1. Thus far, Congress has not reauthorized No Child Left Behind.

35. For more on the Medicare vote, see Thomas E. Mann and Norman J. Ornstein, *The Broken Branch: How Congress Is Failing America and How to Get It Back on Track* (New York: Oxford University Press, 2006), esp. 1–6.

36. Quoted in Jim VandeHei, "GOP Irritation at Bush Was Long Brewing," *Washington Post*, March 16, 2006, A1.

37. Marvin N. Olasky, *Compassionate Conservatism: What It Is, What It Does, and How It Can Transform America* (New York: Free Press, 2000), 8–9.

38. See Joshua Green, "The Rove Presidency," *Atlantic Monthly*, September 2007, 70.

39. Zogby International postelection poll, November 3–5, 2004.

40. Quoted in Joshua Green, "Rove Presidency," 70.

41. "Political Landscape More Favorable to Democrats: Trends in Political Values and Core Attitudes: 1987–2007," Pew Research Center press release, March 22, 2007, 102.

42. Arnold Schwarzenegger, Address to Republican Party Fall Convention, Indian Wells, CA, September 7, 2007.

43. Tom Davis, "Where We Stand Today," memo to Republican Leadership, May 14, 2008, at www.realclearpolitics.com/articles/2008/05/post_38.html.

44. Schwarzenegger, Address to Republican Party Fall Convention, September 7, 2007.

45. Rick Santorum, *It Takes a Family: Conservatism and the Common Good* (Wilmington, Del.: ISI, 2005), 95.

46. Quoted in Steve Goldstein, "Santorum Makes Pitch to Female Voters," *Philadelphia Inquirer*, April 26, 2006, A4.

47. National Election Pool, Pennsylvania exit poll, November 7, 2006.

48. Ibid.

49. Quoted in David S. Broder, "A Prescient Assessment of Reagan," *Washington Post*, December 9, 1992, A23.

50. Quoted in Janet Hook, "Fewer Pledge Allegiance to the GOP," *Los Angeles Times*, March 23, 2007, A1.

51. Quoted in Stefan Lorant, *The Presidency* (New York: Macmillan, 1951), 591.

52. Quoted in Kenneth S. Davis, *FDR: The New Deal Years, 1933–1937: A History* (New York: Random House, 1986), 644.

53. Ronald Reagan, Inaugural Address, Washington, D.C., January 20, 1981.

54. Franklin D. Roosevelt, Inaugural Address, Washington, D.C., January 20, 1937.

55. Daniel Patrick Moynihan, *Came the Revolution* (New York: Harcourt Brace Jovanovich, 1988), 151.

56. Quoted in David D. Kirkpatrick, "Shake, Rattle, and Roil the Grand Ol' Coalition," *New York Times*, December 30, 2007, WK1.

57. Quoted in Bruce Bartlett, *Impostor: How George W. Bush Bankrupted America and Betrayed the Reagan Legacy* (New York: Doubleday, 2006), 203.

58. Ronald Reagan, Speech to the National Association of Evangelicals, Orlando, Fla., March 8, 1983.

59. George H. W. Bush, CNN interview, June 15, 1992.

60. Quoted in Fred Barnes, "Campaign '88: Bush's Mandate," *The New Republic*, November 14, 1988, 12.

61. Thomas B. Edsall, *Building Red America: The New Conservative Coalition and the Drive for Permanent Power* (New York: Perseus, 2006), 5.

62. Quoted in Jackie Calmes, "GOP Is Losing Grip on Core Business Vote," *Wall Street Journal*, October 2, 2007, A1.

63. Gallup Poll, February 2–7, 1940, September 27–October 2, 1946.

64. Ibid., February 26–March 5, 1950.

65. Quoted in Theodore H. White, *The Making of the President, 1964* (New York: Atheneum, 1965), 365; Veronique de Rugy, "President Reagan, Champion Budget-Cutter," *American Enterprise Institute*, June 9, 2004.

66. Bartlett, *Impostor*, 1.

67. Quoted in Calmes, "GOP Is Losing Grip," A1.

68. Quoted in Jay Newton-Small, "Bush: A Born-Again Conservative?" *Time*, September 27, 2007.

69. David Frum, *The Right Man: The Surprise Presidency of George W. Bush* (New York: Random House, 2003).

70. David Frum, *Comeback: Conservatism That Can Win Again* (New York: Doubleday, 2008), 2.

71. Quoted in Eric Lichtblau and Scott Shane, "Bush Is Pressed over New Report on Surveillance," *New York Times*, May 12, 2006, A1.

72. Joe Scarborough, "Joe Scarborough on NSA Phone Database: 'Be Very Afraid,'" MSNBC.com, May 12, 2006.

73. Quoted in Bruce Landis, "Chafee Quietly Quits the GOP," *Providence Journal*, September 16, 2007, A1; Scott MacKay, "Chafee's New Book Is Tough on Pro-War Democrats, Republicans, President Bush," *Providence Journal*, January 27, 2008, A1.

74. Quoted in M. Charles Bakst, "After Chafee, the Picture for Rhode Island's GOP Looks Bleak," *Providence Journal*, September 23, 2007.

75. Mark Arsenault, "Rhode Island's Chafee Backs Obama," *Providence Journal*, February 14, 2008, A1.

76. James M. Jeffords, *My Declaration of Independence* (New York: Simon and Schuster, 2001), 116, 114.

77. Lowell P. Weicker Jr. with Barry Sussman, *Maverick: A Life in Politics* (Boston: Little, Brown, 1995), 169. Weicker left the party in 1990 to become an independent.

78. Christine Todd Whitman, *It's My Party Too: The Battle for the Heart of the GOP and the Future of America* (New York: Penguin, 2005), 5.

79. Quoted in Robert Draper, *Dead Certain: The Presidency of George W. Bush* (New York: Free Press, 2007), 261. At the time, Bush was far off the Reagan mark. His job approval ratings hovered in the mid-40 percent range, a far cry from Ronald Reagan's 57 percent approval rating in May 2004 (Quinnipiac University Polling Institute poll, May 18–24, 2004).

80. Samuel Lubell, *The Hidden Crisis in American Politics* (New York: Norton, 1971), 146.

81. Samuel P. Huntington, *Who Are We? The Challenges to America's National Identity* (New York: Simon and Schuster, 2004), 11.

82. Richard M. Scammon and Ben J. Wattenberg, *The Real Majority* (New York: Coward-McCann, 1970), esp. 45–71.

83. Ellis Cose, *Color-Blind: Seeing beyond Race in a Race-Obsessed World* (New York: HarperCollins, 1997), 5. Other racial minorities added up to just over 1 percent. Hispanics, who could be of any race, stood at 4.5 percent.

84. Edison Media Research and Mitofsky International exit poll, November 4, 2008.

85. Michael Barone and Richard E. Cohen, *The Almanac of American Politics, 2004* (Washington, D.C.: National Journal, 2003), 151. The 2000 Democratic National Convention was held in Los Angeles, further mitigating any need for Gore to spend money on television commercials. Three years later, Republican Arnold Schwarzenegger won the state's governorship with a remarkable 31 percent of this Hispanic vote against a Democratic and Hispanic challenger (Anthony Salvanto and Jennifer De Pinto, "Why Schwarzenegger Won," CBS News.com, October 8, 2003).

86. Edison Media Research and Mitofsky International exit poll, November 2, 2004.

87. Edison Media Research and Mitofsky International exit poll, November 4, 2008.

88. Quoted in Mark Silva, "GOP Chairman: 'Message Received,'" *Washington Post*, November 9, 2006, A1.

89. Edward Gillespie, "Populists Beware: The GOP Must Not Become an Anti-Immigrant Party," *Wall Street Journal*, April 2, 2006, A6.

90. Lou Cannon, *Governor Reagan: His Rise to Power* (New York: Public Affairs, 2003), 152.

91. Barone and Cohen, *Almanac of American Politics, 2004,* 283; Patrick J. Buchanan, *The Death of the West: How Dying Populations and Immigrant Invasions Imperil Our Country and Civilization* (New York: Dunne/St. Martin's, 2002), 139.

92. Of Orange County's 2.95 million residents, 1.49 million are nonwhite (Ronald Campbell and Erica Perez, "Minorities Dominate 'Real' Orange County," *Orange County Register,* October 1, 2004, 1).

93. Quoted in "Robert Dornan," at http://en.wikipedia.org/wiki/Robert_Dornan.

94. Barone and Cohen, *Almanac of American Politics, 2004,* 284.

95. Nancy Frazier O'Brien, "At 29 Percent of 109th Congress, Catholics Remain Largest Faith Group," Catholic News Service, November 11, 2004. Nixon beat Democrat Jerry Voorhis on an anticommunist platform to win Whittier's congressional seat in 1946.

96. Marek Fuchs, "Corzine Selects Menendez to Replace Him in Senate," *New York Times,* December 9, 2005, A1. Menendez, the son of Cuban immigrants, became the first person from a minority group to represent New Jersey in the U.S. Senate.

97. Arian Campo-Flores and Howard Fineman, "A Latin Power Surge," *Newsweek,* May 30, 2005, 20; "Latinos Achieve New Political Milestones in Congress and State Houses," National Association of Latino Elected and Appointed Officials press release, November 11, 2006.

98. Quoted in Eric Green, "Record Number of Hispanics Elected to U.S. House of Representatives," U.S. Department of State, International Information Programs, November 12, 2002.

99. Edison Media Research and Mitofsky International exit poll, November 4, 2008.

100. Quoted in Michael Gerson, "Division Problem," *Washington Post,* September 19, 2007, A23.

101. Quoted in Jake Tapper, "Front-Runner No-Shows at GOP Minority Debates Assailed," ABC News, September 25, 2007.

102. Eli Saslow and Robert Barnes, "In a More Diverse America, a Mostly White Convention," *Washington Post,* September 4, 2008, A1.

103. Quoted in Frank Rich, "The Grand Old White Party Confronts Obama," *New York Times,* February 17, 2008, WK13.

104. Quoted in Michael Barone and Grant Ujifusa, *The Almanac of American Politics, 1996* (Washington, D.C.: National Journal, 1995), 81.

105. Everett Carll Ladd Jr., *America at the Polls, 1994* (Storrs, Conn.: Roper Center for Public Opinion Research, 1995), 124.

106. William Booth, "In a Rush, New Citizens Register Their Political Interest," *Washington Post,* September 26, 1996, A1.

107. Dick Polman, "GOP Drops the Ball on Hispanic Vote," *Philadelphia Inquirer,* September 2, 2007.

108. Paul Taylor and Richard Fry, "Hispanics and the 2008 Election: A Swing Vote?," Pew Hispanic Center press release, December 6, 2007, 1, 3, 11, 6, 5, 4. The poll of 2,003 Hispanics was conducted October 3–November 9, 2007.

109. Reagan, *Reagan Diaries*, 269.

110. CBS News/*New York Times* exit poll, November 6, 1984.

111. "Age Cohorts and Their Party Ties," *Public Perspective*, September–October 1993, 12.

112. Jonathan Pontell and J. Brad Coker, "The Invisible Generation Elects a President," *Polling Report*, November 29, 2004, 7. The Reagan generation vote for Bush in 2004 broke down as follows: Florida, 56 percent; Ohio, 59 percent; Iowa, 56 percent; Nevada, 56 percent; New Mexico, 54 percent.

113. Greenberg Quinlan Rosner Research poll, May 29–June 19, 2007.

114. Democracy Corps/Greenberg Quinlan Rosner Research Youth Survey, "Republican Collapse among Young Americans," press release, June 19, 2007.

115. Quoted in Ronald Brownstein, "A Party Transformed," *National Journal*, February 29, 2008, 1.

116. Greenberg Quinlan Rosner Research poll, May 29–June 19, 2007.

117. Ibid.

118. Democracy Corps/Greenberg Quinlan Rosner Research Youth Survey, "Republican Collapse among Young Americans."

119. Seventy-five Senators and 333 House members were Democrats, and 4 senators and 13 House members belonged to other parties.

120. James MacGregor Burns, *Roosevelt: The Lion and the Fox* (New York: Harcourt, Brace, and World, 1956), 283.

121. Quoted in Kenneth S. Davis, *FDR*, 650.

122. See John Kenneth White, *Still Seeing Red: How the Cold War Shapes the New American Politics* (Boulder, Colo.: Westview, 1997).

123. CBS News/*New York Times* poll, August 2–7, 1980.

124. Roper Organization poll, October 26–November 2, 1985.

125. Tom Wicker, "A Party of Access?" *New York Times*, November 25, 1984, E17.

126. ABC News/*Washington Post* poll, October 24–29, 1991.

127. CNN/*USA Today*/Gallup poll, May 23–24, 2000.

128. Quoted in Draper, *Dead Certain*, 89.

129. Opinion Research Corporation poll, March 9–11, 2007.

130. Quoted in Charlie Cook, "The Coming Challenge," *National Journal*, October 9, 2007.

131. Peggy Noonan, "Breaking Up Is Hard to Do," *Wall Street Journal*, January 25, 2008, W14.

Chapter Seven

1. Obama beat McCain by an impressive 8,366,077 votes, a far cry from the narrow vote margins separating the major party presidential candidates in 2000 and 2004.

2. In 2000, Bush received 271 electoral votes to Gore's 266. (One D.C. elec-

tor voted for another candidate to protest the District's lack of statehood.) Obama's 2008 electoral count included 1 electoral vote from Nebraska, the only state other than Maine to award its electoral votes by congressional district.

3. Iowa and New Mexico, which supported Al Gore in 2000 and George W. Bush in 2004, backed Obama in 2008.

4. MSNBC, November 4, 2008.

5. "Obama for President," *The New Republic*, November 5, 2008, 1.

6. See John Kenneth White, *The Values Divide: American Politics and Culture in Transition* (Washington, D.C.: Congressional Quarterly Press, 2003).

7. Quoted in Evan Thomas and *Newsweek*'s Special Project Team, "How He Did It: The Inside Story of Campaign 2008," *Newsweek*, November 17, 2008, 48.

8. Democrats enjoyed an off-year landslide in the post-Watergate midterm election of 1974, which helped them cement their House majority for two more decades.

9. Richard Cohen, "Party Like It's 1964," *Washington Post*, October 21, 2008, A17.

10. After the 2006 midterm elections, Republicans led 94 Senate filibusters.

11. George F. Will, "What Would Goldwater Do?" *Washington Post*, November 6, 2008, A21.

12. Charlie Cook, "Obama's Short Coattails," *National Journal*, November 8, 2008, 100.

13. See John Kenneth White, "The Death of a Presidency," *The Forum* 3, no. 4 (January 2006).

14. Edison Media Research and Mitofsky International exit polls, November 4, 2008.

15. In 1968, Hubert Humphrey carried Texas as a result of the state's residual support for native son Lyndon B. Johnson and his party. In 1980, Carter won his home state of Georgia. Otherwise, Nixon and Reagan carried every southern state in 1968, 1972, 1980, and 1984.

16. In 1992, Clinton carried Louisiana, Georgia, Arkansas, and Tennessee. In 1996, Clinton won Louisiana, Arkansas, Tennessee, and Florida.

17. Edison Media Research and Mitofsky International exit polls, November 4, 2008.

18. For county results, see Adam Nossiter, "For South, a Waning Hold on National Politics," *New York Times*, November 11, 2008, A1.

19. The Clinton-Gore ticket won Tennessee by just 2 points in 1996, and Gore lost his home state in 2000, a devastating blow since its electoral votes would have given him an electoral college victory.

20. Quoted in Ana Marie Cox, "McCain Campaign Autopsy," *Daily Beast*, November 7, 2008.

21. Quoted in Michael Cooper and Liz Robbins, "At Governors Meeting, Palin Looks Ahead," *New York Times*, November 13, 2008.

22. U.S. Department of Labor, Bureau of Labor Statistics, "Employment Situation Summary," press release, October 3, 2008.

23. Michael M. Grynbaum, "Rattled by Housing Slide, Consumers See Worse

to Come," *New York Times*, October 29, 2008, E1; David Cho, Michael D. Shear, and Michael S. Rosenwald, "Obama Calls on Congress to Act Fast on Stimulus," *Washington Post*, November 8, 2008, A1.

24. John Zogby, "Investors for Bush," *Wall Street Journal*, March 15, 2005, A20.

25. Patrick O'Connor, "U.S. Layoffs Mount, Home Foreclosures Rise," Inteldaily.com, October 24, 2008.

26. Jack Healy, "A Record Decline in October's Retail Sales," *New York Times*, November 14, 2008, E1.

27. Grynbaum, "Rattled by Housing Slide." According to this survey, a reading of 100 represents the consumer outlook on the economy in 1985.

28. Quoted in Peter Wallsten and Janet Hook, "Four Big Questions of the Presidential Election," *Los Angeles Times*, November 2, 2008.

29. "Barack Obama for President," *New York Times*, October 24, 2008, A30.

30. Edison Media Research and Mitofsky International exit polls, November 4, 2008.

31. "Survey Finds President's Job Approval Marks Hit a New Low of 21%," Zogby International press release, October 15, 2008; Gallup poll, August 2–5, 1974. For more on Truman's problems in 1952, see John Kenneth White, *Still Seeing Red: How the Cold War Shapes the New American Politics* (Boulder, Colo.: Westview, 1997), 79–106.

32. Frank Newport, "Americans' Satisfaction at an All-Time Low of 9%," Gallup poll press release, October 7, 2008.

33. Matthew Mosk, "Obama's September Haul Provides Huge Advertising Edge," *Washington Post*, October 20, 2008, A2; Michael Luo, "Obama Recasts the Fund-Raising Landscape," *New York Times*, October 20, 2008, A21. McCain accepted $84 million in public funding and could not match Obama either in paid advertising or in mobilizing supporters.

34. Quoted in Adam Nagourney and Elisabeth Bumiller, "Republicans Voicing Concern after Rough Week for McCain," *New York Times*, October 12, 2008, 1.

35. Quoted in Richard L. Berke, "G.O.P. Leaders Doubtful That Dole Can Close Gap," *New York Times*, October 20, 1996, 1.

36. Gallup Poll, July 30–August 4, 1958.

37. See V. Lance Tarrance Jr., "The Bradley Effect—Selective Memory," *Real Clear Politics*, October 13, 2008; Ken Khachigian, "Don't Blame the Bradley Effect," *Washington Post*, November 2, 2008, B1.

38. Edison Media Research and Mitofsky International exit polls, November 4, 2008.

39. The final Rasmussen poll pegged the race at 52 percent for Obama to 46 percent for McCain. Likewise, Research 2000 showed the race at 51 percent for Obama to 46 percent for McCain.

40. See, for example, James M. McPherson, the renowned Civil War historian and professor emeritus of history at Princeton University, who said of Obama's victory, "It's an historic turning point . . . an exclamation point of major proportions to the civil rights movement that goes back to the 1950s" (quoted in Todd Lewan,

"Historians, Too, Call Obama Victory 'Monumental,'" Associated Press, November 9, 2008).

41. Quoted in Everett Carll Ladd Jr., *Where Have All the Voters Gone? The Fracturing of America's Political Parties* (New York: Norton, 1978), 24.

42. Jeffrey Hart, a former Reagan speechwriter, also saw similarities between his old boss and Obama (Jeffrey Hart, "Obama Is the New Reagan," *Daily Beast*, November 4, 2008). Others, including Caroline Kennedy, compared Obama to her father, John F. Kennedy (Caroline Kennedy, "A President Like My Father," *New York Times*, January 27, 2008, WK18).

43. For more comparisons between 1980 and 2008, see Julian E. Zelizer, "Here We Go Again—Maybe," *Newsweek*, October 20, 2008, 51.

44. John Kenneth White, *The New Politics of Old Values* (Hanover, N.H.: University Press of New England, 1990), 21.

45. Thomas B. Edsall, "For GOP, Reliable Wedge Issues Suddenly Fall Flat," *Huffington Post*, October 16, 2008.

46. McCain-Obama Third Presidential Debate, October 15, 2008; and Jim Kuhnhenn, "Palin Says Obama 'Palling Around' with Terrorists," Associated Press, October 4, 2008.

47. CBS News/*New York Times* poll, October 10–13, 2008.

48. Edison Media Research and Mitofsky International exit polls, November 4, 2008.

49. Ronald Reagan, Acceptance Speech, Republican National Convention, Detroit, July 17, 1980.

50. Adam Nagourney, "A Year Still to Go, and Presidential Politics Have Shifted Already," *New York Times*, November 4, 2007, 24.

51. Gerald M. Pomper, "The Presidential Election," in *The Election of 1980: Reports and Interpretations*, ed. Gerald M. Pomper (Chatham, N.J.: Chatham House, 1981), 65.

52. Decision/Making/Information survey for the Reagan for President Campaign, June 1980.

53. Gallup/CNN/*USA Today* poll, November 2–6, 1994.

54. "Fewer Voters Identify as Republicans," Pew Research Center press release, March 20, 2008. According to the 2008 exit polls, 39 percent of voters called themselves Democrats, 32 percent were Republicans, and 29 percent were independents (Edison Media Research and Mitofsky International exit polls, November 4, 2008).

55. Marjorie Connelly, "Dissecting a Changed Electorate," *New York Times*, November 9, 2008, WK5.

56. "Democratic Party's Image More Positive Than GOP's," Gallup poll press release, November 15, 2007.

57. Quoted in David D. Kirkpatrick, "Voters' Allegiances, Ripe for the Picking," *New York Times*, October 15, 2006, WK1.

58. Edison Media Research and Mitofsky International exit polls, November 4, 2008.

59. CBS News/*New York Times* poll, March 7–11, 2007.

60. Wilson Carey McWilliams, "The Meaning of the Election," in *Election of 1980*, ed. Pomper, 180.

61. Richard B. Wirthlin to Ronald Reagan, December 16, 1988, in possession of the author; reprinted in full in John Kenneth White, *New Politics of Old Values*, 185–89.

62. Jeffrey M. Jones, "Low Trust in Federal Government Rivals Watergate Era Levels," Gallup Poll press release, September 26, 2007.

63. Gallup Poll, September 14–16, 2007; Opinion Research Corporation poll, October 20–22, 2006.

64. Associated Press/Ipsos–Public Affairs poll, June 18–20, 2004.

65. Sean Wilentz, "The Worst President in History?" *Rolling Stone*, April 21, 2006, 2.

66. James P. Pfiffner, "George W. Bush and the Abuse of Executive Power," paper presented at the American Political Science Association Convention, Chicago, August 29–September 2, 2007.

67. Eric Foner, "He's the Worst Ever," *Washington Post*, December 3, 2006, B1.

68. Stephen Skowronek, "The Imperial Presidency Thesis Revisited: George W. Bush at the Point of No Return," in Stephen Skowronek, *Presidential Leadership in Political Time: Reprise and Reappraisal* (Lawrence: University Press of Kansas, 2008), 150–66.

69. Jimmy Carter Interview, *Today Show*, NBC News, May 21, 2007.

70. Chuck Hagel, "A Conversation with Chuck Hagel," Council on Foreign Relations, November 28, 2007.

71. See http://voices.washingtonpost.com/44/2008/10/16post-debate_spots.html.

72. McCain-Obama Third Presidential Debate, October 15, 2008.

73. Quoted in "Endgame: November 1," *New York Times*, November 1, 2008 (available at http://thecaucus.blogs.nytimes.com/2008/11/01/endgame-nov-1.

74. NBC News/*Wall Street Journal* poll, December 5–8, 2008.

75. Franklin D. Roosevelt, Inaugural Address, Washington, D.C., March 4, 1933.

76. Barack Obama, Victory Speech, November 4, 2008.

77. Rick Perlstein, *Nixonland: The Rise of a President and the Fracturing of America* (New York: Scribner, 2008), 14.

78. Cited in John Kenneth White, *New Politics of Old Values*, 54.

79. David Brooks, "Patio Man Revisited," *New York Times*, October 21, 2008, A29.

80. Edison Media Research and Mitofsky International exit polls, November 4, 2008.

81. Richard M. Scammon and Ben J. Wattenberg, *The Real Majority* (New York: Coward-McCann, 1970), 45–71.

82. Ibid., 35–44.

83. Richard M. Scammon and Ben J. Wattenberg, *The Real Majority* (New York: Primus, 1992), 3.

84. Quoted in George Packer, "The Fall of Conservatism: Have the Republicans Run Out of Ideas?" *New Yorker*, May 26, 2008, 2.

85. See John Kenneth White, *New Politics of Old Values*.

86. Associated Press, "Exit Poll Survey Confirms Partisan Shift," November 8, 2008.

87. Frank Rich, "The Terrorist Barack Hussein Obama," *New York Times*, October 12, 2008, WK10.

88. George F. Will, "Kentuckian in the Breach," *Washington Post*, November 13, 2008, A23.

89. Edison Media Research and Mitofsky International exit polls, November 4, 2008.

90. Jeffrey S. Passel and D'Vera Cohn, "U.S. Population Projections: 2005–2050," Pew Research Center, February 11, 2008, 9; Sam Roberts, "A Generation Away, Minorities May Become the Majority in U.S.," *New York Times*, August 14, 2008, A1.

91. Quoted in James Traub, "Is (His) Biography (Our) Destiny?" *New York Times Magazine*, November 4, 2007, 50.

92. Barack Obama, Address to Supporters, Chicago, February 5, 2008.

93. "Age Cohorts and Their Party Ties," 12. These results are based on combined Gallup polls with a sample size of approximately 10,000 respondents.

94. Edison Media Research and Mitofsky International exit polls, November 4, 2008.

95. Richard Florida, *The Rise of the Creative Class and How It's Transforming Work, Leisure, Community, and Everyday Life* (New York: Basic Books, 2004).

96. Voter News Service exit poll, November 2, 2004; Edison Media Research and Mitofsky International exit poll, November 4, 2008.

97. See Everett Carll Ladd Jr. with Charles D. Hadley, *Transformations of the American Party System* (New York: Norton, 1978), 57–60.

98. Ibid., 112.

99. Connelly, "Dissecting a Changed Electorate," WK5.

100. George W. Bush, *A Charge to Keep: My Journey to the White House* (New York: HarperPerennial, 2001), 237.

101. Obama's showing bears out the advice political scientist Thomas F. Schaller gave to the Democrats in 2006, when he advised that they forget about the South and concentrate on the Southwest, where Hispanic votes could carry the party to victory (Thomas F. Schaller, *Whistling Past Dixie: How Democrats Can Win without the South* [New York: Simon and Schuster, 2006]).

102. Quoted in David S. Broder, "Trending away from the GOP," *Washington Post*, November 16, 2008, B7.

103. Bill Clinton, Acceptance Speech, Democratic National Convention, Chicago, August 29, 1996.

104. Cited in Andrew Delbanco, "A Fateful Election," *New York Review of Books*, November 6, 2008, 8.

105. MSNBC, November 4, 2008.

106. NBC News/*Wall Street Journal* poll, December 5–8, 2008.

107. George McGovern, "Why I Believe Bush Must Go," *Washington Post*, January 6, 2008, B1.

A Bibliography of selected books, articles, polls, and speeches is available on the Web site www.press.umich.edu at this book's page.

Index

Lennon, John, 6, 153, 156–57, 269 n. 21
Levi's jeans, advertising on *Queer Eye for the Straight Guy*, 30
Levitt, Peggy, 60
Levitt, William, 15
Lewinsky, Monica, 233
Lewis, John, 137
Lewis, Mark, 121
Liberals, 21
Libertarian Party, 134
Lieberman, Joe, 6
Life magazine, 2, 33, 94
Lifenet (antiabortion group), 20
Lightcap, Vicki, 195
Lighty, Brian, 124
Lincoln, Abraham, 8, 34, 226, 232
Lincoln, Neb., 45
Lindbergh, Charles, 41
Lindsey, Brink, 21
Lipset, Seymour Martin, 11
Lithonia, Ga., 156
Little Rock Nine, 33
Lodewyks, Chris, 121–22
Logan family, 121
Lombardo, Steve, 233
Long, Bishop Eddie L., 156
Long Island, N.Y., 15
Los Angeles, Calif., 57, 64–67, 71, 74
Los Angeles Times, 6, 145, 151
Los Angeles Unified School District, 63
Lost City, The (Ehrenhalt), 153–54
Loudon County, Va., 61, 65
Louis Harris and Associates, 145
Louisiana, 76, 216
Loving, Donald, 73, 252 n. 166
Loving, Fondrey, 108
Loving, Mildred, 48, 72–73, 245 nn. 4–5
Loving, Peggy, 73
Loving, Richard, 48, 72–73, 245 nn. 4–5
Loving, Sidney, 73
Loving Conference, 72–73

Loving v. Virginia, 49, 72–73, 141
Lubell, Samuel, 202
Luce, Clare Boothe, 226
Lundberg, Ferdinand, 23
Lynch, Jennifer, 107–8
Lynch, Lincoln, 50
Lyon, Phyllis, 137

Mableton, Georgia, 4
Mac, Bernie, 77
Machu Picchu Restaurant, 55
Madden, Benji, 96
Madden, Joel, 96
Maddox, Lester, 53, 246 n. 26
Madison Square Garden (N.Y.), 209
Maharidge, Dale, 67
Maine, 79
Mali, 54
Malliaris, Maryanthe, 62
Maloy, Dona, 134
Maneely, Marilyn, 121
Manford, Jeanne, 125
Manhattan, 105
Manhattan Institute, 199
Manuelle, Victor, 66
Marcel-Keyes, Maya, 127
Marcus Welby, M.D., 29
Marini, Diane, 121
Mariscolandia Seafood House, 55
Marley, Bob, 6
Marquardt, Elizabeth, 95, 97
Marriage, 92–106, 108–10, 113–14, 123–24, 130, 134–40, 176, 180, 194. *See also* Family; Gay marriage; Gender roles; Interracial marriage/dating; Values
Marriage: A History (Coontz), 93
Marriage Affirmation Act (Va.), 119
Marriage Protection Week, 102
Marshalltown, Iowa, 62
Martin, Del, 137
Martin, Louis, 81
Martin, Ricky, 66, 78
Martinez, Jose, 71
Martinez, Mel, 205
Maryland, 138